THE LIFE AND WORK OF KWAME NKRUMAH

The Life and Work of Kwame Nkrumah

Papers of a Symposium Organized by the Institute of African Studies, University of Ghana, Legon

Edited by Kwame Arhin

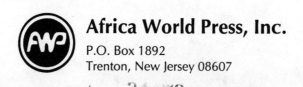

Africa World Press, Inc.

P.O. Box 1892
Trenton, New Jersey 08607

Africa World Press, Inc.
P.O. Box 1892
Trenton, N.J. 08607

Copyright © 1993 The Institute of African Studies
University of Ghana

Book Design — Jonathan Gullery
Cover Design & Illustration — Carles Juzang

Library of Congress Cataloging-in-Publication Data

The life and work of Kwame Nkrumah / edited by Kwame Arhin. - - 1st
    American ed.
     p.   cm.
   Includes bibliographical references and index
   ISBN 0-86543-395-X. - - ISBN 0-86543-396-8 (pbk.)
     1. Nkrumah, Kwame, 1909–1972. 2. Presidents- - Ghana- - Biography.
   3. Ghana- -Politics and government- -1957–1979. I. Arhin, Kwame.
   DT512.3.N57.L54   1993
   966. 705'092- -dc20
   [B]   93-30706
                                      CIP

*To the innumerable villagers who supported
Kwame Nkrumah
in the hope of a better world*

CONTENTS

PART 3   ECONOMY

PREFACE

With the exception of chapters v and xiv, the papers in this volume were read and discussed at a symposium on "The Life and Work of Kwame Nkrumah" held at Legon on May 25–June 1, 1985, and organized by the Institute of African Studies, University of Ghana. Nkrumah believed very much in the Institute of African Studies which he regarded as an intellectual wing of the pan-Africanist revolution; the Institute owed it to his memory to start a dialogue by Ghanaians themselves on his contributions to the making of modern Ghana.

Kwame Nkrumah was born, by his own reckoning, in 1909 at Nkroful in Nzema in Southwestern Gold Coast, now Western Region of Ghana. He was educated in Half Assini on the border with modern Ivory Coast (Cote d'Ivoire) and trained as a teacher at the Government-established Teacher Training College at Achimota near Accra. After a spell of teaching, he went to America in 1935 where he remained for ten years and acquired degrees in Theology, Sociology, Education, Philosophy and Political Science. He also engaged in journalism and undertook the organization of politically-oriented African student groupings. He went to London in 1945 and for two years participated zealously in student anti-colonial politics and the pan-Africanist movement. He returned to the Gold Coast at the invitation of the Leaders of the United Gold Coast Convention (UGCC), the nationalist movement of the Gold Coast, which was formed in 1947 to "fight" for Self-government from the British Colonial Authorities.

Nkrumah was made Secretary and later Treasurer of the UGCC. But in June 1949 he broke ranks with it and formed the Convention Peoples' Party (CPP). That break was a decisive landmark in the history of the Gold Coast Colony and its "dependencies," Ashanti, the

Northern Territories and British Togoland. From 1949 to 1966 when a *coup d'etat* by military officers overthrew Nkrumah as the President of the First Republic of Ghana, Nkrumah dominated the country. The political divide that he opened up in 1949 still runs through Ghanaian politics.

When Nkrumah died in Bucharest in April 1972, there was a fairly general agreement in Ghana among both his supporters and opponents on the main outlines of his achievements. Kwame Nkrumah canalized the discontent of the peoples of the British-ruled territories of the Gold Coast Colony into a highly organized movement of protest against British rule. He stirred the political consciousness of ordinary men and women and awakened them to the real evils of colonialism which he considered as the root of their economic, social and political discontent. He made himself their spokesman and leader and, turning them into a potent political force, was thus enabled to defeat his political rivals. With the support of the "masses" he was able, within the relatively short period of ten years, to bring political independence to the Gold Coast Colony and associated territories on March 6, 1957. The new state was named Ghana. Between 1951 and 1966, as leader of Government Business, Prime Minister and President of Ghana, he laid impressive foundations for the economic and social transformation of the country. His political achievements in Ghana served as a model for African nationalists elsewhere on the continent, and he actively supported other nationalist struggles; in some ways he even sacrificed Ghana's potential prosperity for the larger cause of total African emancipation. He was a pre-eminent founder of the movement for African Unity; more than any other African leader of his time, he symbolized the Black man's self-identity and pride in his race. His name shall endure as the leading emancipator of Ghana, the leading protagonist of African independence and unity, and a statesman of world stature of the twentieth century.

The contributors of the various papers assess aspects of Nkrumah's life and work from the perspectives of their various disciplines and their own "ideological" view-points. The organizers of the symposium did not attempt to impose any theoretical constraints on the contributors and, consequently, the papers must be read and assessed by themselves. It goes without saying that the Institute does not necessarily share in the views expressed by the individual contributors, and is not responsible for the manner in which those views are expressed.

The Institute of African Studies is indebted to the following organizations and individuals for their contributions towards making the symposium possible: The Government of Ghana (PNDC); Mr. Kojo Botsio and friends; Mr. W. E. Inkumsah, Crocodile Matchet Ltd.; Nana Oduro Numapau II, Esumegyahene (Asante Region); Dr. M. N. Tetteh of Uniclean Ltd.; the Ghana National Trading Corporation (GNTC); Ocean Fisheries Ltd.; Mankoadze Fisheries Ltd.; the Ghana Tourist Development Company; Fan Milk Ltd.; Cold Stores Ltd.; State Fishing Corporation; GIHOC Distilleries Co. Ltd.; and Piccadilly Biscuits Ltd.

Miss Joyce Aryee, then PNDC Secretary for Education read the opening address; Dr. Obed Asamoah, PNDC Secretary for Foreign Affairs read a paper on Nkrumah's foreign policy; Dr. R. K. A. Gardiner, the distinguished Ghanaian and intenational public servant and academic, chaired the entire symposium. Mr. Kojo Botsio, Mr. K. B. Asante, Mr. K. A. Gbedemah, Professor E. A. Boateng, Mr. J. V. L. Phillips and Nana (Dr.) Kobina Nketia chaired sessions of the symposium.

Professor Akilakpa Sawyerr, who had at the time of the symposium just assumed office as Vice-Chancellor of the University of Ghana, was kind enough to chair the session on foreign policy.

The Ghana Dance Ensemble under Mr Nii-Yartey, and the Mannyina Choir, led by Dr. S. D. Asiamah, entertained guests at a cocktail party organized at the end of the symposium.

Messrs. F. C. Essandoh and Francis Zonyrah and Ms. Rebecca Narh have been very helpful in typing the manuscript. Mr. S. S. Quarcoopome, Research Fellow of the Institute, gave helpful editorial assistance. Mr. E. Aggrey-Fynn, National Serviceman, has rendered invaluable service in checking the notes and references and putting the bibliography into shape. But I am responsible for any mistakes that may be found in these.

Professor K. A. Dickson, then Director of the Institute, Drs. K. Afari Gyan, G. P. Hagan, Irene Odotei and Ms. Takyiwaa Manuh, all Fellows at the Institute, shared in the responsibility for the management of the symposium.

Kwame Arhin
Institute of African Studies, University of Ghana, Legon.
April, 1988

CONTRIBUTORS

K. Afari-Gyan	Research Fellow, (Political Science), Institute of African Studies, Legon.
Dominic K. Agyeman	Associate Professor of Sociology, University of Cape Coast, Cape Coast.
P. A. V. Ansah	Associate Professor, Director, School of Communication Studies, Legon.
Kwame Arhin	Professor, Director, Institute of African Studies, Legon.
Obed Asamoah	Formerly Lecturer in Law, University of Ghana, PNDC Secretary for Foreign Affairs.
S. Asamoah-Darko	Associate Professor, Department of General and African Studies, Unversity of Science and Technology, Kumasi.
K. B. Asante	Public Servant; Formerly Ghana's Ambassador to the European Economic Community (EEC); Economic Consultant; PNDC Secretary for Education and Culture.
Joseph R. A. Ayee	Lecturer in Political Science, University of Ghana, Legon.
K. A. Dickson	Professor Head of Department of the Study of Religion; Formerly Director of the Institute of African Studies, Legon.

G. P. Hagan — Senior Research Fellow (Social Anthropology), Institute of African Studies, Legon.

E A. Haizel — Director, Institute of Adult Education, University of Ghana, Legon; Secretary, National Commission for Democracy (NCD).

Kwesi Jonah — Lecturer in Political Science, University of Ghana, Legon.

Takyiwah Manuh — Research Fellow, (Legal and Women's Studies), Institute of African Studies, Legon.

Kwame A Ninsin — Senior Lecturer in Political Science, University of Ghana, Legon.

Fui S. Tsikata — Senior Lecturer in Law, University of Ghana, Legon.

J. A. Dadson — Senior Lecturer in Agricultural Economics, University of Ghana, Legon.

NKRUMAH

PART 1

SOCIETY

NKRUMAH'S CULTURAL POLICY

George P. Hagan

One abiding effect of the leadership of Nkrumah is that
the peoples of Africa now have a consciousness of their cultural
identity and possess a definite pride of culture. Africans are also
aware of the need, in fact of the necessity, to discover their cultural
heritage and develop it. In Ghana, by the time of his overthrow,
Nkrumah had established practically all the institutions we now
identify with cultural development, and it is difficult to tell what significant additions have since been made to them.

Those who were privileged to be involved in the great cultural
self-assertion of Ghana in the sixties are unanimous in acknowledg-
ing Nkrumah's personal interest and enthusiastic support for the
arts and the cultural institutions that sprang up at that time. Among
the most outstanding of these are the Ghana Museum, which was
opened on the 5th of March, 1957 — the eve of Independence; the
Arts Council of Ghana, which was created as the Cultural wing of the
Ministry of Education and Culture (1958); the Research Library on
African Affairs (June, 1961); and the Ghana Film Corporation (1964).
In other areas there occurred such expansion and intensification of
activity in the days after independence that operational strategies
experienced a radical transformation. There occurred similar transformations in archival and library services, broadcasting, the theatre
and public entertainment, development of Ghanaian languages, the
development of publications on Ghanaian culture and cultural

events, and art and cultural education. The arts had a proud patron.

From the long term perspective, the advances which Nkrumah initiated for the discovery, interpretation, evaluation, preservation and development of the African heritage would have needed a clear cultural policy to sustain them; and such a policy should have identified the issue of African unity as well as the issue of Ghana's national identity and unity as its logical objectives. The extent to which Nkrumah discerned the need for such a policy and succeeded in constructing one is a subject both of practical and speculative academic interest; and it is this that this paper attempts to explore.

Identifying Nkrumah's Cultural Objectives

Nkrumah first hinted at the need for a Pan-African cultural policy proposition in his opening address to the First Conference of Independent African States on the 19th of April, 1958. Ethiopia, Libyia, Tunisia, Morocco, Egypt, Liberia, the Sudan and Ghana — the participating states — were so diverse in culture that it proved necessary for Nkrumah to suggest a way forward from this cultural mosaic to the grand objective of Pan-African 'nationhood.' And he portrayed at this point a practical concern:

> Addressing ourselves to the cultural aspects of our relationship, we must also examine ways and means to broaden and strengthen our association with one another through such means as the exchange of students and the visits of cultural, scientific and technical missions, both governmental and non–governmental, and the establishment of libraries specializing in various aspects of African history and culture which may become centres of research. There are no limits to ways in which we on this African continent can enrich our knowledge of our past civilizations and cultural heritage through our cooperative efforts and the pooling of our scientific and technical resources.[1]

These were unexceptionable ideas that called for a more systematic elaboration as a cultural policy for the union of independent African States. And one would have expected such a policy to have materialized by the time of the establishment of the OAU. This hope was held out by the Charter drawn up in 1961 for realizing the Ghana, Guinea, Mali accord, but was dashed by the OAU Charter.

The Charter for African States' Unity signed by Ghana, Guinea and Mali, three states that had signalled their willingness to merge as "The Union of African States which shall be regarded as the nucleus of the United States of Africa," stated, as the first aim of the Union:

to strengthen and develop ties of friendship and fraternal cooperation between the member states politically, diplomatically, economically and culturally.[2]

The activities of the Union included under culture were

the rehabilitation and development of African culture, and frequent
and diversified cultural exchange.[3]

If the OAU Charter stands as a document which bears evidence of
the thinking and deepest conviction of its authors, one can glean
from it little of the importance Nkrumah might have attached to culture. In the preamble to the Charter there is no mention of the word
'culture': There is only an indirect reference to culture in the para-
graph (5th) which states that, the leaders of Africa were creating the
OAU, inspired by, among other things, "a common determination to
strengthen understanding and cooperation among our States in
response to the aspirations of our peoples for brotherhood and solidarity, *in a larger unity transcending ethnic and national differences*"
(emphasis mine). This shows a concern only with the problems that
our ethnic cultures could create for African Unity, and not with the
positive contribution that culture can make towards the realization
of that unity.

In the statement on Purposes, the Charter is again silent on culture. One is therefore pleasantly surprised to see high priority being
given to culture in the listing of the specialized commissions deemed
necessary for the operation of the OAU — that is, if the order in
which they were set down should be taken as indicating the order
of priority the Leaders accorded the establishment of the various
commissions. In that order, the Educational and Cultural
Commission comes second after the Economic and Social
Commission; and the Health, Sanitation and Nutrition Commission,
Defence Commission and the Scientific Technical Research
Commission follow in that order of descent. The Charter does not
state the objectives to be pursued by these agencies. Maybe it
should not. But if so, in the absence of a definitive statement of purpose, there has sprung up in Africa a profusion of ideas, if not a confusion of thought, as individual nations have sought to define their
own cultural philosophies and pursued different, often conflicting,
lines of approach to cultural development which can only serve to
divide Africa and make continental unity that more difficult to
achieve.[4]

Another source from which one might expect to obtain an idea of Nkrumah's cultural policy in respect of African unity is Nkrumah's book, *Africa Must Unite* (1963). Nkrumah's declared purpose in this book was "to trace briefly the African background and the effects of centuries of colonialism on the political, economic and social life in Africa as a whole; to place development in Ghana in the broader context of the African revolution; and to explain his political philosophy based on his conviction of the need for the freedom and unification of Africa and its islands."[5] Yet, though the cultural effects of the centuries of colonialism have been more enduring and not less damaging than the political and economic, Nkrumah gave intimations of this awareness in no clear terms. What hints the book gives of this awareness and what the cultural problem demands by way of policy, we only obtain here and there in the chapter on the "Intellectual Vanguard" and in the chapter on "Neocolonialism in Africa."

In one place, however, Nkrumah left us his assessment of the causes of Africa's cultural disorientation, a necessary first step to the determination of policy objectives. He wrote:

> Our pattern of education has been aligned hitherto to the demands of British examination councils. Above all, it was formulated and administered by an alien administration desirous of extending its dominant ideas and thought processes to us. We were trained to be inferior copies of Englishmen, caricatures to be laughed at with our pretensions to British bourgeois gentility, our grammatical faultiness and distorted standards betraying us at every turn. We were neither fish nor fowl. We were denied the knowledge of our African past and informed that we had no present. What future could there be for us? We were taught to regard our culture and traditions as barbarous and primitive. Our textbooks, telling us about English history, English geography, English ways of living, English customs, English ideas, English weather. Many of these manuals had not been altered since 1895. [6]

Further, seeing the cultural problem as largely the outcome of the colonial educational system, Nkrumah projected its solution educational terms:

> We needed to plan an educational system that will be more in keeping with the requirements of the economic and social progress for which our new development plans are aiming.[7]

Nkrumah saw this as a "stupendous task," but he was reassuring:

> This is something that we are, however, getting on with as it is vital
> that we should nurture our own culture and history if we are to
> develop that African personality which must provide the educa-
> tional and intellectual foundations of our Pan-African future.[8]

Nkrumah probably then saw his educational policy as the centre-
piece of his cultural policy and his aim of the development of African
personality. However, if the object of making the content of education more African was to ensure that future generations would see
themselves as African, then it was at once also important to nurture
the consciousness of African identity through the creation or preservation of an African cultural ambience and through due emphasis on
African values and modes of conduct. And this demanded more than
the replacement of one educational system by another. Educational
systems aside, the African cultural disorientation derived from the
imposition on Africa of foreign languages, an economic system
geared to different personal and collective value options, foreign
political systems constructed with different concepts of the ends of
government and a new technology with its own sociocultural values
and implications. A society could not give its educational system an
African content while remaining hostage to the colonial past in terms
of language, politics, economics and technological systems. An
African cultural policy needed to adopt this wider perspective, if it
should provide "the educational and intellectual foundations of our
Pan-Africanist future."[9]

That Nkrumah did not survey this wider cultural view was due
to the fact that he was a thinker Isaiah Berlin might have described
as a hedgehog rather than a fox. He had big visions and had the
instinct for big constructs, often leaving it to others to work out the
small details. He had no natural inclination to compose grand
designs out of minor strands or small pieces. And it was as a hedgehog that he wrote:

> A union of African States will raise the dignity of Africa and
> strengthen its impact on world affairs. It will make possible the full
> expression of the African personality.[10]

This statement puts Nkrumah's Pan-African cultural objective in tan-
dem with his objective of political union. It is noticeable here that
the cultivation of the African personality was to be the outflow of the
Union of African States when it was brought into being.

However, in other places, Nkrumah saw its development as a necessary means for the attainment of continental union.[11]

Whatever be the case no more could cultural attainment be advanced entirely through political action than could political results be attained by cultural means without deliberate political actions. So it was necessary for Nkrumah to define the types of cultural activities that would enable Africans to achieve the fullest development of African personality. While the lack of explicitness in this regard might be construed as a failing, it would appear that the concept of African personality served to provide Nkrumah as well as the masses of Africa an escape from the pains of contemplating the perplexing and paralyzing complexities of Africa's cultural heterogeneity. African personality represented for him the basis on which to examine the policy strategies for Africa. And it served, in the absence of identifiable detailing of policy guidelines at the national level, to provide some principle or moving interest for the quest and preservation of the African heritage. This last point has been evident in Ghanaian official thinking on cultural policy till now.

For Ghana, the first document that suggests Nkrumah might have had a cultural policy is "Cultural Policy in Ghana" published by UNESCO in 1975, which came out almost a decade after the overthrow of Kwame Nkrumah. There is no reference in this document to any policy statement on culture before 1975; however, the document claims that the "philosophy of an African personality" had been "the guiding principle of Ghana's cultural policy from the time of independence to the present."[12] Since this document does not even state what the elements of that policy had been, its claim becomes difficult to evaluate, and it might be taken that it is based either on a source which is not available to the public or on wishful thinking.

The awareness of the need for a cultural policy was present in certain circles of the Convention People's Party government as early as 1957, the year of Independence. On the 20th of August, Mr A. Casely-Hayford put a question to the Minister of Education thus:

What is the Government's cultural policy to assure the preservation and demonstration of the character and traditions of the people of Ghana?[13]

The Minister responded:

The Government is keenly interested in the preservation and demonstration of the character and traditions of the people of

Ghana. The establishment of the Ghana Museum and Monuments Board and the recent opening of the Ghana National Museum are evidence of this interest.[14]

He went on to express the hope "that it will be possible to establish a statutory Arts Council in place of the present Interim Committee during the course of next year".[15]

The Minister also expressed hopes for the establishment and creation of a National Theatre, and a National Art Gallery; and he said a report was awaited from the Interim Committee on an Arts Council whose terms of reference included the drawing up of "detailed and realistic proposals . . . for a national theatre movement."[16] There was no further debate on these matters till 1958. In any case, the response of the Minister indicated that the government had rightly or wrongly left any policy formulation on culture and the arts in the hands of the Interim Committee, whatever the Government's own ideas were.

When in 1958 the Bill establishing the Arts Council of Ghana came up for debate, there was no reference in the debate to the need to develop Ghana's cultural programmes with the aim of entering into cultural exchanges with other African states and achieving African unity; and there was no reference to the concept of African personality as a guiding principle for Ghana's cultural development. These were to come later. The general impression left by the debate was that Ghana's cultural policy had to have a Ghanaian focus and to develop Ghana's wealth of ethnic cultures as the means of projecting Ghanaian "national culture" which was accepted all round as an existing fact. [17]

From the beginning, then, with his mass education programme in place, Nkrumah did not have any other policy on culture, nor was there any awareness that his educational programme should aim at creating consciousness of African heritage. Culture represented to him an enigma which only gradually came to occupy an important place in his thinking.

Nkrumah's Cultural Predicaments— Some Core Cultural Issues

What appears as Nkrumah's failure to spell out a clear cultural policy in the early years of independence can be traced to the predicaments that might have occupied his tactical political mind in respect of African cultures. He perceived these predicaments in the close-up cultural situation in Ghana.

For Nkrumah, culture represented an irksome problem from the very start of the revolution he led. In his mind, traditional culture had two tendencies militating against African progress. It carried in itself forces of resistance to change; and it also bore the seeds of disunity.[18] However, Nkrumah was too well aware that our people's consciousness of their distinct heritage had constituted one of the major bulwarks against imperialism. This awareness was clear in the thoughts and works of Mensah Sarbah, Casely-Hayford, Attoh Ahuma, Kobina Sekyi and his own direct and immediate predecessor and mentor J. B. Danquah. He himself sought to create this awareness of our identity in order to stir up the masses into rejecting European cultural and political domination. In the heat of the nationalist struggle, however, the incipient negative forces of that same heritage became apparent. What most engaged Nkrumah's mind at the time was not only the people's obsession with *aborofosem,* European ways and the European values of the elite, but the divisiveness of the tribal cultures and the reactionary leadership of the chiefs to whom the people owed traditional allegiance. He made all these the object of persistent attack. But he directed his most threatening remarks against chiefs whom he saw as a direct threat to the revolution. Nkrumah's enigma in respect of cultural policy had its seeds in his reaction to chieftaincy, tribalism and *aborofosem.*

a. Chieftaincy

Nkrumah knew that chieftaincy was a central institution of the Ghanaian cultural identity. He knew also the historic role of chiefs in resisting foreign domination of the people of the Gold Coast. He could not discount the people's attachment to their chiefs. And he could not neglect the developmental potential of that lofty institution. Yet in the struggle for national independence, some of the most influential chiefs had become part of the reactionary forces seeking to stem the tide of the liberation struggle, and he was in no doubt that those same forces could resist the efforts to create a strong and viable nation. He was on record as having made at a rally the apocalyptic pronouncement: "The chiefs would run away and leave their sandals behind;" and the chiefs were made never to forget it.[19]

For a chief to step on the ground with his bare foot was a sign of abdication or self-destoolment. A destooled chief has his sandals seized from under his feet. And therefore Nkrumah's words meant nothing but that chiefs would lose their prominent position in the society, even if chiefship would survive in any form.

By the time of independence, enough chiefs had either whole-heartedly, or, under the fear of Nkrumah's threat, grudgingly pledged him their allegiance for him to appear less as an usurper of the natural leadership of the chiefs than as a leader accepted as such within the framework of traditional values. He naturally accepted the accolade *Osagyefo,* and subsequently accepted to be enstooled a chief in his home village in the Nzima area. The expression "the chiefs and people of Ghana" became one of the favorite expressions of Nkrumah. It reflected not only Nkrumah's view of both the unity and cultural identity of Ghanaians, but also his own personal respect for the institution of chieftaincy.

Contrary to the radical expectations he had raised, Nkrumah therefore appeared to have compromised with the cherished but, what he had seen as, reactionary institution of chieftaincy. It is not unexpected that he should have felt the need than to explain this virtual capitulation. And he sought to do so in *Africa Must Unite,* discounting any impression that he had changed his most genuine convictions. In fact, he gave the impression that the radical reading of the facts was correct; and he reiterated his main premise:

> Within a society poising itself for the leap from pre-industrial retardation to modern development, there are traditional forces that can impede progress.[20]

As a leader of his people rather than as a nationalist agitator, however, his judgement of the situation was that while some traditional forces "must be cut at their roots . . . others can be retained and adapted to the changing need" and care in the selection was necessary, he cautioned.[21] Nkrumah himself obviously was not sure which of these forces deserved to be cut at their roots. He was certain however that chieftaincy was not one such force.

> The place of chiefs is so interwoven with Ghanaian society that their forcible eradication would tear gaps in the social fabric which might prove as painful as the retention of other more unadaptable traditions.[22]

The tares of reactions had to be allowed to grow with the good seeds of our culture.

The question naturally arises: who should adapt these institutions to the time? Is it the impatient political radical? Nkrumah's preferred solution was implied in his approval of the advice reportedly given by the Asantehene on the need for chiefs to change.

Nkrumah observed:

> For the most powerful paramount chief in this country to warn that
> chiefs will, by reason of wider educational facilities, in due course,
> be denied one of the main symbols of their office, is tantamount to
> warning of the natural attenuation of chieftaincy under the impact
> of social progress. If, in the interregnum, chieftaincy can be used to
> encourage popular effort, there would seem to be little sense in
> arousing the antagonism which its legal dissolution would stimu-
> late.[23]

And Nkrumah went on to remark:

> The adaptation of our chiefs to what must, for them, be distressing
> exigencies created by the changing relations in the national polity,
> has been remarkable. We could wish that other forces with vested
> interests might have proved as adaptable.[24]

If social progress would itself lead to the attenuation of chieftaincy,
why create unnecessary upheaval with a pre-emptive action that
might prove ineffectual. The irony of fate to which Nkrumah seemed
to be pointing was the historical inevitability of the demise of chieftaincy as he had predicted. He would not chase chiefs away from
their sandals, but as the Asantehene was bold to point out, their
umbrellas will float away in the whirlwind of progress — which
comes to the same thing.

If in chieftaincy Nkrumah had seen a negative force, his tolerance of it came out of understanding its strength and its significance
as the embodiment of the highest cultural values of the people. He
sought to surround his presidency with the symbols of chiefly status. And he enjoyed it.

The presidential stool was of gold and designed in traditional
motif. Kente became his costume on formal occasions, though he
appeared at times uncomfortable in it. (It is reliably learnt that at
least initially his kente was held in place with safety pins.) A state
umbrella occasionally appeared over him; and traditional drummers
and horn-blowers became part of formal state ceremonies. Nkrumah
had a linguist to pour libation and praise him with traditional praise
names from all the major chiefdoms of Ghana. Had he destroyed
chiefship, in what way could he have projected this cultural personality? His appreciation of the elements of traditional ceremony
that surrounded him on state occasions came out in *I Speak of
Freedom*. In his description of the state opening of Parliament on
4th July he wrote:

My arrival at Parliament House was heralded by the beating of traditional drums and the cheers of watching Ghanaians....I was then
escorted to the House in a procession led by the State Sword Bearer
and including the Mace Bearer and eight linguists drawn from many
parts of the country. State horns—*Imenson*— were sounded by the
Juaben State Ntahera. I then took my seat on the Presidential
Throne, carved in the form of a stool and adorned with golden traditional stool symbols.[25]

Nkrumah's predicament was clear: he loved chieftaincy as the
embodiment of Ghanaian culture; but he disliked it as a force of reaction which had to be reduced. But could the powers of chieftaincy
be eliminated or even reduced without at once also eliminating the
glory that surrounded that power which rested with chiefs as tribal
leaders? Such an enigma Nkrumah chose not to pronounce on: To
leave things to the social forces might be construed a non-interven-
tionist policy in culture.

b. Tribalism

If Nkrumah accommodated chieftaincy because in the "inter-
regnum" it could be used to encourage popular effort, he could never
come to tolerate "tribalism." Nkrumah was not only concerned that
Africa should unite, he was also concerned that Ghana should unite.
In a way, he saw that the unity of Africa would make the tribal tendencies of disunity lose their force. African unity however lay in the
future; the reality he was dealing with was a nation which would not
hang together because of ethnic differences. And so long as Ghana
would not unite, so long would his own foothold remain weak and
uncertain and the quest for African Unity more precarious.

Nkrumah would have liked to abolish tribalism; but how does
one root out tribal identity without effacing the culture that gives the
African his cultural identity and awareness? The problem of tribalism was more insidious than that of chieftaincy. One could identify
chiefs and make an order banning chieftaincy. Tribe however is the
skin of the African; one can no more wipe out tribal differences than
remove the stripes from the zebra's back. And tribe confers deeper
spiritual and mental marks of identification on the African than the
facial marks which Nkrumah attacked and banished.

Nkrumah's thinking on tribalism was clear. He could have taken
the long term view that the forces of social progress would sweep
away tribalistic tendencies among our peoples. This was for him
probably a millenarianist dream. Nkrumah probably feared that
before tribalism could disappear in a millennium, tribalism would

have destroyed the new nations of Africa. He had therefore to act.

> We were engaged in a kind of war, a war against poverty and dis-
> ease, against ignorance, against tribalism and disunity. We needed
> to secure the conditions which could allow us to pursue our policy
> of reconstruction and development.[26]

And as if the final solution had been grasped, he wrote:

> My government brought in the Avoidance of Discrimination Bill to
> deal with the control of political parties based on tribal or religious
> affiliations. Its full title was "An Act to prohibit organizations using
> or engaging in racial or religious propaganda to the detriment of
> any other racial or religious community, or securing the elections of
> persons on account of their racial or religious affiliations, or for
> other purposes in connection therewith."[27]

In the parliamentary debate on the Bill, it was clear that
Nkrumah's purpose for the Bill was political — to avoid the fragmentation of the country through tribal-based parties. The Bill made
all the regiona — and religious-based parties in Ghana immediately
illegal, and dealt them a crushing blow. Nowhere was it clearly stated
that the Avoidance of Discrimination Bill was a first step towards creating a national consciousness to replace pride in tribe. Busia, who
appeared to have had that idea as what should be the proper end or
aim of the government in bringing up the Bill, actually thought that
the Bill was not necessary. But our history suggests that he was on
weak grounds.

If the Government side had referred to Ghanaian history and
culture, they could have supported the Bill with the fact that the
Asante law that forbade anyone revealing the origins of another (*Obi
nkyere obi ase*) was one of the pillars on which Asante was built. The
success of that law in stamping out the identities of the congeries of
ethnic groups that came to form the Asante federation would have
appealed to the imagination of all. One has however to hasten to add
that such a law could not alone have created a sense of national
unity. Its complement is public education. Busia's solution was the
complement to the Bill against discrimination; but, from the liberal
perspective he took to the problem, he rejected the law as of no
value. His view was this:

> Our problem is one of nation-building, and you do not do it by
> repressive legislation but by education and the growth of coopera-

tion and leaving parties and policies to the choice of the people (Opposition cheers).[28]

To illustrate his point Busia went on:

Not so long ago, Canada had many parties because of its large regions, but with the passage of the years in order to win the support and command an effective voice in the Government, they had to join and amalgamate. (Mr. Kofi Baako: "We are in Ghana, not in Canada.")[29]

Subsequent events have belied the lessons of the then contemporary experience of Canada. One has only to refer now to the regional and breakaway tendencies in Canadian politics, also in Spain, Ireland and even Great Britain and France, to appreciate how wishful it was to assume that the processes of education and enlightenment could alone be effective in burying discrimination and building up national unity. The effectiveness of anti-discrimination laws in the USA also clearly reveals that Nkrumah's Bill should have been taken, if not as a necessity, certainly as a good prudential step with which to raise the new national consciousness through education.

In the immediate run, the legislation served to unite the fragmentary opposition. From this point in time, it is important to note also how Ghanaians refer back to Nkrumah's days to their pride as Ghanaians and not as Asante, Ewe or Dagbani. The legislation removed from application forms and all government forms, questions about one's tribe, region and religion, compelling personal merits to be seen on equal terms for all Ghanaians.[30]

The question often raised now is: could Nkrumah not have taken a positive view of ethnic differences and built the nation on that foundation? The fact was, Nkrumah was at times so idealistic as to be blind to things he did not like to see. Yet in his idealism he never took his eyes off the practical situation and reality. Thus he emphasized in a speech before independence that "We were all one people" — showing his self delusory desire; but he went on to say that "it was the policy of my government to set up Regional Committees so that the needs of the various regions would be considered in the light of individual wishes of the people who lived in them," recognizing then regional differences. Nkrumah's actions clearly indicated he was aware of the ethnic balance in the political scales, and his appointments and political moves always indicated this consciousness.[31]

C. National Costume

It is necessary for the proper understanding of Nkrumah's thought on culture to place on record a third predicament which proved to be entirely of Nkrumah's own making and is treated here for its symbolic significance.

One matter which issued out of Nkrumah's nationalist propaganda and life-style was whether independence should lead Ghanaians to throw away European attire and wear the traditional cloth to church, school, factory — wherever. Clothing has a great symbolic value in African cultures. Any accession to new status, power or privilege tends to be marked in change of costumes. Clothing is a mode of self-identification and communication. European clothing exposed attachment to European values and cultural forms, and the Ghanaian cloth identified one with traditional values and usages. It is therefore not surprising that this issue should have surfaced in the immediate post-independence years when the one way the people expected to see their "decolonization" emphasized was in change of apparel.[32]

The national good sense suggested that traditional clothing be reserved for use on formal occasions while European clothing be used for the non-regal realms of the farm, factory floor, and classroom. In the issue of clothing, the nationalist movement played out its cultural dilemmas in a medium the people could understand. The African was part of a world culture; thus while he had to find a way of expressing his distinct identity, he could not reject any aspect of world culture that was beneficial in terms of progress and development. Thus the African dress had to live side by side with the European dress. This synthesis—seeing Ghanaian culture as part of world culture—made it also easier for Ghanaians to see their culture as a composite culture of diverse ethnic cultures. Ghanaian culture could be projected through the display of aspects of any of the ethnic cultures within the boundaries of Ghana. And Nkrumah showed how.

Nkrumah made the *fugu* (smock) of the North national in appeal. The *fugu* was his battle dress, as it was for some leaders in the olden days. And he put on *kente* for formal ceremonies. In so doing, he used elements of cultural attire to show that customs from different ethnic cultures were merely different aspects or manifestations of one cultural identity, the Ghanaian identity. In this realm of symbolic thought, it was most African to assume that there was a unifying common element of culture of which the ethnic cultures were a mere manifestation. And the same metaphysical leap became evident in Nkrumah's thought when he turned his mind to reflect on the unity that must exist as the reality behind the African cultural mosaic. Nkrumah assumed this unity of African culture when he began to see the need to justify African unity. But before turning to that justification, it is needful to point to the modes of action that Nkrumah appeared to delineate for handling matters relating to culture.

Nkrumah perceived Africa's cultural predicament in dialectical terms: his mind worked dialectically. Cultural continuity and change presented him with several dialectical opposites. With respect to these polarities, where Nkrumah saw the possibility of a synthesis, he explored and exploited it, as symbolized in the handling of the issue of national attire; where he saw that the polarities resisted a synthesis and yet could not be eliminated, he sought to transcend them. This was the case of tribalism as projected in the Ghanaian situation and on the Pan-African plane. And where he could neither synthesize nor transcend them, he left them to play themselves out; this was his attitude towards things of this order in the words of a prayer:

> Grant me serenity to accept things I cannot change;
> Courage to change things I can
> And wisdom to know the difference.[33]

These then are some of the historical antecedents to the major speech that can be taken as outlining Nkrumah's cultural policy.

The African Genius —
An African Metaphysic and its Strategic Implications for Cultural Institutions

On the occasion of the formal inauguration of the Institute of African Studies, University of Ghana, Nkrumah delivered a speech which, judging by the title and prominence given to it when it was published, was meant to stand as a major policy statement on the issue of African culture. The speech came out under the title "The African Genius." And in it one sees clearly how the cultural problems which Nkrumah had been grappling with might have influenced him to a philosophical turn of mind. From it also, we obtain Nkrumah's strategy for designing the programme of a key cultural institution that Nkrumah might have projected as a model for other cultural institutions. Nowhere else did Nkrumah take as much pains as he did in this speech to explain how the belief in African personality and African unity should determine the strategy of cultural institutions.

In the *African Genius,* Nkrumah identified the dialectical poles in the African cultural situation, aware that these are what should determine the bearings of the African quest for freedom and respectability. First, he identified the polarity of the African past and Africa's future, and from the perspective of the present, insisted that we must re-assess and assert the glories and achievements of our African past, and inspire our generation and succeeding generations with a vision of a better future.[34]

The future of Africa could not be compromised by cultural atavism, and the past could not be denigrated and rejected by any radical commitment to progress and change which would kill the people's sense of historical identity. Nkrumah was aware of this. But Nkrumah, like most members of the African elite, was in the grip of these two conflicting tendencies: primacy of traditions and need for change which, whichever dominated African thinking, was likely to affect African culture and development.

What Nkrumah's attitude to chieftancy suggests is that he himself was not inclined to start tinkering with deep-rooted traditions. He would commit himself to socio-economic development which would, by itself, unleash the forces that would compel the entire people to change aspects of their culture in the historic direction of their own choice. But in the vortex of change Nkrumah felt there had to be something timeless that would span the past, the present and the future, and preserve, or subsist in, the essential cultural identity of the African. For Nkrumah it was necessary to be sure of this factor.

Second, Nkrumah identified the polarity of Africa's oneness and diversity. He sought to assert Africa's separateness and oneness not only in geographical terms — "Africa is no extension of Europe" — but also in qualitative cultural terms. Africa's fragmentation on account of the diversity of ethnic cultures; and fragmentation on account of colonial divisions which imposed on the former in such a way that while, on the one hand, some disparate ethnic groups had come to share common European languages, institutions and modes of thoughts and conduct, viz. Ghana, Nigeria, Kenya, on the other hand, several previously homogeneous or continuous ethnic congeries had come to be separated on account of different European traditions viz. Ivory Coast (Cote d'Ivoire), Togo. Given this diversity, Nkrumah again posited a quality of Africanness that was boundless and common to all the diverse peoples of Africa. To him this too subsisted as a universal existential fact in spite of the specificity of African cultures.

Seeking the permanent and universal in the changing patterns of African culture as one moved in space and time, as it were, Nkrumah postulated the concept of African personality.

To advance the course of African unity, Nkrumah had a choice between two metaphysical positions. He could either choose to assert the reality of Africa's diversity of cultures and then seek to unite Africa through development towards a harmonized or integrated continental culture — the "melting pot" ideology is a case in point; or he could choose to assert the essential oneness of African cultures and regard cultural differences as superficial manifestations or modifications brought about by differences over time and space. Whichever Nkrumah chose, it would have been a matter more of temperament than of logic. And with the intuition of the metaphysician he easily submerged logic when he came to account for what he thought was his distinct and perceptive insight into African cultures. Thus he appeared quite impatient with the realists who did not see the basis for African unity in African cultures. He wrote:

> Critics of African unity often refer to the wide differences in culture, language and ideas in various parts of Africa. This is true, but the essential fact remains that we are all Africans, and have a common interest in the independence of Africa. The difficulties presented by questions of language, culture and different political systems are not inseperable. If the union is agreed upon by us all, then the will to create it is born; and where there is a will there is a way.[35]

Not to be charged with too gross a fallacy, the African Genius emphasized not so much "we are all Africans" as the long known historical connections, common experiences of Africans and their common hope for the future as the basis for asserting a common heritage and a common historical personality. However, neither common experiences, historical connections nor geographical continuity would serve as a basis for claiming a common identity and personality. In fact, not even the family resemblance between cultures which most African cultures evince could justify such a claim. For Nkrumah, however, it was necessary to posit this common personality to enable Africans to overcome or transcend their differences, their many historical jealousies and antipathies, and forge a real family bond. In this light the concept of African personality is just the myth of "one family, one blood" writ large.[36] With reference to outsiders all the members of our continental village (or is it village continent,) are brothers.

From Myth to Action Program

Now, the concept of African personality was born out of Nkrumah's conviction that "we are all Africans." But Nkrumah was convinced that it was a reality which had always been there, only waiting to be restored. He said:

> The personality of the African which was stunted in this process can only be retrieved from these ruins if we make a conscious effort to restore Africa's ancient glory. It is only in conditions of total freedom and independence from foreign rule and interferences that the aspirations of our people we see real fulfillment and the African genius find its best expression.[37]

As it turns up here, if there is any reality or "substratum" to African personality, it is the African genius, and Nkrumah defined the African genius as a step towards determining the strategy which cultural establishments like the Institute of African Studies could use to restore the African glory and bring about African unity. He wrote:

> When I speak of the African genius, I mean something different from Negritude, something not apologetic, but dynamic. Negritude consists in a mere literary affectation and style which piles up word upon word and image upon image with occasional reference to African and things African. I do not mean a vague brotherhood based on a criterion of colour, or on the idea that Africans have no reasoning but only a sensitivity.[38]

He went on to assert:

> By the African genius I mean something positive, our socialist conception of society, the efficiency and validity of our traditional statecraft, our highly developed code of morals, our hospitality and our purposeful energy.[39]

So Nkrumah identified African personality with the African genius, and the African genius with certain cultural characteristics: communalistic social values, efficient institutional structures, and a humane attitude to all humans. Upon this basis Nkrumah proceeded to explain his development strategy with reference to culture.

As the mind is dynamic, the culture of the African cannot be seen in static models; and the way of nurturing the African genius is to infuse the educational system with the right cultural content. The educational system that would take into consideration African culture and seek to bridge the African continental context—the two poles of time and space are here evident—must have as its objective the inculturation of the creative genius of the individual. And such an education would, in Nkrumah's view, be judged by its contextual relevance:

> Indeed, education consists not only in the sum of what a man knows, or the skill with which he can put this to his own advantage ... a man's education must be measured in terms of the soundness of his judgement of people and things, and in his power to understand and appreciate the needs of his fellow men, and to be of service to them. The educated man should be so sensitive to the conditions around him that he makes it his chief endeavour to improve those conditions for the good of all.[40]

This prescription or yardstick would be applicable to education in any milieu. What Nkrumah does, therefore, is to assert by implication that a consciousness not fashioned by education to relate directly to the African environment, not seized of the pressing needs of Africa, and not attuned to African values, cannot give rise to original contributions for the improvement of the life and culture of the peoples of Africa while preserving the African's sense of cultural identity. And this makes the proper cultural education of the African the most important factor in the strategy of African cultural development.

An Institutional Policy—A Model Strategy

Because Nkrumah perceived education as the linchpin of his politico-cultural policy for Africa, it was in respect of the learning process that he demonstrated his thinking on the strategy for preserving and interpreting and creating African culture. And this was a strategy Nkrumah prescribed for the Institute of African Studies, an institution which he charged with the burden of leading the effort to uncover Africa's heritage and make the African aware of his rich heritage.

Expressing the hope that the Institute of African Studies "would always conceive its functions as being to study *Africa,* in the widest sense — Africa in all its complexity and diversity, and its underlying unity,"[41] Nkrumah invited scholars to a consideration "of the implication of the concept of African unity for the study of African peoples and cultures..."[42] He spelt out the implications in a strategy involving two steps. First, studies undertaken on African peoples and cultures must not be limited "by conventional territorial or regional boundaries."[43]

these investigations must inevitably lead outwards—to the exploration of the connections between the musical forms, the dances,
the literature, the plastic arts, the philosophical and religious
beliefs, the systems of government, the patterns of trade and economic organization that have been developed here in Ghana, and
the cultures of other African peoples and other regions of Africa.
Ghana, that is to say, can only be understood in the total African
context.[44]

Now, were this principle to be adopted as a strategy for cultural
activities rather than as a mere strategy for investigating culture, it
would demand that action be oriented outward to reflect the relatedness of different cultural activities—religion, philosophy, art, politics, trade and economics, as well as the relatedness of different
nations and people. Thus, for example, an art programme should be
made to portray the important functions of art in religion, philosophy, politics, and trade, and also bring out the relationships between
the arts of different African countries.

Second, in extension of this approach, Nkrumah urged that even
the continent should not be the limit of the exploration of African cultures. African cultural studies must extend beyond the continent's
perimeters to seek Africa's relationships in the Mediterranean, the
Indian Ocean, Arabia, India, Indonesia, America and even China.

Should these principles guide not only cultural studies but also
cultural development activity, Nkrumah emphasized that such studies as shall be done to African heritage must also lead on to creative
activity. In literature, for example, such studies

must stimulate the birth of a specifically African literature, which,
exploring African themes and the depth of the African soul, will
become an integral portion of a general world literature.[45]

Thus Nkrumah's strategy for cultural development is to use
education to obtain knowledge which would be used in an effort to
contribute the creative output of the African genius to the wealth of
world culture. In this strategy, all facets of culture would be given
equal attention, and the inter-relationship between all facets examined in each society in the wider context of Africa and, in turn, in the
still wider context of world culture.

Summary and Conclusion

Nkrumah had laid the foundations of almost all the major cultural institutions of Ghana by the time of his overthrow. The historical evidence shows that many of these institutions had come into being before he had formulated any cultural policies to guide their operations. Certain practical problems of African culture engaged his mind at home, and called for specific actions: these might have set his mind to work. Once he began to think seriously of laying the foundations of African unity, however, his focus shifted outward: he sought to make clear how he would justify the quest for African unity, especially as his critics never ceased pointing out what a diversity of peoples and cultures the African continent held. This compelled Nkrumah to crystalize his ideas; and he chose the occasion of the inauguration of the Institute of African Studies on 25th October, 1963, to spell out his cultural objectives, his cultural philosophy and the implications of that philosophy for the strategy of study and of creative cultural activity needed to regenerate and develop African cultures.

Nkrumah's major political objectives were national unity and continental unity. The national objectives would be irrelevant if continental unity could be achieved. Because of this, though it was virtually the same issues that plagued him at home that confronted him on a continental scale when he contemplated African unity, he fashioned a cultural philosophy and strategy more suited to Africa than to Ghana.

For this strategy he fashioned a concept of African personality, and defined it as the creative expression of the African genius, the common reality behind the diversities and complexities of African cultures. To obtain a genuine African personality, Nkrumah could posit only an educational system that had African cultural content and sought to create awareness of Africa's needs. Such an educational system had to regard as its frame of reference (a) relationships between all major aspects of people's culture; (b) the specificity of one nation's experiences in the context of Africa as a whole; and (c) the particularity of African experience as a major part and not "a mere appendage of world culture."[46] This had also to be the framework of the African creative endeavour that should flow from the educational programme.

Now if this is the outline of Nkrumah's cultural policy, then it had three major failings. First, for a great leader who saw the masses and their need as a major factor in culture, Nkrumah failed to project any active role for the workers and people of Africa though they constituted the creative source and vitality and guarantors of Africa's heritage. Where Nkrumah mentioned the people, he saw them as recipients rather than as cultural innovators or creators, with the new intelligentsia, of African culture. And this attitude arose out of a second fault in his strategy.

It is clear that Nkrumah saw cultural education in terms of classroom or academic activity instead of a learning process carried out in life and spanning each person's life from birth to death. The strategy he put forward therefore neglected the learning and creative experience which is informal and occurs in the general ambience of African life outside the classroom. The third failing in his strategy is that it neglects to give serious place to the preservation of the African cultural ambience in the process of developments that are likely to change the African way of life and African mores. Are the ways in which our cities, public buildings and modern houses designed, to be influenced by African concepts and conditions of life? This is neglected by Nkrumah's strategy.

Whatever its failing, however, the strategy which Nkrumah uncovered in his speech, *The African Genuis,* would quite likely influence the thinking of policy makers for a very long time to come. History would judge Nkrumah's cultural philosophy and strategy as a very important and necessary stimulus to the examination of how Africa would preserve and develop its cultures in a Pan-African framework.

Did Nkrumah have a cultural policy? It is obvious he had one in the making. He got as far as fashioning the intellectual or philosophical foundations for it. We cannot say he actually succeeded in erecting its superstructure.

NOTES

1. Nkrumah, 1961(b):129
2. Article 3 of the Charter.
3. *Ibid.,* Article 4(e).
4. Apart from Negritude and African Personality we have Nyerere's *African Socialism* or *Ujamaa,* Zaire's *Authenticité* and the Philosophy of African Humanism of President Kaunda of Zambia — not to mention the Third Universal Dimension of Liby and other less well known ideologies of deep cultural significance.
5. Nkrumah, 1963a:xi, Introduction.
6. Nkrumah, 1961(b), op. cit.: 48.
7. Nkrumah, 1963a:49

8. *Ibid.*
9. *Ibid.*
10. *op. cit.* :93
11. *op. cit.* :49
12. UNESCO, 1975: 9
13. Columns 5 and 6 "Written Answer to Questions" 30th August, 1957, in Ghana Parliamentary Debates—First Series Vol. 7, 20th - 30th August, 1957.
14. *Ibid.*
15. *Ibid.*
16. *Ibid.*
17. These sentiments were most clearly articulated by Mr. Joe Appiah who went to the extent of expressing the hope that "The Minister will make it possible for the true heritage of Ghana as a whole to be developed and brought up to its proper proportions." And he went on to explain: "By this I mean that in the appointment of Members of Council care should be taken to see to it that a truly representative council, representative of the entire Ghana is set up." He went on to assert further: "It is not enough to know the heritage of your own individual tribal grouping; it is not enough. We must expand and be true exponent of Ghanaian culture *in toto* (Second Reading, p 306)." While some MPs thought this could make the Council, the notion of all ethnic cultures as representative of Ghanaian culture was distilled as the premise of representation.
18. These impressions emerged in *Africa Must Unite* (Heinemann, London, 1963) and are explained below.
19. In his *Autobiography* (195 7: 99), Nkrumah explained that what he had said could not be construed as a rejection of chieftaincy. His view was that if chiefs would not follow the wishes of the people then they would flee. However, such was the fear that Nkrumah had to explain his stand in many places. (See *I Speak of Freedom*, Heinemann, London, 1961, p. 24.)
20. Nkrumah, 1 963a: 83 .
21. *Ibid.*
22. *Ibid.*
23. *Ibid.:* 84 Nkrumah succeeded in doing precisely this through destoolments engineered by CPP elements and through the use of Gazette notices (indicating government power) to recognize chiefs, or withhold recognition making the position of a chief untenable.
24. *Ibid.*
25. Nkrumah, 1961:238, 239.
26. Nkrumah, 1963a:74.
27. *Ibid.* 74.
28. Ghana Parliamentary Debates Official Reports—First Series Vol. 7, 20th - 30th August, 1957, p. 527.
29. *Ibid.*
30. In the few years before his overthrow Nkrumah started appointing Regional Commissioners to posts outside the regions from which they hailed. This was in apparent pursuit of his policy of non-discrimination. However, some people remarked that he himself had begun to employ more Nzema into the Security Service, which if true would prove how deep tribal sentiments struck when one felt insecure.
31. His Cabinet and party central executive reflected regional and ethnic considerations. And Regional Commissioners were initially always men from the

regions they were sent to head. Much later, he appointed men from one region to be Commissioner in a different one. Also with his theory of democratic centralism the notion of creating regional assemblies went out of consideration.

32. In the debate on the Bill establishing the Arts Council of Ghana, Joe Appiah highlighted the significance of Ghanaian national attire in projecting the Ghanaian national culture, and others concurred. The foremost apostle of this mode of national self-expression were the famous lawyer Kobina Sekyi and the no less famous musician Ephraim Amu.

33. Nkrumah, 1961(b):61.

34. Nkrumah, 1963e:3 .

35. Nkrumah, 196 l(b):xii, Preface.

36. The African lineage or clan is almost always a cluster of people believing that they have one blood, though they might know some are strangers and others slaves. The wish for unity was often made into reality by oath or a symbolic enactment of blood sharing. For Akans *Abusua baako, Mogya baako* (one family, one blood) was the maxim of clan and lineage solidarity.

37. Nkrumah, 1963e:5.

38. *Ibid.:* 5, 6.

39. *Ibid.*

40. *Ibid.*

41. *Ibid.:* 9

42. *Ibid.*

43. *Ibid.*

44. *Ibid.:* 10.

45. *Ibid.:* 8

46. *Ibid.:* 8

THE SEARCH FOR "CONSTITUTIONAL CHIEFTAINCY"

Kwame Arhin

1. Prologue: Power, Authority and Influence

The argument of this paper is as follows: Kwame Nkrumah's government, like the preceding colonial regime, adapted chieftaincy to the demands of their administration. The colonial regime — 1874 1957 — had converted chiefly power into authority for the execution of its plans of imperial rule and made chiefs its agents. Nkrumah and his Convention People's Party saw the basis of authority as the People's mandate; and thought therefore, that power had to be located in the people as a whole, and exercised by their elected representatives. Hence the authority granted to the chiefs by the colonial regime was reduced at best to influence, and even that varied with a particular chief's standing with the Convention People's Party. The end result was a "constitutional chieftaincy."

Chieftaincy under Nkrumah passed through two phases. The first phase began in 1951, when Nkrumah's Convention People's Party (CPP), first formed the government, and ended in March 1957, the year of independence. In this phase, the representatives of the people reduced the authority granted to chiefs by the colonial regime. In the second phase, which began in 1957 and ended in 1966, when Nkrumah was overthrown by a *coup d'etat,* the people's representatives reduced the residue of chiefly authority left in the first phase, and made the chief a passive agent of the central government.

These propositions will be examined in the light of the legislation on chieftaincy in the Gold Coast Legislative Assembly, 1951–1957, and in the Ghana Parliament, 1957-1966, and also of the activities of the Party outside the legislative chambers. But it is necessary to consider, first, the position of the chiefs on the eve of the rule of the Convention People's Party which shaped the Party's views on the institution of chieftaincy.

II. Chieftaincy on the Eve of CPP rule

The period, 1844-1874, was one of hesitant imperialism. It was one during which, while making up their minds about the character and extent of their authority in what they called the Gold Coast Protectorate, the British colonial authorities sought accommodation with the chiefs. But in 1874 they declared the Gold Coast Protectorate a colony[1] and made it clear in subsequent legislation that the chiefs of the Protectorate were subordinate to the Governor of the Gold Coast and his provincial and district agents, and that the chiefs could only exercise authority granted to them by the colonial government.[2] The chiefs of Ashante and Northern Territories (now the Northern and Upper Regions), were placed in much the same position as those of the Gold Coast in 1896 and 1901. It made no difference whether the chiefs were, formally, allies, conquered or protected: they all became subordinate to the colonial authorities who regulated their legislative, judicial and other functions. Also in the north, outside Gonja, Dagomba, Nanumba, Mamprusi and Wa, the colonial authorities converted heads of clans into territorial rulers of the Akan type for the purpose of colonial administration.[3]

The effect of the legislation was that at the beginning of formal colonial rule, the chiefs became the executive agents of the colonial administration. As junior partners of the political officers, who consulted them on customary law matters, *(abibise)* and the planning of local projects, they replaced the "intelligentsia," the educated professionals and businessmen of the coastal towns who, through the Governor's nomination, had been represented on the Legislative Council of the Gold Coast. The intelligentsia lost favor with the British when they promoted the establishment of the Fanti Confederation, 1868-1872, and, in 1897, formed the Gold Coast Aborigines Rights' Protection Society to lead the agitation over the Lands Bill. Again, following the decision, for fairly racist reasons to employ only British senior officers, the educated indigenes could no longer be employed in the senior branches of the civil service.[4]

In addition to the colonial authorities' suspicions of the intelligentsia as "agitators," whom they were later to label as an "irresponsible minority," the British preferred the chiefs as advisers on other grounds. They thought that since the chiefs had signed the treaties that provided part of the legal basis of colonial rule, and since the chiefs, at least in theory, were the elected representatives of their various states (aman), they — and not the isolated educated men ought to be regarded as the legitimate unofficial advisers to the Governor and his subordinates. Before 1925 the British considered it premature to introduce the ballot box even in the coastal municipalities, the centres of British culture; and the educated men did not make easy partners in the Legislative Council. The British, indeed, envisioned the future constitutions of the Gold Coast in terms of a federation of the various indigenous states.

These considerations led the colonial authorities to promote the groupings of head chiefs of the indigenous states in the Gold Coast Colony into the Western, Central and Eastern Provincial Councils of chiefs in 1924-192.[5] The councils were to be consulted on economic and social policy, but also to act as electoral colleges to elect six unofficial members to the Legislative Council, in addition to the three elected members of the municipalities of Accra, Cape Coast and Sekondi-Takoradi under the Guggisberg Constitution of 1925.[6]

In this way Guggisberg met the demand by the West African National Congress for increase in the unofficial representation in the Legislative Council. He argued that the Provincial Councils would "constitute the breakwater defending our native constitutions, institutions and customs against the disintegrating waves of Western Civilization."[7] The British formally restored the Ashanti Confederacy Council on January 31st, 1935, for the same reasons.

The idea of a ruling partnership between colonial officials and chiefs was embodied in the system of indirect rule which was officially formulated in 1927. The British then supported the passage of the Native Administration Ordinance, introduced by Nana (later Sir) Ofori Atta, the Paramount chief of Akim Abuakwa, its subsequent amendments, and its elaborations in the Native Courts Ordinance in the Gold Coast, Ashanti and the Northern Territories in 1932,1935,1939 and 1944.[8]

The "intelligentsia," led by Casely-Hayford, and the remnants of the Gold Coast Aborigines Rights' Protection Society, objected to the establishment of the Provincial Councils as electoral colleges for the Legislative Council and to the Native Administration Ordinance on the following grounds: They argued that in Akan Law and custom a paramount chief could not speak to outsiders without his spokesman (linguist), which he was bound to do in both the Provincial and Legislative Councils; that the paramount chiefs were acquiring powers foreign to the indigenous constitutions; that the chiefs would come under the undue influence of the Colonial political officers (the chief, provincial and district commissioners) and that the effect of it all would be the alienation of the paramount chiefs, not only from their sub-chiefs, but also from the commoners.[9]

These objections expressed the discontent among the "intelligentsia" about the growing alliance between the chiefs and the colonial authorities. They also expressed the claim of the "intelligentsia" to represent the people in place of the chiefs. The apprehension about the alienation of the chiefs from the people was real. In 1942, Sir Alan Bums, the Governor, stated that within the 10 year period, 1932-1942, in the Gold Coast, 22 paramount chiefs had been destooled, 22 others had abdicated in order to forestall destoolment, 7 stools were vacant and only a few paramount chiefs had succeeded in maintaining their places on their stools for any significant length of time.[10] In the era of growing nationalism, the chiefs became the foci of discontent against British rule.

An aspect of the colonial situation was the increasing rivalry between the chiefs and the "intelligentsia" for the people's allegiance. The joint action of the chiefs and the "intelligentsia" over the petition to His Majesty the King on the Sedition and Waterworks Bill in 1934 was a temporary truce.[11] The municipal members of the Legislative Council thereafter clashed with the chiefs in the Council over the imposition of levies for stool treasuries and the bills that tended to augment chiefly authority.[12] Again, although the chiefs and the "intelligentsia" came together to press for political reforms, resulting in the Burns' 1946 Constitution (that permitted the Provincial Councils to elect both chiefs and commoners as their representatives in the Legislative Council), no chief was a founding member of the United Gold Coast Convention (UGCC) whose aim was to obtain reforms in the "out-moded" Bums' Constitution.

So when Kwame Nkrumah joined the UGCC as its General Secretary in December 1947, he found the chiefs, on the one hand, and the intelligentsia in the Convention, on the other, rivals for the people's allegiance.[13] But he considered neither as likely champions of the welfare of the people, who he regarded as his army of liberation from colonial rule and the base of his rise to political power.

Nkrumah himself was apparently not well disposed towards

the chiefs. He professed himself a Marxist Socialist.[14] The rank and file of the Committee for Youth Organization, which in June, 1949, broke away from the UGCC and formed the Convention People's Party, consisted of youth associations, clubs and societies of elementary school leavers[15] who were even more resentful than the intelligentsia of the growing chiefly authority,[16] particularly as manifested in the operations of the Native Authority Courts, and led the destoolment movements against the chiefs.[17] Nkrumah stated on the authority of his mother that he had claims of succession to the stools of Nsuaem in Wasa Fiase and Dadiase in Aowin in the Western Region. But he regarded chieftaincy as a feudal institution, and was seemingly not interested in becoming a chief.[18]

It also became clear, in the intervening period between the publication of the constitutional proposals of the Coussey Committee in 1949, and elections to the new Legislative Assembly in 1951, that both the "intelligentsia" and the chiefs regarded Nkrumah and his party as *parvenus,* and potential usurpers of power from the legitimate heirs to the British, the chiefs and the British-educated "intelligentsia." In 1950, when the chiefs declared their loyalty to the British government, after Nkrumah had declared "Positive Action" in an attempt to advance the attainment of independence, he aroused the hostility of the chiefs to his party with his statement that, should the chiefs refuse to support the people's "just" struggle for freedom, the time would come when they would run away and leave behind their sandals.[19] In the circumstances it was certainly a "tactical action" on his part — a ploy to win the support of the chiefs that he prevailed upon the CPP to ask for a second chamber in the new Legislative Assembly, which would be dominated by the chiefs.[20] But this friendly gesture to the chiefs did not win his party a single representative from the Territorial Councils of Chiefs in the 1951 Legislative Assembly.[21]

In summary, on the eve of the assumption of power by Kwame Nkrumah as Leader of Government Business in the new Legislative Assembly in 1951, the authority the chiefs exercised under the colonial administration had alienated them from both the intelligentsia and their people. Yet the increased number of destoolments showed that the commoners were concerned with the performance of stool occupants and not with the institution itself: one destooled a bad chief in order to preserve a stool. Apparently there was acceptance by the colonial rulers, the intelligentsia and also tho CPP of the view of the Coussey Constitutional Committee that:

the institution of chieftaincy is so closely bound up with the life of
our communities that its disappearance would spell disaster. Chiefs
and what they symbolize in our society are so vital that the subject
of [its] future must be approached with caution.[22]

As will be seen, caution, or, as he would call it, "tactical action," was
an outstanding characteristic of the manner in which Nkrumah and
his Party dealt with the question of chieftaincy in the first phase of
their administration.

III. Watson and Coussey on Chieftaincy

Before Nkrumah and the CPP came into power in 1951, the Gold
Coast (Constitution) Order-in-Council, 1950, defined the place of the
chief in the new Constitution.[23] The basis of the Order-in-Council
was the findings of the Watson Commission of Enquiry[24] into the
disturbances in the Gold Coast (1948) and the Coussey
Constitutional Committee, 1949.[25]

The Watson Commission reported wide-spread criticisms of
chiefs in the Colony and Ashanti. They were impressed by the con-
tentions of many of their witnesses that the people generally had no
political rights, in spite of the considerable educational and socio-
economic progress made since colonial rule, and that:

Only in Native Administration, residing largely in a hierarchy of
vested interests jealously guarded by chiefs and elders, was the
African provided with an approach to political expression. Even
where an enlightened Native Administration admitted entrants into
the fold of the state council, it was conceded as a great privilege
and not conferred as an elementary right.

A large section of witnesses considered the chiefs as instruments
"for the delay if not the suppression of the political aspirations of the
people." They stated as the essence of the radical change in chief-
people relations;

The fact that destooling—once the absolute privilege of a dissatisfied people, if need be exercised capriciously and violently —has
been made the subject of a well-defined code, under the supervision
of the government.[26]

The Commission also found wide spread objections to chiefs as
members of the Legislative Council, into which they reportedly
elected either one of their own number or close relatives, and where

they allegedly served as tools of the government: it was repeatedly pointed out that the place of the chief was among his people. The rather extreme view was said to have been widely held that the function of the chief should be "ornamental." The chief was

> a man not necessarily of any particular ability but of good presence, expressing in his person but never in his voice the will of his people; exercising the office of pouring libations to ancestors; remaining always among his people and never speaking save through his linguist; he must either remain on his stool and take no part in external politics or forgo the office; he should not attempt a dual role.[27]

The chiefs and their more zealous adherents, notably the leaders of the United Gold Coast Convention, naturally disagreed with this view which, indeed, was neither formally nor substantively correct. But the problem remained of how to ensure change in continuity; how to reconcile the demands of the growing African revolution with the claims of tradition. As the Watson Commission noted, it was not easy "to envisage the growth of commercialization in the Gold Coast with the retention of native institution...;" the crux of the problem was to make sure that existing institutions did not stand in the way of making such modifications to the constitution as would ensure the satisfaction of general political aspirations.[28]

   The Watson Commission sympathized with these political aspirations, and also understood the difficulties into which the chiefs had got themselves in consequence of becoming junior partners in indirect rule, as well as the need not to force the pace of change. Therefore, in their proposals for constitutional reform they provided for a large chiefly representation, one half of the seats in all the units of local government—town, district, rural and regional councils— and in the Gold Coast Assembly. But they also insisted that "local government" authorities, should be separated from "traditional" authority bodies, with linkages in the form of chiefly representation in, and presidencies of, the local government bodies.[29] The Watson Commission sought to dismantle the existing "native administration" and recreate government by chiefs and people in a new form.

   It has been considered necessary to go into the findings of the Watson Commission in this detail because the Commission set the scene for the subsequent argument about the constitutional position of the chiefs in the independent state of Ghana. At the time of Watson, the debate was about the relative political weights of the chief, as chief, and of the commoner. Later, the debate became one of the chief's utility given the accepted norm of democratic rule on the basis of universal adult suffrage.

The All-African Coussey Committee of distinguished chiefs and eminent men objected to the view that the chief should have merely "ornamental" functions. As already noted, they held that Ghanaian society was rooted in chieftaincy. They believed that the experience and wisdom of the chiefs should be utilized at all levels of the government of the country. They voted by a majority of one for a bi-cameral legislature in which a second chamber of chiefs and eminent men, too elevated above the ordinary run of men to engage in the tough game of electioneering, would exercise restraint on an overly enthusiastic first chamber of commoners.

The Coussey Committee adopted the Watson Commission's view that local government bodies should be based wherever possible on local states or federations of contiguous states, and provided for one-third chiefly representation in all local government bodies— municipal, district, urban/rural, rural and village area, and regional councils—and chiefly presidents for those bodies. They provided for special seats in the Gold Coast Legislative Assembly for the Territorial Councils of Chiefs of the Colony, Ashanti, the Northern Territories and Southern Togoland. But they agreed with Watson that local government should be kept separate from state and other chiefs' councils which should be concerned with local constitutional and traditional issues, the declaration of customs, and also serve as electoral colleges for electing representatives to the local government bodies and the Gold Coast Assembly; and also that the native courts — a source of friction between the chiefs and their people—should be reformed by appointing panels of lay magistrates with knowledge of local customs or qualified lawyers for the local courts, which would be managed by the local authorities.[30]

The Coussey Committee was careful to emphasize that these proposals were not meant to upset relations of customary allegiance, a point that Mr. E. O. Asafu-Adjei, the Minister of Local Government, repeated in his "Preface" to the brochure on Local Government Reforms.[31] Finally, Coussey also provided that the local government bodies, including representatives of the chiefs, would become trustees of stool lands, collect rates and levies and, by agreement with the chiefs, provide for the maintenance of the latter.

IV. Chieftaincy in the First Phase of CPP Rule, 1951–1957

The Gold Coast (Constitution) Order-in-Council, 1950, — the result of His Majesty's Government's reflections on the recommendations of the Coussey Committee—accepted the Coussey view on the position of chiefs in the new constitution. The chiefs themselves, deliberating in the three territorial councils, rejected a second chamber in the new legislature just as the Legislative Council had done.[33] Although the chiefs had, in the main, opposed them during the election, and though there were features of chieftaincy that the CPP heartily disliked, Nkrumah and his Assemblymen could not launch any significant attack on the institution within the framework of the Coussey Constitution.[34]

The pivot of that Constitution was the Executive Council, over which the Governor presided, and in which Nkrumah, as Leader of Government Business, ranked third. Article(4) of the Order-in-Council reserved chieftaincy matters to the Governor, acting in his discretion, and the Assembly could not discuss bills relating to the institution without the Governor's prior consent. Nkrumah had to act with the support of the thirty-seven Assemblymen elected by the three territorial councils of Ashanti, the Colony and the Northern Territories. It was also fairly certain that the three Ex-official members, as well as the six Special Members representing the Chambers of Commerce, would vote against any radical measures affecting chieftaincy.[35] The Gold Coast (Constitution) Order-in-Council, 1954, gave the country internal self-government and placed chieftaincy under the authority of Nkrumah, his all, African cabinet and his majority in the Legislative Assembly. But the country was still not independent, and the Convention People's Party had to exercise caution in dealing with the erstwhile junior partners of the British authorities.

Therefore, like the preceding colonial regime, Nkrumah's government had to seek peaceful accommodation with the chiefs, while pursuing the goal of majority rule based on "one man, one vote." This would put total power in the hands of Nkrumah and the CPP and, with that power, they could remove what they believed to be the "feudalistic" features of chieftaincy.[36]

Before 1955 all the legislation relating to chieftaincy, initiated by the government, gave effect to the recommendations of the Coussey Committee on the institution. The Local Government Ordinance, 1951, introduced the new local government system envisaged by Coussey. The State Councils Ordinance (1952) for Ashanti, the Colony and Southern Togoland tightened up the procedure for the settlement of chieftaincy disputes by the State Councils, with appeals to the Governor in respect of the Colony and Southern Togoland and to the Asanteman Council in the case of Ashanti.

But the CPP also had "unofficial" ways of contending with the chiefs. The Party was in no doubt that many of the chiefs were antipathetic to it and supported one or other of the opposition groups of the "intelligentsia;" and that the chiefs could influence, to a cert~in extent, the voting pattern of their subjects. As Nkrumah saw it, and stated later, "Instead of supporting the efforts of the man in the street to express himself and to bring pressure to bear on the imperialists, these political opponents of the Party ranged themselves on the side of the British Colonial Government in trying to suppress the great upsurge of nationalism."[37]

The Party dealt with the more pronounced of their chiefly opponents at the local levels through destoolment agitation by the local branches expressed in "resolutions" and "telegrams" to the Minister of Local Government. Such was the spate of destoolment agitation that a harassed state council was moved to put the question, "Does the CPP favor destoolment?"[38] Chiefly opposition to the Convention People's Party reinforced the Party's view of chieftaincy as undemocratic.[39] Nkrumah, Life Chairman of the Party, and Leader of Government Business, reportedly explained the new local government system by saying "One of the pitfalls of the [Native Authority] Ordinance was that members were not properly elected. This has led to a split between the chief and the people. In order to bridge the gap, the local councils have been formed to take over the functions of the Native Authority."[40] Since destoolment agitators, known as "malcontents" were mostly CPP "activists," who had to appear before the State Councils and Native Authority Courts, the Party also pressured the government into reducing the penalties attached to unsuccessful destoolment litigation.[41] Accordingly, while the State Councils Ordinance (1952) seemingly protected the chiefs against baseless destoolment movements, it equally minimized the fees and fines attached to the proceedings, and gave the courts of the central government, and not those of the Native Authorities, the power of enforcing the prescribed sanctions.[42] When a chief appeared to be overly hostile to the CPP, as was the case of the Wenchihene, Nkrumah persuaded, normally through a motion passed in the Legislative Assembly, the Governor to appoint a Committee of Enquiry into his activities.[43] Both officially and unofficially, the party made it clear that the chiefs must adapt themselves to the changing times and accept CPP rule.[44]

Some chiefs, notably Nana Sir Tsibo Darku, Omanhene of Assin Atandasu in the Central Region, rightly read the signs of the times and gave support to the Convention People's Party and the government.[45] Also some of the chiefs were prepared to make use of the new order for their own purposes. In 1952 when the Techimanhene, Nana Akumfi Ameyaw, and the Dommahene, Nana Agyeman Badu, started a serious movement to win Government recognition for the separation of the Brong-Kyempim Council from the Asanteman Council, they decided that their best chance of success lay in giving support to the CPP government.[46] Generally, chiefs in the then Northern Territories and most parts of the country fell back on the practice in the colonial period of supporting the government.

The great exceptions to this rule were the Asanteman Council and the Akim Abuakwa (ƆKyeame) State Council in the Eastern Region, which gave open support to the National Liberation Movement (NLM). Baffour Osei Akoto, a Senior Spokesman (ƆKyeame) of the Asantehene, led the NLM, which was dominated in its leadership by the leading members of the parties opposed to the CPP. The NLM was said to have been formed to secure a federal constitution for the country, in order to provide a safeguard, they said, against the creeping dictatorship of Nkrumah, as well as to ensure that cocoa farmers got a good producer price for their produce. Between 1954 and 1956, a period of "struggle for power," as Austin calls it, the political battle raged between the CPP and the NLM and their allied chiefs, each side using the weapons at its command.[47]

The Asanteman Council construed dissent by chiefs from the decision of the Council to support the NLM as a rebellion against the Golden Stool, and instigated their destoolment, or made it impossible for them to attend the Council's meetings.[48] The Council sanctioned the use of its funds for promoting the political work of the NLM.[49] The Akyem Abuakwa (ƆKyeame) Council did the same. In justification for this, both Councils argued that the NLM was a national movement with the specific objective of securing a federal constitution in which, they supposed, the position of chieftaincy would be safeguarded, and which would secure the country against the "mass" dictatorship of the CPP and the personal one of Nkrumah.[50]

The collaboration of the Asanteman Council with the NLM brought the first major official attack on a chiefly institution. In 1955, Mr. Krobo Edusei, Member of the Legislative Assembly (MLA) for Sekyere East in Ashanti, got a motion passed in the Assembly which read:

This House does request Government to introduce a Bill to amend
sections 8, 9 and 13 of the State Council (Ashanti) Ordinance, 1952,
to allow a chief below the status of paramount status to appeal in a
constitutional matter from the decision of a State Council to the
Governor.

Mr. Edusei gave as his reasons for seeking the amendment that the
Asanteman Council had constituted itself into a political party and
used its powers under the Ordinance against the chiefs who did not
support the NLM, citing cases of the Council's victimization of CPP
supporters among the chiefs. He made it clear that his motion was
not against the "Golden Stool" which had not "picked up a quarrel
with anybody."[51]

The CPP members in the Assembly generally supported Mr.
Edusei while the opposition members, notably Mr. B. F. Kusi
opposed it, denying that the Asanteman Council had identified itself
with a political party or that the Asantehene had misused his powers under the Ordinance.[52]

The debate on the motion clearly illustrated the conflicting
views between the parties on the position of the chief in the constitution and in the politics of the country. The CPP made it clear that
the chiefs must maintain a neutral position in the competition for
power between the various parties, and that they must accept a
position of subordination to whomever emerged as the government,
just as they had done under the colonial government. The parties
opposed to the CPP saw the chiefs as their allies who could help
them turn the tide against the CPP.[53] They did not think that the
chiefs should be neutral in the struggle for a suitable constitution.

In the search for a suitable constitution for an independent
Ghana, which engaged the attention of the CPP Government, its
opponents and the Secretary of State for the Colonies in 195–56,[54]
the Asanteman and the Ɔkyeman Councils, as well as the Northern
chiefs who supported the Northern People's Party (NPP) held the
same view as the NLM. This was that only a federal constitution
could save the country from Nkrumah's imminent dictatorship.[55]

But the chiefs in the North were less open and much less bitter
in their opposition to the CPP than the majority of the members of
the Asanteman and Ɔkyeman Councils.[56] The chiefs in the Brong
district, who wanted secession from the Asanteman, naturally sided
with the CPP as a way of advancing their secessionist aims.[57]

The progress of the Brong-Kyempim Movement illustrates the
pragmatic approach of Nkrumah and the Convention People's Party
to chieftaincy. In 1952, while the Asanteman Council had not openly

allied itself with the opponents of the Party, Nkrumah set up a Committee, under Nene Azu Mate Kole, the Konor of Manya Krobo, to arbitrate between the Asanteman Council and the dissident Brong chiefs.[58] But when in 1954 the Council became openly hostile to the Party, the latter started to make common cause with the Brong chiefs, and to take seriously the possibility of making the Brong chiefs independent of the Asanteman Council. The State Councils (Ashanti) (1955) Amendment Ordinance was, to a great extent, a supporting gesture for the Brong chiefs, and also showed the CPP's operational principle in chieftaincy matters. This was to penalize the chiefs opposed to the party and show favor to those who supported it. Convinced that there was no support for the abolition of the institution, the CPP considered it necessary to secure the voluntary allegiance of all chiefs, first to the Party, which was yet to win the political battle and, second, to the government.

The result of the constitutional agitation, conducted both violently and non-violently by the NLM and the CPP in Ashanti and Akyem Abuakwa, the proposals by the Government of the Gold Coast,[59] and the intervention by the Secretary of State for the Colonies, was that the institution of chieftaincy was given an apparently secure position in the Ghana (Constitution) Order-in-Council, 1957. In order to make it difficult to break up the Ashanti Region and, thereby meet the demands of the Brong chiefs, Section 32 entrenched the sections affecting chieftaincy matters, and Section 33, and its sub-sections 1–7, made special provision for the alteration of regional boundaries and the creation of new regions. Section 66 "guaranteed" the "office of Chief in Ghana, as existing by customary law and usage," and Section 67 stated:

> Within twelve months of the appointed day or as soon as thereafter may be practicable, a House of Chiefs shall be established by Act of Parliament in and for each Region. A House of Chiefs shall have power to consider any matter referred to it by a Minister or the Assembly. A House of Chiefs may at any time offer advice to any Minister. A House of Chiefs at any time, may, and where the Assembly so requests, shall, submit to the Governor General or the Speaker, as the case may be, a written declaration of what in its opinion is the customary law relating to any subject in force in any part of the area of its authority.

Section 68 and its sub-sections required an Act of Parliament to provide for the settlement of local constitutional disputes (a) in other regions and (b) in Ashanti.

In (a) case disputes involving a paramount and subordinate chiefs would be determined in the first instance by the State Council concerned, and, in the second, by an Appeal Commissioner to whom the relevant House of Chiefs would refer appeals. In (b), Ashanti, the requisite Act of Parliament would provide for determination of such disputes by a committee of the House of Chiefs, and appeals from the decision of the Committee would be referred by the Head of the Region "within a prescribed period to an Appeal Commissioner" whose decision, subject to any clarification required by the Head of Region "shall [as also in the case of (a)] be final."

The envisaged Act of Parliament would give the Appeal Commissioner the discretion to sit with or without assessors and "to call upon any person to give him advice ... on local laws and customs." It would also require the Commissioner, after due clarification, if sought by a House of Chiefs or Head of the Ashanti Region, to forward his decision to the appropriate Minister for publication in the Gazette within two months.[60]

The Constitution obviously intended that the Appeal Commissioner would replace the Governor and the cabinet in the settlement of chieftaincy disputes and hence be impartial. Therefore, as noted, in hearing referred cases, sub-section 4 of Section 68 provided that he would act as a public officer appointed by the Judicial Service Commission. Sub-section 5 defined "matters of constitutional nature" which would fall within his competence as:

> the nomination, election or installation of any person as a chief or the claim of any person to be elected or installed as a chief; or

> the tenure of office, deposition or abdication of any chief; or the right of any person to take part in the election or installation of any person as a chief or in the deposition of any chief; or

> the recovery or delivery of stool property or skin property in connection with any election, installation, deposition, or political or constitutional relations under customary law between chiefs.

In effect, the chiefs in their regional houses would become advisers to the government of national and customary matters and, to enable them to do so, they were to be free from partisan political pressures. The constitutional provisions were, clearly, a compromise solution that could only have been imposed by Her Majesty's Secretary of State, and accepted by Nkrumah at the risk of delaying the attainment of independent nationhood.[61]

V. Chieftaincy in the Second Phase of CPP Rule, 1957–66

Subsequent legislation in the Parliament of Ghana, dominated by the Convention People's Party, even without the defections from the NPP, shows that Nkrumah and the CPP did not regard the matter of chieftaincy as decisively settled by the 1957 Constitution.[62] Partly to enable them to carry through the subjection of the chiefs to the Party, which they identified with the Government, they passed the Constitution (Repeal of Restrictions) Act, 1958, and the Constitution (Amendment) Act, 1959.[63] The passage of the two Acts, which permitted the government to act on chieftaincy matters without reference to the chiefs, made it possible for them to appoint Commissions of Enquiry into the financial management and the exercise of customary jurisdiction by the Asanteman, Kumasi State, and Akim Abuakwa State Councils. Consequent upon the findings of the commissions the Government withdrew recognition from Nana Ofori Atta II,[64] the kyenhene, and the Asantehene was obliged to make a statement repudiating his relations with the opposition party and pledging support for "the government of the day."[65]

The enactment of the two Acts also enabled the government to pass the Ashanti Stool Lands Act (No. 28 of 1958) which transferred the trusteeship and management of all lands vested in the Golden Stool and its occupant, the Asantehene, to the Governor-General; and also the Akyem Abuakwa (Stool Revenue) Act of 1958, which provided "for the control of the revenues and property in the Akyem Abuakwa State and for the application of those revenues" by a Receiver appointed by the Minister of Local Government and acting under his instructions.[66] In this way the Government sought to destroy the economic basis of the power of the potentially most powerful chiefs in Ghana.

The enactment of the two Acts similarly facilitated the passage of the Local Court Act (1958) which abolished the Native Authority Courts, the Houses of Chiefs (Amendment) Act, 1959, and the Brong-Ahafo Region Act, 1959; the last validated the creation of the Brong-Ahafo Region. The two Acts enabled the Government to create additional paramountcies in all the regions of Ghana, and to reduce the status of certain paramount chiefs, simply by omitting their stool names from the list of chiefs entitled to attend meetings of their respective Houses of Chiefs.[67]

It was clear by the end of 1959 that a chief could act officially only if the government willed it, and the Chieftaincy Act (No. 81) of 1961, which attempted to consolidate the previous enactments of chiefs, gave statutory recognition of that fact. Its most significant provision was contained in the "Definitions" which stated:

A chief is an individual who:
(a) has been nominated, elected and installed as a chief in accordance with customary law, and
(b) is recognized as a chief by the Minister responsible for Local Government.

The Minister may by executive instrument at any time withdraw recognition from a chief if:

(a) the chief has been destooled and his appeal against the destoolment has been dismissed or the period allowed for appealing has elapsed without an appeal having been brought, or
(b) the Minister considers it is in the public interest to withdraw recognition.

The "Definitions" also set out the categories of chiefs, and made it clear that while it was "unlawful" to undermine the lawful authority of a chief by refusing to "recognize" him, it was nonetheless legitimate to make claims or complaints as part of destoolment proceedings against him.

Parts I–VII of the Act provided for the establishment of chiefs councils and houses, their memberships, functions and procedures, all of which were subject to determination by the Minister of Local Government. For the first time the Government recognized "divisional councils of chiefs" which would perform functions assigned by the Minister. "Traditional States" were to be known as "Traditional Areas" with traditional councils, including those created by the Minister. Their membership was contained in a list drawn up by the Minister who could terminate memberships. Traditional councils would determine chieftaincy disputes not involving the Asantehene or a paramount chief. The Minister would determine the time and place of meetings of traditional councils and appoint auditors of their accounts.

The Act specified the members of the Houses of Chiefs of the various regions. The Minister could change the headship by legislative instrument, and the Regional Commissioner would supervise elections to vacant seats, while the Minister could also fill them with his nominees. The Minister could summon the meeting to elect the Head of a House of Chiefs; appoint a temporary Head of a House; and determine the place and time of the meetings of a House. The

"Standing Orders" of the House of Chiefs were subject to approval by the Minister who under section 26(ii) "may direct a House of Chiefs to exercise its powers under the section, and if the direction is not complied with within a reasonable time may exercise the functions on behalf of the House of Chiefs."

Part V provided for the appointment of a Judicial Commissioner by the Minister to enquire into chieftaincy affairs, with or without assessors and submit a report to the President through the Minister. The President's decision on the report, as published in the Local Government Bulletin, would be final. In view of the history of destoolment movements in the CPP period, section 36(2) of the Act which regulated the Judicial Commissioner's procedure was revealing. It stated:

> A Judicial Commissioner may act on any testimony, sworn or unsworn and may receive as evidence any statement, document, information or matter which in his opinion may assist him to deal effectively with the matters before him whether the same would, apart from the subsection, be admissible in evidence or not.

A Judicial Commissioner would have both original and appellate jurisdiction, to hear any case or matter affecting chieftaincy to which the Asantehene or a Paramount chief was a party and in all traditional areas on instructions from the Minister.

The Act also prescribed regulations for the proceedings of Traditional Councils in chieftaincy disputes: the councils would have the powers of a District Court in summoning evidence, but they had no power to impose fines or imprisonment, their decisions being enforceable in the regular courts.

Part V defined "stool property" and stated that a Traditional Council could alienate any part of it only with the approval of the Minister, who under section 56 would "by executive instrument order any local authority or public officer to take possession of stool property."

Part VII imposed the duty of declaring or modifying customary law upon the Houses of Chiefs who could also make "alterations" in it with the approval of the Minister. Section 61, and its subsections, provided for the Minister to ask a joint committee of the Houses of Chiefs to make declaration of customary law when he considered it necessary.

In effect, as Ollennu has it, a people could elect whomever they chose as their chief but he could perform his constitutional duties only at the will of the government. The institution of chieftaincy went full circle: the Act reduced it to an agency of the government just as it had been under the colonial regime. But in contrast to his position under the colonial regime, the chief was a passive, and not an active, agent.

The Act was subsequently amended in 1963 to "empower the Minister [of Local Government] to make regulations laying down clear rules of procedure governing destoolment proceedings and to preserve the right of persons entitled under customary law to bring destoolment proceedings."[68] The ostensible reason for the amendment was to reduce the spate of destoolment movements encouraged by the procedures laid down under Act 81. But, it was obvious that Government then felt sure that the chiefs would no longer oppose it and it could, therefore, afford to put order in the regulations governing destoolment procedures. In 1965, the Act was further amended in order to abolish the position of the judicial Commissioner in chieftaincy disputes, and empower the President, who now supervised chieftaincy matters through the Chieftaincy Secretariat, to appoint Judicial Commissioners.[69]

By 1965, the party had established its supremacy over chieftaincy as it had apparently done over all other organized bodies in Ghana, under its doctrine that the "Convention People's Party is Ghana and Ghana the Convention People's Party."

The party's "struggle" against chieftaincy had not been conducted only in the National Assembly and Parliament. The local branches had organized destoolment movements against dissident chiefs through floods of telegrams to the Minister, asking for committees of enquiry into the affairs of the relevant Traditional Councils, and sent protest resolutions and delegations to the Minister asking for the removal of dissident chiefs. The village chairman of the party competed with the local chiefs, in certain cases seizing the "gonggong," the means by which chiefs summon the people to meetings, which is also a symbol of authority. Visiting Ministers ignored dissident chiefs, denied their areas "amenities," and re-sited the headquarters of Local and District Councils, symbols of prestige, sources of employment, and often the loci of improved living conditions so that their subjects were forced to destool them. Rural dwellers in general, have a horror of litigating against *aban*, the government: all prayers in the stool room include one for protection by the ancestors and the gods against *aban amanae*, disputes with government.

On the other hand, the party and government gave tangible favors to their supporters among the chiefs: the creation of the

Brong-Ahafo Region was a political reward. Paramount chief status was another. Ambassadorial appointments, membership of boards of directors of state enterprises, the headship of the government's "cultural institute," and positions in the chieftaincy secretariat were awarded to chiefly supporters of the party.[70]

Nkrumah and the party may have started with a position of hostility to the chiefs, the most prominent among whom more than reciprocated the sentiment. Also, Nkrumah's own personal ideology and the party's commitment to "mass" democracy was incompatible with hereditary chiefship and aspects of the chief's relations with their "subjects." From the " modernist" viewpoint, "citizenship" and "subjecthood" could be reconciled only if the chiefs existed and functioned within a political order approved by the majority. Only a "constitutional" chieftaincy was tolerable.

At the same time, Nkrumah, with his doctrine of "African Personality," realized that the distinctive "culture" of Ghana was eminently embodied in the institution of chiefship, and he was not averse to using the rituals of the institution in order to emphasize his own position as the Head of State of Ghana. He was the paramount chief among paramount chiefs. Early in his career he accepted the position of "Tufuhene," a captaincy of an armed unit of Saltpond, and a sub-chiefship of Techiman in the Brong-Ahafo Region. He adopted the official title of *Osagyefo* (Twi) "victor in battle." The ceremony of his installation as the President of Ghana in 1960 blended Ghanaian chiefly tradition with alien borrowings. Towards his last days in office a state appointed bard greeted Ghanaians in his name with appellations borrowed from Akan court poetry, on the radio. This was all in aid of manipulating local political vocabulary in order to advance nation-building. Powerful chiefs were harmful; indigenous political rituals were useful as symbols of communication. Chiefs without power or authority were tolerable. They could be instruments of political stability.

VI. Conclusion

This paper has attempted to show the evolution of the policy of Nkrumah's governments (1951-1966) towards the institution of chieftaincy. It is clear that whatever may have been his own ideological position, and, in spite of the experiences of the rank and file of his party with the chiefs, particularly with their courts,[71] which were certainly perverted and corrupted in response to the pressures of cash — as Busia found in the case of Ashanti[72] — the CPP at first had no settled policy towards the institution. The party may also have been constrained to exercise caution in dealing with the chiefs. The constraints were (i) a fairly general consensus, reflected in both the Watson and Coussey reports, that the institution must be preserved; (ii) the composition of the 1951 Legislative Assembly; and (iii) the British surveillance over the legislative process. In those circumstances a radical attack on chieftaincy would have jeopardized advance towards self-government.[73]

But there is, really, no evidence for supposing that the CPP contemplated any such radical attack. The party's view was simply that the chiefs should be impartial in the struggle between the contending parties, and accept the popular choice of government. So that, before independence, it only dealt with specific issues and individual chiefs whose activities appeared to negate the "one man, one vote" principle, the premise of the African revolution, and who appeared unwilling to accept the logical implications of universal adult suffrage. Such chiefs were, in the party's eyes, reactionaries who, even within the framework of the indigenous system of government, deserved to be removed from office.[74] It is possible that the CPP would have continued to deal with the chiefs on the basis of the Coussey recommendations if there had not been the challenge of the National Liberation Movement 1954-1956. Pragmatism was the keynote of the CPP's relations with the chiefs.

The close identification of the Asanteman and ꓚkyeman Councils with the Movement implied the rejection of the CPP Government's policy of accommodation by the richest and most powerful of Ghanaian chiefs, and pointed starkly to the potential dangers of chieftaincy as a rallying point for centrifugal forces and a potential impediment to progressive nationalism.[75] It was the CPP's perception of these dangers and the chiefs' apparent repudiation of the principle of universal adult suffrage that led the Party to deal the crippling blows to the two powerful councils; to remove the residue of judicial authority left the chiefs in the 1951-1957 period; remove them from the local councils; and break the financial backbone of the chiefs' councils.[76]

To be sure, the CPP aimed at total power for the party, and did not envisage its co-existence with competitive centres of power, so that chieftaincy, like most other institutions in Ghana, would have eventually been reduced to an agency of the government. But the NLM episode was enough of a danger, as the party saw it, to hasten the drastic measures that were taken immediately after independence to remove the chiefs from a position of minor partners in government — as had been the case under colonial rule — to that of helpless dependence upon the government.[77]

In sum, the reaction of the most powerful chiefs in Ghana to the democratic revolution, and their insistence on ethnic or regional interests, as well as the CPP's commitment to the supremacy of the party, in theory and practice, prevented what could have been a useful experiment in local government centered around the chiefs. The apparent instability at the central government level and the current growth of interest among Ghanaians of all status groups and regions in chieftaincy suggest that Ghana may well turn to modified chieftaincy in an attempt to secure an efficient local government system.

NOTES

For a general picture of chieftaincy before colonial rule see Busia: 1951, Apter: 1963, and Arhin: 1985.

1. The present Central, Eastern, Greater Accra, Western and Volta Regions.
2. See appendices, Sarbah, 1897; Ollennu, 1976:44; Apter, 1963: 120-123, 130.
3. Rattray, 1932; Fortes, 1940: 239-271.
4. Kimble, 1963: 457-505.
5. Speech of Sir Gordon F. G. Guggisberg in the Legislative Council of the Gold Coast; Legislative Council Debates (LCD) 22nd February, 1926, in Metcalfe, 1957: 600; also Apter, 1963: 134-135.
6. On 19th April, 1927, LCD in Metcalfe, 1957: 617-619.
7. See *Papers Relating to the Restoration of the Ashanti Confederacy,* Gold Coast, Government Printer, Accra, 1935.
8. See *Report to His Excellency the Governor by the Committee on Constitutional Reform;* London: HMSO, 1949; otherwise known as the *Coussey Report,* pp. 12,15.
9. Nana Ofori Atta summarized these views when introducing the Native Administration Ordinance; Metcalfe, 1957: 619; also Casely-Hayford in the debate on Guggisberg's address to the Legislative Council in 1926; Metcalfe, 605. Casely-Hayford predicted unrest among the people as a result of the lack of representation of the educated classes outside the municipalities in the Legislative Assembly and the division between the Municipal and Provincial members: to him the conception of a division of interests of educated and uneducated people was false.
10. Speech of Governor Sir Alan Bums in the Legislative Council, 29th September, 1942, in Metcalfe, 666.
11. Signatories to the petition were:

Sir Nana Ofori Atta	Dr. J. B. Danquah
Dr. Nanka-Bruce	Mr. E. O. Asafu-Adjei
Mr. K. A. Korsah	Mr. I. K. Agyeman
Mr. Akilakpa Sawyerr	

Metcalfe: 640-644; also Gold Coast Aborigines Rights' Protection Society, Metcalfe: 646 .

12. For example, on 25th February, 1936, Kojo Thompson, the member for Accra, sought the deletion of sub-section (2) of Clause 18 of the Native Jurisdiction (Amendment) Ordinance relating to "The imposition of levies or tribute by a Paramount Chief with the concurrence of the State Council, the fixing of the amount to be raised by means of such levies or tribute" on the ground that "where there is going to be imposition of taxes then there must be representation." Metcalfe; 1957: 649.

13. The leading members of the Convention were:

A. G. (Pa) Grant	- a merchant of Sekondi-Takoradi, Chairman
R. S. Blay	- lawyer, Vice-President
Dr. J. B. Danquah	- lawyer, Vice-President
R. A. Awoonor-Williams	- lawyer, Treasurer
W. E. Ofori-Atta	- graduate teacher
E. A. Akuffo-Addo	- lawyer
J. W. de Graft-Johnson	- lawyer
Obetsebi Lamptey	- lawyer
John Tsiboe	- newspaper proprietor; Ashanti Pioneer)Kumasi; and
Cobbina Kessie	- lawyer from Kumasi; see Austin, 1964: 52 53, notes 6 and 7.

14. Nkrumah, 1957: 1044.
15. Nkrumah, 1957: 79, 80; Austin, 1964: 81-84.
16. See Busia, 1951: 189-194: Apter, 1963: 145.
17. Nkrumah, 1957: 21.
18. Nkrumah, 1957: 183.
19. Nkrumah, 1957: 99.
20. *Coussey Report*, 1949: 5 5 .
21. *Coussey Report*, 1949: 5 5ff.; Austin, 1964: 145-148.
22. *Coussey Report*, 1949: 91.
23. Appendix I, *Coussey Report*, p. 78.
24. Appendix 11, *Coussey Report*, p. 80.
25. Report of the Commission of Inquiry into Disturbances in the Gold Coast; Watson, 1948: pp. 24-29; See also Austin, 1964: 49-102.
26. *Watson Report*, 1948: pp. 2425 .
27. *Watson Report*, 1948: p. 25 .
28. *Ibid.* See UGCC: *Letter to Nananom in Council: Touching the Controversial Issues in the Coussey Report,* also Dr. Danquah's motion on Second Chamber in the Legislature Council: *Legislative Council Debates,* 1950, Issue No. 2, pp. 247 ff.
29. Watson, 1948: 26-27.
30. *Coussey Report:* The Legislative Council, in particular, the chiefs' representatives, oddly voted against a Second Chamber in spite of an emotional speech in its favor by Dr. J. B. Danquah, ably supported by Mr. Obetsebi Lamptey. The Secretary of State for the Colonies upheld the decision of the Council. Dr. Danquah suggested that the chiefs, influenced by the political officers of the Government of the Gold Coast, opposed the motion for a Second Chamber because Nkrumah had supported it. He said: "I personally think that the greatest single achievement of our unfortunate compatriot, Mr. Kwame Nkrumah, was his acceptance of the Coussey majority recommenda-

tion that the future structure of the Gold Coast Legislature should not be of the chamber, but two chambers." Leg. Co. Debates, 1950, No. 2, p. 254. In 1953 the chiefs asked for a second chamber but Nkrumah rejected it. See *Gold Coast Constitution in Outline*. Government Printer, Accra, 1950. *The Government's Proposals for Constitutional Reform*. 1953

31. *Local Government Reform in Outline*, 1951.

32. *Ibid.*, v.

33. *Coussey Report. op. cit.:* 18.

34. Different arrangements were made for the then Northern Territories where chiefs did not have to contend with the claims of too many educated commoners; Austin, 1964: 43.

35. The representatives of these chambers had long been allies of the chiefs in the Legislative Council.

36. Nkrumah, 1957: 128.

37. Nkrumah, 1968a: 55.

38. The Breman-Asikuma State Council in the Daily Graphic No. 387, February 4, 1952, p. 1.

39. See debate on the Governor's Sessional Address, *Gold Coast Legislative Assembly Debates;* Session 1952, Issue No. 1, First Meeting, 21st and 26th February. It was alleged that the CPP crowds at the entrance of the Assembly building demonstrated against the chiefly Assemblymen by booing and hooting at them; and there were complaints that the Governor's Address had deliberately ignored mention of the chiefs.

40. *The Daily Graphic*, No. 387, February 4, 1952.

41. State Councils (Ashanti) Ordinance, No. 5 of 1952: date of *Assent,* the 27th March, 1952, Section 3; *Daily Graphic* (D.G.) No. 389, 6th February, 1952, p. 5, reports Mr. Krobo Edusei, CPP member of the Legislative Assembly, as saying that fines imposed on "malcontents," leaders of destoolment movements, were being considered with a view to making them moderate.

42. *Daily Graphic* Nos. 412 and 413, 4th and 5th March, 1952.

43. *Daily Graphic* No. 390, February 7, 1952; 395, February 13, 1952; also Legislative Assembly Debates (LAD) Vol. 3, Col. 5, 1953 ff.

44. *Daily Graphic* No. 452, of April 21, 1952, reported Nkrumah as warning the chiefs to "steer clear of opposing the CPP and party politics in general" and that his party would "deal blow for blow if the chiefs interfered with the activities of the party. The party was not against chiefs," also Prime Minister's Statement in the Legislative Assembly in (LAD) Vol. 4 of 1954, Cols. 1557-1558.

45. Nana Sir Tsibu Darku became Chairman of the Gold Coast Cocoa Marketing Board; Nana Kobina Nketsia, Omanhene of British Sekondi, later headed the 'Cultural Institute'; an Oxford D Phil., and Interim Vice-Chancellor of the University of Ghana; he was one of the "staunchest" supporters of the party, having been imprisoned for party activities; See Hodgkin, 1961:

46. See Drah, 1979: 119-162 .

47. Austin, 1964: 250-312.

48. For example, the Kumawuhene, Nana Otuo Acheampong, an active supporter of the CPP, took refuge in Accra; see *Minutes of the Asanteman Council,* 2nd - 5th and 9th of August, 1955.

49. *Daily Graphic* No. 2383, and No. 2452, June 13,1958.

50. See Dr Danquah's evidence on the Jackson Enquiry into the Akim Abuakwa

State Council, *Daily Graphic* No. 2293, February 5, 1958.

51. *LAD* Issue No. 2 of 1955, cols. 545 ff. The 'Golden Stool' was the Asantehene's Stool; See Rattray, 1929.

52. Mr. Kofi Baako, for example, stated that the Asanteman Council had identified itself with a political party. *LAD op. cit.* col. 606. Mr. B. F. Kusi denied this, saying that the Asanteman Council had never become a political body, but had been supporting a demand for a federal constitution made by the whole of Ashanti; cols. 577-579.

53. Minutes of the Asanteman Council, *op. cit.;* Also Dr Danquah's evidence, *op. cit.*

54. Gold Coast Government, Report of the Constitutional Adviser, Government Printer, Accra, 1955, Gold Coast Government, Report of the Achimota Conference, Accra, 1956.

55. *Ibid.*

56. Not all members of the Asanteman Council supported the NLM; and several *ahene*, chiefs, directly subordinate to the Asantehene were active supporters of the CPP. The latter were promoted to paramount status in 1959 and 1961; See Nkrumah, 1957: 181; 1963: 71.

57. See Drah, *op. cit.*

58. See Drah, *op. cit.;* and Austin, 1964: *op. cit.*

59. The government insisted on assembling views from identifiable bodies, collating them and writing its own constitution, and would not allow a specially convened Constituent Assembly to discuss the constitution, as demanded by the opposition parties, Nkrumah, 1957: 198-209.

60. In Gyandoh Jnr.and J. Griffiths, 1972: 128.

61. Nkrumah, 1957: 239-240; 1963: 59-60.

62. Austin, *op. cit.;* Nkrumah, 1 963a: 62.

63. Gyandoh Jnr. and Griffiths, 1972: 149; Nkrumah later said of chieftaincy: "On reflection even though I trusted too much in the power of a reformed chieftaincy I was not mistaken in attempting to use popularly chosen chiefs within the framework of the government. It was then essential to have broadest possible grouping of interests at home if we were to be sufficiently united to deal with the essential issue, namely, the political unification of the African continent," 1968: 65-66.

64. *Daily Graphic,* No. 2452, June 13, 1958.

65. Statement issued by the Kumasi State Council at Manhyia held on 31st March,1958, Appendix "B" to the Minutes of the Asanteman Council for April 15, 1958.

66. *Parliamentary Debates* Official Report, First series, Vol. 11, 1st July - 5th September 1955, col. 2196; *The Laws of Ghana.* "The Akim Abuakwa (Stool Revenue) Act., No. 8 of 1958."

67. See Schedules to the Houses of Chiefs (Amendment) Act, 1959, and the Brong-Ahafo Region Act, 1959.

68. *Parliamentary Debates.* 18th June - 5th July, 1963, cols. 102 ff.

69. *Parliamentary Debates,* Vol. 36, col. 104 ff.

70. *Parliamentary Debates,* 17th - 27th September, 1963.

71. See further: Arhin, 1985.

72. Busia *op. cit.,* Arhin, 1976.

73. Hodgkin, 1961: 27.

74. Busia, 1951;Arhin, 1985.

75. Bretton, 1967: 71, is surely mistaken in saying that "at no time did they (the chiefs) pose a substantial security threat to Nkrumah." There was some threat to the integrity of the state-nation in 1954-56.
76. Bretton, 1967: 73.
77. *Ibid.*

EDUCATION IN GHANA, 1951-1966

E. A. Haizel

Background

Opening the Lever Brothers Soap Factory at Tema on 24th August, 1963, Dr. Nkrumah, among other things, made this statement:

> It is not only the favourable climate for investment created by the Government of Ghana which has resulted in industrial development such as the soap factory now before us. The education policy inaugurated by the Convention People's Party in 1951, when for the first time we had a limited degree of control over our own affairs is now bearing fruit. We have a growing number of skilled technicians, and in some fields the technical ability of our workers can today compare favourably with that of any country in the world. This is an important factor in encouraging foreign investment.[1]

This was Dr Nkrumah's judgement of the educational policy started in 1951, and a restatement of his conviction of the link between education and national development. The story has, however, to be taken a bit further back in time.

From 1923, the educational policy of the British Colonial Office for dependent territories began to assume a definite form with the establishment of the Advisory Committee on Education in the Colonies. A flow of memoranda started issuing from the Advisory Committee, all aimed at improvement of "native education." During and after the Second World War, the documents assumed a tone of urgency.

In 1943, the Advisory Committee published the document entitled "Mass Education in African Society" In this document, the aims of mass education were described as follows:

1. The wide extension of schooling for children with the goal of universal schooling within a measurable time.

2. The spread of literacy among adults, together with a widespread development of literature and libraries without which there is little hope of making literacy permanent.

3. The planning of mass education of the community itself, involving the active support of the local community from the start.

4. The effective co-ordination of welfare plans and mass education plans so that they form a comprehensive and balanced whole.[2]

The document on "Mass Education" was followed in 1948 by "Education for Citizenship in Africa." The purpose of this document was to "study the technique needed to prepare people for responsibility, and examine generally the problem of building up a sense of public responsibility, tolerance and objectivity in discussion and practice, and an appreciation of political institutions, their evolution and progress."[3]

The "fresh wind of change" was blowing, and decolonization and self-government were in the air, and with them the need to train men and women as responsible citizens of free countries. The task ahead was going to be arduous, and the 1948 report "Education for Citizenship in Africa" stated clearly:

The pace of life is faster, the economic structure is immeasurably more complicated, nations are more closely linked, and democracy has replaced aristocracy. In this matter, as in so many others, the Colonial peoples are setting themselves the task of passing one generation through a development over which the leading nations of the West have spent two, by no means leisurely, centuries.[4]

It was now clear that educational development in the colonies had become a "political project of the greatest magnitude." [5]

The other area in education to receive attention from Britain was higher education. The Asquith Commission of June 1943 was "to consider the principles which should guide the promotion of higher education, learning and research and the development of universities in the colonies, and to explore means whereby universities and other appropriate bodies in the United Kingdom may be able to cooperate with institutions of higher education in the colonies in order to give effect to these principles."[6] The Inter-University Council and the special relationship with London University were an outcome of the Commission.

For us in this part of the colonial world, the Elliot Commission was "to report on the organization and facilities of existing centres of higher education in West Africa, and to make recommendations regarding future university development in that area."[7]

The Minority Report of the Commission had advocated a single university for West Africa to be established in Nigeria with constituent feeder colleges in the other territories. The Majority Report, however, asked that each territory should have its own university, even if the fear of the Minority Report that there would not be enough students were justified.[8]

Ghana, at first, accepted the Minority Report but came round by a somersault to accept the Majority Report, and established the University College of the Gold Coast in 1948. As early as the following year, the Legislative Council accepted the report of the Committee on Africanisation, which had called "for an immediate expansion of the University College to the limit of facilities which could be provided at Achimota,"[9] the temporary site.

The Principal's report on the University College for the period 1948-1952 provides the reason:

> The College's planned rate of growth would have been a total output by 1960 of about 400 students. By providing additional temporary buildings and service as quickly as possible, and by increasing the College's teaching and administrative strength, it was estimated that the output could be raised from 400 to 1,000.[10]

The demands of the country on higher education were demonstrated very early in the life of the University. Higher education was confirmed as an integral part of the programme for national development, and this development was not to be left to proceed at a leisurely pace. Skilled manpower was urgently required, and the country was prepared to pay the price.

Colonial Office guidance on secondary education and technical education in the country was scanty if not non-existent. However, the Gold Coast Education Committee reported in 1941 that the aim of general secondary education was narrow and exclusively materialistic; bore little relationship with the needs of the country; that the existing facilities were inadequate, and those in existence in danger of creating unemployment; and that there was no provision for the control of secondary education.

The Committee's greatest concern was over the quality of the final products of the secondary schools:

> . . . the chief danger is not the creation of unemployment, but the production by the examination ridden secondary school of a class of unemployables who over-estimate their own achievement and worth.[11]

This was the time that the secondary schools in the country could be counted on one's fingers and were all situated in the colony.

By 1948, in the Colony and Ashanti, it was estimated that half of the children of infant–junior school-going age were at school. But the report of the Education Department for that year had this to say:

> . . . the basis of the educational system is the six year's infant-junior course. Selected pupils proceed to a further four years' senior primary course, but it is estimated that for many years to come the Gold Coast will be unable to afford this course for more than a third of the children who complete the infant-junior course.[12]

This was the situation of schools directly under the Department of Education and the recognized Education Units. Yet the pressure was on, relentlessly and from below. The Education Committee had observed:

> Despite all the war-time difficulties, the development of education went on throughout the 1939–45 period. On the one hand, there was a severe reduction in the amount of inspection and supervision possible, and, on the other, there was a rapidly increasing and insistent demand which showed itself in the opening of hundreds of non-assisted infant-junior schools. Of these many were started by local communities without reference to either recognized Education Units or the Education Department. No notification of their founding was given and their existence was not registered. The majority of them were ill-housed and almost without exception staffed with untrained teachers.[13]

So what was the position in 1948? The strictures on secondary school products notwithstanding, the country was in a position to embark on university education, using the very products of the secondary system as its main recruits. The broader network of infant junior schools and the limited senior-primary schools was the result of voluntary effort, mainly missionary, supplemented by the Government. But now another dimension was developing. Communities were providing themselves with schools which were mushrooming without Government recognition and without support of the Education Units. These schools had grown up in an effort to satisfy the demands of the people whose faith in education seemed without limit. Secondary education and teacher training had developed mainly through mission effort. Government's role was to have overall direction through the Department of Education by means of regulations, recognition, inspection and grants-in-aid. It also built its own schools and colleges to fill in gaps.

The education scene in the country, taken together with the aims of the Colonial Office, the unplanned community effort and with the fact that financial provision for education was limited to areas only in the Colony and Ashanti, posed a problem which had to be solved. Nkrumah and the CPP were prepared to attend to the problem, especially as the rank and file of the Party were also imbued with faith in education. In doing so, however, Nkrumah and the CPP decided on a novel approach. For the first time in the history of the country, the Central Government was to assume full responsibility for educational policy and practice. Educational development itself had passed the stage where it was a political project of the greatest magnitude. It had become both fundamental and crucial to the political economy, and was to find full expression in the Seven-Year Development Plan of 1964, the CPP's programme for "work and happiness."

Primary Education

The education policy of the CPP Government evolved over a number of years. But it started with the Accelerated Development Plan for Education, 1951. The Accelerated Development Plan envisaged a six-year primary school which was eventually to be followed by entrance to secondary grammar school, secondary technical school, technical institute or the newly named middle school, or to a training college for two years, in the first instance, for a Certificate 'B' award.

The aim of the Accelerated Plan was "to provide as soon as possible a six-year primary course for all children at public expense."[14] This aim seemed to satisfy the faith expressed by the opening of unrecognized schools through community effort. It also

met an aim of the report on "Mass Education," namely, "The wide
extension of schooling for children with the goal of universal schooling within a measurable time."

The primary school itself was "to provide education in the basic
skills of reading, writing and arithmetic for everyday life, with the
usual complementary learning deemed to be essential for the children in the age group 6–12." The end purpose was "to provide a
sound foundation for citizenship with permanent literacy in both
English and the vernacular."[15]

The system and the hectic efforts made to make it work are
arresting enough. But the reactions to it, in and outside Parliament,
touched the fundamental issue that was at stake. This was the
Government's clear intention to take over control of education in the
country.

The Plan stated categorically:

> In future no new primary school opened by a denominational reli-
> gious body or by a person or group of persons will be eligible for
> assistance from public funds unless prior approval of the local
> authority concerned under powers delegated by the Central
> Government has been obtained.[16]

Further, it was "expected that considerable numbers of educational
unit schools will be handed over to Local Authorities."[17] The missions were not only virtually barred against future expansion of their
primary schools. They were also expected to give up their existing
schools. It was permissible for any person, or group of persons, to
open and conduct a private school. But while no public funds would
be granted to any such school, it could be closed down by law if it
was potentially dangerous to the physical and moral well-being of
the pupils. And, as if in anticipation of a counterattack, the Plan went
on to say:

> This policy is one which the people themselves already regard as
> their own. It implies no disregard for the devoted services and the
> great achievements of the Missionary Societies and the Churches.
> Far less does it imply any disregard for moral training and religious
> education. Opportunities have been provided for them in all institu-
> tions supported by public funds.[18]

It was clear that the old partnership which had existed between
Government and voluntary effort, especially by the Churches, was
completely ruptured and that the Government had made a deliber-

ate move to take over primary schools where church influence had been strong. The churches were left with no other option but to attach their names to local authority schools and take a back seat.

Technical Education

As already noted, the educational policy of Nkrumah and the CPP evolved over a period of time. Free primary education came into existence in 1952. Ten years later, in 1962, progress in primary education was regarded satisfactory enough to warrant the announcement of compulsory primary education.

Dr. Nkrumah was to refer to these two measures when he presented the Seven-Year Development Plan for National Reconstruction and Development to Parliament in 1964. The link between education and economic development was clearly stated. As has been said:

> . . . We must look to industry and agriculture to provide an increased standard of living, but these two sectors of the economy are dependent on an adequate supply of suitably educated and trained manpower. In a sense, education takes precedence over the other two as the mainspring of economic progress...[19]

Dr Nkrumah went on to develop his idea of education as a function of economic development. He stated:

> In the context of economic development, education may be viewed in two aspects. First, in order that productivity of the people may improve they ought to be made generally receptive to new ideas. Secondly, education should have the function of teaching the population the specific skills that are required to produce the goods and services needed by the economy.[20]

So far the emphasis had been on education producing skilled personnel for economic development. But as he continued talking about education, other dimensions, the individual returns to education and social justice, became discernible in the educational conceptualization of Dr. Nkrumah. After referring to the free and compulsory primary education schemes, he continued:

> These measures have laid the foundation of the greatest revolution in Ghana's history. It is possible now to envisage the date when every child without regard as to whether his parents are rich or poor will be able to develop his talents to the fullest degree. Eventually, this revolution will make it possible for every child, provided he has the ability, to get an education from the primary to the

university level without any hindrance from his financial circumstances. Already, university education and teacher training are virtually free. It is intended that by the end of the Seven-Year Development Plan, secondary education will also be free.[21]

In the meantime, to avoid the situation where place of birth and where schools were situated determined who should proceed beyond the primary stage, scientific selection methods were to be developed and applied "uniformly throughout the country in selecting young people for the various levels of further education."[22]

But back to education in the context of economic development, Dr. Nkrumah stressed that with the Development Plan, "the stage has now been reached where educational policy must increasingly concern itself with the second great purpose of education, the teaching of skills and other attainments."[23] In this enterprise, the burden was not to be borne by the school alone. Because of the expected changes in demand for certain types of craftsmen, it was time to re-examine the entire structure of the apprenticeship programmes so as to bring these into better alignment with future employment demands.

The Accelerated Development Plan had envisaged technical education based on the Kumasi College of Technology, secondary technical schools, trade training centres, technical institutes and mobile training units. Most of this was formal school education. In 1964, the CPP added a further dimension. In-service education was to assume its proper place, especially as there was the need to update and upgrade people's skills on the job. It was stated in the Seven Year Development Plan:

> This upgrading process will require the introduction of in-service training programmes and improvements in employee selection methods. Hitherto, with a few notable exceptions, employers of labour in Ghana have paid insufficient attention to the training of their workers. It needs to be more widely appreciated that the formal education system cannot provide all the training required in a modern economy. Employers, both public and private, will be expected to make a far greater contribution to labour training through individual factory and farm schools, industry-wide training schemes, day release, payment for attendance at short courses and evening classes.[24]

And the issue was not just left there. Contracts for new enterprises were to include a clause requiring the new industry to provide "pre-employment training for the operative personnel which will be employed."[25] An incentive system was to be provided by way of tax-relief and imports allocations.

There was a limit to what the schools could do and do very well. If they were allowed and supported to perform the function of transmitting the fundamentals of skills, on-the-job training could take over and develop these skills in the actual work situation. This seems to be what Dr. Nkrumah was suggesting.

But this was Dr. Nkrumah speaking in the context of education and economic development, and in relation to the Seven-Year Development Plan. Earlier on in 1960 and 1961, he had made certain statements on technical education which are worthy of comment. On July 19, 1960, Nkrumah used the occasion of the opening of the Hall of Trade Unions to throw up an idea on technical education he had on his mind. Primary Technical Schools were to be established "by Executive Order and not subject to any regulations of the Education Department." These schools were to run alongside primary schools and give concurrent training to boys and girls "so that by the time a pupil leaves primary school he or she will have gained sufficient training to make him or her a semi-skilled worker."

The scheme was to continue at middle school and secondary school levels, where a student would be ready "to complete a technological education within a short time at our schools of technology." He concluded 'we must begin to produce our technicians and technological experts."[26]

Dr Nkrumah pursued this line of thought when he spoke to Ghanaian teachers on April 6, 1961, and said:

It is necessary that technical courses should be provided at all levels in addition to the "grammar school" type of course which exists.[27]

It would seem that Dr. Nkrumah's concern was with the content of the curriculum. He was not against the grammar school type of education. He wanted something more added to it. His emphasis on technical education did not constitute a de-emphasis on general education. For in that same speech, he continued by saying:

At the primary level we have to aim at a completely literate working population. We need to expand the teacher training system to provide the teachers for universal education. We need to expand the secondary school system itself to feed our universities continuously. Facilities for technical education should be extended so that our industrialisation can move forward without over-dependence on imported skills. We need finally to expand and adapt our university system to provide a greater variety of courses which will have relevance to the needs of our country.[28]

The emphasis on technical education without de-emphasizing general education was repeated when Dr. Nkrumah gave the sessional address to Parliament in 1963 and outlined the role of the University College of Science Education at Cape Coast. The College was to be responsible for the training and production of professional and graduate science teachers "who are required to teach in our secondary schools and polytechnics." To this end, and in order to make the College of Science Education the centre for research and teaching in eduction, he declared that:

> Our Government has also decided that the Institute and Department of Education at the University of Ghana and the Science Research Unit of Kwame Nkrumah University of Science and Technology should be transferred to Cape Coast.[29]

But what was the practical outcome of all this rhetoric, one would ask. There was a lot of technical and vocational education on the ground and away from the formal system under the Ministry of Education. Many departments ran training schemes. For instance, the Agricultural Department had training centres at Kumasi, Tamale and Bunso. The Forestry Department had a Rangers school at Sunyani. The Medical Department had the NTC at Accra for the training of SRN's while selected hospitals provided three-year courses leading to the QRN. In 1951, the Local Government Training School was established to be followed in 1952 by the establishment of the Government Secretarial and Typing Training School to train a secretarial class within the new Civil Service structure as recommended by the Lidbury Commission.

Besides the departmental institutions, the Ministry of Education was busy. In 1956 a Chief Technical Education Officer was appointed. And the report for the year stated that the Kumasi Technical Institute was commissioned early in 1956 and the new building of the Accra Technical Institute in the latter part of the year. Trade courses began for the first time at the Kpandu Trade School in January, 1956. The Report concluded:

> These developments increased the number of Government Technical establishments to four Technical Institutes at Accra, Takoradi, Kumasi and Tarkwa and four Trade Schools at Asuansi,

Mampong (Ashanti), Tamale and Kpandu. Thus all regions were provided with an institution offering technical training.[30]

In September 1960, the Technical Teacher Training Centre was opened in Kumasi to ensure a steady flow of instructors. In the following year, 1961, the Apprentice Act was passed, and

> ... provided for the establishment of an Apprenticeship Board to have general oversight of the conditions of Apprenticeship and for National Apprenticeship Committees in respect of individual industries.[31]

But by far the most interesting action taken in connection with technical training was the Artisan Training Scheme:

> In consultation with the Colonial Office and the UK Ministry of Labour, a scholarship scheme was devised for the training for artisans and tradesmen in the United Kingdom. The purpose was to raise the level of work of alrtisans and tradesmen in this country until training schemes which are in the process of being developed (e.g. technical institutes) come into full operation.[32]

A total of 107 artisans and tradesmen went to the UK under the Scheme in 1952. A breakdown of the number reads as follows:

Bakers	5	Laundrymen	3
Watch Repairers	2	Moulders	3
Potters	6	Painters	4
Typewriter Mechanics	4	Tailors	5
Dressmakers	2	Masons	4
Carpenters	6	Shoemakers	4
Brick and Tile Makers	4	Upholsterers	1
Turners	7	Electricians	13
Cabinet Makers	4	Welders	3
Fitters	14	Printers	7
Blacksmiths	6		

To many, this was a strange phenomenon, against the trend of sending would-be "scholars" to the U K. But the fillip given to "manual" work was great, even though today technical education and training is still the "cinderella" of the national educational effort. One hopes that the National Vocational Training Institute will be encouraged to recapture that spirit which fired the Nkrumah regime in its concerns about technical education.

Secondary Education

The expansion of education at the primary and middle school levels meant that sooner than later there was going to be pressure on secondary education. At the same time, the siting of the older secondary schools was such that certain areas of the country had no such schools. The Cocoa Marketing Board had to come to the rescue. The Board realized that the cocoa growing areas had no secondary schools, and also took the view that the cocoa industry involved labour from all over the country. With funds provided by the Cocoa Marketing Board, Dr. Nkrumah founded the Ghana Education Trust with the purpose of building secondary schools and colleges all over the country. And before long, secondary schools and colleges sprang up from Half Assini to Keta, and from La Bone through Acherensua and Tamale to Tumu.

Under Nkrumah, secondary school facilities were expanded, both for the older schools and Ghana Education Trust schools. Sixth form facilities were expanded, commercial subjects found their way back on to the curriculum, and "subject Association" began to flourish. The West African Examinations Council became an integral part of the education system.

But the real novelty of the period was the establishment of the Ghana Education Trust whose schools ran parallel to those under the Ministry of Education. When Dr. Nkrumah spoke to Ghana Teachers on April 6, 1961, he had nothing but praise for the Trust:

> The Ghana Education Trust which I established to build Ghana Schools and Colleges is doing magnificent work. The Trust has so far built thirteen new secondary schools, has rehoused five others, and will be opening eight more in September this year. As a result largely of the work of this body, the number of secondary schools within the public system has arisen from thirty-nine in 1960 to fifty-nine. The annual increase in pupil intake to forms one and two has been most encouraging, and is now well over 4,000.[33]

There was linear expansion alright, but one wonders what the situation would have been if the Trust had not gone ahead to establish these schools even though there was opposition to the dilution in teacher effectiveness which the rapid expansion was bound to cause. Luckily, Dr Nkrumah was not the person to wait for ideal conditions before acting in the field of education. And his vision went further. In the sessional address to Parliament on October 2, 1962, he declared that by the end of the period of the Seven-Year Plan, secondary education would be free and compulsory. In the meantime, the Botsio Commission on University education had reported, and the Institute of Public Education was to use its Workers' Colleges to provide opportunities for working adults to pursue GCE 'O' Level courses in order to improve their efficiency at work and to help those desirous of pursuing higher education.

Teacher Training

The Nkrumah Regime saw that the provision of teachers was fundamental to the success of both the Accelerated Development Plan and the role of education in the Seven-Year Development Plan.

The Accelerated Development Plan worked out a concrete scheme to meet the dilution in teaching which was inevitable with the rapid expansion the scheme entailed. Formal teacher training was to consist of a two-year Certificate 'B' course to be followed by a further two year course for the Certificate 'A' after a period of classroom work. The Certificate 'A' (Post-Secondary) course was to continue. To supplement these, the Emergency Training Centres were to continue functioning; staffing in primary and middle schools was to be so arranged that headteachers could give in-service training to unqualified staff and at the same time help them in supervising their classroom work. District Assistant Education Officers were to be appointed with responsibility for the professional training of classroom teachers.

By 1964, when Dr. Nkrumah presented the Seven-Year Development Plan to Parliament, conditions for teacher training had improved considerably. New training colleges had been built and older ones expanded. Supervision in the field was no longer policed by "inspectors" and mutual professional respect of classroom teachers and education officers was growing. But a new problem was steadily developing. Teacher training and teaching were becoming stepping stones to other jobs, even with the establishment of the University College of Cape Coast on the grounds of the Osagyefo Training College originally established by the Ghana Education Trust. Dr. Nkrumah touched on this problem in his 1964 address to Parliament.

> The recruitment and retention of teachers of all types has become increasingly difficult because of the unattractive salaries and conditions of service in the teaching profession relative to other occupations. It is proposed to adjust salary scales of teachers to make them at least comparable to those in other occupations for which similar qualifications are required.[34]

This was the measure to even out matters. But Dr. Nkrumah realized the main causes of the trouble. As he put it, it was the discrepancy at the top salary levels that was particularly discouraging because it provided no incentive for making a career of teaching.[35] Even today, to remain at the "school" section of the Ghana Education Service is not as attractive as to be in the "office" section, whilst the relative unattractiveness of teaching persists.

University Education

The Minority Report of the Elliot Commission had argued its case on the inability of the territories of West Africa to provide enough students from secondary schools to feed a university. Yet under the Nkrumah Regime, two more universities were added to the one established in 1948. Indeed, a fourth university, solely for agriculture, was proposed.

Towards the end of his regime, Dr. Nkrumah had this to say on university education in his sessional address to Parliament in 1965:

> Enrolment at the universities increased from 2500 in 1964 to 3480 in 1965. Our plan is to increase enrolment of regular students in university institutions to about 25,000 by 1970 . . . University Education in Ghana is free and will continue to be free. It will be accessible to all those who are capable of higher learning.[36]

We have not, in 1985, attained the enrolment figures Dr. Nkrumah envisaged. Indeed, it has become necessary to set up cut-off points and other criteria in order to eliminate normally qualified candidates from entering university because of restricted accommodation and lack of facilities.

However, in 1963, Dr. Nkrumah was twice on the campus of the University and used the opportunity to state his opinion on education and the role of the University. On February 24, 1963, he spoke at a dinner at Legon and made a speech which has been published under the title "The Role of Our Universities." There was tension in the atmosphere, especially following a speech at the Arena at the tenth anniversary of the CPP.

In 1959, Dr. Nkrumah had stated that "with a few exceptions University College is a breeding ground for unpatriotic and anti-Govemment elements." He had gone further to state:

> We do not intend to sit idly by and see that these institutions which are supported by millions of pounds produced out of the sweat and toil of the common people continue to be centres of anti-

Government activities. We want the University College to cease being an alien institution and take on the character of a Ghanaian university, loyally serving the interests of the nation and the well-being of our people.[37]

So much for the role of the University. Dr. Nkrumah wanted reforms to come from within. Otherwise, and in his own words:

If reforms do not come from within, we intend to impose them from outside, and no resort to the cry of academic freedom (for academic freedom does not mean irresponsibility) is going to restrain us from seeing that our university is a healthy university devoted to Ghanaian interests.[38]

These were strong words, and, indeed, the CPP did subsequently 'invade' the University to set an example which has been followed a few times during subsequent regimes. But the reasons have been political and the question whether those in the universities have a right to their political views and their expression has yet to be resolved either on the principle of academic freedom or freedom of speech.

In February, 1963, Dr. Nkrumah's mood was only less restrained but appropriate to the occasion and setting. In his after dinner speech, he said:

The role of a university in a country like ours is to become the academic focus of national life, reflecting the social, economic and cultural and political aspirations of the people. It must kindle national interest in the youth and uplift our citizens and free them from ignorance, superstition, and, may I add, indolence.[39]

He then went on to remind his listeners about the realities of the situation:

A university does not exist in a vacuum, or in outerspace. It exists in the context of a society, and it is there that it has its proper place. A university is supported by society, and without the sustenance which it receives from society, it will cease to exist.[40]

To this D. M. Balme would say "the man who pays the piper may call the tune, but he does not try to tell the piper how to play it; he trusts him to know that. The tune has been called in the Ordinance: University education, learning and research."[41]

At the dinner in 1963, Dr Nkrumah accepted the stand. He promised,

I would like to assure you of my readiness to defend at all times this right of the University and to encourage all those who work within it—students, research scholars and professors—to work with honesty and objectivity.[42]

But thus far and no more. Any other interpretion was to him unacceptable.

There is however, sometimes a tendency to use the words "academic freedom" in another sense, and to assert the claim that a university is more or less an institution of learning having no respect or allegiance to the community or the country in which it exists or purports to serve. This assertion is unsound in principle and objectionable in practice. The university has a clear duty to the community which maintains it, and which has the right to expect concern for its pressing needs.[43]

On October 25, 1963, Dr. Nkrumah returned to the University of Ghana, this time to open the Institute of African Studies. He used the occasion to express his understanding of education and elaborated on the purpose of the Institute. On the interpretation of education, he had this to say:

. . . education consists not only in the sum of what a man knows or the skill with which he can put this to his own advantage. In my view, a man's education must also be measured in terms of the soundness of his judgement of people and of things, and in his power to understand and appreciate the needs of his fellow men, and to be of service to them. The educated man should be so sensitive to the conditions around him that he makes it his chief endeavour to improve those conditions for the good of all.[44]

Dr. Nkrumah's educational idealism had a practical base. On the purpose of the Institute of African Studies, he was unequivocal. He declared:

One essential function of this Institute must surely be to study the history, culture and institutions, languages and arts of Ghana and of Africa in new African-centred ways — in entire freedom from the propositions and presuppositions of the colonial epoch, and from the definitions of those professors and lecturers who continue to make European studies of Africa the basis of this assessment. By the work of this Institute, we must reassess and assert the glories and achievements of our African past and inspire our generation and succeeding generations, with a vision of a better future.[45]

This was how Dr. Nkrumah defined the purpose of the Institute of African Studies and spelt out its historiography. Both were to be in the service of Ghana and the African Revolution. The Research Fellows of the Institute were therefore to search for, edit, publish and make available sources of all kinds.

Reference has already been made to the desire to make Cape Coast University the centre for education and educational research. Kumasi University was to be responsible for producing the top applied scientists and technologists the country badly needed for economic development. But this was not the end of the story in Nkrumah's scheme of things.

Science, Research and Technology

The Nkrumah scheme of things envisaged top academics and top scientists directly influencing Ghanian society. To this end, the Academy of Learning and the National Research Council had been inaugurated in 1959 by the Duke of Edinburgh. These were later amalgamated to form the Academy of Sciences. On 30th November, 1963, Dr. Nkrumah explained in his speech entitled "Strength and Power" as follows:

> The Academy of Sciences was created . . . as a new and dynamic body to assume full responsibility for the co-ordination of all aspects of research and the promotion of scientific pursuits and learning. In this way we have combined in one institution the fundamental academic functions originally envisaged for the Academy of Learning and the applied scientific research so vital to our national development. We expect that from this amalgamation will grow strength and power which will push us faster in the development of the sciences and literary arts.

On the functions of the Academy, he was very specific:

> We do not conceive the functions of the Academy as passive, or as the mere collection and compilation of data from our universities and research stations. The Academy is expected to design and carry out research programmes related to the life, changes and growth of our society. For this reason, the Academy has under it about twenty research institutes.[46]

Dr. Nkrumah thought about science in the light of this wider ideology. There was the need to popularize science to make the mass of the people science-conscious. Children were to be given a lively interest in science and scientific pursuits from the earliest stages in education, and taught to realize that science is not just something which works in the laboratory, but is all around us in nature and in the things we see in our daily lives. And the reason for all this:

A socialist state can only be maintained by a people who have a correct understanding of nature, and who hold within their grasp the knowledge and the means to master and transform nature for their common good faith.[47]

Dr. Nkrumah's emphasis was on the means to master and transform nature as the way to a just and prosperous society. As he declared in his speech of November 30, 1963:

We have the resources to create a better life for our people. What we need is widespread conviction in the correctness of our ideology, the will and the effort to mobilise our intellectual, social and material resources in a dynamic effort to establish the just and prosperous society.[48]

The Academy was therefore charged "to become a vital force and the intellectual and scientific centre of the vigour of our nation, committed entirely to the purpose of our society, and bending its talents to the realization of those purposes." And this was because Dr. Nkrumah declared that his concern was not with plans to explore the moon, Mars or any of the planets. His concern was here on earth "where so much needs to be done to make it a place fit for human effort, endeavour and happiness," and science could be "directed towards fighting and overcoming poverty and disease and in raising the life of the peoples of the earth."[49]

Dr. Nkrumah was at pains to point out that the Ghana Academy belonged to our society and the African revolution. Like the universities, the Academy could "justify its status in our society only by the contribution which it (made) to the progress and development of the nation."

While the Academy was to carry out this fundamental role, there was also a great need to train more scientists. It had become necessary to supplement local effort in the production of scientists abroad. Dr. Nkrumah declared that the number of state scholarships which would enable Ghanaians abroad to qualify in science, technology, medicine and agriculture had been increased. And scholarship holders were to be found not only in the United Kingdom, Western Europe and America but also in the Soviet Union, China and in other socialist countries.

A further step was taken in establishing the scientific base of Ghanaian society when Dr. Nkrumah laid the foundation stone of Ghana's Atomic Reactor at Kwabenya on November 25, 1964.

In his speech, Dr. Nkrumah expatiated upon what he had said previously elsewhere and introduced some entirely new elements in his conception of a scientific society and what was to be done to achieve this. He felt there was the need to:

  i.   raise the quality and number of science graduates;
  ii. raise the standard of science teaching;
  iii. reach out to the mass of the people "who have not the opportu-
       nities of formal education . . . We must use every means of mass
       communication—the press, the radio, television and films—to
       carry science to the whole population;"
  iv. mount science exhibitions, whilst the National Science Museum
       was to provide "this kind of exhibition in a permanent form "[50]

All this was going over old ground. But Dr. Nkrumah did put out something novel at Kwabenya. Not only was the Ghana Academy of Sciences to produce a first seven-year national programme for the promotion of science in the country. For science to become part and parcel of the life of the people, Dr. Nkrumah contemplated the creation of a special scientific community where scientists of the Academy from different fields would live and work.

This was the Science City which was to have a main central building to be known as the "Palace of Science," and to contain a whole range of laboratories and other facilities. The city was to accommodate a number of research institutes and be a centre where the Academy would undertake pilot industries based on its discoveries. The Academy would then be in a position not only to recommend the setting up of any full scale industry, but would also be able to give expert advice on the type of industrial plant to be established and make the necessary economic appraisal.

Dr. Nkrumah was also concerned about the quality of products. He stated therefore:

> One of the most important projects planned for the Science City is a
> National Bureau of Standards where the testing of the quality of
> both imported and locally manufactured products will be under-
> taken to ensure that they conform to acceptable standards.[51]

Dr. Nkrumah then proceeded to spell out the justification for the creation of the Science City, both in terms of the Ghanaian situation and of theory and practice in science:

The Ghana Academy of Sciences should not be just a body of
learned men elected for their distinction and eminence. It should be
part of our national life, serving the people of Ghana, working with
them and helping to bring science and scientists into the closest
possible relationship with their lives.

It is only through this practical union of theory and action that the
life of man can attain the highest material, cultural, moral and spiritual fulfillment in the service of his fellow man. This ultimately is the
only justification for the pursuit of knowledge and the discoveries of
science.[52]

But the occasion was the laying of the foundation-stone of Ghana's
Atomic Reactor. Dr. Nkrumah was at pains to point out that Ghana's
interest in atomic energy was only in its peaceful uses, and he felt
that Ghana had to be part of the scientific revolution which could not
be ignored. On this occasion too, the major reasons, political and
ideological, came out clearly.

We in Ghana are committed to the building of an industrialised
socialist society. We cannot afford to sit still and be mere passive
onlookers. We must ourselves take part in the pursuit of scientific
and technological research as a means of providing the basis for
our socialist society. Socialism without science is void.[53]

While speaking about atomic energy, Dr. Nkrumah charged the
Ghana Atomic Energy Commission to investigate and expand
research on the possibilities of solar energy. This was to supplement work already begun at the University of Science and
Technology.

Ideological Education

Dr. Nkrumah had declared that socialism could be built only by
socialists. In his scheme of things therefore ideological education
was of paramount importance. His dream of African unity and his
conception of the African personality came to reinforce his ideas
about African socialism. Aleady, some of the productive agencies in
the public sector had become integral wings of the Party. These
were the Trade Union Congress, the Farmers Council and the Co-
operative Council.

On July 9, 1960, Dr Nkrumah said at the opening of the Hall of
Trade Unions:

I wish to seize this opportunity to announce today that the CPP have finished plans for the immediate establishment of a school to be known as the Kwame Nkrumah Ideological Institute at Winneba.

It will give educational ideological training to Party activists, trade union officials and our co-operators of the National Co-operative Council. In addition it will train freedom fighters from all over Africa who wish to come to Ghana for ideological and educational orientation.

He then outlined the details of the organization of the Institute as follows:

The Institute will comprise two sections, namely, the Positive Action Training Centre and the Ideological Training Centre. The Kwame Nkrumah Ideological Institute will be controlled exclusively by the Central Committee of the CPP and will not be subject to any regulations of the Education Department or the Ghana Education Trust.[54]

It was just as well since the Institute would have been beyond the control of the Education Department or the Ghana Educational Trust whose roles in education in the country were radically different from that of the Ideological Institute. They were engaged in the linear expansion of the system that existed, while the Institute's aim was to be

The chief means of counteracting the miseducation which has continued for so long and will in due course effectively direct the freedom movement for African emancipation.[55]

And this should come as no surprise when one remembers Dr. Nkrumah's March 6, 1957, statement. "The independence of Ghana is meaningless unless it is linked with the total liberation of Africa."

Non-Formal Education

The CPP's manifesto for the 1951 general elections stated, with regard to social development, that

The country needs a unified system of education, with free and compulsory elementary, secondary and technical education up to the age of 16 years . . . The Party lays special importance on Adult Education and will see to it that a planned campaign to liquidate illiteracy from this country in the shortest possible time is vigorously undertaken.[56]

The attempts made by Dr. Kwame Nkrumah and the CPP to redeem the 1951 election pledges so far as formal education was concerned has been recounted already. What remains to be said concerns out-of-school education, popularly referred to as non-formal education.

The country did respond to the Colonial Office document on "Mass Education" as it affected non-formal education. By 1948 a Mass Education Officer had been appointed "to advise on the initiation of mass education and social development work in the rural areas." This was followed by a trial run in Trans-Volta Togoland of a pro-gramme in mass education.

In 1951 the CPP presented the "Plan for Mass Literacy and Mass Education" to Parliament. Unlike the Accelerated Development Plan which preceded it, the Plan for Mass Literacy and Mass Education received the unanimous approval of the National Assembly. This was in August 1951. In April 1952, the Plan was launched with a dec-laration that

> Prominent in a mass education campaign must be an attack on illit-eracy, but mass education for community development is some-thing more than this. It is an attack on ignorance, apathy and prejudice, on poverty, disease and isolation. It is an education which is designed to teach people, not merely how to read and write, but how to live. Passive reception of ideas or information is not enough; every programme should be designed through the stim-ulation of initiative or the encouragement of local self-help to action either by individuals or by the community or both.[57]

The programme as carried out by the Department of Social Welfare and Community Development had clearly defined objectives. These included campaigns to reduce illiteracy; improvement in farm meth-ods of cultivation; better employment prospects on the land; improvement in water supplies through wells and bore-holes; better care for existing sources of water supplies; promotion of indigenous handicraft; small scale industries; child care; methods of food preservation; balanced diets; first aid and home nursing; and the construction of feeder roads, latrines and town centres.

The Department seemed to have carried out what a host of new departments and organizations have now been created to do, thus breaking the effective integrated approach to community education and development. However, while the Department was at it, it car-ried on special campaigns for other government agencies. As Kwa Hagan puts it, the Department "functioned like an omnibus govern-ment agency for the promotion of a whole range of projects, many of them carried out on behalf of other government departments, for community betterment in rural areas."[58]

It is ironical that with the overthrow of Nkrumah, the National Liberation Council decided that the Department should spend its expertise in eradicating the image of Nkrumah in the rural areas whilst the Government invited experts from Unesco to advise the Department on the eradication of illiteracy.

But when we come to agricultural extension, the Seven-Year Development Plan breaks new grounds, for there is a deeper grasp of the principles of non-formal education. The Plan noted that there had grown up a cadre of new agricultural manpower trained in the ways of modern farming. Hitherto, this skilled manpower had been used rather ineffectively as a sort of supervisory bureaucracy, standing over and outside agricultural production. There was thus a gap between agricultural service and agricultural practice. The new extension and development service officer was expected to work with the farmers. There was to be joint planning in the production targets and methods to their implementation and then to co-operate with the farmers in implementation. To achieve this required "the establishment of confidence over time in the farmers" own community.'[59]

Broadcasting as a Tool of Education

Ghana Broadcasting had a television (TV) component added to it. Dr. Nkrumah had already stated that TV, sound broadcasting and films were to enhance general educational programmes. At the State Opening of Parliament on October 15, 1963, he declared that "Ghana's television will not cater for cheap entertainment or commercialism; its paramount objective will be education in its broadest and purest sense." It is of interest therefore to see what he made of the broadcast media himself.

There was the Dawn Broadcast with its sequel of some Ministers losing their portfolios. The process could truly be described as non-formal education with the aim of bringing some sanity into the body politic and within the ruling party.

But the broadcast of April 30, 1963, published under the title "Revive Our Virtues," is a straight example of non-formal education. Dr. Nkrumah seemed worried by the "insolence and laziness of boys and girls, young men and women at work and in public places," at bars and dance halls, and the falling standards in courtesy and politeness of the youth.

On the eve of the May Day Celebrations, therefore, he used the occasion of his broadcast to address the youth, and not specifically the workers. To revive "those virtues and values in our society on which our fathers based their high standards of moral conduct and behavior," he proposed the following measures:

i. the expansion of the Young Pioneer Movement;
ii. the establishment of Gliding School at Afienya;
iii.the institutionalisation of a National Pledge and salute of the National Flag every morning at parade at school;
iv. a system of National Training:
   (a) three months immediately prior to admission to secondary school for boys;
   (b) three months at the end of secondary school prior to attendance at university, also for boys;
   (c) six months for all graduates on leaving university and before taking their place in life in society.

The whole purpose of this exercise, Dr. Nkrumah declared, was

to inculcate in our young people and our youth the virtues and disciplines such as the spirit of service, love for work, a sense of responsibility and dedication, of devotion to Ghana and Africa, of respect for superiors and of self-discipline and earnestness.[60]

One could take Dr. Nkrumah on, because the categories he specified did not include all "our young people and our youth." Even when it came to "schooled" children, only at the university level was the feminine gender included in national training. And up to now, national service is envisaged for the minority of our children and youth who enter second cycle and tertiary institutions. Whether it is national training or national service, the scope has to be widened since we all have to pledge to serve our motherland.

Conclusion

The education programme of Dr. Kwame Nkrumah has come in for some comment, some unfavorable, some eulogistic while others have based their critique on the performance of the economic plan which education was to support.

There are people in Ghana, in various occupations and of varying status who swear that but for Nkrumah they would not have had this start in life. On the other hand, a Jones-Quartey would dismiss the programme as:

the rapid take-over of most public affairs by the Convention People's Party of the Nkrumah regime. From its highest level at the University of Ghana to the village primary schools, education became not just the legitimate concern of government but one of the media of party ideological propaganda.[61]

That is one dimension of evaluation. But a more fruitful orientation is to look at the legacy and to decide where we go from there. Some analysts claim that formal education has not only proved costly, but it has also been dysfunctional. It has also not reached all the people and while a large proportion of the working population do not have a complete cycle of primary education there is a growing number of educated unemployed and of under-utilized manpower.

During the Nkrumah period, the economists had discovered education, and "education and economic growth" had become a credo in development planning. It was in this period that Harbinson and Myers produced their "composite index of human resource development." For a country to reach a high level of income it must first increase its score on the index. And the index was based on secondary and tertiary level enrolment, "the IS 5H formula," where S and H represent ratios at secondary and University level respectively, with the co-efficient 5 as an arbitrary weighting to higher education. Therefore manpower requirements at the higher and middle levels became the goal of educational effort. In Ghana, Dr. Nkrumah's model of development was "modern sector growth," with the expectation that with the creation and expansion of a modern industrialized and high productivity sector of the economy, the benefits would spread. With the growth in the GNP the benefits would trickle down.

This development policy does not seem to have worked: According to Rafael L. Irizarry, Third World countries wanting to develop through industrialization have had to import consumer goods; intermediate and semi-processed goods have had to be imported. Internally, industrial plants have not carried on any significant exchange with each other.

They do not produce materials required by other firms nor do they buy materials they need from one another . . . In consequence, new industries do not generate additional industrial activity. Overall then, the new industrial firms constitute a series of disconnected units which duplicate the pattern of a disarticulated economy that is characteristic of dependent societies.[62]

This is an interpretation based on dependency theory.

An economist will be in a better position to make a realistic appraisal of the performance of Nkrumah's economic policy. An educator can only state that the expansion in education provision under Nkrumah and the CPP was in part the outcome of the economic policy. It was linked with economic development, especially the Seven-Year Development Plan. Unfortunately the economic programme did not expand both far enough and fast enough to absorb the growing number of graduates from the primary schools and when the expectations of school leavers in respect to job openings are not met, the education system has become dysfunctional.

Just now, there is the need to rectify the imbalance between education and employment by improving the quality of it between education and jobs available and at the same time removing disparaties and irregularities that exist in education. The state bureaucracy, during and after Nkrumah, has tended to employ graduates and stimulated the demand for higher education. Governments have given discriminatory fiscal support in favor of secondary and higher education. There is prevalence still in the curriculum of skill and value orientations leading to job-seeking rather than to self-employment or entrepreneurial values. We still have the problem of over-education and under-utilisation of educated manpower.

We may attribute all these difficulties and challenges to Nkrumah. But the times are changing, and we have to rethink our way through these difficulties and challenges.

The Ideological Institute of Dr. Nkrumah, for instance, was anathema in 1966. Yet we have followed the idea in the establishment of the Centre for Civic Education, the Charter Secretariat and the National Commission for Democracy. It is an inescapable fact that we have to strive to find how we are going to organize our society. We require an orientation, an ideology of the state and the CPP under Nkrumah saw this need and initiated action.

The challenge thrown to the country by Dr. Nkrumah in the search for a scientific and technological base in the transformation of our society still stands. The empty shell of the Science Museum stands as a constant reminder of this unfinished business.

The need for "Mass Education" to bring in all of us to the task of national reconstruction still exists. In 1951, the Minister of Education and Social Welfare stated in his introduction to the Plan:

The Plan for Mass Literacy, Mass Education and Community Development . . . is a large scale, balanced plan to help every part of our country to achieve literacy and go far beyond and transform its whole life. The government will do all in its power to secure success. But the success with any plan for mass education and community development depends on the spirit of self-help among the members of every community and on willingness to co-operate with those who seek to help them.[63]

Central government initiative and support, dialogue with the people and the participation of the people in the effort to improve upon their standard of living are the three elements of a successful plan for mass education that have stood the test of time. When Dr. Nkrumah and the CPP introduced the measure in 1951, it received the unanimous support of Parliament. We need to revive that spirit of urgency and purpose which the CPP provided in the fifties.

With the benefit of academic hindsight, some critics have maintained that Dr Nkrumah's educational policy was only that of linear expansion. On the other hand, some commentators have maintained that people had to be "schooled" to man the modernizing sector. Today the student slogan is "education is a right." Dr. Nkrumah and the CPP attempted to make education open to every Ghanaian child. If there is anything worthwhile in formal education, if education can also be evaluated in terms of individual returns and personal satisfaction, and if it is right for a government not only to think of markets for education but also publics for it, then there is something to be said for the educational policies of the CPP under Dr. Nkrumah.

It is possible now to envisage the date when every child, without regardless to whether his parents are rich or poor, will be able to develop his talents to the fullest degree. Eventually this revolution will make it possible for every child, provided he has the ability, to get an education from the primary to the university level without hindrance from his financial circumstances.[64]

Dr. Kwame Nkrumah deserves to be judged also on his idea of the democratization of education put forward when he presented the Seven-Year Development Plan to Parliament. But at least the Ghana Educational Trust (GET) schools stand as concrete evidence that Nkrumah was not only engaged in rhetoric.

Notes

1. Nkrumah, 1963b: 1
2. Lewis, 1954~3
3. *Ibid.* 24
4. *Ibid.* 25
5. *Ibid.* 3
6. *Ibid.* 33-34

7. *Ibid.* 34
8. *Ibid.* passim
9. Balme n.d.
10. *Ibid.* 6-7
11. Lewis, op. cit.,: 29
12. Austin, 1964:15
13. *Ibid.* 15
14. *Accelerated Development Plan for Education,* 1957.
15. *Ibid.*
16. *Ibid.*
17. *Ibid.*
1 8. *Ibid.*
19. Office of the Planning Commission, 1964:141.
20. *Ibid.* 141
21. *Ibid.* 141-142.
22. *Ibid.* 142
23. *Ibid.* 142
24. *Ibid.* 147
25. *Ibid.* 144
26. Nkrumah, 1960:6
27. Nkrumah, 1961c:3
28. *Ibid.* 3
29. Nkrumah, 1965a: 16
30. *Annual Report of Education in the Year 1956*: Government Printer, n.d 2
31. *Report of the Education Department for 1960-62*, Government Printer, n.d 'N'
    27
32. *Annual Report of Education Department in the Year 1952*, Government Printer,
    1954: 21.
33. Nkrumah, 1961c:3
34 . Nkrumah, 1 964c: 5
35. *Op. cit.*
36. Nkrumah, 1965c :6
37. Nkrumah, 1961c :167
38. *Op. cit.*
39. Nkrumah, 1963f: 1
40. *Op. cit.*
41. Balme, op.cit.,:52
42. Nkrumah, 1963f :2
43. *Op. cit.*
44. Nkrumah, 1 963d :1
45. *Ibid.* 3
46. Nkrumah, 1 963d: 2
47. *Ibid.* 4
48. *Ibid.* 5
49. *Ibid.* 5
50. Nkrumah, 1 964b: 7-8
51. *Ibid.* 9
52. *Ibid.* 9
53. *Ibid.* 2
54. Nkrumah, 1960:6

55. *Op. cit.*
56. Hagan, 1975:15
57. *Ibid.* 20
58. *Ibid.* 25
59. *Seven-Year Development Plan,* 1964:76
60. Nkrumah, 1 963c
61. Lowe, 1970: 24
62. Irizarry, 1980: 349
63. *Plan for Mass Education and Literacy,* 1951
64. *Seven-Year Development Plan, op. cit.,* 1964:141

KWAME NKRUMAH AND THE MASS MEDIA

P. A. V. Ansah

Introduction

From the time he entered the political arena in the Gold Coast to the time of his overthrow, Kwame Nkrumah dominated the scene not only in his native Ghana but also on the whole of the African continent. Through the activities and pronouncements of Nkrumah, the small country of Ghana acquired a reputation that was far out of proportion to its size or the actual resources it commanded.

Since his regime came to an end in 1966, political scientists and other scholars have been assessing his achievements and his failures, and even though there seem to be as many judgements on Nkrumah as there are scholars with different political orientations, there is general agreement that he profoundly influenced the evolution of Ghana's history. He wielded tremendous power and exercised great influence on the lives and thinking of his people. Despite his personal charisma and other qualities, a close analysis would seem to lead one to the conclusion that the influence he exerted from 1947 to the end of his regime in 1966 was made possible largely through the masterly use of the mass media. He became actively involved with the press as an editor and years later could "still be excited by the smell of the printer's ink and the clatter of the printing machine."[1]

His personal experience of the potential of the press for organizing people and influencing the course of events no doubt influenced the way in which he regarded and treated the press under his rule. He also devoted considerable energies to the development of the other aspects of the mass media: radio, television, the national news agency and a professional training institute. Assessing Nkrumah's contribution to the development of mass communication in Ghana, one scholar observed: "At relatively great expense (certainly more than the Ghanaian economy could afford), he did build one of the most comprehensive national media systems in black Africa."[2]

If it is generally agreed that there was considerable expansion in the provision of machinery, plant and equipment for the mass media there is, however, some debate about the use to which these facilities were put. Liberals see Nkrumah's media philosophy as unalloyedly authoritarian; while progressives consider that, for the circumstances of a developing country with a large illiterate population, the draconian measures he took against the press and the monopolistic control he exercised over the media were justified in that particular historical context.

There is no doubt that Nkrumah's media philosophy was informed by a large dose of authoritarianism, but perhaps it might be more accurate to see it as a mixture of authoritarianism, paternalism, revolutionary theory, developmental media theory and other varieties which are all as far away as possible from the classical libertarian theory of the press. Nkrumah himself provided a consistent ideological rationale that characterized his relations with and handling of the mass media; and it is Nkrumah's own rationale that will form the basis of this discussion.

We do not propose to pass any value judgements on Nkrumah's relations with the press. Our main purpose is to use Nkrumah's own writings and pronouncements as primary source material to analyze his concept of the place and function of the media in the kind of society he tried to build in Ghana. There shall therefore be very little historical reference to his conflicts with individual newspapers or editors; the emphasis will be more on his media philosophy and how he used the media to pursue his objectives both at the national and continental levels.

The Press as a Revolutionary Tool

In the struggle for African emancipation, the newspaper became an indispensable tool. As part of the strategy for displacing colonial institutions, it was felt necessary to establish an indigenous press to counter the propaganda served by the colonialist or foreign-owned press. It was for this reason that many African nationalist leaders established or edited newspapers in the early stages of their political activities. In this regard, some of the examples that readily come to mind are Azikiwe's *West African Pilot,* Jomo Kenyatta's *Muiguithania* published in Kikuyu in the 1920's as the mouth-piece of the Kenya Central Association, Julius Nyerere's *Sauti ya TANU,* Leopold Senghor's *La Condition Humaine* and Kwame Nkrumah's *Accra Evening News.*

The main reason why the nationalist leaders used the newspaper to organize the people was that it was the only mass medium open to them, radio stations being entirely under the control of the colonial government. They were very much aware that in a largely illiterate society, the newspaper is an elite medium that does not reach the majority of illiterates in the rural areas. But they also knew that it could still make a great impact because "even in those areas the people can always be reached by the spoken word. And frequently the written word becomes the spoken word."[3]

Nkrumah saw the medium of print as an important tool for political education and mobilization. Already while in the University of Pennsylvania, he started organizing the African Students Association of America and Canada and he arranged for the publication of the *Africa Interpreter* as the organ of the Association "to revive a spirit of African nationalism."[4] Back in the Gold Coast he suggested that a newspaper should be established for political education, but this suggestion was spurned by his colleagues on the Executive Committee of the UGCC. After he left the UGCC he founded his own party, the CPP, with its own newspaper, the *Accra Evening News.* He wrote:

For the whole time that I was Secretary General of the movement (the UGCC), I had done my utmost to impress on the Working Committee the importance of establishing a newspaper as an organ of the movement. Personally I failed to see how any liberation movement could possibly succeed without an effective means of broadcasting its policy to the rank and file of the people.[5]

Nkrumah described the *Accra Evening News* which appeared on September 3, 1948, with only one sheet as "the vanguard of the movement and its chief propagandist, agitator, mobilizer and political educationist."[6] In January, 1949 he established the *Morning Telegraph* in Sekondi with Kwame Afriyie as editor, and in December of the same year he also set up the *Daily Mail* in Cape Coast with Kofi Baako as editor. These papers played such a prominent role in the launching and maintaining of "Positive Action" that the colonial government which had been using the radio to appeal to people to go back to work decided to close down all the three papers. The editors of the *Evening News* and the *Daily Mail* were charged with sedition and the editor of the *Morning Telegraph* was jailed for contempt of court.[7] As Nkrumah wrote in the January 14, 1949, issue of the *Evening News,* "The strength of the organized masses is invincible . . . We must organize as never before, the organization decides everything." Nkrumah had then the most effective, and an indispensable tool for this organization and mobilization which was the newspapers.

Nkrumah's concept of the newspaper as a revolutionary tool was a reflection of his reading of Lenin. Addressing the Second Conference of African Journalists in Accra, 1963, he said:

> To the true African journalist, his newspaper is a collective organizer, a collective instrument of mobilization and a collective educator—a weapon, first and foremost, to overthrow colonialism and imperialism and to assist total African independence and unity.[8]

The view expressed by Nkrumah closely echoes what Lenin said in 1901-2:

> A newspaper is not only a collective propagandist and collective agitator, but also a collective organizer. In this respect, it can be compared to the scaffolding erected around a building in construction; it marks the contours of the structure and facilitates communication between the builders, permitting them to distribute the work and to view the common results achieved by their organized labour.[9]

Development of the Mass Media

The importance Nkrumah attached to the mass media was demonstrated in the rapid expansion of media facilities in the country under his rule. In 1957 he established the Ghana News Agency (GNA) to collect and disseminate information at home and project Ghana's image abroad. The GNA was liberally provided with funds, and within two years its teleprinter service was extended to all regional capitals. By 1966 it had 8045 km of teleprinter lines inside Ghana with bureaux in Lagos, London, Nairobi and New York.

Radio was considerably expanded under Nkrumah. Because of the large percentage of illiterates in the country, radio, considered the best means of reaching them, was singled out for development.

Transmission and studio facilities were vastly improved, more relay stations were established and an external service was inaugurated in 1961. This was one of Nkrumah's most successful ventures. The external service broadcast in English, French, Arabic, Swahili, Portuguese and Hausa. With four lOOkw, and two 250kw transmissions, it broadcast 110 hours a week and the signal was clearly received in several parts of Africa and Europe. The aim in setting up an external service was partly to counter the "vile and vicious propaganda designed to cast doubts on the ability of the Africans to manage their own affairs."[10] Another objective of the Ghana Broadcasting Corporation (GBC) external service was formulated by Nkrumah thus:

> From this station, symbol of the true voice of Africa, we shall continue to fight for our complete emancipation, assisting in the struggle for the total liberation of the African continent and the political unification of the African states.[11]

For all practical purposes, then, the GBC External Service became an instrument of foreign policy.

On July 31, 1965, a television service was inaugurated as a noncommercial, public service station. It was also to be an ideological tool to "assist in the socialist transformation of Ghana."[12] The service started with the aim of devoting itself completely to education, information and nation-building.

Seeing the importance of professional training for media personnel, Nkrumah established the first institution for training journalists in Africa, the Ghana Institute of Journalism, in 1959, which attracted both Ghanaian and other Africans. It was liberally endowed with funds and its courses included not only professional disciplines, but also ideological training.

The development in the electronic media was not matched by a corresponding development in the print media. If anything, the print media shrank under Nkrumah as a direct result of his policies. The political atmosphere created after the passing of the Preventive Detention Act in 1958 and other laws specifically designed to limit the freedom of expression and of the press adversely affected the development of the press. While the state-owned or party press expanded, the private press shrank out of existence with the result that at the time of Nkrumah's overthrow the print media had become a state or party monopoly. Nkrumah had stated categorically on the ownership of the press:

It is part of our revolutionary credo that within the competitive system of capitalism, the press cannot function in accordance with a
strict regard for the sacredness of facts, and that the press, therefore, should not remain in private hands.[13]

It was this type of thinking which had led Nkrumah to acquire the private, foreign-owned *Daily Graphic* in 1962 from the London based
Mirror Group of newspapers, after he had established the Guinea
Press Limited in 1958 to publish the *Ghanaian Times* to offer competition to the *Daily Graphic*. It was the same company that took
over the printing of the *Evening News*. A few other papers were sponsored by the government, including six in the local languages to provide reading material for the new literates who had acquired literacy
in their mother tongues from the mass literacy classes. By far the
most ambitious effort of Nkrumah in newspaper development in the
early 1960's was the publication of *The Spark,* an ideological weekly
of analysis, "socialist in content and continental in outlook."[14]

By the time of Nkrumah's overthrow in February 1966, government control of the newspaper was total. From about ten newspapers at the time of independence, with most of them privately owned
by Ghanaian nationals, by 1966, the government or the party owned
and controlled all the newspapers, the resilient *Ashanti Pioneer* having been subjected to consistent censorship from 1960 and eventually closed down in October 1962.[15] With the passage of the
Newspaper Licensing Act, 1963 (Act 189), which required a person
to obtain a licence before publishing a newspaper, it became virtually impossible for anyone outside government or party circles to
establish or continue to operate a newspaper.

Policy on Broadcasting

At independence, one of the most urgent problems facing an
African country is that of national integration. National symbols have
to be forged and projected to the people to create a sense of identity, belonging and loyalty. Ethnic and regional loyalties have to give
way to national loyalty and a national cultural identity has to be created. Because of its ability to overcome the barriers of illiteracy and
distance, radio becomes an essential tool for reaching the masses of
the people. This is the reason that led Nkrumah to develop and
expand broadcasting in the country. With the unhappy memories of
seccessionist moves in certain parts of the country in the period
immediately preceding independence, it was decided that radio
should operate as a centralized system in order to serve as a tool for

unification. Speaking to the National Assembly on the expansion of radio services in the country on the occasion of the erection of two new transmitters at Prang in the Brong-Ahafo Region to improve reception in other parts of the country, the Minister of Education and Information, the Hon. Kofi Baako, said:

> I wish to stress that these new transmitters will relay the national programme and there is no intention whatever of initiating regional programmes . . . The radio is a great unifying agency in our country. Through it, people all over Ghana can appreciate that we are all of the same nation with the same ideas and aspirations . . . Ghana is a unity and in this small country there is no room for regional and tribal groups each emphasising their own differences from the rest of the country, at the expense of national unity. We do not want separate programmes on the radio for separate regions or tribes.[16]

A year later, the then Minister of Information and Broadcasting, the Hon. Kwaku Boateng, also told the National Assembly: "I wish to emphasize that the radio is a unifying influence and there is no intention of regionalising the broadcasting system . . . I have no intention of encouraging either regional or class or cultural distinctions among our people."[17]

Because of the great importance it attached to the issue of national unity, the CPP government was very consistent in its opposition to any form of decentralization or even proliferation of channels. Inaugurating television in Accra on July 31, 1965, President Nkrumah devoted a few words of his address to radio:

> In order to improve the standards of our national broadcasting service, the Government has recently taken certain decisions which are to be put into effect immediately. First, all the existing three national networks of the Broadcasting Service will be converted into one single network, and all our national transmitters will carry the same programmes throughout the country . . . The new broadcasting transmitters at Ejura will be used to reinforce those in Accra. They will, however, carry the same single network.[18]

The very tight and centralized control of broadcasting was reflected in the Instrument of Incorporation of the Ghana Broadcasting Corporation (GBC) in 1965. Because of the crucial role that broadcasting can play in educating people, enlightening them on their national responsibilities and the need for development, and especially because of its potential as a tool for national unity, the corporation's statutes did not leave much freedom of action to the professional broadcasting personnel. The Minister of Information and Broadcasting was given "powers of direction" which could override the decisions of the Board of the Corporation; but the largest amount of power was reserved to the President in Section II of the Legislative Instrument (L.I. 472 of 1965) which is worth quoting in full:

> Notwithstanding anything to the contrary in this Instrument, the President may, at any time, if he is satisfied that it is in the national interest to do so, take over the control and management of the affairs or any part of the functions of the Corporation and may for that purpose —
>
> (a) reconstitute the Board;
> (b) appoint, transfer, suspend or dismiss any of the employees of the Corporation; and
> (c) do, in furtherance of the interests of the Corporation, any other act which is authorised or required to be done by any person under this Instrument.
>
> Provided that the President may in addition to or in lieu of the exercise by him of any of the foregoing powers issue direction of a general or particular nature to the Board not inconsistent with the Provisions of this Instrument and that when issued, such directions shall be binding on the Board.

Radio under Nkrumah, then like the other media, became not a forum for free public discussion on national issues, but a closely guarded and tightly controlled propaganda machine for achieving the major objective of political education, the promotion of socialist ideals, national unity at home, the projection of Ghana's image and foreign policy abroad and for the liberation and unification of Africa. Another important objective was to counter the "vile and vicious propaganda" to which he and his government were being constantly subjected. For these, he believed that he needed total control of broadcasting which he obtained from L.I. 472.

Nkrumah's Concept of the Media

In trying to understand Nkrumah's concept of the place and role of the mass media in society, it is pertinent to recall that "the press always takes on the form and coloration of the social and political structures within which it operates. Especially, it reflects the system of social control whereby the relations of individuals and institutions are adjusted."[19] Nkrumah's political career was centred around certain basic ideas: the elimination of imperialism, colonialism and neo-colonialism, the establishment of a one-party state with control in the hands of the Central Committee of the Party, the supremacy of the party, the development of Ghana and Africa along a socialist path and the political unification of Africa.

Nkrumah's theory of the media was characterized by a certain eclecticism, containing elements of the authoritarian, paternal, communist, developmental and revolutionary theories of the press.[20] Some of the basic tenets of this blend of press theories are that the press should be always subordinated to established authority and that deviations from official policies or unacceptable attacks on, or criticisms of authority could be treated as criminal offences; and prior censorship could be justified for the purpose of maintaining public order, ensuring national stability and reinforcing the legitimacy of political authority. The media should also serve positive functions in society by informing, educating, mobilizing and motivating the people for national development. They were also expected to inform the people about events in other developing countries which are geographically, culturally or politically close. In terms of ownership, the state has the right to restrict media operations or exercise direct control in the interest of national development.

In addition to his views on the role of the press spread throughout his numerous writings, President Nkrumah gave the most comprehensive exposition of his views on the African press when he addressed the Second Conference of African Journalists in Accra in 1963. As far as ownership was concerned, Nkrumah expressed his opposition to the private ownership of newspapers, despite the fact that he had privately owned a press which he had used to criticize the colonial administration and mobilize the people. Or perhaps it was his awareness of the powerful role that the press could play, in the light of his personal experience, that shaped his thinking on the matter. Commenting on the attitude of African leaders to the press, Dennis Wilcox writes: "Many of them especially those who used the press to garner political power, fear the press because they are familiar with its potential for changing current political elites."[21] This might at least partly explain Nkrumah's almost morbid hatred of an opposition press.

Nkrumah's socialist approach in economic matters was reflected in his opposition to a media system that is commercially supported through advertising, as in the libertarian press theory that operates in a free-market economic environment. He believed that advertisers could exert undue and undesirable influence on the content and direction of the press and other media. Even when he had enormous difficulties running the *Evening News*, he refused to take advertisements "for fear that the advertisers might try to influence the policy of the paper."[22] His fear was that the interests of the advertisers as a class were opposed to those of the masses whose interests the newspaper was expected to project:

> As in a capitalist or neo-colonialist environment, profit from circulation and advertising is the major consideration, the journalist working within it is caught by its mechanics . . . Consciously or unconsciously, he is forced into arranging news and information to fit the outlook of his journal. He finds himself rejecting or distorting facts that do not coincide with the outlook and interest of his employer or the medium's advertisers. Willy-nilly, he adjusts his ideas to that of the class which his journal represents. Under the pressure of competition for advertising revenue, trivialities are blown up, the vulgar emphasised, ethics forgotten, the important trimmed to the class outlook.[23]

For the same reason, he decided that advertising should not be allowed in the electronic media. Inaugurating television services in July 1965, he reiterated what he had told Parliament two years earlier; namely that "it (television) will not cater for cheap entertainment nor commercialism."[24]

On the question of commercial broadcasting and the introduction of advertising into programming, Nkrumah's government was very consistent. Already in 1960, the then Minister of Information, the Hon. Kwaku Boateng, addressing Parliament, said:

> It is because I am conscious of the great power for good or ill that is inherent in broadcasting that I will ask Honourable Members to exercise the greatest caution when considering the introduction of Commercial Broadcasting features into our programmes. . . . I am personally convinced, and I hope Honourable Members agree with me, that whatever slight additional revenue may be obtained by this means, this advantage is by far outweighed by the inevitable deterioration in the quality of the programmes. For the same reasons I think we should be extremely careful in considering proposals for the introduction of Commercial Television. I do not think we should sell television time simply for the sake of establishing some sort of television service regardless of quality . . . I am happy to report that Government has decided that television, when it is introduced, shall be a state-owned system operated by the Ghana Broadcasting System itself.[25]

Nkrumah did not believe in professional objectivity, detachment and neutrality. Owing to the need for the journalist to serve as an educator and mobilizer of the masses, the journalist had to be fully committed to the ideals of the party; for all intents and purposes he was to be a dedicated party functionary. In his own words:

> The true African journalist very often works for the organ of the political party to which he himself belongs and in whose purpose he believes. He works to serve a society moving in the direction of his own aspirations.[26]

For this reason, he believed that professional education of a journalist was not enough. The journalist had to understand the relations between the press and society and the society in relation to the rest of the world.

The Role of the Media

Nkrumah saw the mass media as playing a crucial or even decisive role in the consolidation of African independence, the liberation of the countries still under colonial domination and the political unification of Africa. Inaugurating the External Broadcasting Service on October 27, 1961, he drew up the following agenda for the station:

> From this station, symbol of the true Voice of Africa, we shall continue to fight for our complete emancipation, assisting in the struggle for the total liberation of the African continent, and the political unification of the African states.[27]

This continental vision was not confined to the external service of Radio Ghana. Nkrumah believed that at the intellectual level, Africa could be emancipated and united only if her people, especially the intellectuals, were properly oriented ideologically. This was the reason that led him to found *The Spark*. To Nkrumah, the most important tasks facing African countries after independence were the political unification of Africa and the construction of socialism to replace "the imperialist system of colonialism." These two objectives constituted the basis of a new ideology that was to be scientifically formulated and vigorously propagated.

Writing on the occasion of the one-hundredth issue of *The Spark* which was started in 1962 and which Nkrumah compared to "the first Russian prototype *Iskra*,"[28] he explained:

The new Africa needs a new ideology, socialist in content and continental in outlook. The propagation of such an ideology demands an
ideological journal or journals serving all Africa. Hence *The Spark.*[29]

The newspaper was to "specialize in ideological work and thought
and provide the intellectual revolution which could dispel the
doubts and confusion concerning the ideology of the African revolution."[30]

Nkrumah believed that at the initial stages of independence,
special efforts were needed towards the mental decolonization of
Africans because the forces of imperialism operating through the
mass media were formidable. The Spark was thus to become the
"primary weapon for the conduct of the ideological battle in
Africa."[31]

It was Nkrumah's firm conviction that imperialism was a strong
force that could not be successfully challenged by individual African
countries. It was necessary, therefore, to fight it at the continental
level, and to prepare for that fight, people had to be ideologically prepared. For this reason, Nkrumah's vision embraced the whole of
Africa, and sometimes extended to the rest of the Third World
through the non-aligned movement.

Already, at the formation of the Organization of African Unity
(OAU) in 1963, Nkrumah was one of the leaders who proposed the
idea of a Pan-African News Agency. In December of 1963, Ghana again
proposed the establishment of PANAF as an inter-African news
agency to correct the distorted image of Africa that was being projected in the foreign media. But even before then, in 1961, he had
endowed the Ghana News Agency with considerable funds for expansion to serve as a nucleus of an All-Africa News Agency with offices
throughout Africa.[32] The strains on the economy frustrated these
plans. The arguments which Nkrumah put forward at the time and
the criticisms he addressed to the western media in their coverage
of Africa are precisely the points raised in the 1970's in the debate
on the New World Information and Communication Order (NWICO).

Nkrumah's preference for an ideologically committed and cru-
sading press did not blind him to the needs for maintaining professional journalistic standards. It was for this reason that he set up the
Ghana Institute of Journalism. Within the limits of ideological constraints, he called for the "faithful presentation of truth and fact" and
professional integrity. He said:

Truth, we say, must be the watchword of our African journalists and
facts must be their guide. These tenets, however, must not excuse

dullness in our newspapers and our journals. They must not be
used as an excuse for shoddy writing and ambiguous intentions.
The African journalist is not only expected to communicate the
facts and aims of our African Revolution, but to do so compellingly
and without fear . . . . He must acquire technical proficiency and literary skill . . . . We must make our publications attractive to the eye
and easy to handle and read.

We cannot self-righteously or contemptuously dismiss the appeal or
under-rate the seductiveness of the brightness in which imperialism
clothes its journalistic offerings. Bright colours and gay forms are
used to cover insidious suggestiveness .... You will not beat the spu-
rious and seductive output of western journalism except by publications of high quality and popular appeal. The answer is not to copy
them but to excel them— to educate the taste of the African reader
to the point of rejecting the undesirable foreign wares.[33]

One of the traditional roles of the press is to act as a watchdog of the
people's rights and monitor a government's performances by scru-
tinizing its actions and those of its officials. Given the tight control
that Nkrumah exercised over the press and the rest of the media in
Ghana, it is a little surprising to learn that he believed that the press
had the right to criticize the government. He declared in 1963:

Because we want strong and yet democratic governments in our
African Revolution, we must guard against the dangers inherent in
governments whose only opposition to tyranny and abuse lies in
the folds of the ruling party itself. A ceaseless flow of self-criticism,
an unending vigilance against tyranny and nepotism and other
forms of bribery and corruption, unswerving loyalty to principles
approved by the masses of the people, these are the main safeguards for the people under one-party rule. Who is best able to
exercise that vigilance, to furnish the material for self-criticism, to
sound warnings against any departure from principles, if not the
press of Revolutionary Africa?[34]

This means, in effect, that a certain amount of criticism or self-criticism could be tolerated or even encouraged, provided that it came
from within the ranks of the ruling party. This type of criticism could
be considered "constructive" whereas criticism from outside the
folds of the party could be, and indeed was, characterized as
"destructive" or "subversive."

Nkrumah and Press Freedom

Nkrumah's concept of the press saw it as a subservient tool of the government or the party in power. The role of the press was to advance the national cause and help in the achievement of national objectives as defined by the party leadership. He did not believe in the liberation theory of the press which tolerated a clash of different views in the "market-place of ideas." He made no pretenses about his contempt for neutrality or objectivity as an ideal to be pursued by the media. If the media were to be used for the ideological education and intellectual emancipation of the masses, it was essential that definite positions should be taken. He said:

> We do not believe that there are necessarily two sides to every question: we see right and wrong, just and unjust, progressive and reactionary, positive and negative, friend and foe. We are partisan.[35]

Still on the question of partisan commitment, Nkrumah did not mince words about the direction to be followed by the African journalist in a revolutionary situation. The principal aim of the press was not to make money for the owners or provide entertainment to its readers. It was to be a tool for political emancipation and enlightenment.

> It is an integral part of our society, with which its purpose is in consonance. Just as in the capitalist countries the press represents and carries out the purpose of capitalism, so in Revolutionary Africa, our Revolutionary African press must present and carry forward our revolutionary purpose. [36]

His attitude towards press freedom was later to be expressed in one of his publications (1963). Nkrumah claimed that the freedom of expression that he had tolerated in the years immediately following independence had been abused by the opposition which never missed an opportunity to stigmatize the government and subject him to "special attack, abuse and ridicule." Press freedom had been "debased into licence."[37] For this reason, he tightened his control over the press and all the repressive laws on the press date from 1960.

Nkrumah believed that the attacks on him and his government through the opposition press undermined national unity and rendered more difficult the task of nation-building. He described the situation as follows: "This was not freedom of expression. This was irresponsible licence, and if allowed to continue unbridled, it would have undermined our state, our independence and the people's faith in themselves and their capacities."[38]

What was Nkrumah's reaction to what he considered the degeneration of the freedom of expression into licence? He wrote:

> We came to the point where it was obvious that the government must take action if we were to avoid the dangers inherent in a false situation. The imposition of any form of press censorship was an idea most repugnant to me, since it ran counter to everything I had always believed in, everything for which I had struggled in my life. Freedom of expression had been one of the essential rights for which I had fought. I had gone to prison for daring to say things the colonial administration had not liked.[39]

Censorship was effectively imposed by the Criminal Code, Act 29, 1960. Section 183, sub-section (2) of the Act said in part that whenever the President was of the opinion that any publication contained

> matter calculated to prejudice public order of safety, or the maintenance of the public services or economy of Ghana, he may make an executive instrument requiring that no future issue of the newspaper, book or document shall be published, or, as the case may be, that no document shall be published by, or by arrangement with, the said person, unless the matter contained therein has been passed for publication in accordance with the instrument.

This law was initially applicable only to the press in Ghana, but on the strength of the Act, an Executive Instrument (274) was signed by L. R. Abavana, Minister of Information and Broadcasting on September 28, 1962, requiring foreign correspondents to submit their material for vetting before publication.

Anticipating that a situation might arise in which democratic freedoms would need to be curbed, Nkrumah had written:

> Even a system based on social justice and a democratic constitution may need backing up by measures of an emergency nature in the period which follows independence.[40]

In the case of the press, he believed that a young, independent country could not allow itself the type of freedom of expression "which established democracies have taken generations to evolve."[41] He saw freedom of expression, then, as an ideal to be pursued, but considered that his people were not sufficiently politically mature to enjoy that freedom.

Conclusion

Nkrumah's concept of the press has been described as author-itarian, but given the role he assigned to the media, perhaps it may be more accurate to describe it technically as paternal, meaning, "an authoritarian system with a conscience: that is to say, with val-ues and purposes beyond the maintenance of its own power . . . In a paternal system, what is asserted is the duty to protect and guide. This involves the exercise of control, but it is a control directed towards the development of the majority in ways thought desirable by the minority."[42]

The mass media under Nkrumah may have been instrumental in the development of Ghana, but that they were not free is not in dis-pute. Whatever judgement one passes on Nkrumah on this score will depend on the importance one attaches to the freedom of the press or of expression in general in a civilized, democratic society. It is very debatable whether the series of repressive laws passed to muzzle the press were necessary to maintain national stability and progress or were designed to ensure Nkrumah's own undisputed leadership and political survival. The purposeful use of the mass media for development implies a certain measure of direction and control, but the question really is: how much control need be exerted so that the media can discharge their developmental func-tions while some regard is shown for the right to self-expression?

A distinction can be made between positive and negative con-trols over the press; the controls are negative when they are intended to stifle criticism of a government's actions or policies, and positive when they are intended to direct and guide the press towards the achievement of political, social, economic, cultural and ideological objectives.[43] Even if the evidence from Nkrumah's own pronouncements ostensibly indicates that the controls he imposed were positive, they certainly had the effect, intended or unintended, of stifling all criticism so that they became negative. Certain schol-ars have tried to explain the imposition of authoritarian controls in developing countries by articulating the argument advanced by Third World leaders. John Lent writes:

> Because Third World nations are newly emergent, they need time to develop their institutions. During this initial period of growth, sta-bility and unity must be sought; criticism must be minimized and the public faith in government institutions and policies must be encouraged. Media must cooperate, according to this guided press concept, by stressing positive, development inspired news, by ignoring negative social or oppositionist characteristics and by sup-porting governmental ideologies and plans.[44]

This is a rationalization which does not find much favor with liberal scholars of the media in Third World countries or beyond. The monopolistic control which Nkrumah gained over the mass media can be seen only as a logical consequence of his establishment of a one-party political system in Ghana. The virtue of that particular arrangement is open to debate, and so were Nkrumah's concept and handling of the press. An assessment of Nkrumah's relations with the press and the repercussions they had on his own perception of national realities is provided by one scholar who writes:

> A less fettered press might have demonstrated that many programs lacked public approval. But Nkrumah himself made a dissenting press forbidden in theory, criminal in law, and non-existent in practice. Like all rulers, he had to strike a balance between freedom and control, information and coercion. Nkrumah tipped the scales too much, and lost his own balance.[45]

The present writer endorses this assessment of the use Nkrumah made of the mass media system which he developed in Ghana.

NOTES

1. Nkrumah, 1963a: 1
2. Hachten, 1971:172
3. Nkrumah, 1963 a: 5 5
4. Nkrumah, 1957:35-36
5. *Ibid.*, 76
6. *Ibid.*, 76
7. *Ibid.*, 98
8. Nkrumah, 1963a:5
9. Lenin, 1965: 202
10. Nkrumah, 1961d:2
11. *Ibid.*, 3
12. Nkrumah, 1965d: 3
13. Nkrumah, 1963 a: 4
14. Nkrumah, 1964d: 3
15. Gazette October 19, 1962
16. Debates, Vol. 16; 1959-1960, Col. 630
17. Debates, Vol. 20;1960-1961, Col. 934-935
18. Nkrumah, 1965d:5
19. Siebert, F S; Peterson, T and Schramm, W (195 6) 1974: 1-2
20. For further details on Press Theories - See Siebert, Peterson and Schramm, *op. cit.* Merrill and Lowenstein 1979:153-172; McQuail 1983:84-98; Williams, 1962:116-124; Hachten 1981: 80-96.
21. Wilcox, 1975:12
22. Nkrumah, 1957:77; Nkrumah added "in any case most of the people who

could afford to advertise were the imperialist and capitalist merchants who would not in any case have been willing to associate themselves with our paper."

23. Nkrumah, 1963a:4
24. Nkrumah, 1965 d: 3
25. Debates, First Series, Vol. 20, Session 1960-19611Col. 936, August 29,1960. The Impression seems to have been gained that Commercial radio or television necessarily leads to a lowering of cultural tables. It all depends on the volume and quality of advertising allowed. The ITV in Great Britain allows advertising but this is never allowed to intrude on programming and the quality of production compares very favourably with the best television anywhere in the world.
26 . Nkrumah, 1963 a: 3
27 . Nkrumah, 1961 d: 3
28. Nkrumah, 1964d:5
29. *Ibid.,* 3
30. *Ibid.,* 3
31. Nkrumah, 1964d:3
32. Hachten, 1971:170
33. Nkrumah, 1963a:7
34. *Ibid.,* 16
3 5. Quoted from Hachten, 1971: 43
36. Nkrumah,   1 963a: 8
37. *Ibid.,* 76
38. *Ibid.,* 76
39. Ibid., 77
40. Nkrumah,1957: viii
41. Nkrumah, 1963g: 77
42. Williams, 1962:117
43. Merrill and Lowenstein, 1979:165
44. Lent, 1977 :18
45. Rivers, 1970:176.

WOMEN AND THEIR ORGANIZATIONS DURING THE CONVENTION PEOPLES' PARTY PERIOD

Takyiwah Manuh

Introduction

Women cannot be ignored in any assessment of the "Life and Work of Kwame Nkrumah" since it is clear from even a cursory study of the Convention Peoples' Party (CPP) period that they played a significant part in events as well as constituting an important base for the CPP. Nkrumah himself suggests this by his axiom that "the degree of a country's revolutionary awareness may be measured by the political maturity of its women."[1] Inasmuch as Ghana under Nkrumah was in the forefront of the struggle for African Unity and against neo-colonialism, it would be instructive to discover what advances occurred in the lives of Ghanaian women and how these contributed to their political maturity. This paper then focuses on some important and intersecting spheres of problems of the roles and activities of women during different historical periods, culminating in the anti-colonial struggle. The core of the paper centres on women in the post-independence state and on the measures taken by Nkrumah and the Convention Peoples' Party to enhance women's participation in politics, the economy, social and family life, and the quest for African Unity.

I. Women in Ghanaian Society

The Convention Peoples' Party, which came to power professing to speak for the masses, had women among its strongest supporters. C. L. R. James notes in his book *Nkrumah and the Ghana Revolution* that, "in the struggle for independence, one market woman . . . was worth any dozen Achimota graduates . . ."[2] Together with the workers, young men educated in primary schools and the unemployed, women became some of Nkrumah's ablest, most devoted and most fearless supporters. Women followed Nkrumah across the country on his speaking tours, vigorously championing the struggle for independence. They took part in the struggles and boycotts of the period, and as James again records, during the general strike of 1948, the cooks of the Europeans found it difficult to buy food in the markets because the women were reserving it for the strike days.[3] These women fed Nkrumah and his followers and financed them, and it is alleged that without the support of some of these women, Nkrumah could not have survived in Accra.[4] In addition, they were efficient organizers who could bring thousands of people together for a rally at the shortest possible notice.

In order to comprehend the reason why women as a group identified with the CPP and worked to realize its aims and objectives, we need to discuss briefly the position of women in traditional and colonial Ghanaian society. Women played varied roles in the social, economic and political activities of different Ghanaian societies. They worked inside and outside the home mothering and nursing children, cooking, processing and storing food.They participated in agricultural work, farmed different crops and marketed produce. Women made pottery, wove cloth and engaged in other crafts according to the resources available. In addition, some women possessed knowledge of the healing powers of plants and herbs and were skillful medical practitioners. In general, women held their households and families together and were expected to function within the domestic household unit, and marriage and child-bearing were considered the essential vocation of women in society.[5] But women performed other roles and functions which varied with the societies. In some societies, women held political, religious and ritual offices and participated in some limited ways in the lives of their communities. Nevertheless, it is true to say that women occupied subordinate positions in all societies in Ghana and were not regarded as the equals of men.[6]

Arhin (1983) and Aidoo (1985) have attempted to reconstruct the social, economic and political roles of Ghanaian women, particularly the Akan, in the 18th century and 19th century. The central theses of both authors is that the matrilineal core of Akan political and legal institutions guaranteed women's political, social and economic roles, and there existed a complementarity between males and females in society. Aidoo's detailed study provides a wealth of historical information on Akan social organization and of women's roles and activities in the then prevailing social and economic conditions of the 19th century. Aidoo makes comparisons with other non-Akan Ghanaian societies which practiced patrilineal or bilateral descent and where women were markedly subservient to men and suffered many restrictions in their legal, political and economic rights.[7] While it is not intended here to enter into the controversy of the "unique" position of the Akan woman, one may note in passing that even among Akan women, "royal" females possessed statuses and rights which were not applicable to Akan females in general. A similar point is made by Gwendolyn Mikell (1985) in her review of *Female and Male in West Africa* (Oppong, ed. 1983), that the issue is one of complementarity for females in general, and not just royal ones. Further, she notes that the growth and expansion of the patricentric stools, the *mmammadwa*, in Ashanti in the 18th–19th century dealt a critical blow to male/female political complementarity long before colonial rule.[8]

Within traditional Ghanaian societies, women formed associations and groups for social, ritual and military purposes.[9] Some of these groups were age-graded and initiated young women into puberty and adult life. There were as well many music and dance groups which performed at funerals, festivals and other occasions. Arhin (*op. cit.*), refers to the Akan *mmomomme* groups which had military and religious functions and performed dances, mimes and rites to ensure success in war while their men-folk were away at war. Aidoo also makes mention of female wings among the patrilineal Asafo groups of the coastal Akan.[10] These were the *Adzewa* or *Adenkum* bands which provided support to the Asafo companies in war.[11] There were also female captains and the Asafo *nkyeremmaa*, a type of rear-guard, who performed support services in war.[12] With colonial rule, some of these female military associations particularly among the Fante, were co-opted for military services and acted as carriers.[13] Similarly, the participation of women in communal labor in their societies was transformed into forced labor, and in Northern societies, a position of Magazia, an organizer of women, was created to organize women for forced communal labor.[14]

During colonial rule, prevailing Victorian values and morality were super-imposed on the traditional order, and this created many conflicts and tensions. These Victorian values which defined men as heads of households meant, for example, that while Ghanaian women were hardworking and engaged in the cultivation of food and cash-crops, they received little recognition or remuneration and were ignored in the provision of extension services.[15] As well, women's access to the limited health and educational facilities was poor and this led to their being further disadvantaged in the society.

The limited educational opportunities which became available for girls sought to continue their domestic functions by emphasizing good behavior and feminine skills such as needlework, crochet and cookery. In this way, it was intended to create a pool of "better wives (for) the rising crop of educated clerks, teachers, catechists and few professional men."[16] Given the reluctance of parents to educate girls whose services were needed at home and who were ultimately expected to get married, few women got educated. Those who became educated found employment as school teachers, nurses, clerks and telephone operators on a salary scale lower than that of their male counterparts. However, even this employment was regarded as temporary, and women were expected to resign on getting married or pregnant.[17] In 1936, the colonial government, which had embarked on a policy of retrenchment, ruled that the resignation of pregnant women should be made a condition of appointment.[18] In addition, certain positions in the civil service were closed to women, and until 1963, the administrative class remained the presence of men, as women, no matter their qualifications, were deemed incapable of fulfilling all the duties of an administrative officer.[19] Besides the above, discriminatory provisions existed in workplaces, and while dependents of male employees were entitled to free medical treatment and other facilities, the dependents of female employees were denied such rights.[20]

Within the educational set-up dominated by mission-run schools, strict morality prevailed, and female teachers who became pregnant, but could not produce marriage certificates, were dismissed. As well, women who took several maternity leaves had their promotions retarded, and as late as 1951, it was recommended that all serving female officers should be called upon to leave the service on their second pregnancy.[21] These harsh provisions, which were thought to be justified on the grounds of efficiency, rather reflected the values and prejudices of British Victorian society. Women were either to strive for a career, limited though this was, or to marry and remain at home. Thus it was not unusual to find several educated women of the period who devoted themselves to careers remaining unmarried and childless, in a society which based a woman's worth on her fecundity above all else.

For illiterate women in the towns, "hawking" and petty trading developed as the main economic activity to supplement the meagre earnings of their husbands. It was in this way that the "pass-book" system evolved under which some women were supplied goods on credit by the large expatriate trading firms on commission basis. The women then became customers of UAC, SCOA, CFAO, and sold cloth, "provisions" and general trade goods.[22] Women with less capital, who could not open pass-books, bought on credit from the large brokers and retailed their wares in the markets, suburbs and villages of Ghana. As Nkrumah noted "the women play an important part in our internal trade distribution, but are reliant for their supplies on the monopoly firms, for whom they provide the cheapest kind of retail distributive system."[23]

In turn, some of the women bought foodstuffs from the villages and sold them in markets throughout Ghana, and established elaborate systems of supplies, distribution and controls in the markets.[24] Women also set up 'chop-bars' in the towns and around work-sites to provide quick meals to workers, laborers, and the growing numbers of town-dwellers. These trading activities enabled some women to become really wealthy and a few even imported goods on their own account and sent their children abroad to be educated. However, petty trading was not so lucrative for the mass of traders, and the little profit gained was quickly expended on urgent family needs. In order to survive in town, therefore, the women had to rely on help in the form of foodstuffs and occasional loans or gifts from kin in the villages. As well, there was constant interaction between town and villages as children were sent from one place to the other to be fostered by kin and to receive education and other training.

It was in this atmosphere of uncertainty and insecurity of town life that many benevolent and mutual aid associations, credit unions and other voluntary groups were formed by both men and women.[25] In the markets, women formed groups for the various commodities traded in, and each had its "queen" and other leaders. There were also women's groups within the churches and all these sought to relieve tension and foster cohesion among their members.

One women's association which was prominent during the period was the National Federation of Gold Coast Women.[26] It was founded in 1953 and soon established branches in the Colony, Ashanti and the Trans-Volta Togoland, and worked through women's church groups, benevolent and mutual aid societies, market women's associations and other voluntary bodies. The Federation concerned itself with improving the lives of women and children through the recognition of customary marriages by the colonial authorities. It sent many petitions to the Governor and the Joint Provincial Council on discriminatory practices in employment, marriage, inheritance and social life affecting women.[27] It was recognized by the colonial government which supported its work, and operated as a non-political body within the confines of colonial society. It published a periodical, "The Gold Coast Woman." However, its influence and reach were limited, and it failed to attain the status of a national women's movement.

II. Women in the Anti-colonial Struggle

With the return of Nkrumah to the Gold Coast and his breakaway from the United Gold Coast Convention (UGCC) to form the CPP, women's involvement in politics on a national scale became possible for the first time. While some of the women in the towns had identified with the UGCC, the lack of a mass base of the UGCC to successfully prosecute the struggle for independence had prevented meaningful action, and some of the first women to join the CPP had started out with the UGCC.[28] With the birth of the CPP, a *Women's Section* was formed almost simultaneously, and these women worked tirelessly within it, for the achievement of "self-government now." Women such as Mabel Dove Danquah and Akua Asabea Ayisi worked side by side with Nkrumah on the *Evening News* writing articles, demanding independence and exposing themselves to the risks attendant on political activity in a colonial regime.[29] Women took part in the "Positive Action Campaign" and Leticia Quaye, Akua Asabea Ayisi and others went to prison.[30] Memorable among them was an old lady in her sixties, Arduah Ankrah, who used to call herself "Mrs Nkrumah," and who was convicted for the contempt of exhibiting unruly behavior in court during the trial of some of the campaigners.[31] It is said that she was very cheerful and kept up the spirits of her fellow detainees while in prison.[32]

During this time, women used to attend the rallies of the CPP around the country and, as has been already stated, the women were skilful organizers. They were powerful orators as well, and, inspired by the events unfolding around them, responded wholeheartedly. Nkrumah recounts in his autobiography that:

much of the success of the CPP has been due to the efforts of women members. From the very beginning, women have been the chief field organizers. They have travelled through innumerable towns and villages in the role of propaganda secretaries and have been responsible for the most part in bringing about the solidarity and cohesion of the party.[33]

While Nkrumah was in prison, he had learned that at a rally in Kumasi, a woman party member who had adopted the name "Ama Nkrumah" got up on the platform and ended a fiery speech by getting hold of a razor blade and slashing her face. She smeared the blood over her body and challenged the men present to do likewise, in order to show that no sacrifice was too great in their united struggle for freedom and independence.[34] These women are variously described as the "unknown warriors of the party" and as "playing a glorious part" in the struggle for independence.

In May 1951, the CPP appointed four women, namely, Mrs. Leticia Quaye, Mrs. Hanna Cudjoe, Madam Ama Nkrumah and Madam Sophia Doku, as Propaganda Secretaries.[35] They travelled around the country, enrolling men and women into the CPP and into its Women's Section and Youth League. Wherever there were CPP branches, women's wings proliferated, and these women's wings sponsored rallies where the Propaganda Secretaries spoke about CPP policies and collected contributions for the Party. Some of the female members showed initiative and the Asikasu branch of the Women's Section, for example, organized a singing band which performed at CPP rallies. A few women also served free water at rallies and contributed in these small ways to the growth of the Party. The women combined a variety of methods, both traditional and novel, to rally support for the CPP and drew heavily on the historical experience of Ghanaian women. Thus, at a CPP rally at Dzodze, Nkrumah was received by women in Party colors who fired guns and danced in front of the cars.[36] Inasmuch as independence sought to end colonial domination and create better conditions of life for the population in the form of more schools and hospitals, better drinking water and greater access of all to these amenities, women had more to gain from independence. As has been shown above, women were discriminated against in education, employment and family life, and they had fewer stakes in the maintenance of the colonial state as they were largely unrepresented in its political, social and economic structures. It is noteworthy that even with the attainment of limited self-government in 1951, the electoral provisions placed impediments in their way as electors or candidates, and only one woman,

Mabel Dove Danquah, managed to get elected on the ticket of the CPP to a seat in the colonial legislature.[37]

III. Women in the Post-Independence State

At independence, the tasks confronting the new Ghanaian state in relation to women could be grouped into five broad categories:

i. The task of enhancing women's political and civic rights;
ii. educational, social and economic measures aimed at realising the full potential of women in society;
iii. family, marriage, and inheritance reform;
iv. organizing women centrally to speak with one voice; and
v. women and African Unity.

It is to these that we now turn.

III.(i) Political and Civic Rights

In 1959, the Representation of the People (Women Members) Act was passed.[38] This Act made special provision for the election of women as members of the National Assembly, and reflected the conscious desire of the newly-independent state to have women participate in national affairs at the highest levels. It made provision for the election of ten women as additional members of the National Assembly who were to hold office and be subjected to the same rights and disabilities as elected members of parliament under the Electoral Provisions Ordinance of 1953.[39] There was to be a Women's Electoral College to carry out the election, either in a special election or contemporaneously with any general election. This law, though enacted, never came into operation. New legislation in 1960 repealed the 1959 Act and provided for a different method of election for new women members.[40] Elections were held in June 1960 for the special Women's seats, and the names of the new members were published in the *Ghana Gazette* in July, 1960.

Accordingly, ten women parliamentarians took their seats at the first session of the First Parliament of the Republic of Ghana.[41] This move was not without its critics. The Honourable Mr. Victor Owusu, Opposition Member of Parliament, in his comments on the President's Sessional Address, referred to the women parliamentarians as "a sprinkling of 'lip-sticked' and 'pan-caked' faces of doubtful utility to the deliberations of the House."[42] This was met with a swift rebuttal from Sophia Doku, woman member for the Eastern Region, and he had to apologize hurriedly.[43]

Nkrumah catapulted women onto the political scene in a way that was new both in Ghana and Africa. For him, this was part of the attempt at projecting the African Personality and at raising the status of African Womanhood.[44] Thus, in addition to the women parliamentarians, a woman deputy minister and women district commissioners were appointed. It was not without significance that the woman deputy minister hailed from the North. For long isolated from the rest of the country in political, social and cultural terms, the Northern Territories had functioned as a labor reserve under colonialism and was at a lower level of development than most other parts of Ghana.[45]

Nkrumah was deeply concerned about this state of affairs, and the measures introduced in relation to Northern education reflected this concern.[46] The appointment of a woman from the Northern Territories as a Deputy Minister as well as women parliamentarians and District Commissioners therefore constituted a conscious and dramatic attempt to incorporate women into national life, break the isolation of the inhabitants of the Northern Territories, and do away with the disrespectful and contemptuous attitudes shown towards them by many Southerners.

As well, women were appointed to serve on the boards of corporations, schools and town councils. Most of these women had been with the party from its inception, and their occupations as teachers, housewives and the like, reflected the class composition of the CPP. The main criterion for appointment seems to have been loyalty to the party, a principle similarly applied to the men who rose into prominence with the CPP.

A few women served on the CPP's Central Committee, were influential and formed part of Nkrumah's entourage when he travelled abroad. This was to enable them to observe the standards and achievements of women elsewhere and to emulate them. It is alleged that where a woman could fill a post, Nkrumah would give it to her, and rather than the showpieces that a largely chauvinist society assumed them to be, Nkrumah expected women to work hard and be strong, and insisted that they did better than their best.[47]

III.(ii) Educational, Economic and Social Measures

As well as enhancing women's political and civic roles, the CPP government pursued measures to advance women's educational levels and enhance their social and economic roles. Nkrumah was concerned about the education of women as he saw them as the architects of a nation. Like Aggrey, he believed that educating a woman meant the education of a whole nation, and the Accelerated Development Plan for Education introduced in 1952 reflected this concern. Its implementation resulted in a tremendous increase in the numbers of public primary and secondary schools and teacher training colleges, and the Education Act of 1961 making education compulsory for school-age children raised enrollement figures considerably. Thus by 1965-66, the 1951 figures of 1700 primary schools enrolling about 226,000 children had increased to almost 11 000 schools enrolling nearly 1.5 million pupils.[48] The access of girls to education, particularly at lower levels, was facilitated, and by 1965-66 girls constituted nearly 44% of total primary school enrollments, 35% in middle school and 25% at secondary school.[49] In addition, many elderly women participated actively in the mass education campaigns of the period.

The policy of providing segregated education for girls in mission schools was combined with the establishment of mixed secondary schools which provided places for the increased numbers of girls leaving middle schools. At the level of training colleges, however, no such policy seems to have been pursued, and many women's training colleges opened during this period to meet regional needs. One of these was the Tamale Women's Training College, and in a speech to inaugurate its opening, Nkrumah recounted the hitherto existing difficulties in the way of Northern girls who had completed Standard VII and wished to teach.[50] Nkrumah noted his gratification at the presence of "a lady of Northern extraction on the staff of the college."[51]

More women entered the Universities and higher institutions of learning, and others were sent abroad, together with men, to pursue courses in medicine, dentistry, and other technical courses to meet the requirements of the development plans. Women went on short courses to Israel, the Soviet Union and other Eastern-bloc countries for courses in co-operatives, trade unionism, and fisheries, among others. These courses meant diversification in the fields of employment open to women, and while the result of colonial education had been that the principal profession open to women was teaching, women could now be found working in many other areas. By the end of CPP rule (1966) there were a number of women doctors, dentists, lawyers, graduate teachers, administrative officers, parliamentarians and a judge of the Supreme Court. As the then Minister for Education put it, the government was "dedicated to raising womanhood mentally and morally, and to increasing their general efficiency in the vital roles they have to play."[52]

Furthermore, discriminatory provisions relating to women's work were abolished, and equal pay was instituted for equal work and maternity leave with full pay was assured. With the adoption of the *Seven-Year Development Plan and the Programme of Work and Happiness*,[53] new employment avenues were opened for women through the establishment of many factories, enterprises and state farms. Later, when the Workers' and Builders' Brigades were established, many women were trained and employed as tractor and motor drivers.

For the CPP, some of these enterprises were regarded as avenues to provide employment for party loyalists, and it was urged that illiterate women members of the party in particular should be assisted to obtain jobs as sweepers and cleaners in the offices, factories and towns.[54] In this way, it was hoped that the Party's aims on full employment could be vigorously pursued.[55] At the same time, women were encouraged to enter hitherto male preserves, and some women underwent pilot training at the Ghana Air Force Training School at Takoradi. In the Party Journal, Women were called upon to enter the army in their numbers to serve in the infantry battalions, to train as gunners, work in the intelligence and service corps, and train as electrical and mechanical engineers.[56] According to the authors, the days had passed when women were "considered only suitable for the nursing branch of the army and other auxiliary duties connected with the kitchen." In his Sessional Address to Parliament in 1965, Nkrumah also spoke about the establishment of a women's auxiliary corps which would enable young women to work together shoulder to shoulder with the men.[57]

In spite of all these attempts, however, agriculture and trading absorbed the largest proportion of women workers. While the CPP government introduced a number of measures in relation to agriculture which is the subject of another contribution in this collection, not much information exists on the impact of agricultural schemes on women farmers.[58] Certainly, some women joined the Farmers' Council and the Co-operative Movement fostered by the CPP and a few benefitted from its credit schemes. By and large, however, not much improvement occurred in the lives of women farmers in general, and the various legislations on land which were enacted did not work to their benefit.[59]

Petty trading was a different story, and market women formed some of the most enthusiastic supporters of the CPP, and could be seen at rallies dressed in party colors. They were an extremely vocal

group and could be regarded as a temperature gauge of political
and economic conditions. In almost all the markets across the country, CPP women were very strong, and emerged as the "queens" in
the various trades, and contributed vast sums of money to the
party.[60] Together with City and Town Councils, they controlled the
allocation of stalls and space within the markets, as well as the commodities traded in, and some had strong contacts with the trading
firms. The Abraham Commission of Enquiry into Trade Malpractices
revealed the oligarchy which some of the women had formed and
their manipulation of the pass-book system. After the 1966 coup,
much evidence was presented before Commissions of Enquiry of
the roles of some CPP women in the allocation of import licences and
in the trade malpractices which ensued.[61] Basil Davidson says of
these women that "business was what they understood to their fin-
ger tips and the interest of business were the driving interests in
their nationalism."[62]

These women made full use of the establishment of the Ghana
National Trading Corporation and utilized connections within the
party and state hierarchy to acquire pass-books and goods to trade
in.[63] Even though some women had initially opposed the establishment of local textile firms to produce cloth in place of the imported
"Dutch wax," they soon overcame it, and submitted designs and
names for the new prints, and began a brisk business in the new
"Akosombo" cloth. Up till 1965 when Ghana's balance of payment
became increasingly problematic, petty trading flourished and new
products appeared on the market and were rapidly distributed all
around Ghana.

In addition to the educational and economic measures, we may
note briefly certain socio-cultural and moral matters affecting
women which Nkrumah and the CPP attempted to resolve. The first
concerned the state of nudity which existed among women in parts
of then Northern Territories. While this state of affairs reflected environmental and cultural factors, it was also seen as a manifestation
of a state of under-development. Nkrumah was concerned about it,
and instituted measures to deal with it, including the provision of
second-hand clothing for the purpose. Mrs. Hannah Cudjoe, who
had been a CPP Propaganda Secretary was put in charge of the job,
and it is alleged that to this day, among the older women in parts of
the Upper West Region, a certain type of clothing bears her name.[64]

A second matter affecting Ghanaian women in general concerned dress and aesthetics. It has been alleged that Nkrumah was
very susceptible to beauty, vivacity and intelligence, and enjoyed to

see women dress up colorfully.[65] On one occasion, he stated that even though women were being asked to do men's jobs and to consider themselves equal to men, they should remain "women."[66] For Nkrumah, women were "still the mothers of the nation, the beauty that graced the homes and the gentleness that soothed men's tempers."[67] It is ironic that while Nkrumah projected the concept of the African Personality and expected Ghanaian womanhood to reflect it, the period under review witnessed the mass importation of skin lightening creams and wigs, often by the the wives and mistresses of ministers and leading party officials.[68] Marais has it that Nkrumah personally hated the wearing of wigs and even banned their use for a while, but to no avail.[69]

Allied with the issue of dress and aesthetics was the morality of Ghanaian women. After 1966, much criticism was levelled against Nkrumah and the CPP for the corruption of the morals of young people, especially women.[70] It was during this period that the "sugardaddy" syndrome emerged. Young women were lavished with gifts, found jobs, and had apartments rented for them by older men. It would appear that Nkrumah at least was also concerned with the problem, and in a speech entitled *Revive our Virtues,* he inveighed against the laziness and insolent attitude of many young men and women at work and in public places.[71] He pronounced himself "appalled" at the reports reaching him about the behavior of young women in the bars, dance halls and other public places, and called on them "to maintain the highest standards of health, decency and morality in the society."[72]

It may be noted as a response to the criticisms against Nkrumah and the CPP that the period of their rule must be situated within the context of a society in transition, in which the contradictions and discontent of previous epochs were coming to the fore. Women by virtue of their position as among the most oppressed and exploited in the society were making their voices heard, and were reacting against their age-old oppression, as well as exploiting the avenues which became available to them.

III.(iii) Family, Marriage and Inheritance Reform

A pressing problem that needed to be addressed by the CPP government was in the area of relations between the sexes concerning marriage and divorce laws, inheritance practices and the maintenance of children. This problem arose out of the plurality of laws in existence governing marriage and inheritance, namely the various systems of customary law and the Marriage Ordinance.[73] Under customary law, wives had no share in the estate of their deceased husbands, and in matrilineal systems, children also did not have any specific shares. While in traditional societies there might have been compensatory mechanisms which mitigated the effects of such laws and practices, under the changed economic and social conditions introduced by colonialism these laws were regarded as harsh and unjust.[74] And despite the representations made to the colonial government to effect reforms, these appeals were not heeded to, and it was left to the churches and traditional state councils to regulate such matters.[75] We have already made mention of the petitions sent to the colonial government by the National Federation of Gold Coast Women asking for legislation on customary marriage and a look into inheritance practices, in an attempt to improve the position of wives and children and accord them rights similar to those granted to wives and children under the Ordinance. By the provisions of the Ordinance, wives and children were accorded certain rights which even extended to the offspring of a person whose parents had been married under the Ordinance, but who had not himself married thereunder.[76] However, Ordinance Marriage accounted for about 0.3% of total marriages.[77]

In 1959, the government appointed the Inheritance Commission to investigate customary provisions for inheritance and possibilities for their modification.[78] This Commission was headed by Justice Nii Amaa Ollennu, and included representatives from the Protestant Churches as well as from the Federation of Ghana Women.[79] The Commission received memoranda and heard reports on the inheritance practices of different communities. At the end of its work, the representatives of the Federation of Women refused to sign the report because they felt that the recommendations to be made would not protect wives sufficiently.[80]

But what brought into sharp focus the issue of the relations between the sexes occurred in February, 1961, with the attempt to amend the Criminal Code in order that bigamy and related offences would constitute civil rather than criminal offences. As Vellenga explains, under the Criminal Code, bigamy was committed where one contracted two marriages under the Ordinance without an intervening divorce. The penalty was seven years in prison. However, where a person married under customary law and then married a different person under the Ordinance without divorcing the first person, this was not bigamy, but an offence punishable by five years in prison. Similarly where a person married under the ordinance contracted marriage with a different person under customary law, this was not bigamy, and was merely an offence punishable by two years in prison.[81] However, as Allott states, there were practically no prosecutions under the Criminal Code for this sort of offence.[82]

The attempt to amend the Code appears to have been misunderstood, as evidenced in the Parliamentary Debates of the period.[83] The popular conception was that there was an attempt to abolish polygamy, and Vellenga mentions "worry" expressed by women parliamentarians who claimed that the ratio of women to men in Ghana was 9 to 1, and who feared the consequences of the abolition of polygamy.[84] After explaining what the amendment was really about, the Minister of Justice summed up his impressions of the feelings of members by advocating that the Marriage Ordinance should be modified so as to allow anyone in Ghana to marry one or more wives if he so chose, and to register them.[85]

Such sentiments as expressed by a Parliament dominated by the CPP reflected the contradictions which had emerged in the society, and especially from among its ranks of the party. Many party functionaries, members of Parliament and Ministers of State, had married younger educated women ostensibly to fit the new positions they now occupied. These marriages created problems in relation to their former wives who were, for the most part, illiterate. Vellenga also cites two articles which appeared in the *Evening News,* the Party paper, captioned "Polygamy or Monogamy — which is which?"[86]

It was against this background that in May 1961, a White Paper was published setting out proposals for a marriage, divorce and inheritance bill.[87] The White Paper proposed a marriage law for all citizens of Ghana which would preserve the essence of customary law marriage instead of the two parallel systems of marriage then operating. It provided for the registration of one wife who would be the publicly recognized wife. Where the man subsequently married or had issue with another woman, this would not constitute an offence and a ground for divorce. On the death intestate of the husband, only the registered wife would be entitled to a share of the property in accordance with the rules governing inheritance, but his children by other women would be entitled in the same way as the children of the registered wife. For the purpose of the new law, a woman married under the existing Marriage Ordinance was to be regarded as the registered wife.[88]

The White Paper also proposed new procedures for divorce which drew heavily on customary practices, and stressed the necessity of reconciliation in divorce proceedings, with divorce being granted only as a last resort. Arbitration was to be the procedure used, and a divorce petition in the courts was to be referred to an *ad hoc* panel of four members to arbitrate on the case.

In the matter of inheritance, the White Paper proposed that the surviving spouse (defined as the registered wife or husband) would inherit one-third of the property and all the children of the deceased, irrespective of their mother's status, would receive the remaining two-thirds of the estate. None of the property was to devolve under customary law where the deceased left both a spouse and children, and it was only in the event of neither spouse nor children remaining that parents were to inherit.

The *White Paper* generated much controversy and debates around the country. According to Vellenga, the marriage provisions aroused much concern on the part of many women since they felt that if such a law was enacted, there would be no system under which a woman could contract a legally binding monogamous marriage.[89] The Secretary of the National Council of Ghana Women is reported to have expressed fears about the possible encouragement of polygamy implied in the bill, and is said to have considered it " . . . an assault on Ghanaian womanhood. Men will be mischievous when polygamy is legalized and there would be no peace in homes. . . . there should be a law making a man responsible for the proper upkeep of any child he has with any woman . . . "[90] Other women considered the provision for registration of only one wife unjust and suggested that none of the wives be registered at all.[91] The inheritance provisions generated the widest controversy since they were considered as being too opposed to customary law regarding inheritance.[92]

In 1962, with the adoption of the Party Programme for Work and Happiness in the Seven-Year Development Plan, it was proclaimed that the Party stood for complete equality between the sexes and found this incompatible with polygamy. The Party accordingly asserted its belief in one form of marriage, monogamy.[93] However it recognized prevailing social relations and the existence of polygamous marriages, and stated that there could be no legal or social discrimination against children in the form of illegitimacy. Subsequently, the *Uniform Marriage, Divorce and Inheritance Bill* was published and went through three versions. It could not however become law because of mobilized opposition from the Sarbah Society, a group of leading legal experts, and the churches, and it was deferred indefinitely, and finally dropped in June, 1963.[94]

Although no law could be passed on marriage and inheritance, it was relatively easier for the Maintenance of Children's Act to be passed in 1965.[95] This followed a memorandum submitted by the Department of Social Welfare to secure legal sanction for fathers to maintain their children.[96] The issue of maintenance was a pressing social problem especially among urban dwellers, and the Minister was empowered to set up conciliation committees to hear complaints against fathers who neglected to maintain their children. Afterwards, the Committee could recommend a reasonable allowance not exceeding ten cedis a month, for the maintenance of a child.[97] Where a mother was dissatisfied with the ruling or the father failed to comply, the mother could go to court. The Act made no provision for the punishment of the father if he failed to pay, although his salary or pension could be attached.[98] However, as one commentator has commented, the Act has serious limitations as the award of ten cedis per month, even in 1965, was inadequate. Moreover, it ignored the actual circumstances of most of the applicants who were often illiterate and poor, and did not possess either the resources or time to institute an action for redress.[99] The conciliation committees established also differed from the previous arbitration procedures where the parties and arbitrators knew and respected each other and certain social pressures could be brought to bear.[100]

III.(iv) The National Council of Ghana Women (NCGW)

In the period between 1953 and 1960, there were two predominant women's organizations. One of these was the National Federation of Gold Coast Women which has already been mentioned. The other was the Ghana Women's League formed by Mrs. Hannah Cudjoe. In addition there were many women's benevolent associations, mutual aid and church groups.

The Ghana Women's League seems to have been very political, and concerned itself with local, nationalist and continental issues. Its leader, Mrs. Hannah Cudjoe, who was also a CPP Propaganda Secretary, appears to have combined the insights gained in the nationalist struggle with her work among women. The League toured the Northern, Brong-Ahafo and Central regions and gave talks and demonstrations on nutrition, childcare and the distribution of cloths.[101] It was indeed on these tours that the issue of nudity in the then Northern Region was picked up, and it was no surprise that Mrs. Hannah Cudjoe was put in charge of the campaign. The League also saw its task as explaining issues of national concern to women, and it toured the Northern Region in March, 1960, to explain the impending national census.

In addition to these national issues, the League engaged itself with more general issues of immediate import. Such an engagement was over the French atomic tests in the Sahara, and it led a demonstration of over 600 people including market women against the French atomic test. It also picketed outside the French Embassy and took pictures with a Frenchman protesting against these tests. But it was not only the League which addressed these concerns. The Ghana Federation of Women presented a cheque to the Ghana Council for Nuclear Disarmament as its first contribution to support the protest campaign against the French government's decision to test the atomic bomb in the Sahara.[102] The Cape Coast branch of the Federation organized a house-to-house educational campaign to explain the census in the fishing areas of Cape Coast. However, there were differences between the two organizations consisting mainly in the avowedly political nature of the League and the politically neutral posture of the Federation. This was to come to a head in the proposals for a merger between the two organizations and other smaller ones to form the National Council of Ghana Women.

In 1960, a conference was called of all women of Africa and of African descent. Before this conference took place, it was considered necessary to unite the various women's groups into one organization, operating as an integral wing of the CPP. To this end, invitations were sent to the Federation of Ghana Women led by Dr. Evelyn Amarteifio and to the Ghana Women's League of Mrs. Hannah Cudjoe. As well, invitations went to several women's benevolent associations.

Tawiah Adamafio, then Minister of Information, records the difficulties in the formation of the organization, and the tactics he had to adopt to force the merger.[103] He had been charged by Nkrumah with the task of organizing the women into a great organization. However, if Adamafio is to be believed, he had actually been charged with the organization of a "Regiment of Women."[104] In not a very coherent account, he says that the formation of the organization was the first step in a bid to get women to take over institutions and factories in Ghana. The women would then select their candidates for training in the various skills and disciplines. According to him, Nkrumah wanted the women to take over completely as private secretaries, stenographers and copy typists. They could also branch into engineering services, pharmacy, bus and taxi-driving, law, medicine and all the other fields. Adamafio did not want the task as he thought it was more properly a function of the Department of Social

Welfare. He found it a "disgusting" duty to be involved in dealing with the party women and feared his shirt might be torn into shreds and his face all scratched. For him, the women's section of the party was the most difficult to deal with as they were a vigorous lot, organized and stubborn, and could not be bullied into submission by any party leader, including even Nkrumah.

Between Nkrumah, Adamafio and Tettegah, plans were laid for the new organization, and they even chose the name! It was afterwards that Sophia Doku, the Secretary of the Bureau of Women's Organization, was summoned and concrete plans outlined. The main conflict, as Adamafio again records, seems to have centred around the incorporation of the organization into the CPP as an integral wing, and the position of people like Dr. Amarteifio who disagreed fundamentally with the CPP and did not want a "political" organization. Adamafio says he was rude to them and used threats to get his way. In the end, only the YWCA stayed out of the new organization.

The Council was inaugurated by Dr. Nkrumah on 10th September, 1960, as the only recognized body under which all Ghanaian women were to be organized to contribute their quota to the political, educational, social and economic reconstruction of Ghana. Branches were soon established throughout the country under the party's auspices. As an integral wing of the party, it had representation on the Party's Central Committee and participated in its programmes with some of its members wielding considerable influence in national affairs. In what has become known as the Dawn Broadcast, it was decided that there should be no separate membership cards for the integral organizations of the party, the party membership card alone being sufficient.[105] As well, it was decided that all appointments to the Council and to the other integral organizations would be made by the Party's Committee and that with the formation of the NCGW, the women's section of the Party had ceased to exist.[106] Sophia Doku, who was Secretary General of the Council from its inception, was replaced by Stella Abeka, a barrister and a staunch member of the party. Miss Abeka was succeeded by Mrs. Margaret Martei, another party stalwart, who held the position until the *coup d'etat* of 1966. It was as Secretary General of the Council that the latter entered Parliament in 1965.[107]

Members of the Council formed part of the President's delegation on his travels abroad and they visited many countries to learn about organizing women and to see the standards achieved by other women. On such trips a different programme would be drawn up for the women in the entourage or Nkrumah would draw attention to particular matters when there was no separate programme.[108] The Council also participated in continental and international meetings and established links with fraternal organizations in other countries.

Through the auspices of the Council, many young women were sent abroad for further studies and to pursue short courses. Others were found employment in state organizations and corporations as a reward for services to the party or more commonly, through family connections and other nepotic practices. Market women constituted a big proportion of the membership of the Council, and mention has already been made of their control of space and goods within the markets. These women contributed vast sums of money to the party and were vocal at party gatherings and were fanatical in their support of the CPP. They could be seen spreading clothes on the ground for party functionaries to walk on at rallies and harassed opponents of the party and its policies. Typical of such tendencies was the *CPP Emashi Nonrl*, described as "a militant women's group with headquarters at Bukom (a quarter of Accra) which sprang up as a reaction to the adverse criticisms of the 1961 budget."[109] Basil Davidson referred to the CPP as a "traders" party with a trader's attitude to politics and these women played no mean role in it. Erica Powell gives an example of the alignment of business to politics in her account of a delegation of market women, almost all illiterate, who had called at the Castle to congratulate the President on the publication of his book, *Consciencism*.[110]

The Council organized rallies for women around the country and initiated some programmes for women such as the establishment of day-care centres in the big towns to cater for the needs of working women. Although it took part in the debates on the unsuccessful family reform law, as well as the issue of paid maternity leave, the Council does not appear to have directly concerned itself with the problems of rural women nor even of the majority of urban women. When the CPP was overthrown, the Council collapsed like the other integral wings and the individual women within it were vilified and disgraced as happened to other CPP functionaries. They were summoned before Commissions of Enquiry, had their assets confiscated to the state and were barred from holding public office for specified periods of time. In all this, the mass of Ghanaian women stood passive and felt no identification with them. It was not the women's organization which was on trial but these individual women.

III.(v) Ghanaian Women and African Unity

The commitment to the realization of African Unity by Nkrumah and the CPP was made to form part of the concerns of women during this period and Ghanaian women staged marches and demonstrations to protest against brutal murders of Angolans by the Portuguese colonialists. In July, 1960, the Conference of Women of Africa and of African Descent was held in Accra. It was opened by the President who used the occasion to make an appeal to African Women.[111] He declared that the women of Africa had a mission to fulfill by creating better conditions of life for their sons and daughters. They were therefore to work hand in hand militantly with their men to end colonialism and imperialism. He asked the women to reflect on the burning issues of the time — why women of South Africa had to be in possession of passes in order to go about their ordinary business; why the apartheid overlords should mow down defenseless women and children; the French presence in Algeria, and South Africa's disregard of the United Nations resolutions on Namibia.[112]

Nkrumah saw the role of women in this direction as messengers, and as bringing their feminine influence to bear in persuading their brothers, husbands and friends of the importance of African Unity as the only salvation for Africa. The women were to rise up in their millions to join the African crusade for freedom. In addition, they had the task of projecting the African personality to the rest of the world .

In furtherance of the Ghana-Guinea-Mali Union, a Council of Women of the Union of African States was formed. Meetings were held in member countries for the promotion of the foundation of the movement which would co-ordinate and harmonise the activities of organizations of African women throughout the continent. Nkrumah opened the Second Conference in Accra, and after recounting the sufferings of the people of the Congo, Angola, Mozambique, South Africa and Namibia, he spoke about Africa's need for a new woman, one who was dedicated and inspired by the high ideals of patriotism and devoted to the Unity of Africa.[113] Africa's new woman had to be a woman of virtue, vision and courage, capable of the highest sacrifice. For Nkrumah this was nothing new, but the heritage of the mothers and grandmothers who excelled in these qualities. Much was therefore expected of women in whatever capacity they found themselves. Citing the firm stand taken by African women in all their struggles, he declared that:

A strong and reliable womanhood is a firm and worthy foundation
for the building of any nation.[114]

At the end of the Conference, the Council of Women of the Union of
African States reaffirmed once more its strong desire to strengthen
its efforts towards the realization of the total liberation of Africa as
well as her unity and social and economic reconstruction. In a com-
munique, the women pledged to work for the effective liberation
and rapid emancipation of African women, to fight against illiteracy
which is one of Africa's greatest setbacks, to protect children and
safeguard their interests and to harness all their efforts towards the
establishment of world peace.[115]

Conclusion

We may conclude by offering an evaluation of the impact of
CPP rule on Ghanaian women — especially as regards their political
maturity and their participation in local, national and continental
issues. Without a doubt, women played a decisive role in the anti-
colonial struggle and worked tirelessly in various capacities, often
at great personal risk, till independence was achieved. The CPP government after independence enabled women, albeit a minority, without necessarily being of royal birth, to occupy public positions. This
reflected a conscious desire to project women onto the political
scene as well as a recognition of their roles in the anti-colonial struggle. The results of the educational, economic and social measures
pursued led to high enrollment figures for women in basic education. With the new facilities for post-basic education that were provided and the removal of discriminatory practices in employment,
women were able to enter new occupations and professions previously closed to them. However,these new educational and employment facilities were not uniform and varied according to region and
locality.

As well, younger women were better placed to take advantage
of these facilities and of changing attitudes towards women and their
roles in society. Thus at the end of the period, female illiteracy rates
were still high especially in the 25–49 years range, and female participation rates in the economy still low, and were confined largely
to the agricultural and saleswork/commerce sector.

At the level of family life, the failure to enact the proposals of the
Uniform Marriage, Divorce and Inheritance Bill into law meant that an
issue of pressing importance to the majority of women was left unre-
solved. Even the Maintenance of Children's Act which had been

passed was fraught with problems, and it was left to the courts to find solutions to the many cases of neglect, desertion, maintenance and property rights which found their way before them. And yet for every case that reached the courts, a hundred others did not, and it was left to the women to devise their own strategies to cope. This failure arose from the petty-bourgeois character of the CPP and the contradictions that this engendered. The National Council of Ghana Women, an integral wing of the CPP, and the umbrella organization of all Ghanaian women, also failed to mobilize around this issue and confined itself to calling for a law making a man responsible for all his children but not the women. This again reflected the petty-bourgeois character of its leadership and their desire to protect the "Missuses" as against the masses of women for whom polygamy was a reality of life. The Council, although notionally a women's organization, seemed to have considered its Party role more important and was more concerned with the monumental and nebulous task of "nation-building." It was in this connection that more educational and employment facilities were desired for the women, to enable them to contribute their quota to national development. The provisions of day-care centres for example was to make for more efficient workers, and not to lessen women's domestic chores.

Indeed in the Council's journal, few issues of theoretical nature were discussed and there appears to have been no questioning of the subordinate positions of women in their societies. Again, given the scant attention to issues of democracy and mass participation within the CPP itself, the Council whose beginnings were not democratic, does not appear to have picked them up. The market women who dominated the Council were concerned with furthering their own interests within it, and the Council was the female version of the petty-bourgeois class in the Party, organized to reap the gains of independence. No issues of particular concern to rural women such as access to credit, agricultural extension services or land were picked up, and even as the Council had branches in the rural areas, it remained an urban phenomenon.

Positively, the exposure through the Council to the conditions of women in other countries provided models and inspiration for Ghanaian women and served in some way to challenge the widespread belief in the inferiority of women. In addition, through meetings with other African women and women of African descent, Ghanaian women were linked up with the struggle for the liberation and unity of the African continent. The presence of other African refugees in Ghana and the many meetings and conferences in Ghana at this time also helped to reinforce these feelings of solidarity and Africanness for both Ghanaian men and women.

NOTES

1. Nkrumah, 1968b:8 1 . This is a paraphrase from the French Utopian socialist, Charles Fourier(1772-1837) who declared that in any given society, the degree of woman's emancipation is the natural measure of the general emancipation, See F. Engels, 1975. 2. James, 1977:56 3. Ibid.,: 130 4. Interview with Mrs Margaret Martei, Osu, March 1985. 5. For a discussion of this, see UNECA, 1984. 6. Ibid.

7. Aidoo, 1985 :19
8. Mikell, 1985 . See also Oduyoye, 1981.
9. As yet there has not been much systematic treatment of traditional women's groups and associations in Ghana unlike for Nigeria or East Africa societies. Arhin, 1983, and Aidoo, 1985, discuss some of these for Akan societies.
10. Aidoo,op.cit.,: 141
1 1. *Ibid.*
12. *Ibid.*
13. *Ibid.,:* 142
14. UNECA *op. cit .,:* 8
15. Boserup, 1970
16. Graham, 1971: 72
17. UNECA *op. cit.,:* 50
18. Greenstreet, 1971
19. Wontumi, 1978:252
20. Interview, Koforidua, 1985
21. Greenstreet *op. cit.,* 1971
22. Acronyms for the United Africa Company, *Societe Commerciale Occidentale d'Afrique and Compagnie Francaise de L'Afrique Occidentale*, respectively.
23. Nkrumah, 1963a: 26
24. Personal communications
25. Little, 1974, discusses voluntary associations in African towns and cities.
26. Information for this section is derived from an interview with Dr. Evelyn Amarteifio at her Adabraka residence in February, 1 982.
27. Archives of the Federations, located in the home of Dr. Evelyn Amarteifio.
28. Interview with Mrs Margaret Martei. She said that her first knowledge of Nkrumah was through the UGCC in Saltpond, where she was cooking for them.
29. The organ of the CPP, founded by Nkrumah in 1948.
30. The campaign of civil disobedience and non-violence embarked upon by the CPP to demand self-government. See also Nkrumah, 1973: 5
31 . Interview with Akua Asabea Ayisi, Barrister-at-law who then aged 17, worked with Nkrumah and Mabel Dove Danquah on the *Evening News*. She also served a prison term for participating in the Positive Action Campaign.
32. Interview with Akua Asabea Ayisi, *op. cit.*
33. Nkrumah 1957:89
34. *Ibid.*
35. Evening News. May 1951.

36. *Ibid* ., May 28th, 1951.
137. Austin, 1964 :109-110, 203; sets out the qualifications for the 1951, 1954 and 1956 elections which included the ability to read and write in the English language, property qualifications and payment of basic rate all of which tended to work against women.
38. No. 72 of 1959, Volume of the Acts of Ghana enacted during 1959 and the 1st half year of 1960, Government Printer, Accra, 1961 .
39. Ibid ., S.3
40. No. 8 of 1960. Annual Volume of t,he Acts of Ghana, op. cit.
41. These were:

Mrs. Susanna Al-Hassan	- (Northern Region)
Ms. Lucy Anin	- (Brong-Ahafo)
Ms. Regina Asamany	- (Volta Region)
Ms. Comfort Asamoah	- (Ashanti Region)
Mrs. Grace Ayensu	- (Western Region)
Mrs. Ayanori Bukari	- (Northern Region)
Ms. Sophia Doku	- (Eastern Region)
Ms. Mary Koranteng	- (Eastern Region)
Ms. Victoria Nyarku	- (Northern Region)
Ms. Christiana Wilmot	- (Western Region).

Source: The National Assembly list of Members returned at General Election 17th July, 1960, in Parliamentary Debates official Report Vol. 20, 2nd July - 5th September, 1960.
42. Parliamentary Debates, Official Report, First Series, Vol. 20, 2nd July - 5th September, 1960, p. 24.
43. *Ibid.,:* 25
44. Nkrumah, Speech at Inauguration of the National Council of Ghana Women, 10th September, 1960 .
45. For a discussion of the political economy of Northern Ghana see Bening, R. B., 1972; Thomas 1973, Konings, P., 1981; Songsore,J., 1979.
46. George, 1976:36
47. Marais, 1972.
48. George, *op.cit.,:* 5 1
49. Ministry of Education Reports, 1960-75, cited in UNECA 1 984, *op. cit.*
50. Obeng, n.d.: 205 .
51. *Ibid.*
52. The Ghanaian Woman No. 15 of 1961.
53. The CPP's Programme for the construction of a socialist state. The Seven-Year Plan was launched in 1964 while the programme of Work and Happiness was adopted in 1962. See Nkrumah, 1973:181.
54. Group discussion at Seminar for Regional Commissioners and Party Attaches at Winneba, 24th November, 1962.
55. *Ibid.*
56. The Party No. 19, February 16 - 28, 196 2: 6; CPP Bureau of Information and Publicity 1962:6.
57. Ghana Government, 1965 .
58. But see Dumor, 1983.
59. These included the Land Development (Protection of Purchases) Act, the Farm Lands (Protection) Act and Rent Stabilisation Acts.
60. Cutrufelli, 1983: 99

61. See for example Ollennu Commission of Enquiry into the Assets of Specified Persons, 1967.
62. Davidson, 1973 :124
63. Office of the President, 1965
64. Personal Communication
65. Marais, *op. cit.*
66. Speech at Inauguration of National Council of Ghana Women, *op. cit.*
67. *Ibid.*
68. Interview with women in Accra and Kumasi, 1984/85
69. Marais, *op. cit.*
70. See generally reports in newspapers of post-February, 1966
71. Government Printer, 1963
72. *Ibid.*
73. For a discussion of this see UNECA *op. cit.:* 20-34, Ollennu, 1966.
74. Asante, 1975:267-271
75. Ollennu, *op. cit.:* 144-152
76. S. 48 of Cap. 127. See also Ollennu, *op. cit.* :239
77. This is an approximation from Gaisie and De Graft Johnson, 1974 Population of Ghana, Accra cited in UNECA, *op. cit.*
78. Vellenga 1971:125, sees this as reflecting a change of emphasis from the colonial practice of leaving such matters in the hands of traditional authorities and the churches to a more activist posture by the state.
79. *Ibid .:* 139
80. *Ibid.*
81. *Ibid.*
82. *Ibid.:* 140
83. Parliamentary Debates Vol. 22, No. 4 (13th February, 1961)
84. Vellenga,op.cit.: 140
85. Parliamentary Debates Vol. 22, No. 4, *op. cit.:*71
86. Vellenga, *op. cit.:* 141
87. Ghana Government, 1961
88. *Ibid.*
89. Vellenga, op. cit.:142
90. *Ibid.:* 143
91. *Ibid.*
92. *Ibid.:* 144
93. Programme of the CPP, n.d.: 34-35
94. Vellenga, *op. cit.:* 145
95. Ghana Government, Law of Ghana, 1965
96. But see Jones-Quartey, 1974, for a discussion of the background to the Act. Incidentally a woman, Mrs. Susanna Al-Hassan, was the Minister for Social Welfare in 1965.
97. Ghana Government, 1965; in Sec. 4a
98. *Ibid.:* S.2
99. See UNECA, *op. cit.* :33, 101; *Evening News* January 5th, 1960
100. *Ibid.*
101. *Ibid.*
102. *Ibid.*
103. Information for this section is derived from the interview with Mrs. Margaret Martei, op. cit.; Adamafio, 1982:114-119 and Vellenga, 1971,

    op. cit.
104. Berger, 1975, quoted in Oduyoye, *op. cit.* :14, she says "this is a satire described by the publishers as 'an outrageous novel of sex role revesal.' "
105. Nkrumah, 1973:158
106 . Obeng, n.d .: 7 5
107. Interview with Mrs. Margaret Martei
108. *Ibid.*
109. *The Ghanaian Woman,* No. 20, March 1-15, 1962.
110. Powell, 1984: 202 described *Conscienism* as a philosophical work which left her "utterly mystified."
111. "Appeal to African Women" found in *The Ghanaian Woman* No. 3, March, 1961.
112. *Ibid.*
113. *The Ghanaian Woman* No. 18 February 1-15,1962.
114. *Ibid.*: 14
115. *Ibid.*

RELIGION AND SOCIETY: A STUDY IN CHURCH AND STATE RELATIONS IN THE FIRST REPUBLIC

K. A. Dickson

The wording of this title calls for an explanation. The first part of it may give the impression that this essay is focused on what Nkrumah might have said or written on religion (for reasons that will become evident I have Christianity in mind). I had hoped, when I agreed to write a paper on the subject, to put together as much as possible of such material; indeed, the possibility of doing a serious analysis of such material had excited me, if only for the reason that, as far as I knew, such a study had not been attempted before. However, my hopes of achieving this 'first' were dashed when it became clear that Nkrumah himself did not make any significant public remarks on the subject of religion, nor did he, as far as I have been able to discover, cause anything to be done that was specifically aimed at influencing, for good or ill, the practice of religion.

That Nkrumah had had more than average grounding in the subject of religion may not be doubted. After all he had studied at the Catholic Seminary at Amisano, near Cape Coast, and had subsequently pursued his interest in theology at Lincoln University in the United States of America. He was later to describe himself as a non-denominational Christian.[1]

While I am making introductory remarks on my subject, I must recall a situation which caused quite a stir in my first year as a lecturer in this university: The government appointed a Commission in 1960 to look into university education in Ghana. There was one point in the course of the 1960-61 academic year when I was made to understand by my senior colleagues, rightly or wrongly, that our department, the Department of Divinity, had become the focus of attention: rumors had filtered through to the effect that it was being wondered by some members of the Commission whether such a department as ours had a place in the University. Apparently, it was rumored, Nkrumah considered our department too "sectarian" for his liking. I have hesitated to make this reference because I have since that time searched diligently without discovering any documentary evidence of this. At that time, however, the threat seemed real, and I had to take time off to speak to a member of the Commission whom I had got to know in another university and to explain to him what my department was about.

Whether Nkrumah did actually express that opinion about my department or not, it is a fact that the department's subsequent actions seemed to have been aimed at making such an opinion inappropriate: not only did it propose to change its name to the present one, Department for the Study of Religions, so as to indicate its non-sectarian character, but it also took steps to ensure that the lecturers represented a wider range of religious backgrounds. I might add that the Commission's published report, to my surprise, contains not a word about that department. The only reference to religion in the report is in connection with the Commission's proposal regarding the setting up of an Institute of African Studies where, among other things, religion would be studied.

In the absence of the kind of material that I had thought to be available for study and exposition, there are other possibilities: situations which brought the Church and State into discussion or potential conflict; the religious or quasi-religious language used by the Convention People's Party Press in support of Nkrumah's ideas and role as leader; pronouncements by the Party faithful which had a religious flavor, and lastly, what Nkrumah did not say. It is evident from this last reference that I have refused to ignore the fact that Nkrumah apparently did not say anything on religion, for while silence may not necessarily be used as evidence, it can nevertheless be suggestive particularly given the possibility of silence being seen by the interested as providing warrant for the pursuit of certain actions.

It is essential, in discussing the role which religion played in Nkrumah's time, to give some attention to Church and State relations in Ghana before and after Nkrumah; this would set the scene, providing material for comparison with the situation in Nkrumah's time.

In 1967, the then Clerk of the Eastern Region House of Chiefs, Mr. E. Odoi-Atsem, wrote as follows to the General Secretary of the Christian Council, Rev. W. G. M. Brandful:

Sir,
At a recent meeting of the Eastern Region House of Chiefs, the growing waywardness of young men and women in this country came up for serious discussion. This appalling situation is evident in the form of strikes and disregard for law and order which are sweeping through our Secondary Schools and Training Colleges. It was agreed that this disregard of elders and authority shown by the youth is due to the little attention paid to the teaching of the Christian religion in our schools. The origin of this unfortunate trend can be traced to the doors of the old regime which deliberately indoctrinated our youth with baseless and empty ideologies in its bid to destroy the Christian religion and turn the youth into a Godless people.
I am directed to appeal to your Council to bring this serious matter before all the Churches which are members of your Council in order to take a nation-wide action to arrest the situation. It is the view of the Chiefs that the teaching of Scriptures has been relegated to the background in the schools and that if the nation can be saved from this backward trend, the teaching of the Christian religion should be resuscitated and pursued more energetically in all the schools right from the Primary to the Secondary School and Training College levels.[2]

This post-Nkrumah assessment is quite clear: Nkrumah's time had seen an erosion of Christian values, which erosion was considered by the Eastern Region House of Chiefs to have been caused by policies pursued by the Nkrumah regime. For the moment I do not wish to go into the question of whether or not this assessment was soundly based; I have quoted this letter merely in order to draw attention to one view of the effect of the State on Christianity and what it stood for during the First Republic.

As far as the period before Nkrumah is concerned, some Ghanaian Church personalities, even before the turn of the century, had loudly proclaimed the Church's interest in politics; this was particularly true of some personalities in the Methodist Church. For example, the Methodist missionaries began to worry when the Ghanaian, Rev. Samuel Richard Brew Attoh-Ahumah, editor of the *Gold Coast Methodist Times,* fought through the pages of his paper the colonial government's plan to pass the Lands Bill which would vest land in the Crown. Attoh-Ahumah wrote in 1897:

> We have been indoctrinated as to how a religious paper should be conducted . . . we do not intend to wrap up our religion for Sunday use only: we shall continue to go on, so long as we are permitted to be organically connected with this periodical. Our silence on matters political, so far as they traverse the fundamental principles of the Christian faith, will only synchronise with our absence from the editorial chair which position, or course, we occupy on sufferance.[3]

To come closer to our time, in August 1949, the Christian Council issued a statement of "the moral and spiritual" principles underlying political issues. One of these principles recognized "that the Gold Coast, like any other country, has a natural right to Self Government . . ." The fourth principle in particular is worth quoting:

> The Church contains people of goodwill who hold different views on the affairs of their country and support different political, economic and social programmes. The Church, therefore, cannot become identified with any particular party or programme. She does not condemn any party so long as its object is in accordance with Christian principles and the means employed to reach that end are honest and good. Such a party needs the help of Christians who share its views but the question of joining it must be left to the conscience of the individual.[4]

This statement, coming as it does in 1949, the year before which had seen the country in turmoil following the arrest of the so called Big Six is of interest. Theologically, it appears unexceptionable, though its timing suggests an anticipation of conflict. The fact that in that year (1949) all the principal officers of the Christian Council were expatriates is probably not significant.

The point of the references to the times after and before Nkrumah is this: they demonstrate a definite understanding that religion has a part to play in the life of a people. To say this in 1985 is to make an understatement, for theological activism has blossomed in recent decades and issued in a variety of postures, from the Latin American situation of priests serving in a secular government, which development has exercised the Vatican considerably, to the general desire of the Church to speak to situations of mismanagement, cruelty, oppression, and military take-over. Thus it is not enough to say that religion has a role to play in a people's life. The question must be asked: What precisely is that role, in this or that set of circumstances? There is the rub, for diverse views have been expressed. Instead of attempting to characterize at this point the understanding that seemed to prevail within the ranks of the Convention People's Party, I shall proceed to survey, in order of occurrence, a number of situations which highlighted religion in the First Republic.

Earlier I referred to 1949, the year in which the Christian Council of Ghana issued a statement on the Christian and politics. In the very next year, on the 17th of January, 1950, the *Accra Evening News*, the Party's voice, contained the following:

> Blessed are they who are imprisoned for self-government's sake, for theirs is the freedom of the land.
> Blessed are ye, when men shall vilify you and persecute you, and say all kinds of evil against you, for Convention People's Party's sake.
> Blessed are they who hunger and thirst because of self-government, for they shall be satisfied.
> Blessed are they who reject the Coussey Report, for they shall know freedom.
> Blessed are the parents whose children are political leaders, for they shall be thanked.
> Blessed are they who took part in Positive Action, for they shall have better rewards.
> Blessed are they who now love CPP, for they shall be leaders in the years to come.
> Blessed are they who cry for self-government, for their voice shall be heard.

That this is a kind of adaptation of the biblical Beatitudes (Matthew 5: 3-12) hardly needs to be pointed out, and the fact that this adaptation contains eight rather than nine 'Beatitudes' is of no consequence. This kind of composition was probably meant to serve more than one purpose. A former colleague of mine, Professor John S. Pobee, has observed that it was "intended to inculcate. . . devotion to the CPP."[6] This is obviously true. Pobee further observes: ". . . the adaptation of biblical language to political ends is evidence of the deep impact the Church has made on the African society, so much so that her biblical language could be used to inculcate nationalism with the implication that it was powerful language that could be appreciated."[7] However, it seems to me that to argue that such a composition was meant solely to inculcate nationalism is to leave a great deal unsaid, for by that very fact attention was being drawn away from the reality for which the particular religious teaching adapted stood in its original context. To be sure, such formulations imply the recognition of the Christian reality, but they could also have been intended to draw attention away from the Christian faith. That such compositions constituted an assault upon Christianity must be recognized, for they taught what was politically desirable, but in such a way as to relegate the religious faith behind the language to the background. This reasoning may be considered far-fetched by some, but it has been known for a show of religious interest to be really intended to be a means of destroying religious sentiments. Thus in the nineteen-twenties the Soviets allowed a schismatic group, the Living Church, to emerge in order to ensure that the religious establishment of Orthodoxy was attacked from within.[8] This reference, I must admit, does not constitute an exact parallel to the Ghanaian situation in Nkrumah's time, but it does underline the point already made that a show of interest in religion and its language could be a disservice to the religion, if the motives behind the interest were wrong; parodying religious language with a view to highlighting what is politically desirable could have the effect of devaluing religious sentiment.

The next situation I wish to refer to occurred in 1958, the year in which Nkrumah's statue was erected in front of Parliament House. The pedestal of the statue carried the inscription: "Seek ye first the political kingdom and all other things shall be added unto you." I hardly need to point out that his inscription was based on the words of Jesus: "Seek ye first the kingdom of God and his righteousness; and all these things shall be added unto you" (Matthew 6:33, Authorized Version). The Christian Council sent off a protest to the then Minister of Works which read in part: "If intended seriously, it is a denial of one of the best-known sayings of our Lord and Saviour Jesus Christ — otherwise it is an irrelevant parody of it." The protest was not ignored by the Minister, but not in the way the Christian Council had expected; its Chairman, Rev. G. T. Eddy, and Secretary, Rev. P. I. Dagadu, were called in twice and verbally roasted. On this, Roseveare, then Anglican Bishop of Accra, was to write: "Threats were uttered that such an action from the Christian Council was an offense against the recently enacted *Avoidance of Discrimination Act* since in this the Christian Council was virtually becoming a political party, and therefore, liable to elimination."[9]

Commenting on this episode Pobee writes that in making the protest the Christian Council was being "frivolous," though he goes on to observe that the description in question represented an unrealistic view in so far as it saw political power as making all things possible. I am in agreement with Pobee when he criticizes this conception of politics as implying boundless power. Nkrumah himself was aware that self-government was only the beginning of a journey, so that a deliberate choice was to be made for a constant striving in order to arrive at the journey's end of self-fulfillment and what he called "the good life." All the same, he probably had a great deal of faith in power, *qua* power, which, without the proper safeguards, is capable of causing incalculable harm. The history of the application of political power in Africa since the late fifties has sadly shown that power has the potential for encouraging thoughtlessness and divisiveness.

Whether it is right to describe the Christian Council as "frivolous" and "misguided" in its protest to the government is another matter altogether, especially when one looks at that inscription a little more closely and in the light of scholarly work on certain aspects of nationalism.

In 1926 the American scholar, Carlton Hayes, published an essay in which he wrote of nationalism as deriving its strength from its idolatrous appeal to what he described as man's "religious sense," a theme to which he returned in 1960 in his book *Nationalism: A Religion,* in which he wrote: "Since its advent in western Europe, modern nationalism has partaken of the nature of a religion."[10] In another publication, *Essays on Nationalism,* he wrote: "Nationalism's kingdom is . . . of this world, and its attainment involved tribal selfishness and vainglory, a particularly ignorant and tyrannical intolerance . . ."[11] Given his background as one who had converted to Roman Catholicism, Hayes argued strongly for a religion-based attack on political structures.

Hayes' approach to nationalism is only one of several. I should like to refer to another writer who looked at nationalism from the point of view of its religious connotations. The German writer, Hans Kohn, had his ideas shaped by the First World War. He recognized, as apparently Hayes did not, that nationalism was a product of the Judeo-Christian tradition, but that it had developed excesses which must be countered, not by religion as Hayes proposed, but by nationalism's desacralisation. "Nationalism," he wrote, "is itself neither good nor bad, as little as capitalism, socialism . . . are,"[12] The destructive tendencies it has assumed are the result of its being undergirded by religious sanction.

Now, it is widely recognized that the nationalistic feelings which finally led to independence in Africa had something to do with biblical teaching. So then that inscription, "Seek ye first the political kingdom . . ." is, on the one hand, an acknowledgement of the

Church's role in the development of the people's consciousness regarding freedom; on the other, however, it does suggest a sacralisation of nationalism which could have the effect of giving the Christian faith a less than authentic character. One might refer in this connection to the theologian Paul Tillich who wrote in 1959: "Modern nationalism is the actual form in which space is ruling over time, in which polytheism is a daily reality . . . The 'beside-each-otherness' necessarily becomes an 'against-each-otherness' in the moment in which a special space gets divine honor."[13]

Thus the Churches' protest was neither "frivolous" nor "misguided." Whether the Churches were in a position to work for the desacralisation of nationalism is another matter. To this point we shall return. Meanwhile we shall take a brief look at another occurrence in the history of Church-State relations in Ghana.

By 1962 the Christian Council of Churches was becoming exercised about the Young Pioneer Movement, the youth wing of the Convention People's Party. The movement had been set up with the sole aim of giving the young political instruction and awareness, with Nkrumah's ideas and ideals set before them as an example. The heads of Churches made it known in 1962 to the then Minister of Education, Mr. Dowuona-Hammond, that they, to use the words of Bishop Roseveare,

> found it impossible to give our support and co-operation in the development of the Movement as at present constituted. It is an affront to our agelong traditions that, in Ghana of all countries, a National Institution for the training and development of boys and girls should entirely ignore the existence and claims of Almighty God. Moreover, it seems the Movement confuses the work and example of a great man with Divine Acts which are unique in history. The incipient atheism is quite foreign to the traditional concept of the African personality."[14]

Once again we are in agreement with Pobee when he argues that the charge of atheism was not soundly based. However, there are indications, in a denial of the charge of atheism in the Party's *Accra Evening News* of 9th August, 1962 (the very month in which Bishop Roseveare made his accusation public), of an understanding of Christianity which is disturbing, to say the least. In that denial we read:

> Surely, self-appointed mentors like Roseveare cannot bamboozle the world into believing that our Pioneers are a godless organisation because imperialist-inspired scriptures are not actually known in the instructional programme of the Young Pioneers Organisation.

Also,

> What is more, the democratic organisation of the Party itself makes
> room for the grace and presence of God.

The reference to "imperialist-inspired scriptures" is significant, for in fact the scriptures are the story of a people who throughout Biblical times knew slavery and various forms of oppression and deprivation, but who doggedly refused to give up the struggle for freedom. Indeed, the scriptures can be described with considerable justification as freedom-inspired. To describe them as imperialist-inspired is to show considerable ignorance regarding their evolution, and possibly also of the faith which inspired them and out of which came the Christian Church. The Convention People's Party, to be sure, had in its midst a number of ordained clergymen: one of them, Rev. Stephen Dzirasa, a Methodist Minister, wrote a book on Nkrumah's political thought; another Rev. J. S. A. Stephens, also a Methodist Minister, was appointed Rector of the Young Pioneer Movement; a third Rev. S. G. Nimako, again a Methodist Minister, served as an ambassador. The presence of these Methodist Ministers in the Party would probably have gladdened the heart of such as Rev. R. B. Attoh-Ahuma of *Gold Coast Methodist Times* fame, but it did not seem to have prevented theological misjudgement. Incidentally, there were other denominational ministerial members in the Party: one Evangelical Presbyterian and two Anglicans, one of the latter being an expatriate.

Then there is the matter of the Party being a "democratic organisation" which "makes room for the grace and presence of God;" the exact import of these words is not easy to determine. In the absence of any reasoned official explanation one is left to make one or two guesses as to their basis. Thus at Party rallies Christian hymns were often sung. What was the real significance of this? Was this a recognition of "the grace and presence of God?" Some of the hymns adopted by the Party were evidently chosen for their nationalistic import. There was, for example, Cecil Spring-Rice's

> I vow to thee, my country, all earthly things above,
> Entire and whole and perfect, the service of my love;
> The love that asks no question, the love that stands the test,
> That lays upon the altar the dearest and the best;
> The love that never falters, the love that pays the price,
> The love that makes undaunted the final sacrifice.

This particular hymn was meant to be repeated by Party members at sunset and at sunrise.

It is worth pointing out that the practice of using Christian hymns in situations which are not specifically Christian, by organizations which neither corporately nor severally evince any particular interest in the Christian tradition pre-dated independence. Thus as far back as the thirties football teams in the country would sing hymns as part of their preparations towards important football matches. I can recall as a little boy being awakened from sleep on a number of occasions by the Dwarfs football team of Winneba singing in the night before an engagement, John Henry Newman's hymn:

Lead, kindly light, amid the encircling gloom
Lead Thou me on!
The night is dark, and I am far from home;
Lead Thou me on!
Keep thou my feet; I do not ask to see
The distant scene: one step enough for me.

This was precisely the hymn that became one of the Convention People's Party's favorite rally hymns. Pobee has concluded that the use of Christian hymns was evidence "that Christianity whether in terms of language or themes or philosophy was evidently a great influence in Ghanaian society and politics."[15] While as a general statement it is true, that is, that Christianity has exercised influence, nevertheless the use of hymns by the Party, and by football teams, is capable, at least in part, of being given a less flattering explanation.

Throughout the history of religion—and I include Christianity — the superstitious attitude has from time to time reared its head. By superstition I mean that pose of reverence which is misdirected because it is based upon a less than authentic understanding of a religion. Let it be emphasized that superstition involves the practice of a religion, or the adoption of an attitude to it, that is based on an irrational fear of or on credulity regarding the unseen world. Thus it is superstition when the Anlo of Ghana, in some of their traditional ritual practices, apologize to any gods who might be present on a ritual occasion but who cannot be specifically addressed by name because they are "unknown." It is this attitude which makes a football team sing "Lead, kindly Light ...," say the Lord's Prayer or some other prayer in the centre of the pitch just before a game begins, and take the further precaution of burying in the stadium grounds traditional preparations with the intention of putting the opponents at a disadvantage; and all this despite the fact that the team has the expert services of a western coach. Similarly, some of the CPP stalwarts who sang "Lead, kindly Light ..." at rallies were not beyond taking other precautions, before elections, for example. It was revealed by a candidate at one Mature Students selection meeting which I chaired at this university in the sixties, that some of the Party members sought the help of magic-religious practitioners before elections.

I am submitting that though it is incontextable that Christianity has had a great deal of influence, the attitude to it in some circles and on some occasions had been superstitious, and the singing of hymns at Party rallies may be seen in this light.

Again, how does the Party's claim to make room for "the grace and presence of God" relate to what Pobee describes as the "divinisation" of Nkrumah? Pobee examines eight honorifics which were used of Nkrumah, and comes to the conclusion that of the eight only one, *Asomdwehene*, "certainly looks at Nkrumah as Messiah after the fashion or order of Jesus. The ordinary Ghanaian would upon hearing it recall Messiah Jesus of the Bible."[16] The other seven, Pobee argues, were used of Nkrumah as a description of his role in the political history of Ghana, and were in accord with traditional practice. Pobee is right when he concludes that the Churches' attitude to the seven honorifics used of Nkrumah failed to take account of traditional usages.[17] As he expresses it, "... when the Church leaders attacked the use of Osagyefo of Nkrumah as a blasphemous equation of Nkrumah with Jesus the saviour, they were showing their ignorance of the traditional African background."[18]

It is with respect to the honorific *Asomdwehene* that Pobee finds himself agreeing with the Church leaders in their censure. This honorific does recall the "Prince of Peace" of Isaiah (9:6), an expression which came to have a Messianic interpretation, and is thus used of Jesus the Messiah in the Christian tradition. The fact that this term is not known to be used in traditional practice of the Chief would seem to argue for the view adopted to it by Pobee. However, one cannot help observing that this honorific *Asomdwehene* is no less significant than *osagyefo* (one who saves in battle), a term applied to warrior chiefs, and also of God in those traditional lyrics which have come to be extensively employed in the Mfantse-speaking Methodist Churches. Thus on the surface of it, at least, it would be as legitimate to suppose that *Osagyefo* as used of Nkrumah would strike some as implying his divinisation, as it would be to suppose that *Asomdwehene* would remind Christians of the Messianic figure. In fact, however, it is doubtful whether these two terms could have struck Christians with any particular force, belonging as they did with an array of terms of such magnitude as *Oyeadeeyie*—one who rights wrongs, and *Kasapreko* — one who speaks once and for all. Indeed, the Churches' objection to *Osagyefo* would have been more credible if they had reflected seriously on the significance of the other honorifics.

Incidentally, I have so far questioned, at more than one point in the foregoing, the Churches' understanding of certain ideas and practices which developed around the Convention People's Party and its founder, Kwame Nkrumah. At a later stage I shall address myself to the question of how one explains the Churches' less-than authentic attitude at various times in the days of the First Republic.

To return to the issue of the divination of Nkrumah, certain things were said and done by the Party and its supporters which are of interest. On more than one occasion the Party paper, *Accra Evening News,* enthusiastically painted Nkrumah in colors which ranged in import from the mildly other-wordly to the totally otherworldly. In the issue of 4th February, 1960, we read: ". . . the whole phenomena of Nkrumah's emergence is second to none in the history of the world's Messiahs from Buddha and Mohammed to Christ." There is nothing on record to indicate that Muslims reacted in one way or the other to this. Christian leaders, however, were unhappy about this linking of Nkrumah and Christ. Then, in that same year, from 21st March, the *Accra Evening News* featured daily a piece on "the Seven Days in the Wilderness" during which Nkrumah apparently meditated and fasted. That this was likely to recall for Christians Jesus' forty days in the wilderness when he was tempted would not have been lost upon the editor, I suppose. Later in that same month a photograph of Nkrumah appeared with the caption: "This is our Messiah Kwame Nkrumah, in the hour of Transfiguration."

It is my judgement that there was a great deal of imprecise thinking behind these pictures painted of Nkrumah. On the one hand the mention of Nkrumah and Transfiguration in the same breath would seem to give the term Messiah a certain theological specificity. On the other hand, it is clear that no such specificity was intended; the term Messiah is being used in the sense of someone who plays a significant role, and in that sense is on a par with those traditional honorifics to which reference has already been made. After all what is common to Buddha, Mohammed and Christ is that each of them started a religious revolution; they were great religious personalities. Nkrumah did not set out to be a religious personality; he was an important political personality. How, then, does one explain this use of the specific Christian images of Temptation and

Transfiguration, among others, in connection with Nkrumah? There are three possible explanations, and these are a re-statement of critical comments already made.

First, it may be speculated that those who adopted these modes of expression had what I have chosen to describe as a theo-political motive, and that is, to widen and solidify Nkrumah's political base by drawing the attention of a sizeable proportion of the population away from Christ to Nkrumah. Now is this a fanciful possibility? The largest organized body in the country was the Christian Church, and it would have suited the Party's purposes for the Church to submit entirely to Nkrumah and the Party. It would not surprise me if this had been a motivating factor; however, the evidence available does not permit me to say categorically that the Party and its various organs were out to change radically the Church's understanding of its significance and mission; in any case, it is doubtful if they could have succeeded, even considering the fact that the Church's theological understanding was in certain respects defective.

Were the Party and its organs acting out of ignorance of the religious realities from which they drew their language? It is difficult to run away from the conclusion that in some respects the Party and its organs had a less than authentic understanding of religion, in general, and Christianity, in particular. I have already suggested that it does not say much for one's understanding of religion to link Nkrumah and Buddha, Mohammed, and Christ. Quite apart from the fact that there is a common denominator which excludes Nkrumah, there is also the fact that a superficial viewing of the three religious revolutionaries together is likely to involve glossing over certain important doctrinal matters which distinguish the religions founded by them. Thus "Christianity believes in one God, Creator of the universe, while Buddhism supposes that an indefinite number of deities exist, and that while they share a higher form of existence, they, like we, are subject to the universal laws of becoming and of suffering. . . For Christianity man is saved by the grace of God, but for Buddhism, in its original form, salvation depends on individual effort."[19]

The third possibility could be that the Party and its organs were bent on the sacralisation of nationalism. My earlier references to the American Carlton Hayes and the German Hans Kohn suggest this as a real possibility: that is, nationalism was being raised to the level of the sacred, so that fostering its goals becomes a sacred duty — on a level with religious obligation. It would not surprise me if some Party officials thought of nationalism in such terms.

I suspect, in fact, that the motives of the Party and its organs were mixed, and that it is not a question of one or the other of these three explanations operating to the exclusion of the others; it is quite likely, given the fact that there was no attempt made to undertake a serious analysis of the religious language utilized, that different understandings prevailed, or that various combinations of motives came into play, at different times.

Now I move on to a line of thought which poses considerable problems, and to which I referred at the start of this paper. For a theologian, the most intriguing thing about the use made of religious ideas in Nkrumah's time is that Nkrumah himself, who had received theological education, and one who in his *Autobiography* described himself as having a "longing for things supernatural," did not once, as far as it is·known, make public his attitude to this.[20] One is tempted to say that it is an eloquent silence, but in what direction? Did he approve of this misuse of religious ideas?

It seems to me that to say that he approved of this is to say something damaging. Thus he did not, as far as I know, restrain people from addressing all those traditional honorifics to him, but was he not aware that by accepting all those chieftaincy titles and then ruling dictatorially he was giving a wrong impression of what chieftaincy was all about? A number of Chiefs know to their cost that Ghanaian society does not suffer dictatorial rule indefinitely. Nkrumah was a very intelligent person. He could have, I suspect, been amused by Idi Amin's words reportedly spoken on the eve of a celebration marking the fourth anniversary of the *coup d'etat* that brought him to power: "God is on my side. Even the most powerful witchcraft cannot hurt me." Despite his own claim to have had a longing for things supernatural, I am strongly of the opinion that Nkrumah could not have overtly approved of the excesses which surfaced in the Party's adoption and application of religious ideas and concepts; he could not have directly encouraged it.

That being so, one is led to conclude that Nkrumah did not restrain his followers in this matter because this application of religious concepts served a useful purpose. It did no harm to his personality build-up if people could be encouraged to see him in the company of Mohammed, Buddha and Christ; besides, since he had not gone on record as expressing any positively anti-religious sentiments himself, those who objected to the Party's misapplication of religious concepts would not readily accuse Nkrumah personally. However, to say that Nkrumah did not restrain the Party and its organs in this matter for reasons of the advantage it might give him to have such thoughts expressed is to say what is equally damaging, particularly as Nkrumah was otherwise a discerning person.

Finally, I should like to approach this issue of the State and religion by commenting, in a general way, on the efforts made by the Church leaders; as I have already indicated, these, as far as I know, were the ones who protested about the misapplication of religious concepts by the Party and its organs.

More than once in the foregoing I have indicated that the Church was not always clear in its own thinking about those matters which gave rise to its protests. That the Church leaders sometimes demonstrated a defective understanding of certain matters of interest to both the Church and the State is beyond doubt, and the reasons for this are worth exploring in concluding this paper.

First, Nkrumah emerged at a time when the Christian Churches in Ghana were tied, in their theology and ethos, to the founding Churches in Europe and America. This does explain the fact that while the Church leaders in Ghana were willing to express views on the Church and politics, their views were not always soundly based in terms of the specificity of the local situation; moreover, their concern often lacked consistency. For an illustration of the latter there is the 1955 Christian Council conference on Christianity and African Culture, at which the analysis done of the cultural situation and its relevance was narrow in the sense that it neglected all reference to socio-economic and political matters, precisely those matters which are among the concerns of African culture. To make a personal reference, I was one of the recorders at that conference, and I confess that the defectiveness of the understanding of culture displayed did not register, because of my theological up-bringing in the context of colonial theological thought.

This brings me to the second reason why the Church's understanding displayed certain defects. It has been said of the French Church in the nineteenth century that its greatest weakness was its educational programme in seminaries which "seemed designed to exclude the cultivation of the mind."[21] This is a harsh judgement which must not be applied without modification, but it is a fact that seminary training in this country is only very recently beginning to adjust to the realities of our time. The Church's theological stance, which had serious defects, as I have shown elsewhere,[22] influenced theological training; furthermore, since theological education embraced only a very small minority of Christians, the majority of Christians were not in a position to think of their faith seriously in relation to the realities of the life in which they found themselves. This explains why the ordinary members of the Churches, during the days in the First Republic when protests were made from time to time by their leaders, were not seized by the urgency of the situation. For one thing, the Churches' leaders were, generally speaking, very circumspect, to make an understatement, when making their protests to the government on religious grounds; so circumspect in fact that the first time many ordinary Christians got to know that protests had been made was after the overthrow of Nkrumah's government; for another — and consequently—the ordinary membership of the Church does not seem to have been in a position to comment meaningfully on the misapplication of religious ideas.

The third reason why the Church's position often lacked realism is this: the events of that time indicate that following Nkrumah's accession to power, the Church almost always played the role of reactor to situations initiated by the Party or government; that is, it was when something or other had already happened, such as a misapplication of religious concepts, that the Church would feel called to assert its position as a body entitled to express an opinion. That role only made the Church's theological image even more uncertain.

Thus the Church and the State, in the time of Nkrumah, were both operating under a misapprehension regarding their own and each other's fields of competence. In the circumstances they merely sparred at a distance — they never meaningfully engaged each other.

NOTES

1. Nkrumah, 1957:10
2. Anquandah, 1979: 12
3. Debrunner, 1967:33-234
4. Anquandah, *op. cit.,*: 119
5. Kwame Nkrumah, J. B. Danquah, Ako-Adjei, E. Akuffo-Addo, William Ofori Atta and E. Obetsebi-Lamptey.
6. Pobee, 1984:8
7. *Ibid.:* 8
8. Rossler, 1969:
9. Quoted in Pobee (ed.) 1976:1~9-130.
10. Hayes, 1960:164
11. Hayes, 1966:125
12. Kohn, 1956:328
13. Tillich, 1964:33
14. Quoted by Pobee, 1976:132
15. *Ibid.:* 129
16. *Ibid.:* 137
17. *Kukuduroni, Kantamanto, Oyeadieyie, Osuodumgya, Kasapreko, Abrofosuro, and Asomdwehene.*
18. Pobee, 1976:137

19. Pettazzoni, 1954:194.
20. Nkrumah, *op. cit.*: 7.
21. McManners, 1973
22. Dickson, 1984 *passim,* but especially the last chapter.

Social and Political Outlook

Dominic Kofi Agyeman

Introduction

In the Prologue to his book, *Black Star—A View of the Life and Times of Kwame Nkrumah,* a book which is best described as a biography of Dr Kwame Nkrumah, Basil Davidson remarks that Nkrumah "was not, in any ordinary sense, a clever politician. In quite a large sense, he was not a politician at all."[1] This remark is likely to surprise both admirers and adversaries of Kwame Nkrumah. At least this author was surprised by it, for, scanning through Nkrumah's autobiography (published in 1957) one gets the impression that Nkrumah spent the greater part of his life-time engaged in political activities and movements and devoted most of his writings to formulating political ideas and philosophies. Twelve years of life in America and England, "years of sorrow and loneliness, poverty and hard work," provided the background that helped Nkrumah to formulate his philosophy of life and politics.[2] In fact so much of his life was devoted to political activities and political philosophy that the commentator who would seek to pigeon-hole his thoughts into those of sociological, political and philosophical ideas would soon find himself engaging in an exercise in hairsplitting. Indeed the richness of Nkrumah's thoughts lies precisely in the unity of his political, philosophical and sociological ideas. I shall therefore try to follow the holistic system of his thought in this essay. Let me state by way of an apologia that what I intend to do is not a presentation of a philosophical treatise of Nkrumah's thoughts; it is rather an attempt to examine from a sociology of knowledge point of view the social circumstances and forces that helped to mould Nkrumah's social ideas, and the effects of those ideas on the society (within which he operated). Our task is not that of a biographer who pieces together views on the life and times of a great thinker, but since we intend to examine his social thoughts against the background of the social environment and social forces that influenced him, we cannot avoid outlining his life and times for this purpose. We shall use as our source of information Nkrumah's own autobiography.

The Man Evaluates His Own Life

Nkrumah was born on 18th September, 1909, and grew up at a time when the wind of national movements was sweeping across British West Africa. In his own native land, Ghana (then Gold Coast), there was the Aborigines Rights Protection Society led by the educated elements of the society at the close of the 19th century; then in 1920 Casely-Hayford and others organized the "National Congress of British West Africa." In between these two political movements there was what David Kimble calls "Cultural nationalism."[3] Nkrumah left the Gold Coast at the age of 26, in 1935, so that he was old enough to have had a mature experience of the evils, and the virtues, if any, of colonialism as well as a good grounding in the sociology of his people. Yet, as he rightly admits, the conceptualization of his philosophy of life and politics really began during his University student days in America and reached its climax during his active practical political training in England.

As a student Nkrumah read widely, and in diverse fields which were to shape his thinking in later years. He read Theology, Sociology, Economics, Politics and Philosophy. In his final B.A. degree, however, he majored in Economics and Sociology at Lincoln University in 1939. It was in 1942 that he obtained a B. A. in Theology from the Seminary at Lincoln. In the same year he obtained a Master of Science degree in Education from the University of Pennsylvania. Meanwhile, after his first degree, he was appointed assistant lecturer in Philosophy at the Lincoln University. It is not surprising therefore that when he took his Masters Degree in Arts in 1943 it was in philosophy from the University of Pennsylvania. And he would have gone on to take a Ph. D in Philosophy were it not for persistent financial difficulties. Strangely enough when he left for Britain in 1945 it was Law that attracted his attention; it was his involvement in active political training in the form of political conferences, demonstrations and organizations that prevented Nkrumah from becoming a lawyer like most of his political predecessors, including J. E. Casely-Hayford and J. B. Danquah.

In addition to his involvement in these diverse political activities he kept up with his reading which covered an impressive range of authors including Kant, Hegel, Descartes, Schopenhauer, Nietzsche, Freud, Marx, Engels, Lenin, Mazzini, Marcus Garvey and Gandhi. He also showed interest in Logical Positivism under Professor Ayer. The outcome of this wide reading and studies is reflected in his own worldview which, according to Nkrumah, makes him "a nondenominational Christian and a Marxist socialist."[4] Interestingly, Nkrumah maintains, " I have not found any contradiction between the two," i.e. a "Christian" and a "Marxist." Not unnaturally he has not found any favor with the disciples of the two worldviews, for Christians reject him as one of them; and Marxist Socialists reject him as a Marxist.[5]

In point of fact, his synthesis of the Christian and Marxist worldviews makes his position unique, for as shall be argued later, even though he confessed on his deathbed that he became a "Marxist" only in his last days, his political activities reflect the synthetic ideas derived from his position as a "non-denominational Christian" and "a Marxist;" and the epitome of this synthesis is found in his social philosophical treatise, *Consciencism,* which was first published in 1963. Indeed in his actions, too, he was a synthesizer of the two apparently irreconcilable worldviews. For instance, as a politician fighting against colonialism and knowing fully well that the colonialist would never give freedom to his subjects on a silver platter, he resorted to the philosophy of non-violent methods with effective and disciplined political action which he christened "Positive Action."

His synthesis of ideas is again reflected in his attitude to cultural fusion in Africa. In 1948 while opening the Ghana National College at Cape Coast he argued that "the times are changing and we must change with them. In doing so we must combine the best in Western culture with the best in African culture." Indeed this is the point of justification for the judgement (by both his critics and himself) that Nkrumah was never a convinced Marxist socialist and this to a large extent may account for his failure to establish socialism in Ghana.

Considering his ambivalent attitude to Marxist Socialism it is questionable whether Nkrumah is justified in labeling himself as "revolutionary" as compared with the leaders of the United Gold

Coast Convention whom he labeled as "reactionary." This labeling is not just a mere semantic exercise. Nkrumah made this remark about himself and about his political opponents in his autobiography. He must have arrived at his judgement after careful examination of his own political philosophy and practice and those of his opponents. Judging from the events that ushered in decolonization and independence in Ghana, one is tempted to agree with a critic like Henry Bretton[7] that Nkrumah does not qualify for a revolutionary leader. But this criticism would be valid only if one adopted the orthodox concept of "revolution." According to the orthodox view, a revolutionary change is one that is brought about by force and through armed struggle, is abrupt and discontinuous with the past. Empirical evidence suggests that such a revolutionary change exists only in novels. In the reality of history all social changes are continuous. Besides not every "revolutionary change" is caused by force of armed struggle. We speak of industrial revolution, scientific revolution and the like. Rex D. Harper therefore defines a revolutionary change as "precisely that kind of social change which occurs when the basic institutional (i.e. legally enforced) values of a social order are rejected and new values accepted."[8] For the same reason Prof. Walter Buhl of the University of Munich criticized what he calls the "dogmatic narrow definition of revolution" when applied to the societies of the Third World.[9] In its wider definition the concept of revolutionary change is applicable to the social change that the world has been witnessing in the African context since the days of decolonization.

But this is not to argue that every political or social upheaval or movement organized by every African leader is qualified to be labeled as a "revolutionary change." Since the basic tenets of a revolutionary change, according to Rex Harper, are the rejection of the legally enforced values of a social order and the acceptance of new values, it follows that only movements and leaders who reject the *status quo* and seek to replace it can be revolutionary. It is in this context that Nkrumah qualifies to be called a revolutionary leader, whereas his contemporary political opponents do not qualify for the label. For whereas Nkrumah challenged the *status quo* of the colonial order and sought to replace it with a novel sociopolitical order, his opponents, such as J. B. Danquah, sought to uphold the *status quo ante* of the colonial order, their political aim was to replace the colonial personnel with an African personnel while maintaining the *colonial social structure*. Indeed Danquah and his associates saw themselves as the natural or the legal successors to the colonial administration. For that reason they adopted the British parliamentary system and guarded it against any injections from the Marxist ideology.

Purely from the point of view of ideological orientation Nkrumah can lay claim to being a revolutionary, not so much because he had Marxist inclinations — in fact his flirtation with Marxism would rather disqualify him — as that in contrast to his opponents who sought to emulate and protect the British parliamentary system he sought to synthesize the African, Islamic, Christian, Capitalist and Marxist socialist worldviews in order to establish a new doctrine which would transform society (Ghanaian and African) into a new structure and order. That Nkrumah did not succeed in transforming the society into this new order before his overthrow and death is an issue which is premature to discuss now. After all great men do not always succeed in transforming their societies during their lifetime; their works and ideas live after them. The question that may be justifiably asked at this stage therefore is: Has Nkrumah's social thought or world view any hopes of surviving him and becoming the cornerstone of social, economic and political development in Ghana in particular, and Africa in general? It is to answer this question that we have set ourselves the task of evaluating the nature of his social thought against the background of the society he lived in and to try to project them to the future of the same society. The path that we traverse is that of the sociology of knowledge and thus we begin with the premise that "knowledge is a product of social life" and therefore whatever knowledge we have springs from life experience.

Nkrumah's Economic, Sociological and Political Experience

Even if Nkrumah did not study enough economics to become an economist of repute, his whole life as a student and graduate in America and in Britain was one of practical economics. Nkrumah was not an affluent student. He was a "worker–student;" working most of the time in order to finance his studies and to survive as a man. This situation brought him face-to-face with the hard facts of capitalism. While washing dishes or sleeping in forbidden public places or living in slums, he participated in the lives of the proletariat or even the declassé of the capitalist society of America and England. One positive outcome of this "participant observer" role Nkrumah was forced to play was the shaping of his ideas as a radical sociologist and politician and his emergence as a champion of the oppressed and the exploited

This socialization later became a political asset and while in prison it served as a shock absorber against the social problems that he witnessed there. Among other things, he witnessed the way criminals were treated; how capital punishment was executed with "bestial sadism" by the law enforcement agents; and how such experiences affected the personality of the prison inmates. He was able to remark while in prison: "No man is born a criminal; society makes him so, and the only way to change things is to change the social conditions; it is only from the social standpoint that crime and punishment can be effectively approached." He went on to condemn the death penalty as "a relic of barbarism and savagery," something which "is inconsistent with decent morals and the teaching of Christians ethics."[10]

But it seems to me that Nkrumah did not have enough "socialization" in radical sociology and politics to push him to extremes, for even though he went on to observe that "The aim of punishment should be that of understanding and correction,"[11] there is hardly any evidence that when he became the Head of Government and State he revolutionalized, or at least reformed, the prisons in Ghana to make them more civilized and humane.

Again, Nkrumah had first hand experience with racism in both America and Britain. He spoke with emotion about how the Black man in search of accommodation is degraded in both Britain and America.[12] Yet he does not show any resentment against the White race. What he hates, he repeated often, is imperialism, the domination of one society by another; therefore he sought to fight against British imperialism and not against British racism. This fight was naturally and logically a political one, and for this he had a store of practical political training. His first book, *Towards Colonial Freedom,* which he wrote while still a student, was actually a political treatise.

His practical political training was rather rich. He took part in students' politics in Pennsylvania by forming the African Students Association of America and Canada with Ako Adjei and Jones Quartey — both Ghanaians. Together with them he established a newspaper, *African Interpreter.* He also took part in the activities of the Republicans, the Democrats, the Communists and the Trotskyites and learnt through them political organizational methods. This training became richer while in Britain. There he organized with George Padmore, Makonnen and Peter Abrahams, the Fifth Pan–African Congress which, in his own words, was unique and marks the turning point of the Pan-African Movement; for he was able to attract a great number of African politicians who later became leaders of various African countries in their struggle against colonialism. It is indeed this rich, practical political training which gave him the edge over his opponents, both Africans and whites. He also organized the "Circle" which was more or less an underground Pan–African movement.

This rich, practical political experience was however marred by Nkrumah's lack of in-depth sociological knowledge. Had he balanced his rich practical political experience with in–depth sociological knowledge he probably would have foreseen the probable effects of his two-front approach to Pan-Africanism and West African Union, which was to culminate into a Union of West African Socialist Republics. Apart from the fact that his conception of Pan-Africanism and the Union of West African Socialist Republics was "wholly idealistic,"[13] he thought that he could achieve his goal in a gradualist manner by first securing the independence of each African country *at their own pace* before uniting them to form regional groups and then finally transform them into a Pan-African Union. He failed to realize that a gradualist approach to the achievement of independence by the various states would lead to difficulties in uniting them. Again, he failed to realize that regional groupings would inhibit the formation of the Pan-African Union. The rivalries between the Casablanca and the Monrovia groups testify to this political myopia.

I have argued elsewhere that Nkrumah cannot exonerate himself from the charge that he contributed to the failure of Pan-Africanism as originally conceived by DuBois and George Padmore.[14] For by shifting the emphasis from Pan-Negroism, to geographical, area-oriented, Pan-Africanism, as a geographical entity, he destroyed the original spirit of Pan-Africanism and from that moment separated the African interest from the Afro-American interest. In the words of Frantz Fanon: "Negro and African-Negro culture broke up into different entities because the men who wished to incarnate these cultures realized that every culture is first and foremost national, and that the problems which kept Richard Wright or Langston Hughes on the alert were fundamentally different from those which might confront Leopold Senghor or Jomo Kenyatta."[15]

In spite of these realities Nkrumah remained idealistic about his confused concept of Pan-Africanism for the greater part of his life. In spite of the stark realities that confronted him he remained convinced that "the forces that unite us Africans are far greater than the difficulties which divide us at present."[16] Had Nkrumah been a realist, the course of events in Ghana and Africa might have taken a different turn. Unfortunately, this idealism permeated Nkrumah's thoughts and actions and dictated his course of actions even while in exile in Guinea. For example, writing on class struggle in Africa while in exile he jumped to the conclusion that there is class consciousness among the working class of Africa. It is strange that Nkrumah did not realize that to speak of class consciousness was to speak of the existence of a "class for itself."[17] It is doubtful whether the working class in most African countries today qualifies as a "class for itself." By suggesting to himself that class consciousness had already emerged among the "oppressed"classes of African societies, Nkrumah ignored the need to involve himself in the organization of the working class to develop class consciousness and to lead a really revolutionary struggle with the oppressed against the oppressors.

　　We are therefore back to our starting-point, namely, the question of whether Nkrumah qualifies to wear the label of a "revolutionary." We find ourselves constrained to answer this question by saying that as a theoretician, contributing to the world of ideas, history will very likely judge him as a revolutionary; as an activist and a political strategist, however, Nkrumah is far from deserving to be ranked with the revolutionaries who have shaped this world. We are told that while in Guinea he learned the practical art of Guerrilla warfare. But he never had the opportunity to demonstrate his prowess as a practical revolutionary. We therefore stand on a firmer ground if we examine Nkrumah's contribution as a cultural revolutionary, as found in his exposition of the concept of "African Personality."

The African Personality

　　As has been pointed out already, the ultimate aim of Nkrumah's Pan-Africanism was to delimit what is African from the non-African and thus free the African from all forms of colonialism and neocolonialism. It was this goal of delimiting the "Africanness" from the "non-Africanness" that led Nkrumah to pursue the concept of the African Personality. The African Personality, according to him, is "defined by the cluster of humanist principles which underlie the traditional African society."[18] On the surface Nkrumah's conception of the African Personality does not differ from Senghor's view of Negritude. Senghor defines Negritude as "the whole complex of civilized values — cultural, economic, social and political—which characterize the black peoples, or more precisely, the Negro-African world."[19] However, according to Senghor, Negritude does not include Arabite. Geographically, Negritude covers only that part of

Africa between south of the Sahara and north of the Republic of South Africa. Senghor therefore derives his view of Pan-Africanism from Negritude and thus delimits his Pan-Africanism from Nkrumah's continental Pan-Africanism.[20] In contrast, though Nkrumah's concept of Pan-Africanism derives from the African Personality, it embraces geographically the whole of the continent of Africa and therefore has a broader frame of reference than Senghor's Negritude.

Nkrumah conceived of the African Personality in terms of the total African continent because, on the one hand, he did not recognize the legitimacy of the Republic of South Africa, on the other, he saw both the Arabic and the negroid parts of Africa as constituting one total culture; and his aim was to revive and revolutionize this total culture which has a long history and which is as old as other great cultures. One characteristic feature of the African Personality is the non-exploitative, co-operative communalistic life of the traditional African. Nkrumah saw this as compatible with scientific socialism and argued that the African Personality should be conceived as the true culture of the African peasantry which is characterized by the non-exploitative and co-operative relationship that existed between members of the peasant society. He also argued that if the cultural revolution of the African Personality was to succeed — and it should succeed — then the African revolution should be brought to its rightful place, i.e. to the peasantry.

Unfortunately Nkrumah did not succeed in bringing the revolution to the people, the peasants, and the workers whose cause he championed in the exposition of his ideas. And for this failure Nkrumah rightly deserves the criticism of the young African Marxist-Leninists of today who claim that he was an idealist. This criticism, however, applies not only to Nkrumah but also to those who shout slogans of socialism and African revolution without recognizing the proletariat and the peasants as the true vanguard of the revolution. For those who want to see the African revolution carried to its logical conclusion let these words of Nkrumah be the guiding principles: "As in other areas of the world where socialist revolution is based largely on the peasantry, African revolutionary cadres have a tremendous task ahead of them. Urban and rural proletariat must be won to the revolution, and the revolution taken to the countryside. It is only when the peasantry have been politically awakened and won to the revolution that freedom fighters—on whom the revolution largely depends in the armed phase—will be able to develop and to expand their areas of operation."[21]

The Lessons of Nkrumah's Thoughts

Nkrumah's last minute acceptance of the fact that the urban proletariat must be won to the revolution and that the revolution must be carried to the countryside is the most significant development in his political thought and practice. The lesson that can be derived from this is that Nkrumah realized that the ideas he developed could not be put into practice unless he mobilized the people he was fighting for. Indeed this may sound commonplace, but it is not that common. It is not unusual for those who develop ideas—especially philosophical ideas—to miss the chance of putting them into practice. The work of putting such great ideas into practice is usually left in the hands of disciples to complete. In this context we suggest that the best way to put Nkrumah's ideas into practice and thereby honor him is to translate them to the level of the rural peasantry and the workers so as to make them internalize them and act on them to the level of the rural peasantry and the workers so as to make them internalize them and act on them, for it is through practice that ideas can be tested and nourished and they in turn lead to a fruitful development of society. This is an age-old maxim which has been couched in the expression "practice without thought is blind; thought without practice is empty," and this has been repeated by many a great men, including Kwame Nkrumah himself.[22]

NOTES

1. Davidson, 1973 :15
2. Nkrumah, 1957:7
3. Kimble 1963:517
4. Nkrumah, *op. cit.:* 12
5 . *African Red Family,* n.d. Vol. 1, No. 2: 21-31
6. Nkrumah, *op. cit.:* 52-53
7. Bretton, 1967:7476
8. Harper, 1957:311
9. Buhl, l970:219
10. Nkrumah, 1957: 132
11. Nkrumah, l957: 132
12. *Ibid,* :48-51
13. *African Red Family, op. cit.* :25
14. Agyeman, 1975
15. Fanon, 1970:174
16. CPP Programme for Work and Happiness, Act 176, 1962
17. Amin and Cohen, 1977 of.
18. Nkrumah, 1964a:79
19. Senghor, 1967 196

20. Senghor, 1967
21. Nkrumah, 1973:515
22. Nkrumah, 1964a:78

NKRUMAH

PART 2
POLITICS

Nkrumah's Ideology

K. Afari-Gyan

In this essay, I attempt an outline of Nkrumah's ideology around four themes: Colonialism, Socialism, Unity and Social Justice. In Nkrumah's writings, these themes form an inter-related body of ideas with a focus on reconstructing an ex-colonial society.

Influences on his Thought

Before outlining the salient themes in Nkrumah's thought, it may be worth our while to briefly indicate some possible sources of influence on his thought. Admittedly, it is a tricky exercise trying to establish linkages between a person's background and his ideology; but there is no doubt that a person's ideology is often as much the product of his experiences as they are of his thought processes.

We have found no evidence of Nkrumah's involvement in the early nationalist movement in Ghana. However, judging from his profuse admiration for the nationalistic writings of Nnamdi Azikiwe in Ghana in the 1930s and his utter revulsion at the Italian invasion of Ethiopia in 1935, one could say that he had a sense of nationalism before he went to America in 1935 to further his education.[1]

Nkrumah's early days in America were apolitical. But later he got involved in a wide range of political activities covering a wide spectrum of political perspectives from capitalism to communism.

According to him, in doing so his basic aim was to learn the techniques of political organization, and to find a formula for solving the problems of colonialism.[2]

The quest led him to the reading of radical literature, of which he says the writings of Marx, Lenin and Marcus Garvey influenced him most.[3] As we shall see later in this essay, the Marxist-Leninist influence on Nkrumah was intellectual and profound. It is most evident in his first book, *Towards Colonial Freedom* (1961), and in three of the books he published after his ouster from office, namely, *Dark Days in Ghana* (1968), *Handbook of Revolutionary Warfare* (1968), and *Class Struggle in Africa* (1970).

In contrast to the Marxist-Leninist influence, the Garveyist influence on Nkrumah was largely inspirational. Garvey's basic concern was with the relation between black and white peoples in America: and he saw the only alternative to perpetual white domination in blacks building a strong nation of their own in Africa.[4]

Nkrumah appears to have drawn great inspiration from Garvey's idea of Africa for Africans, his glorification of Africa's past and optimistic vision of her future grandeur, his emphasis on the need for unity, organization and self-reliance as necessary for the liberation of a subject people, and his very success in attracting large scale support to his movement in America.

Nkrumah left America in 1945 and went to live in Britain until late 1947 when he finally returned to Ghana. During his stay in Britain, he took advantage of the presence of students and workers from the colonies and the existence of several anti-colonial movements and personalities to learn more about the colonial problem. Equally important as a possible formative influence on his ideas was his involvement in the Pan-African Congress held in Manchester in 1945. Nkrumah took an active part in organizing the meeting and in formulating its platform.

We find four of the conclusions that emerged from the Manchester meeting to be significant in view of Nkrumah's later activities. They are as follows:

a. Colonialism could be eradicated only through the concerted action of the colonial peoples themselves;
b. the job of ending colonialism could not be done by a few intellectuals alone, but through a mass movement and the creation of institutions responsive to the needs of the people;
c. Pan-Africanism should be seen as an independent ideological system, a counterpoint to capitalism and communism;
d. peaceful civil disobedience in the form of strikes and boycotts

should be used in the struggle against colonialism. Violence was not to be used unless circumstances made it the only viable option.[5]

To the foregoing possible sources of influence on Nkrumah's thought are to be added his experiences from his role in the Ghanaian independence struggle. In sum, Nkrumah came to see the divisions in the nationalist movement as a drag on progress, to build a more deep-seated distrust of the colonial government and the chiefs and intellectuals of the old nationalist movement, and to realize the enormity of the task of national reconstruction.

We shall now proceed to outline Nkrumah's ideas about Colonialism, Socialism, Unity and Social Justice.

Colonialism

Nkrumah reiterates the Leninist view that colonialism arose from the need for raw materials to feed European industries. According to this view, at the onset of colonialism, capitalism in Europe had reached a stage where the lure of greater profits impelled the capitalist to export investment capital abroad. Colonialism was a self-serving venture. And in order for the colonialist to be free to repatriate the immense profits he made on his investments, it was necessary for him to take control of the economy and the politics of the colony.[6]

Once in firm control, the colonialist proceeded consciously to exploit the resources of the colony, while wilfully neglecting the needs of the people. Thus, in their experiences of colonialism, African countries differed only in detail and degree and not in kind. For everywhere the colonialist exploited and oppressed the subject people; he placed his interests above theirs, circumscribed their rights and liberties and degraded them.

In view of this single-mindedness of the colonialist, the colonial record everywhere was broadly similar. In the colonial economy, trade and commerce were controlled by European buyers and sellers, who effectively manipulated prices. Extractive industries were promoted at the expense of manufacturing; and monocrop and cash economies were pushed to the detriment of comprehensive national agricultural programmes. In the area of education, the colonialist left behind mass illiteracy and inadequate educational facilities. Moreover, the few educational facilities that existed were literary in content and were clearly intended to spread European ideas and to serve European needs. In terms of social infrastructure, one sees poor health and living conditions, slums and squalor, ignorance and superstition, malnutrition and disease, poor drinking water, and scarce transportation and communication facilities. As for the civil service, Nkrumah says it was by and large efficient but thoroughly alien in orientation. And as regards the subject people, they were treated as inferiors in practically all aspects of life. The result was that they came to be ridden with fear and apathy, to lack confidence in themselves, and to adore things associated with the colonial master.

In sum, then, according to Nkrumah, at the time of independence colonialism left behind immense obstacles to development. The physical and social infrastructure necessary for progress were absent. That aside, the people were either uneducated or had been miseducated; they had been taught no skills relevant to nation-building; their economic initiative had been stifled; and they suffered a general feeling of inadequacy and helplessness.[7]

Against the foregoing background, Nkrumah saw one major task which faces an ex-colonial country to be the removal of the obstacles to progress left behind by colonialism. Unless this was done, an atmosphere congenial to development could not be created. Thus, he likened the obstacles to mines left behind by a vanquished army that have to be cleared in order to make the land usable again.[8]

He indicated the broad outlines of what an ex-colonial country needs to do in this connection.[9] It must diversify its economy in such a way as to enable it to provide for both domestic needs and exports. It must vigorously promote industrial growth in order to lessen its dependence on the outside world. It must make its agriculture able to produce enough food for a rapidly expanding population, raw materials for industry and cash crops to pay for needed imports.

An ex-colonial country must also expand its educational system, give it local content and gear it toward satisfying the country's manpower needs. It must develop a civil service whose members are patriotic, fully conscious of their country's problems, and who blend harmoniously into the programmes of their government. Finally, the generality of the people need to rebuild their self-confidence, develop a personality of their own, and seize the initiative and become creative pioneers in their country's development.

Nkrumah says that these are difficult tasks in themselves; but they are made even more difficult by the phenomenon of neo–colonialism. He defines a neo–colonial country as one that has all the outward trappings of independence, but whose major policies are in reality controlled from outside.[10] He sees neo–colonialism as a device by which the developed world seeks to retain the new nations in essentially the same status as during the colonial period. Thus neocolonialism is the most dangerous obstacle to the true development of an ex-colonial country.

Neo-colonialism is primarily, but not solely, an economic phenomenon. For through its control of the economy it also exerts control over the other aspects of society. Its methods of control are most subtle and varied than those of the old colonialism. It usually establishes its grip through intricate webs of interests and influences, from which it is difficult to disentangle. Such interests and influences may be established through the dominance of international corporations and banking and financial institutions, through aid and a whole host of cultural, social and ideological factors.

Nkrumah says that no new nation is going to be able to do away entirely with western capital or the international corporations. In fact, it is the indispensability of foreign capital for the development of the new nations which brings them face to face with neo-colonialism. Thus, what requires critical examination is the relationship between a new nation and a western financier that results from the infusion of western capital. In this regard, the question is whether the new nation is able to retain such integrity and control over its resources and institutions that western capital is not used to impoverish its people. Thus, for Nkrumah the essential difference among the new nations is between "those states that accept neo-colonialism as a policy and those which resist it."[11]

How then can neo-colonialism be resisted? According to Nkrumah, the first step is for the peoples of the new nations to become knowledgeable about neo-colonialism and to realize that it is a drag on their progess. Secondly, they must also realize that the forces of neo-colonialism are too strong for any one nation to defeat alone. Thirdly, in the final analysis, the only way to ward off neo-colonialism is to create a socialist system.[12]

Socialism

Nkrumah saw capitalism and socialism as the two competing models of development. He rejected the capitalist model for several reasons. In the first place, the problems that the new nations have to solve have been created by capitalism . Secondly, he considered socialism as the only way to defeat neo-colonialism. Thirdly, capitalism is characterized by "unfeeling competition and pursuit of supremacy" plus unfair distribution of the fruits of national growth. Fourthly, he considered government initiative and active involvement in the development process to be necessary.[13]

But equally important as Nkrumah's rejection of capitalism was his caution against an uncritical adoption of socialist measures used elsewhere. The caution was necessary because even though "There is only one true socialism, and that is scientific socialism," there are different paths to socialism, dictated by the "specific circumstances and conditions of a particular country at a definite historical period."[14] The crucial thing is that every socialist experiment should aim at creating a society in which all citizens have equal opportunity, where there is no exploitation, and where "the free development of each is the condition for the free development of all." For Nkrumah such a society has four essential features:

1. the common ownership of the means of production and exchange;
2. production for use rather than for profit;
3. planned industrial and agricultural development; and
4. political power in the hands of the people.[15]

With this conviction, Nkrumah set out to give the universal principles of socialism "the institutional forms that take into account our African background and heritage."[16] This task entailed the analysis of contemporary African society. That analysis shows some differences between his ideas before and after his ouster. For example, before his overthrow he believed that Marxian-type classes had not yet crystallized in Africa and so socialism could be achieved by reform. He changed his view after his overthrow. He now saw Marxian class lines clearly drawn and so concluded that violent revolution is essential to achieve socialism in Africa. Again, before his ouster he had said that what he sought to do was to create "a welfare state based on African socialist principles;" but after his ouster he considered any socialism "derived from communal and egalitarian aspects of traditional African society" as a myth used to deny the class struggle and thus to "obscure genuine socialist commitment." Once again, before his overthrow he had said that foreign capital was indispensable to the development of the new nations, but after his ouster he claimed that the private sector had been tolerated in Ghana simply because the country lacked the means to switch to a full socialist economy soon after independence.[17]

Nkrumah's perspective on the *coup* that ousted him from power may help to explain some of the changes in his ideas.[18] As is to be expected, he saw the *coup* as a reactionary one carried out by the

internal allies of neo-colonialism at the prompting of powerful external forces. Its aim was to put an end to Ghana's socialist experiment
and its lessons for the rest of Africa. Such *coups* represent a new
offensive by imperialism to re-establish firm control over the new
nations by installing puppet governments. Thus, at core the struggle in the new nations is between capitalism and socialism, and not
between democracy and dictatorship.

From this analysis of the *coup,* Nkrumah concluded that the
class lines in Ghanaian society, as indeed elsewhere in Africa, were
now clearly drawn. The *coup* would soon bring the contradictions in
the society into sharp focus, and eventually lead to a *counter-coup*
which would decisively reverse the direction of the original *coup.*

It is not surprising then that in the two books that came after
the *Dark Days in Ghana,* Nkrumah did a more detailed analysis of
contemporary African society than ever before, with a view to clar-
ifying what he perceived to be Africa's class structure.

It is appropriate at this point to briefly outline Nkrumah's thinking on the development of classes in Africa. According to him some
time ago a collectivist ethos pervaded traditional African social organization and imposed duties on society on behalf of every member.
During that time, there were no Marxian-type classes, i.e., there was
no horizontal social stratification accompanied by such dispropor-
tionate economic and socio-political power as to make the class
above able to hold the one below down. But this traditional society
was changing on its own even before it was subjected to influences
from two other cultures, the Euro-Christian and the Islamic. In fact,
by the time Europeans arrived, the traditional classless society was
already passing away and gradually being replaced by a feudal order.
Colonialism speeded up the process toward a class society. In contrast to the traditional collectivist ethos, Christianity introduced the
accountability of the individual conscience. Then colonialism produced an urban petty bourgeois class of merchants, doctors,
traders, intellectuals, politicians, trade unionists, landlords, etc.,
who assumed new prestige, rank and power in the society. On the
other hand, as the colonies became integrated into the international
capitalist system, subsistence agriculture declined, private enterprise grew, and consequently a working class developed.[19]

During the colonial period, the class cleavages within the
indigenous people were effectively blurred by two factors. One was
that, in relation to the whites, all the indigenous people were
regarded as a subject class. The second was the need for united
action during the struggle for independence. But the blurred class

situation changed after independence. The reactionary *coups* that have taken place since then have clearly demonstrated the reality of the class struggle.

What then are the class divisions in Africa? Nkrumah identified three broad class groupings—the bourgeoisie, the proletariat and the peasantry.[20] The bourgeoisie are small in number, comprising about one percent of Africa's peoples. They are made up of traditional leaders, large rural farmers, lawyers and judges, doctors, top civil servants, police and army officers, intellectuals, businessmen and leaders of political parties. The members of this class are by and large imbued with western ideology and subscribe to the bourgeois conception of freedom. In this conception, freedom is viewed primarily as the absence of constraints and justice is sacrificed for law and order. Also, in social organization emphasis is placed on the individual and government is said to exist to protect private property. Thus freedom has only political meaning for all, and no economic content for those who have no property. In the circumstances, democracy is at best competition between oligarchies. As a class, the bourgeoisie distrust change and prefer capitalist institutions. Some members of this class participated in the struggle for independence, but they did so to enhance their position in society and to create more room for their upward mobility. Finally, as a class the bourgeoisie fear socialism and the masses.

The proletariat consist of an urban sector and a rural sector, and together make up about seven percent of Africa's population. But their real problem is not so much their small size as their lack of consciousness as a class, due mainly to their low education and skills and the low level of industrialization. Thus, they are not completely revolutionary, and some even have bourgeois aspirations. However, their consciousness and revolutionary potential can be aroused by trade unions dedicated to socialism.

The peasantry are the underprivileged, exploited class of rural society. As a rule, they cultivate small patches of land for their subsistence and tend to be conservative and submissive. They clearly need to be awakened to the realities of their situation; but once so awakened, their numbers will make them the real backbone of a socialist revolution.

Nkrumah concludes his analysis of Africa's classes by saying that the continent's socialist revolutionary potential still lies dormant. As such a genuine socialist revolution will require concerted action by the proletariat, the *lumpenproletariat*, the peasantry and revolutionary intellectuals under the leadership of a vanguard party.

Such a revolution must be guided by a new ideology which takes into full account the three cultural influences existing in uneasy equilibrium in contemporary Africa—the traditional African, the Euro-Christian, and the Islamic. It is to be understood that the interaction of these cultures produced dynamic changes in African society which cannot be simply reversed. For example, one cannot, as it were, "return" to traditional African social organization and practices. What socialist thought in Africa must recapture then is not the structure but the spirit of traditional African society.[21] Using that spirit as the base, the Euro-Christian and the Islamic influences should be treated as experiences of African society with a view to creating an ideology that harmonizes the three cultural strands.

For this purpose Nkrumah proposed philosophical consciencism. There is a popular tendency to regard consciencism as an ideology. But it is not. Rather, it is a "philosophical statement which gives the theoretical basis for an ideology."[22] The ideology of philosophical consciencism is socialism, for consciencism seeks to end exploitation and the solidifying of class divisions, and to promote planned, egalitarian development and social justice.

UNITY

In this section we shall summarize Nkrumah's views on both national and continental (Pan-African) Unity.

National Unity

Nkrumah was firm in his belief that national unity is essential for stability and purposeful development. But what kind of unity?

He argued that in a post-colonial setting the exigencies of national development amount to a national emergency requiring overall central planning and united action. In the circumstances, any diffusion of governmental power such that bodies are created with powers "wide enough to impinge on those of the central government" makes the central government less sovereign than it should be. Thus, centralization of power and authority is necessary for the exercise of "positive leadership," meaning the ability of the central government to initiate and carry through its programmes without any hindrance whatsoever.[23]

In order to get a clearer picture of the kind of centralization of authority Nkrumah desired, we must add to the fore-going his views about his own political party—the Convention People's Party (CPP)

— and its role in Ghanaian society. According to him, the party embraced "all the progressive elements in our community" and was "the uniting force that guides and pilots the nation.... Its supremacy cannot be challenged." He believed that Ghana's fortunes were irretrievably bound up with those of the party: hence "the Convention People's Party is Ghana and Ghana is the Convention People's Party."[24] Elsewhere he writes that "the aspirations of the people and the economic and social objectives of their government are synonymous"[25] and that "the true welfare of the people does not admit of compromise."[26]

On occasion Nkrumah said he believed in a strong and well organized opposition party, and even suggested in 1955 that all the opposition parties should come together to form one such party.[27]

However, taken together his views about centralized authority and about his party left virtually no room for an organized opposition party. In fact, Nkrumah conceived sovereignty, in Hobbesian fashion, to be indivisible. This, plus his conception of the ruling party as the embodiment of the national will, made opposition to the ruling party no less than opposition to the very essence of the nation. An opposition party is thus rendered illegitimate.

It should not be surprising then that Nkrumah saw the political opposition as an irresponsible one seeking to add to the difficulties of the government instead of complementing its efforts.[28] Elsewhere Nkrumah described the members of the opposition as "disgruntled and disappointed politicians who were against the common man and were determined to undermine the democratic process;" and "reactionaries" carrying out "vicious and treacherous" activities.[29]

Nkrumah's position on national unity and the centralization of authority was at the basis of his objection to the Independence Constitution which sought to give a measure of autonomy to the regions: It conditioned his handling of the political opposition; and it finally culminated in the vesting of all power in the central government in the Republican Constitution (1960) and the declaration of the one party state (1964).

Continental Unity

Nkrumah considered pan-Africanism to be a higher level of ideological development than nationalism. He argued that while nationalism is necessary for gaining independence, it cannot be a final solution, because genuine decolonization cannot be achieved within the existing national boundaries. He stressed that only a united Africa can effectively resist the pressures of neocolonialism, and so continental interests must take priority over the interests of any one country. He believed that although Africa is diverse in race, culture and language, its common colonial past means that "the forces making for unity outweigh those which divide us."[30]

Ultimately, Nkrumah envisaged a politically and economically united Africa. But initially he thought regional economic co-operation would precede common political action, and he envisaged a gradual evolution whereby the artificial boundaries would give way to "viable economic units, and ultimately a single African unit."[31] He later changed his view on the unity programme. From 1960 on he persistently emphasized that the African struggle for independence and unity must begin with a political union, because only a strong political union can safeguard Africa's independence and provide the right framework for economic, social and cultural advance. He now objected to regional groupings because they might produce hardened regional loyalties inimical to continental unity.[32]

A united Africa would operate on the principle of the equality of all member states. It would have a common economic, defence and foreign policy, leaving the residual powers in the hands of the national governments.

Nkrumah found the advantages of continental unity to be legion.[33] First, unity would make Africa strong enough to project her personality more forcefully and to be able to practise positive neutrality and non-alignment so as to keep the big powers out of Africa's affairs. Secondly, being a large unit, a united Africa could more easily attract foreign capital and thus end the senseless competition among African countries for small doses of foreign aid. Thirdly, a united Africa would provide a more rational economic setting for development. For example, it would make possible the pooling and sharing of natural and human resources, the joint exploitation and development of economic resources, and a common currency and monetary zone. Fourthly, rational planning would eliminate duplication and waste and thereby reduce the cost of development to the individual countries. A united Africa with a common land, sea and air defence strategy would also make it possible to abolish standing national armies and establish in their places people's militias. Nkrumah considered peoples' militias to be the best guardians of society because they cannot be subverted.

According to Nkrumah, the benefits likely to come from unity will be meaningful only in a socialist context. Thus he found African unity and socialism to be "organically complementary."

Social Justice

For Nkrumah the goal of the reconstruction of post-colonial society is to achieve social justice. A socially just society is one in which, at the minimum, the general run of the people have access to the basic needs of life. Creating such a society requires the removal of the obstacles to progress left behind by colonialism and the rapid expansion of education, health, and other social infrastructure and services. To make all these possible, the economy must be planned, rapid industrialization must be achieved, agriculture must be modernized, and investments must be directed into desired channels. Moreover, the problems of low productivity must be solved, and economic surplus must be created.[34]

Nkrumah maintained that in the drive to achieve social justice particular attention ought to be paid to developing the rural areas. To this end the "vestiges of rural feudalism" must be destroyed; industries must be built in the rural areas to provide employment and to arrest the drift of the population to the towns; and co-opertive banks must be established to give easy credit to rural dwellers. In addition, the people must be taught preventive medicine and sanitation, and health facilities, good drinking water and feeder roads must be provided.[35]

Nkrumah says that the initiative and major responsibility for achieving social justice must fall on the government, because it requires government control of national production and a conscious effort to distribute the fruits of growth and social progress more evenly. However, the people through self-help projects can play an important role. Also, institutions like the trade unions have an important role to play. In this regard, unlike their counterparts in the west, African trade unions must do much more than "safeguard the conditions and wages of their members." They need to be an integral part of the attempt to solve the problems of productivity and to create economic surplus.[36]

Nkrumah maintained that social justice could be achieved only in a democratic society. In a speech to the National Assembly in 1956, he included the following among the factors that make for a democracy:

a. all citizens are equal, entitled to the same rights and subject to the same laws;

b. sovereignty belongs to the people, who exercise power through free institutions and popularly elected representatives responsive to them;

c. individual rights — freedom from arbitrary search, arrest or confiscation of property, freedom of speech, association, religion,
access to law courts, and a free press.[37]

However, he considered the "western style parliamentary
democracy" as unsuitable to African conditions and cautioned
against blindly importing the "trimmings" which have developed
over a long period of time and "have become the accepted norm in
the older nations."[38] As we saw earlier on, Nkrumah also did not
think that traditional institutions were suitable to contemporary
Africa. Thus he concluded that an African country in search of
democracy has to create new institutions that differ from both the
traditional and Western forms.[39]

In creating the new democratic institutions four things were to
be borne in mind. First, democracy consists essentially in universal
adult suffrage and free and regular general elections. Secondly, social
justice can be achieved only in a socialist state. Thirdly, a socialist
democracy is based on the principles of democratic centralism. He
explained that principle as follows: "All are free to express their
views. But once a majority decision is taken, we expect such decision to be loyally executed, even by those who might have opposed
that decision."[40] The fourth thing to bear in mind is that the multi-
party system is a "ruse for carrying out the struggle between the
haves and the have-nots." On the other hand, a one-party non-social-
ist system is an instrument used by the few to suppress the many.[41]

Thus Nkrumah's new institutional framework for achieving
social justice was a one-party socialist system based on the principles of universal adult suffrage and democratic centralism.

Conclusion

Nkrumah's ideology must be seen against the background of his
analysis of colonialism. He considered colonialism to have literally
battered African society, and he sought to provide an ideology suitable for its reconstruction.

He maintained that political independence is crucial to reconstruction, because without it reconstruction is a non-starter. But he
emphasized that political independence is only the first stage of the
victory to be won. He realized fully well that post-independence
reconstruction would present more difficult problems than did the
struggle for independence. The thrust at this stage should be placed
on achieving economic self-sufficiency.

Nkrumah emphasized that the ultimate goal of reconstruction

should be the realization of social justice. To this end, he adopted four main positions to guide the reconstruction exercise:

1. It is essential for the government to take the initiative and become actively involved in the development process;
2. new institutions suitable to the African environment ought to be created, because the solutions to Africa's problems will be different from those adopted elsewhere;
3. a socialist, one-party system is the best framework for achieving social justice; and
4. continental unity is essential to development, because no one African country can succeed all by itself.

In the main, these positions formed the basis of Nkrumah's ideology. The ideology is collectivist in its conception of power and authority.

NOTES

1. Nkrumah (1957), 1971: 22, 27 .
2. *Ibid.:* 4445.
3. *Ibid.*
4. Garvey, 1967; also Nkrumah, 1971:45 .
5. Padmore, 1955:128-129.
6. Nkrumah, 1962(a); 1972;1970a.
7. Nkrumah, 1972: passim and xviii, 20, 31, 3 2, 83-84, 95 .
8. Nkrumah 1961(b):92.
9. Nkrumah, 1972.
10. Nkrumah, 1965(b):1x.
11. Ibid.: x, 20-21.
12. Nkrumah, 1965(b):25-26;also 1961:253.
13. Nkrumah, 1970(a):50.
14. Nkrumah, 1 970(a): 165; also 1972:14.
15. Nkrumah, 1969:28.
16. The Spark Publications, 1964:14.
17. Nkrumah, 1970(a):69ff.; 1969:89.
18. Nkrumah, 1969:19, 90, 132.
19. Nkrumah, 1970(a):69-70.
20. *Ibid.*
21. Nkrumah, 1973 :10.
22. Nkrumah, 1970(b):70.
23. Nkrumah, 1972:64-65; 74, 82.
24. Nkrumah, 1961(b): 209.
25. Nkrumah. 1972:126.
26. Nkrumah, 197 O(a): 99-101.
27. Nkrumah, 196 1(b):43.
28. Nkrumah, 1972:68.

29. Nkrumah, 1961: 90 and passim .
30. Nkrumah, 196l(b) :132, 185, also 1973(b) :16.
31. Nkrumah, 1961:218.
32. Nkrumah, 1961(b): 127, 253, and 1972:63.
33. Nkrumah, 1972:xvi, 164ff., also 1969:15, 65.
34. Nkrumah, 196 lb
35. *Ibid.,:* 53.
36. *Ibid.,:* 87-88.
37. *Ibid.,:* 76-78.
38. Nkrumah, 1972:74.
39. Nkrumah, 196 l(b): 158.
40. *Ibid.,:* 63-64.
41. Nkrumah, 1970(a):91-101; also 1969:64-67.

NKRUMAH'S LEADERSHIP STYLE — AN ASSESSMENT FROM A CULTURAL PERSPECTIVE

George P. Hagan

In this paper, I have taken the liberty to define "leadership style" in a way suited to highlighting the socio-cultural dimension of achieved leadership.

Style is generally defined as a manner and method of acting or performing, distinctive or characteristic of an individual, a group, or an epoch; or, as a way or manner of living or behaving that is elegant or in accord with fashion.

Leadership style is, I take it, a leader's manner and method of acting in seeking and entrenching his influence and power with individuals and groups, especially if this manner is considered elegant or in accord with the fashions of the people and the customs of the time. Thus in treating the leadership style of Nkrumah, I have considered it necessary to describe how Nkrumah took over the leadership of the nationalist struggle in the Gold Coast by securing the key position in its vanguard organization, and how, after the break with the United Gold Coast Convention, using certain methods of communication and certain leadership gifts, he consolidated his influence with the peoples of the Gold Coast.

Nkrumah's leadership style changed after independence in the way in which it then became fashionable for him to communicate with the people mainly through institutionalized governmental channels; and I indicate that this new manner eventually led to the collapse of his leadership. By pointing to and emphasizing this change, it becomes easier to define the dominant characteristics of Nkrumah's leadership style.

It is necessary to make two points clear. First, if this paper appears not to delve into issues of substance, it is because style of leadership concerns more of the external forms, symbols and signs used in self-expression and communication, and the manner of getting and using power and influence, than the substance of leadership, or the powers at the leader's disposal. Second, though it is Nkrumah's leadership with which this paper is concerned, this paper brings into focus aspects of Nkrumah's party organization. A leader and his followers are like husband and wife: one can discover a lot about the one from a close observation of the other; especially, when the bond between them is as close as Nkrumah desired his bond with the Convention People's Party to be. "The CPP," he said, "is Nkrumah, and Nkrumah is the CPP."

This paper is not on Nkrumah's personal lifestyle. It is not on Nkrumah's style of government. It is on Nkrumah's style of leadership. It is, therefore, an attempt to portray and assess the leadership of Osagyefo Dr. Kwame Nkrumah in terms of the perceptions, attitudes, modes of thought and action of his followers, and also, in terms of the modalities of leadership of the culture of the people of Ghana. In so doing, it relies on well-known facts and interprets them in an unfamiliar manner. But it also relies on what Ghanaians believed to be facts, or believed to be reasonable to believe to be facts about Nkrumah and the movement he led. Nkrumah's success in mobilizing the people of Ghana for the independence struggle throve as much on myth as on reality; and perhaps the myth was even a more important device for conscientising the people than fact. This paper is therefore also an attempt to draw attention to the importance of the kind of material and interpretations the political scientist might not be inclined to use, and which is yet needed for a fuller understanding of the success and eventual failure of Nkrumah's style and instrumentalities of leadership.

The Making of a Leader—A Prophecy

Nkrumah did not drop into a leadership vacuum. When he returned to the Gold Coast after twelve years of studies abroad

(1935-1947), he came to join a nationalist movement which had evolved a leadership of its own. This leadership had a definite traditional, if not, conservative colour. The most prominent figures in it were connected to chiefly houses and belonged to the professional class. The leadership had an objective Self-government for the Gold Coast, and was set to go. What it lacked was a programme and a person with the organizational ability to mobilize all sections of the community to achieve its goal. Nkrumah was invited to come back to the Gold Coast to provide that programme and fill that organizational vacuum.

If anyone had thought Nkrumah would come home and become a mere cog in someone else's political machinery, the sermon he gave at the Presbyterian Church in Philadelphia, if it had been given in the Gold Coast, should have served to divest him of that idea.

There he intoned his vision, which he recalled years later:

> My text was, 'I saw a new heaven and a new earth' and I reminded the people of how history repeated itself. Just as in the days of the Egyptians, so today God had ordained that certain among the African race should journey westwards to equip themselves with knowledge and experience for the day when they would be called upon to return to their motherland and to use the learning they had acquired to help improve the lot of their brethren . . . I had not realized at the time that I would contribute so much towards the fulfillment of this prophecy.[1]

If the Mosaic leadership model had only as much as flashed through his mind, it would have been a powerful motivating force. In this case, however, Nkrumah had used the allusion to Moses in making a prophecy about himself. And it was not likely that when fate extended a hand of invitation to him, he saw this opportunity as offering him but an errand-boy role in the nationalist movement. Nkrumah's success when he landed on the Gold Coast depended not only on the force of his personality or on his personal conviction in his pre-ordained role, important as these were. It also depended, in practical terms, on his deployment and use of organizational devices, ideas and methods that appeared to owe much, or to be sensitive to the culture of the people. The spontaneity of the people's response might have created in Nkrumah the confidence in the force of his vision as in the pull of his charisma.

The Idea of the Chosen One

People make leaders after their own image, the way Durkheim postulated they make their gods. They perceive or project in their leaders virtues they value — which they themselves do not possess or possess only fractionally. One fact that aided Nkrumah's prospect as a great leader was that, right from his arrival in Ghana, the people of the Gold Coast began to credit him with virtues they sorely wanted to see in their leaders. The prime virtue they sought at this time was the capacity to achieve results, which capacity had to be beheld with the eye of faith before its existence could be demonstrated. The circumstances surrounding Nkrumah's return seemed to have sowed the seeds of such a faith.

It was this realization that lay at the basis of the grievances that the Working Committee had against Nkrumah. They needed to take that power from him or whittle it down, and they searched him — both literally and metaphorically —to discover one good reason to sack him.

Of course by the time the Committee decided to act, Nkrumah's dismissal had long ceased to be a pragmatic proposition. As Nkrumah put it: "It was known that already I had a strong personal following, and it was feared that movement might fail if I left it entirely."[7]

But why would the convention fail if one person left it? The strength of Nkrumah's position was that the Working Committee could not justify Nkrumah's dismissal, when he was already so popular. Nkrumah must himself have read the thinking of the people— at least this is the impression he gave later.

> As far as the rank and file of the UGCC were concerned, the intentions of the Working Committee appeared highly illogical. They felt that if I was considered to be unworthy of the job of general secretary and incapable of managing the affairs of the convention, how was it that I was considered suitable to undertake the job of treasurer? And coupled with this, the words of Danquah were still fresh in their minds, 'if all of us fail you, Kwame Nkrumah will never fail you.'[8]

The delay in giving Nkrumah the sack served his purpose admirably: while the Working Committee feared to sack him, Nkrumah himself must have been uncertain whether he would succeed outside the UGCC. His only guarantee of success, when he broke away, was if he could take away a sizable section of the popular backing of the UGCC. By the time of the eventual break, so effective had been

Nkrumah's campaign to organize the youth to weigh into the leadership struggle that in the end, it appeared, and it was made to look like, it was the youth who had chosen Nkrumah as a leader and compelled him to leave the UGCC.

On the very day on which he ceased to be the General Secretary of the UGCC, the first issue of his paper, *The Accra Evening News,* appeared. This was another venture Nkrumah must have kept away from the Working Committee. If the elders had seen this as an omen, they did not in any case act. It is also surprising that they did not uncover the intensification of Nkrumah's activities and nocturnal tours. Looking back, Nkrumah wrote: "I knew that sooner or later a final split would have to come. I was determined, therefore, to organize things in such a way that when this break came I would have the full support of the masses behind me."[9] And he succeeded in doing this when the split came.

Now then, if Nkrumah had seen his leadership as resting on "divine guidance" as pronounced by J. B. Danquah, he now also had the voice of the people. Nkrumah's consciousness of these two aspects of his leadership considerably influenced his style of leadership.[10] His style was based on his conviction that his power was both sacred and profane. Another element of his style was the use of the masses to gain his ends — he himself giving the impression he had no knowledge of the people's intentions. Of course such tactics would have helped only one who had the gift of foresight and could anticipate moves. And such a gift Nkrumah displayed in the one year he was spared dismissal from the UGCC.

After the break, Nkrumah carefully doctored the perception of his followers. Up till that break, the ordinary people of the Gold Coast had not seen their leaders as a class apart. If they did, they did not see this as a cause for war—a class war. Now Nkrumah described the leaders of the UGCC as the bourgeois, privileged, professional group, and began to cast them in the role of enemy within. From that point, the Gold Coast society became class conscious, and this consciousness became sharper as time went by, and has persisted till this day.

The Spread of the Party— The Great Communicator

Politics is the use of information dissemination in and for the end of controlling people's individual and collective power of action.[11] Without communication, politics is an impossible art. Nkrumah became a leader by his adept use of the instrumentalities of mass communication in the culture of the Gold Coast.

One great asset of Nkrumah as a person was his ability to communicate not only ideas but also sentiment. As a politician, his greatest gift in this regard was his ability to give the people simple slogans and phrases which facilitated the spread of his message and gave their peddlers a sense of a new awareness and importance. What were his vehicles of communication?

In a society divided into the urban and the rural, the literate and the illiterate, with the majority largely rural and illiterate, Nkrumah adopted a strategy for reaching the majority while not neglecting the educated and semi-educated urban located minority. He correctly discerned that political propaganda in a culture in which communication is mainly face-to-face, had to be face-to-face. This meant he had to communicate his ideas through direct contact. He had to see and touch the people, and the people had to see and touch him. His body and his voice became the medium of communication — and that medium became identified with the call to arms and with *independence*. He and the people drew fresh energy from their mutual encounters. Recording his visit to Kumasi in May 1948 he wrote he was given a "tremendous welcome." "A crowd gathered at the station to meet my train and as I stepped from the compartment a burst of cheering greeted me. I was swept off my feet and carried shoulder high to the waiting taxi . . . The cheers of the crowd made me very happy."[12]

Nkrumah's attempt to cover every piece of Gold Coast territory and speak everywhere to all manner of gathering was deliberate. He himself was a willing medium of the spirit of independence. He loved to meet the people, and he loved to draw the crowds. The crowds demonstrated his strength and popular support. And he let everyone know this. Assessing his own method of communication, Nkrumah wrote:

My speeches were usually reported in the papers, and so my words reached people, all over the country, and sometimes abroad. I spoke without notes, sometimes for hours. Some journalists were flattering. They spoke of personal charm, a lively manner and an infectious enthusiasm. What I think more important is the ability to communicate with the people. Not just with any particular class; not only with professional men but with everyone, and at any time. If I have any special gifts in speaking, I count that the greatest.

Nkrumah claimed further that his success depended also on the message he carried:

Perhaps my success as a speaker may also be put down to the fact that my mind is clear and my policy decided. People listening to my speeches throughout the years could not have failed to notice two recurrent themes. The first is freedom of the individual. The second is political independence, not just for Ghana or West Africa, but for all Africa. I do not know how anyone can refuse to acknowledge the right of men to be free.[13]

But Nkrumah communicated also with his body. In the early years, he allowed people to touch him; and he shook hands with everyone — and endlessly, having a word to say with each person. Those he met, shook hands with, and spoke to, came away with a distinct thrill, and never stopped saying to everyone that they had met and shaken hands with Nkrumah. Through this he secured their friendship and long lasting admiration.

For the educated, Nkrumah saw the need for a press, and he founded several. Besides the *Accra Evening News* (established on or about, 6th September, 1948) he established the *Sekond Daily Telegraph* and the *Cape Coast Daily Mail.* The *Accra Evening News* carried his clarion call: "We prefer self-government with danger to servitude with tranquility." That has proved prophetic. Ghana has had a history of dangers: it has had little servitude, but much less tranquility. And the papers lived dangerously, their editors often being carried to court for libel and sedition.

As the papers gained notoriety through court cases, their circulation increased. Looking back, Nkrumah wrote: "My pen, as well as my voice, had entered the campaign."[14] These were the instruments of war in a campaign which had to be bloodless.

Nkrumah probably used the libel cases to indicate that he was fearless and that the fight through the pen did not need less courage than was required to face violence. This might have helped rid the elite and the people generally of a certain traditional and almost pathological fear of court cases *(amanenyasem).*

The newspapers themselves were written in a style which everyone with some education could read, though not all could be expected to understand. They had a combative and at times bombastic style; and they were jingoistic and jargon-filled. While putting forward party material, the papers attacked Nkrumah's opponents with vitriol, exposing them as turn-coats, traitors and enemies of the people.

A special feature of the newspapers was their political use of cartoons. At times the papers sold more for aspersive cartoons, which on occasions filled a whole page or half, than for their verbal news content. While Nkrumah appeared in the cartoons in the best light his opponents were ridiculed as caricatures. Both the language and the images suited the youthful minds of the political broad spectrum.

Because of the restricted scope of newspapers, and the lack of access at that time to radio time, rumors also became an important vehicle of information, misinformation and disinformation; and Nkrumah was not unaware of its force for good or ill. Nkrumah would have been concerned with what proportions of true information to combine with the quantities of disinformation and the carefully prepared misinformation to produce an effective, even if unhealthy, grist for the political gossip mill. It was the task of propaganda secretaries to prepare the combinations suited to local palates and digestion.

Sensational but libelous concoctions which could not be printed were custom-made and "mongered" under the label of confidential "news flash." Rumor became an institutional complement to printable material — it was uncensored; it needed no check on its source or veracity; and each peddler embroidered it according to his or her imagination and powers of rhetoric. Nkrumah himself eventually became a victim of this dangerous instrument which he took from the "mouth-to-mouth" or "hearsay" culture of the people and sharpened with an expert hand. And he bequeathed his style of political journalism and the use of rumor to Ghana's political culture; and, in some senses, these two broadcasting media have become sensational as the proper channels of communication have fallen under exclusive government control.

Communication: The Use of Symbols

Another aspect of our cultural heritage which Nkrumah carefully exploited was the Ghanaian love of the external symbols of collective and individual identification. Just as the *Asafo*[15] has its colors, so did the party he organized have its colors and flag. And just as the clan has its totemic symbol, so did the party.

Nkrumah gave his CPP a "flag" in colors Ghanaians loved— red, white and green - and Ghanaians had an intuitive traditional understanding of the meanings of the colors: Red for blood, danger, determination, military alertness, sacrifice; White for purity, hope and success; and Green for youthfulness (a virgin is called *Obaabun,* a green woman), fertility, and viability. In physical representation, in some places, Red stands for the Earth *(Ntwema);* White for the sea or sun; and Green for the vegetation—the fundamental elements or sources of life.

The party's colors were made into shirts, caps, flags; and they were painted on propaganda vans and the fronts of houses. The umbiquity of the party was made highly visible through these.

Those who had suffered persecution for the party's sake had the symbol of their martyrdom. They wore white caps with the sign "P G" written on it. The Prison Graduate (PG) cap was proudly worn by the few, including Nkrumah himself, who had been imprisoned in the struggle for independence. Going to prison became as nothing to the members of the CPP.

The party selected the red cockerel for its symbol, and though many joked about it (that one day the party would be put under a basket, was one such joke one heard) the advantage gained by the CPP in the use of that symbol was overwhelming. And the advantage was on account of the cultural notions associated with the cock.

a. The cockerel was known in every place and had ritual uses in virtually every ethnic group.
b. The cock crows at the crack of dawn—an ever ready reminder of wakefulness and a call to a new dawn of life.
c. The symbolism of the cock was most explicit in proverbs. And a few might here serve to show the significance of that choice.
  i.   When the chicken drinks it shows to God its dependence on God's power.
  ii. No one buys a cock for the cock to crow in someone else's village—no cheating or exploitation.
  iii. The hen knows the break of a new day, but waits for the cock to announce it—one must look to leaders to lead or for them to give the right information or to announce time; order in society.
  iv. The fingers of the hen do not crush its chicks— leaders must tread gently on their followers.
  v.   And Ghanaians express thanks by saying: "When at break of day, the cock crows, know that it is I offering you thanks."

In the CPP it was understood that whoever the Party chose as a candidate in an election had to be voted for without question. This loyalty was translated as loyalty to the Party symbol. Thus the rank and file was told that even if the Party stuck the red-cockerel on a goat (this was their language) that goat had to be voted for. This was a way of ensuring the Party's victory at polls on the strength of the popularity of the Party and its leader rather than of the candidate at the constituency level.

Besides these collective symbols, Nkrumah made himself into

a symbol of the people's physical, mental and spiritual force, through the use of certain articles. He himself projected himself as an excellent specimen of humanity. He much later concealed his myopia and used contact lens, for, traditionally, a leader could have no deformity, blindness was a tabooed sickness for a chief.

Describing his meeting with his mother upon his arrival, Nkrumah referred to the only physical feature he would ever describe as a handicap:

> The first shock she had was when I smiled at her and she noticed my teeth. When I left her my two top front teeth were divided by a fairly wide gap. In the United States I found this a handicap whenever I made a public speech. . .[16]

Nkrumah referred to the gap in his top incisors which forced him to replace the first two teeth, probably knowing and confident that it added to his looks in the minds of the people. That gap is considered a sign of beauty. His pigeon gait was beautiful. The name "Show Boy" summed up the people's perception of his physical adequacy.

Nkrumah's favorite colour was white. He carried a swish or horse-tail on occasions. His white handkerchief became proverbial. With it he roused the people to great ecstatic ovations anywhere he went. People thought of Nkrumah's white handkerchief as his magic wand for mesmerizing the crowd. He had a walking stick to which was attributed, I recollect, all kinds of powers. He did not part his hair (a whiteman's habit) - often making it look matted. These recall the accoutrements of traditional fetish priests; and Nkrumah made himself more or less into a "sacred" figure. He cut such a distinct figure in this kind of apparel that the youth started imitating him. School boys would no longer part their hair—doing this in a spirit of open defiance; and headmasters had the task of enforcing the old habit of neatly combing, parting and brushing the hair, a practice that soon became identified as *colo*.[17]

Nkrumah had an infectious *joie de vivre,* a gift he shared with his countrymen, and he consciously or unconsciously exploited it. His face, which at rest looked serious and even a little somber if not sad, glowed and radiated warmth as his lips parted and let off shafts of toothy smiles which warmed every heart.

It was in this spirit of joy in living that he led the struggle to set his people free, not giving them the impression the road ahead could be full of adversity.

The battle for self-government went on, not with weapons and bloodshed, but with words. The wonder is that new words could be found for the ceaseless reiteration of the call for freedom. I once told a gathering of dancers that they were dancing their way to self-government. They might have replied that I was talking my way to Freedom.[18]

It was with a shock that this country realized that a nation might dance its way to freedom, but might not dance its way through the thorny problems of self-government. Yet this is part of Ghana's political culture. We do not only dance around serious problems we laugh at them, very much to the annoyance of outsiders. But no one has ever suggested that our smiling faces suggest lack of resolution or determination to solve our problems.[19]

Blitz—The Propaganda Vans and the Hailers

Nkrumah realized the importance of keeping communication between himself and party agents throughout the length and breadth of Ghana.[20] He introduced propaganda vans which gave speed to his agents. They were painted with the party's colors and symbol. This was an innovation that caught the imagination of the people. In their traditions they had the gong-gong beater who went around to communicate the chief's laws and wishes to them. The vans did the same, but with greater power and mobility—and with music. Occasionally, they found local people speaking through this modern device.

The vans brought the news of Ghana's independence struggle directly to the ears of everyone. This was a struggle in which radio and television played no part — the former was a government monopoly, and the latter had not yet been born. The radio boxes were few, however, and they were largely in the rural areas, and had the greatest impact there. The control he had in the rural areas made up for the uncertain grip he had in some urban areas where people were subject to all kinds of propaganda counter-currents. This has left the impression that the rural folks could not be relied upon to vote with, and for, the intellectual class in the society, a belief that has created the conviction that the ballot is not used properly and responsibly, and, therefore, cannot he relied upon as an effective mode of mandating a party to rule. From being an urban based party, the CPP spread like wild fire and found its greatest support in the rural areas where apart from confrontations with the chiefs, it had no challenge. Thrown into the balance were Nkrumah's personal visits to the rural areas and the mystique and charisma that enveloped his person.

Mystique and Mysticisms—Christian and African Notions of Mystical Powers

The mystique that surrounded Nkrumah has a peculiar cultural undertone. He himself did much to foster the idea that he had mystical powers, but whatever he did, he took as its premise the ideas which the people had.

The mystique associated with Nkrumah had two strains. It had a Christian strain, and a traditional strain. The Christian strain took its source from the belief that Nkrumah had been picked at the beach and educated by a Catholic priest who had gone there to contemplate. It was entirely by divine coincidence that he had an education. Then it was known that he had been to Amisano, a Catholic Seminary near Cape Coast. Some said he went there to train to be a priest. Others, that he went to teach. Whatever was the case Nkrumah's three years at the Catholic Seminary (and in actual fact he was there to teach at a Teacher Training College) before he left for the USA were used to impress people with his love of spiritual and contemplative life. And it was also indicative of his spiritual calling which, as it turned out, was not to be a priest but a leader of his people.

In the USA he had led a hard life, but besides studying and taking the degree of Bachelor of Sacred Theology at the Lincoln Theological Seminary, he had led a priestly life, preaching to several congregations.

During the struggle, Nkrumah liked to reinforce this notion of his spirituality by retreats conducted in secluded places; sometimes along the beach. Saint Francis of Assisi must have held a very strong attraction for Nkrumah.

In the minds of the people, he was the chosen leader, the anointed of God who sought to renew his spiritual strength through solitary contemplation. "Pictures" and cartoons appeared of him kneeling or sitting to receive from Jesus or the angels his crown or scepter. Many party songs were Christian religious songs; and rallies often began with prayers—Christian, Muslim and traditional. The culmination of this was the eventual use of the word "Messiah" to describe him in his role as "Redeemer of his people" from colonial bondage.

The African mystical notions associated with him arose out of the fact that Nkrumah was an Nzema. The Nzema are famed for witchcraft. In the mind of the average Gold Coaster, Nzema witchcraft, besides being powerful — perhaps, the most powerful witchcraft power anywhere—was reputed to be capable of being used for good ends. Besides Nkrumah's staring gaze under which people squirmed, or at least blinked, his personality and voice inspired intense love or fear. And his fearlessness confirmed him as having the natural gift of every Nzema in exceptional good measure.

Some people believed that his mother's witchcraft complemented his and protected him. And they saw Nkrumah's haste for independence as an attempt to gain his objectives before the death of his mother which would leave him weakened and exposed to his enemies. This mystique about Nkrumah's mother was more inflamed because few ever confessed to having ever seen her, and one never saw the mother of the leader in pictures.

No one was prepared to say Nkrumah walked on his head at night. But quite a few people were prepared to believe that he had power to make himself invisible, power to disappear when he found himself in danger, and power to be in several places at once.

This belief grew because while Nkrumah was in jail (25th January, 1950), his influence was as palpable as if he were not behind bars. The explanation which Nkrumah offered for the party's continued vitality when he was the King's guest, was that he continued to give directions for party organization, and Gbedemah faithfully and authoritatively kept the party machinery turning. It is not, however, impossible that Nkrumah might have had a few nights out of prison — the prison guards and police often displayed nationalistic sympathies — but this is generally discounted.

One account of Nkrumah's disappearing act given by someone who was then close to him is worth recording here. According to this account, certain that he had seen Nkrumah in his house at Kokomlemle, a Lebanese who lived in a house across the road phoned the police who were on the look out for him. A platoon of police scoured all the rooms to find Nkrumah, but Nkrumah was nowhere to be found. The Lebanese swore he had seen Nkrumah. Where was Nkrumah? He had disappeared.

What according to this account had happened was this. As soon as the alarm went about the arrival of the police, the women there quickly dressed Nkrumah in women's clothes, complete with headkerchiefs and make-up, and Nkrumah succeeded in making his escape when the women were driven out of the house. It is not unlikely that this was how Nkrumah contrived to pass through hostile crowds and police cordons and barriers undetected and also materialized in places where his arrival had not been noticed.

Whether true or untrue, these ideas that the Gold Coast people had of Nkrumah's powers helped to swing them behind him. Few who were close to him dared say things or scheme behind him. Those close to him generally remained faithful to him till dissensions arose among the following through competition for posts and the perquisites of office. Kofi Baako, of blessed memory, summed it all up in Parliament during a debate on a motion to honor Nkrumah on the occasion of his 52nd birthday.

It was said of Aggrey that the man is a saint,
damn his colour;
let it be said of Nkrumah that the man is a God-sent,
damn his race.[21]

Nkrumah was perhaps aware of these notions people had of him, and fanned them in his *Autobiography*.

Related to this was another gift of extreme importance to a leader. Nkrumah had the ability to identify the personal gifts of individuals and use them where and when necessary. Thus the motley crowd that followed him had the feeling, almost to a person, that each had a peculiar role, and that his gift was recognized and needed by the leader. What enhanced this gift of Nkrumah's was that he saw the sterling qualities of men and women, even when these qualities were obscured by darker character traits through which no ordinary man would see the jewel of a person's character.

Further, Nkrumah was able to mix characters of different backgrounds, and often succeeded in creating a team in which each played for all and all for each.[26] Having created such a team, however, he found it difficult to alter its composition even when this became an obvious necessity. Also he saw those who left the team as traitors. And this was a weakness.

This gift was evident when one looked at the individuals that he led with. He had men of great experience—Agbeli Gbedemah, Kojo Botsio, Hutton Mills, Ako Adjei, Casely Hayford; and men of little or no experience—students who had had no time to finish school, but were brilliant, enthusiastic—Kwesi Plange, Kofi Baako. He had highly educated people, and people who had little education. He had traditional believers, Muslims, Christians of various denominations, and professed atheists and priests. He had wealthy men and women and very poor people. He put them together into one family. Nkrumah crowned these gifts with his ability to take decisions — an ability which, over-exercised, proved his undoing. The decision-making process he adopted has been described by some of his followers. Nkrumah is said to have liked to discuss issues with individuals as a matter of form. Before putting them before a committee, he liked to expose his ideas to people. He did this to help him take his own line, or get his line accepted so that at a committee meeting he might not appear to be ramming things down the throats of everyone else. Thus, ideas that came from others, Nkrumah seized upon as if they were his own. And he happily also allowed to pass the impression that what he held most dearly and pushed hardest actually came from someone else. He sought to avoid confrontational and divisive discussions and therefore sought to get people to the same point of view before meeting.

The Nature of Nkrumah's People

A populist, Nkrumah relied on the lower classes to form his party, the CPP. The notion of the masses as constituting the source of power was a relatively new idea in the Gold Coast. Prior to Nkrumah, the intelligentsia had had discussion groups as their forum. The widest popular movement ever canvassed was the Rate Payers Association, which more or less confined the franchise to a property owning or tax paying group, and adopted a means test that certainly excluded the bulk of the people from direct involvement in the political process of the day. The age hurdle of 25 also meant that a large percentage of the young tax payers could not vote. Kwesi Plange (1950) representing the CPP tabled a motion that amended this.

Nkrumah turned the power structure on its head. He asserted that power was not with the chief, power was not with the educated elite — certainly not exclusively; power was not with rate payers; power was with the masses. If the term "the masses" had ever been used to refer to any section of the Gold Coast society, Nkrumah now gave it a new significance. It referred to the workers and people— so long as they did not belong to the book people; the bourgeoisie, the mercantile and professional groups. But this was not all.

Nkrumah took the women—even the illiterate ones—abroad to see the world. They flew their flag side by side with the national flag, as it were. The younger ones he advanced in the party and government. Nkrumah gave Ghana not only the first woman tractor driver, the first woman police and soldier, but the first woman District Commissioner, High Court Judge and the first woman Minister of State.

Solidarity

Nkrumah built the CPP as a mass party in which solidarity was manifested at every given opportunity. Nkrumah transformed the political culture of the Gold Coast by what was another innovation—

the mass rally. He made use of large assembly halls for several speeches, but when he wanted to display the collective strength of his party, he used the open air rally — something, again, very close to the traditional Asafo gathering at their totem posts.

The rally had its own qualities as a mass gathering. It created close bodily contact and individual freedom of action was restricted. Not only was one shoved and pushed in all directions physically, one was also subjected to the emotional currents in the audience. Also the rally had people on their feet, singing, dancing and joking. A sitting audience could not do anything but listen rather passively. And the remarkable feature of the CPP rally was that the platform had not just the elite on it, but also the ordinary man. Any individual member of the audience could be asked to come on stage and make a contribution. Rallies began with Christian, and Muslim Prayers and Traditional libations. If anything like this had happened before Nkrumah's time, it was certainly not on this phenomenal scale and intensity .

But rallies were more or less for the faithful who took the trouble to go to the rally grounds. To manifest the party's strength, Nkrumah's party used — the Picnic or Parade, by which, like the Asafo, the CPP turned out and displayed its numerical strength and its different wings—the youth, women, the workers and the entire rank and file. The long routes these parades took was to enable the stay-at-homes to see the CPP as it was. The slogan the CPP loved to shout was: "We are many, they are few." And no one was left in any doubt about this.

Funerals became another kind of situation in which the CPP manifested its solidarity. In fact, at times the CPP appeared to displace the bereaved family to an extent to which it began to become the "family" of those who belonged to it. Many families were happy to sit aside and watch the party display.

Having given themselves an ethos and solidarity relations more or less like the *Asafo* or the Clan, complete with its songs and rituals and priests, the CPP unwittingly gave rise to two tendencies in Gold Coast society as a whole. First, members of the same family had to belong to the same party. Where they did not, serious, even permanent divisions developed within families and lineages. The Mercers must have had a great deal of trouble. Lawyer Mercer, one of the twins, was in the CPP and became Ghana's High Commissioner to Great Britain. His twin brother was out of it. And a lot of people talked about this. Second, one could not socialize with members of other political persuasions, especially if they were openly identified with opposed political camps. As a result the CPP had become almost an endogamous organization; the sensational exception having been created by Nkrumah's own son who married the daughter of one of Nkrumah's stalwart opponents.

By the nature of the party he founded, Nkrumah had succeeded in creating a cohesive phalanx against imperialism; but he had also divided the national front and Gold Coast society at several levels, and permanently.

Image Building

Nkrumah must have been aware that to lead the people of the Gold Coast he had to avoid all signals which would create tensions that would fracture the popular front. In this regard he was fortunate in one respect. Deriving from a relatively small ethnic group, it was unlikely that anyone would see his leadership as likely to lead to the domination of one ethnic group over all the others. Even so, Nkrumah distanced himself considerably from his kinsmen and his ethnic group to the extent that, at some point, it appeared it would create disaffection among his own people.

Nkrumah must have been aware that this distancing was necessary in a society whose segmentary character compelled a leader to be above all factional groups though he be a member of one of them. To strengthen this image as a national leader, he made two disavowals which stayed in the mind of the public.

Nkrumah had been brought up a Roman Catholic. He allowed his mother to receive visits from a priest and a lay woman who gave her religious instructions. Many of the men and women who surrounded him were Catholics. Yet he disavowed his Catholic faith and called himself "a non-denominational Christian."[29]

Nkrumah's break with the Catholic Church must have occurred back in the United States where he moved among Afro-Americans who were predominantly of Protestant persuasion. When he returned to the Gold Coast, he could have identified with Presbyterianism as he had done in the States, but he did not. By calling himself a nondenominational Christian he was not just denying his long standing affiliation with the Catholic church; he was also, in effect, denying any links with any organized Christian group. He thus avoided the trouble of either being with one group and appearing to be against all other groups, or being in one group and sharing himself among all the others — an almost impossible task. Not surprisingly Islam became the only religion that some people attempted to use as the basis of political organization in the Gold

Coast, and that organization was opposed to Nkrumah. Nkrumah moved quickly to ban the organization .

This same attempt to avoid identifying with, or attaching himself to, any group must have been his motive for not marrying at all during the period of the nationalist movement — and marrying outside Ghana when he felt he had to. Nkrumah would only explain this in terms of his early fear of women: "In those days my fear of women was beyond all understanding." By the time he came back to the Gold Coast he had "outgrown that feeling towards women."[30] And, yet, kept away from them. He did this "for something deeper" as he wrote. As one can discern, Nkrumah would have been concerned not only with his personal freedom, but with a desire to avoid the same structural problem he identified with being a member of the Catholic church. For, marriage would have tied him down to one ethnic group thus alienating all other groups, or it would have multiplied his problems by alienating all women. Marrying from all ethnic groups was another way out of his predicament, but this would have taxed his energies.[31]

By marrying outside Ghana, Nkrumah avoided these problems and further succeeded in projecting his greater affection for Africa, and uniting Africa north and south of the Sahara.

Transformation of Leadership Role and Style: The International Dimension— Higher Leadership Levels[32]

The image of Nkrumah underwent a radical transformation after independence. This was because his status and role in the nation had changed. At first, Nkrumah was a leader of a party. He became the Leader of Government Business; and then Prime Minister and Head of State of Ghana. This change occurred as much in Nkrumah's own perception of himself as in his followers' perception of him. Not only had Nkrumah risen in status; he had, through that rise, also distanced himself from the rank and file of the people. And this distance became bigger as his leadership acquired and added international dimension.

After independence Nkrumah ceased to be a leader within the restricted universe of Ghana. He had pledged on the eve of Independence to seek the total liberation of the whole continent, without which Ghana's independence was meaningless. His quest for continental freedom meant he had assumed the leadership of African liberation. His position in Africa was unique: the first blackman to assume leadership of a modern state. And this distinction made Nkrumah the model of achievement—a man of unequelled distinction and the unchallenged spokesman of freedom for Africa.

Again, having led Ghana to independence, Nkrumah chose to let Ghana stay in the Commonwealth. This gave him a role in an international forum of leaders of practically all races, and gave him a voice in the transformation and preservation of the Commonwealth, helping that comity of nations to define its new identity.

The Commonwealth was a reality. At independence there was no grouping of Independent African nations. Nkrumah helped to create the OAU. The surprising thing is that the Commonwealth and the English speaking members of the OAU did not see themselves as a group within the Pan-African movement, though within the Commonwealth the African group began to see themselves as a distinct interest group and often took African issues to that forum on a collective basis. Nkrumah helped to initiate the new trend in world politics for the third world: belonging to two international groupings that often had no love lost between them, the reasoning being that each gave such a small nation a peculiar benefit.

This is a style of leadership that must have helped to set up the non-aligned movement which gave Nkrumah another dimension of leadership. The non-aligned movement embraced nations or states of Marxist Socialist leaning, as well as Capitalist leaning. It brought together leaders from different countries, languages and cultures. It brought together leaders who were members of other political blocks whose interests did often clash. This was still a bigger forum than the Commonwealth, and a different universe and called for a higher level of leadership. Nkrumah thus assisted in creating a world in which international friendships were so concatenated that there could not be deep cleavages—the friend of a friend was not necessarily a friend, but he was certainly less an enemy. The ideological cleavage between East and West had a middle ground.

One impact that this ascent to international leadership made on Nkrumah's image at home was that it placed him far beyond the reach of the ordinary man in Ghana. For one thing, the ordinary man in the street could not have seen how his own interest would be served by his external ventures. Indeed the opposition succeeded in demonstrating that the increasingly intractable economic conditions at home were the result not only of Nkrumah's reduced interest in the management of the nation's business, but also of his deliberate diversion of scarce financial resources to foster an ambition for international leadership which demonstrably created more enemies than friends among leaders of African nations and among Ghana's traditional friends elsewhere.

A successful foreign policy is one that a nation can see to foster the nation's self-interest. A foreign policy which is too idealistic or too unclear in the definition of its material objectives is pursued at the risk of losing the support of the electorate. To have clarified his leadership role on the world platform in relation to Ghana's interest, a clear prioritization of objectives was necessary —the immediate objectives, the medium range objectives, and the long term objectives should have been spelt out, and made known to the public. Nkrumah did not succeed in doing this. But there was another aspect of the transformation of the leadership role in terms of its new dimensions.

Nkrumah, the great communicator, appeared now to speak over the people's heads to a wider audience—a world audience. Government business made less time available for party rallies. The people began to see less of him. In fact, Nkrumah appeared to have become so international that more often than not he spoke to the people of Ghana from airport gangways on his way to and from a foreign country. Members of organizations and school children could not see him except at airports or along the streets as he met and drove past with international dignitaries. And as the domestic scene became more disturbed, international visits appeared to be a way of diverting attention from the burning issues at home and providing the people with a tension release valve. It had become difficult for ordinary Ghanaians to meet Nkrumah face-to-face.

It is worth noting that the style of leadership which Nkrumah developed as an international statesman differed from the style of a traditional ruler. The traditional leader stayed at home. The simple practical reason behind this, though ritual ones are offered for this, is that in the absence of the cat the mice come out to play, and when beads break in front of an elder none gets lost. Not to add that the wandering child does not witness her mother's funeral. Nkrumah learnt the truth of this on his way to Hanoi.

Leader of Thought

As an international leader and spokesman for Africa, Nkrumah had to articulate the urgent concerns of the people of Africa to the world.

His first message was freedom or self-government for the colonial peoples of Africa. Thus when Ghana became free he said that "The Independence of Ghana is meaningless until linked with the total liberation of Africa." He put this quest into a book: *I Speak of*

Freedom. But, then, he had to answer the question: what was to be Africa's future, considering exigencies of the peoples who would become free.

Nkrumah saw that strength lay in unity. And he therefore asserted that "Africa Must Unite." The problem of African unity occupied his dreams till the end of his life. What he sought was something which Akan language equipped him to see as a distinct possibility. Abibiman (The Black Nation) had long been a subject of national songs in Ghana.

Nkrumah identified the major forces militating against the realization of this dream. He named one "Neo-colonialism" and described it as the use of economic power to control the political fortunes of Independent African states, while Africans maintained a semblance of independence.[33] Nkrumah feared that an exploitative world economic system and Africa's dependence on world commodity markets and international financial management and technology as source of economic development would rob African states of the power to take their own decisions. In this he has been amply justified.

Nkrumah might have added a rider to his axiom of neo-colonialism; namely, that the degree to which African states will weaken, and the extent of their dependency on international agencies, would correlate directly to the extent to which Africans mismanage their own affairs. In other words while Nkrumah claimed for Africans "the right to manage or mismanage ourselves" he should have added a caution, that mismanagement was the surest way of putting Africans back in the clutches of the more powerful economic powers.

For Nkrumah the way of attaining unity lay in recognizing the need to cultivate in every African an awareness of Africa's distinct identity. In place of the dependency mentality, "colonial mentality," which Nkrumah named as the second major obstacle to unity, Nkrumah saw the need to posit an ideology or a myth of African's self-consciousness. Whence *Consciencism* (1963) which shocked the world till "conscientisation" became a popular revolutionary word.

It was clearly in this line of thought — to maintain Africa's identity and independence of thought in a world in which the dominant powers see small nations as either for or against them — that he pronounced the principal axiom of Ghana's foreign policy: nonalignment. And this principle has become the policy principle of most African states—even those that are more or less aligned. These then were the dominant ideas Nkrumah originated as his position in the world compelled him to spell out more clearly his vision of the African role in the world.

The Party Transformed—Its Problems

Nkrumah's ideas were clearly of a greater significance for the outside world than for the world of Ghana. Yet Nkrumah could not neglect Ghana. Internally, the new idea he put forward as a serious proposition was that Ghana needed to be conscious of its Africanness as far as political culture was concerned. And he postulated that since the Western type of democracy based on a multi-party system had no kinship with any political system in Ghana or elsewhere in Africa, it was bound to fail. Nkrumah averred that the Western parliamentary model was unsuited to the pace of development African nations required. He proposed, therefore, that Ghana should be a one party state. Not stopping to ask whether the one-party state was also African, Nkrumah proceeded to bring the one-party state into being.

It is necessary to point out here that a clear manifestation of change in Nkrumah's leadership arose out of the use of more of the power of legislation than that of persuasion. And an aspect of this change was the use of the coercive forces of government—the police and the army to gain his ends.

To introduce the one-party state Nkrumah could have used persuasion to get all parties to agree. At least, he should have tried to call a national conference of all parties so as to be seen to be consulting all opinions on this issue. But he did not.

Further, Nkrumah had at least two alternative paths he could have pursued: either to try by persuasion to merge all parties, making them lose their individual identities, or abolish all parties but one. In the event, Nkrumah chose the latter. Its consequence was that, since the CPP had an ethos more or less like the *Asafo,* all other parties were made to feel they were losing their distinct identity to join another *Asafo* or family in which they would be considered strangers and second class members, or those not of the "royal lineage" (the founding group). The one-party state was thus inaugurated in total disregard of the feelings of Nkrumah's opponents.

By the time of this move, moreover, the party divide had become a blood feud divide, due to the violence of the NLM days and the subsequent harsh reprisals with which the opposition was put down. The one-party state therefore flew in the face of social facts.

Having decided to make the CPP the one-party within Ghana, Nkrumah also decided it should be the central and supreme body within the nation.[34] To many Ghanaians not identified with the CPP, this meant, if you were not a member of the party you had a lower status in the society, and your allegiance to the nation was suspect.

And yet the CPP was obviously not in such a state of strength that it alone could bear the heavy burden it was required to carry.

Nkrumah had his fears.[35] First, already a cleavage had emerged in the CPP. There had been factional strife, I am told, between the followers of Nkrumah's two lieutenants, Botsio and Gbedemah, and the departure of Gbedemah is thought by some to have weakened the party. A further serious weakening of the party later occurred when for some reason Nkrumah sacked Botsio.

Second, a generation gap had developed in the CPP between the Old Guard and new comers. Some of the youth who were seen by the aging foundation members of the party as opportunists and fortune seekers were favored by Nkrumah, and the Old Guard did not like it much.

Third, a "competence gap" had also developed in the CPP. The burden of government demanded competence and intellectual equipment; and not enough men in the party leadership had the competence to make the party capable of being supreme without the help of new hands. Younger and brighter elements were introduced into the party hierarchy and parliament and encouraged by Nkrumah to the chagrin of the old hands. These were serious internal problems for the CPP.

Fourth, careerism in party work had replaced voluntarism in the party. Graduates of the Winneba Ideological Institute became an articulate self-conscious group in the party; and they thought they had a right to fill party posts.

Fifth, wealth differentials had emerged in stark form—often on account of the corrupt practices of the higher party functionaries.

And sixth, the party structures had become static. A party which claimed to take its power from the people should have had a mechanism by which the people would have elected the party's officers, even at the highest level. This would have offered the younger party followers a way of climbing to the top without having to seek favors from the top—a practice which created a stimulus to clientship and factionalism within the party hierarchy.

Elections would also have placed in the hands of the people a powerful device for eliminating from office individuals the public judged to be abusing their positions in the party and government. Without this, discipline had to come from the top alone. And Nkrumah created hatred for himself with every disciplinary action he took. There had been discussions of the possibility of instituting elections in the CPP, but it had been dropped for fear it might divide the party. But, without this, the party could not renew itself; and interest in it began to die.

Now, all these problems occurred at a time when already Ghana was experiencing some of the effects of Nkrumah's educational policy. Such had been the spread of higher education in Ghana that the CPP propaganda against the educated class was beginning to be counter-productive. Gradually, most districts of Ghana were getting their own graduates and "beentos" (Ghanaian slang for those who have been abroad). Most villages had secondary school graduates and teachers who could counter the party's propaganda in the rural areas.

Nkrumah had seen the change coming, and he had sought more and more to identify himself with the intellectuals in his bid to give them confidence in his interest in them. His propaganda machinery was, however, too late in catching on as demonstrated on the Legon campus in 1963. The younger elite, the university students and their younger brothers, gradually saw themselves as opposed to the party and the government; an opportunity lost. This trend could have been countered if the party had not transformed its political education strategy.

Having put party education in a college, the Winneba Ideological School, the party lowered its interest in the mass education of the people, especially the rural folk. Nkrumah attended fewer rallies after Independence especially after the Accra bomb throwing episodes; and practically none at all after Kulungugu. He became isolated, speaking through the radio and, subsequently, the TV which the party had virtually monopolized. These devices were confined to urban areas and Nkrumah's strength lay in the rural areas. The people who were the source of his inspiration were cut off. They no longer saw their leader face-to-face, and he could never be assured of what support he had in the populace. When he was overthrown, divinity appeared to have left him and the people to have withdrawn. But had the rural people withdrawn? The rural areas now complain that only Accra soldiers and populace make and unmake regimes— because of their demands for imported goods. Governments in power either focus on the rural people and suffer from the insidious propaganda of the urban dwellers; or they satisfy urban dwellers and do nothing for the rural people.

These problems aside, the CPP failed to evolve acceptable modalities of interaction between the party and some of the institutions of state that had every reason to consider themselves supreme in the state structure. In fact by declaring a one-party state and making the CPP supreme, Nkrumah merely succeeded in creating institutional opposition between the CPP and the vital organs of state and nation: the civil service, the army and police, and the TUC.

The Civil Service

Nkrumah would have liked to have party men in top civil service posts. He did not have such men in the party, so he compelled the men at the post to receive party education. But this did not make for a happy state of mind.[36]

At the regional and district level, the District and Regional Commissioners were replaced by Party cadres most of whom had little or no education at all. Government business therefore suffered from incompetence and neglect. And there was in some cases uncontrolled interference of party men in government business.

The Army

Nkrumah tried to introduce party education into the army. However, aware that this would take time, he set up the special and privileged Presidential Guard in the army, and, by so doing, alienated the bulk of the army. The Presidential Guard was not a CPP core; but they were made to appear to be identified with the party especially in their use of arms and equipment from Russia and China whose personnel were in the country believed to be training the special army core. The Police were equally alienated through the setting of the Special Branch which was loaded with semi-educated party members.

The TUC

The Trades Union Committee was in concept a wing of the CPP. But the workers' interest had not been closely identified with the party's programme. Was the party to carry out the TUC programme or vice versa? Furthermore, though structurally the TUC was said to be a wing of the CPP there were many elements in the TUC who were not members of the CPP. When seeking the workers' interest therefore the TUC displayed workers' solidarity, not party solidarity, and it became opposed to the CPP. Towards the end, Nkrumah had a lot of trouble controlling it, going to the extent of detaining some of its most prominent leaders.

Whatever might have been the failure of Nkrumah, the most staggering failure of leadership judgement was to have made the party supreme when it least could take on the burden, and when it had not carefully evolved a modality of coexistence with the major centres of power in the modern state. For in each of these centres there was an ethos, and a corporate spirit that the party had not modified or penetrated. And the party had failed to reach a rational accommodation with them. This, however, was nothing compared to the alienation of the people.

An Assessment of Nkrumah's Leadership Style—Analysis

How might we judge Nkrumah's leadership style? Nkrumah identified the youth and women, the poor and the illiterate, the urban worker and the rural dweller as his target group, and he oriented himself to them. He played on the people's perception, using the traditional modes of face-to-face communication. He used the force of his personality to enforce belief in what he believed to be his own mystical or psychic powers. He initiated new trends in thought and behavior, yet based on the people's culture. He captured the thought and the imagination of his target groups.

Nkrumah's mode of life and conduct emphasized equality between leaders and followers; and it gave the impression of great personal humility. He fostered the communalistic way of life in his party. He carved an image that made it easy to avoid divisions in his following. He remained single during the struggle and disavowed institutional Christianity. He did not forget that sexuality and physical force were potent human forces not to be suppressed. He manipulated information and, as has often been said, he always sought to keep one step ahead of his opponents. He played the part of the folkloric Kwaku Ananse, the Hare, or the Tortoise, as dictated by the needs of the moment, relying on his strong sense of foresight. His style was initially informal and intimate.

Nkrumah's face-to-face and personal style was such that he focused, or appeared to focus, on the individual even in the crowd. When waving to the crowd he would turn and wave frantically in one direction giving about a hundred people the impression, at once, that he had recognized them, each particularly, in the crowd. When talking to the individual he concentrated his gaze on the face of the individual giving him his full attention. One had the impression that no one else really mattered at that moment.

Nkrumah retained the faithful allegiance of many because he also discerned and recognized individual ability; and he respected merit and rewarded it. Those whose merits he recognized, he gave ample trust, and he exacted in return trust and hard work by throwing them great challenges. Nkrumah exploited the talents of all the men he brought round him by emphasizing team work. He built up great solidarity among his men and through their mutual support neatly covered the individual weaknesses of his men.

Nkrumah's leadership style underwent a tremendous change from the time he became Leader of Government Business and, subsequently, President. The change was on account of change of roles and functions.

First, Nkrumah changed from a leader to become a ruler. He was no longer exclusively for the party. He had no longer to rely only on his own party men. The civil servants around him appeared to be nearer him than were his party officials. Nkrumah had to take advice from the civil servants and from his party men; and these often clashed. The incompetence of some of his party men became all too apparent to him and he must have then started pushing them into the background, where the running of the state was concerned.

Second, as a ruler, Nkrumah had acquired instrumentalities of power not dependent on the people's will. He had the army and the police at his command. He could enact laws against his opponents—and these often caught friends too. This meant he had become less dependent on the party. However, he could not use the army and the police as he could the party.

Third, Nkrumah had now at his disposal the communication channels which the colonial regime had used: radio, subsequently, the TV. He used these rather than the propaganda vans. The effect was that Nkrumah's communication style began to be impersonal and long distance, emphasizing the distance which his role transformation had brought. The rallies became fewer and his personal contacts with ordinary people became formal.

Fourthly, Nkrumah's official engagements meant that he had to adopt a certain style of life to project Africa's pride. His profile rose, and this affected his style of presenting himself. The gimmicks had to drop. He used Dinner Jackets and Lounge suits more often than *fugu;* and posh official cars and not taxis. The people no longer carried him. State protocol was controlling the president's movements and manner of behavior.

Fifthly, Nkrumah had given his followers a down to earth—bread and butter, health and clothing—interpretation of the benefits of freedom. As he became more and more engrossed in pushing Ghana's role outside in Africa and the world, he began to speak over the heads of his followers, and their interests and his began to diverge.

The net result of all this was that to gain access to Nkrumah, the people, the membership of the party rank and file, had to pass through individuals close to Nkrumah. By the time of independence therefore the individuals close to Nkrumah had carved up their own sub-constituencies within the party, and party unity and solidarity had begun to collapse.

The party had in all senses collapsed before Nkrumah was overthrown, torn by several internal differences. Most marked were:

a. a generation gap: the old guard against the new boys;

b. a competence gap: the party ranks versus the professional groups;

c. a communication gap: the lower ranks versus the top party echelon and the leader;

d. a means gap: the wealthy versus the poor.

And these were a direct consequence of the change in Nkrumah's style of leadership, resulting from the change from being a mere party leader to being a Head of State.

Summary and Conclusion

If Nkrumah built the CPP by intense use of his personal leadership gifts and his well tested communication capabilities, when his regime collapsed he had ceased to use those instrumentalities of Ghanaian culture which he exploited. Face-to-face communication, dialogue with the people and had been replaced by remote impersonal broadcasts. He hid behind "bunkers" and the people could not reach him. He had placed his life in the hands of the few. His party too had become the ruling elite and others were excluded from the promises and spoils of freedom. No institutional modalities were established to involve the army, civil service or TUC. The economic situation aside, Nkrumah was a leader who collapsed, because he rose so high and went so far he left his followers behind.

Having made the party supreme, Nkrumah had failed to evolve a system whereby it could still be accountable to the populace. The experience of one party states in Africa reveal that leaders, constituency executives and parliamentary candidates and ministers, would tend to entrench themselves if they are not made to appeal to the electorate and derive their mandate from the people. This mechanism whereby Nkrumah could have renewed his own mandate and also used to achieve upward mobility in the party ranks through popular involvement, was never institutionalized, and the people were cut off.

Was Nkrumah's leadership style successful? Nkrumah's leadership passed the only test that really mattered in the African revolution—creating a precedent - winning independence. He mobilized the majority of the people and made them strike for freedom. And in so doing he set Africa ablaze with the fires of freedom.

Folk wisdom judges those who venture high rather sympathetically. *Nyimpa beye bi, wambeye ne nyina* (Fanti Akan): Man comes to achieve something; he does not come to achieve everything. And this is why Nkrumah is appreciated today. Those who proclaimed Nkrumah's overthrow, said: "The myth surrounding Nkrumah is broken!" Assessing public opinion since, one might well ask: Is it?

NOTES

1. Nkrumah, 195 7: 13 7.
2. *Ibid.,:* 50.
3. *Ibid.,:* 62.
4. *Ibid.,:* 63.
5. In traditional African Societies, the right of a leader to lead is explained in a myth: It is social Anthropologists who describe such myths as providing a 'Mythical Charter.' In the political struggle the CPP often used Danquah's declaration to justify the adoption of Nkrumah as the leader of the struggle.
6. Nkrumah, 1957:70.
7. Nkrumah, 1 963(a) :10.
8. Nkrumah, 1957:75-76.
9. Nkrumah, 1973(a):79.
10. When an Akan chief is destooled people often say "*Osoro eyi wo, Asaase eyi wo*"—Heaven (God) has disavowed you, Earth (the people) have disavowed you.
11. This is the author's own definition of politics. In the Information Age, control of information media has become such an important way of controlling other elements of power that such a definition is easily justified. Most likely, this definition or one like it has been offered elsewhere.
12. Nkrumah, 1963(a):9.
13. *Ibid.,:* 5.
14. Nkrumah, 1961b:10.
15. This is the traditional military organization of the Akan.
16. Nkrumah, 1957:16.
17. Most Ghanaian men do not part their hair.
18. Nkrumah, 1963(a):14.
19. There is however a Ghanaian Akan proverb which should make the Ghanaian proverbial grin better understood. "It is when I squeeze my face that you can say that I am angry, what about when I squeeze my anus?"
20. Dei-Annang, 1964:138.
21. Quoted in Arthur, n.d. :17 .
22. Nkrumah, 195 7: 3 .
23. *Ibid.,:* 7

24. *Ibid.,:* 8 It is interesting to see how seriously Nkrumah took this story. It reveals not only how strong his own belief in his psychic powers was but also how strongly his mother must have held his belief. This is an attempt by Nkrumah to support the popular belief that both he and his mother had the "Nzema gift."
25. Nkrumah, 1963 :10; also Dei-Annang, op . cit. :133 .
26. Nkrumah had a problem later in replacing some of the not so good characters. This would have been signal that he was throwing the ordinary people away to take in the respectable educated people he needed to help him rule. He was faithful to them, and they were to him. (*Dark Days in Ghana,* passim.)
27. Nkrumah, 1 963(a):8. Quoted from the *Accra Evening News,* 8th May, 1949 .
28. Nkrumah, 1957:89-90.
29. *Ibid.,:* 10.
30. *Ibid.,:* 30. Nkrumah does not express any very strong disapproval of sexuality here. In fact, people suspected he had girl friends who were good at keeping their cherished affairs secret.
31. This, in fact, was the practice of traditional rulers in Ghana. They took wives from many major segments of the people they ruled.
32. This section is intended to give structural reasons for Nkrumah's loss of contact with the people. He has himself dwelt on his isolation indicating the bombs thrown at him as a major cause (cf. *Dark Days in Ghana*). However, the change derived from the isolation imposed on him by the trappings of office and the new personality he assumed as Head of State. This occurs with most leaders. Alexander the Great was said to have kept near him a slave whose duty it was to remind him thus: "Sir, Remember you are mortal."
33. Nkrumah, 1 965d
34. Nkrumah, 1961a:209.
35. Nkrumah, 1968(a):67.
36. *Ibid.,:* 76.

TOWARDS AN AGENDA OF CONSTITUTIONAL ISSUES UNDER THE KWAME NKRUMAH REGIME

Fui S Tsikata

PERHAPS A WORD of justification and explanation is required for this topic, which does not attempt a specific assessment of any aspect of "the life and work of Kwame Nkrumah."

One of the most persistent criticisms made of the post-Independence Governments presided over by Kwame Nkrumah is their alleged disregard for constitutional norms adjudged to be basic. J. B. Danquah, for instance, who was one of the leading intellectuals among Nkrumah's critics, was concerned about the inconsistency between the practices and objectives of the CPP and the demands of an institutional framework for pluralist electoral party politics. He was also critical of both the post-independence judiciary and the CPP for the failure to develop independent and effective judicial perspectives for the control of the executive, administrative and legislative arms of government.[1]

Similar criticisms have indeed been made to varying degrees and in varying quarters of governments subsequent to those of Nkrumah. An interesting article by Robin Luckham[2] records a range of views of lawyers and judges concerning, interalia, the relationship

between the judiciary and the executive under different post-independence Governments. One of the most striking passages presents
a conversation between Luckham and an unidentified lawyer member of Dr. Busia's Progress Party Government, leading critics of
Nkrumah's shortcomings in the area of constitutional legality.

If I had my way we would have sacked the whole lot of (the judges).

Interviewer: But surely you couldn't do that? the Constitution protected them?

We could have done it, we could have done it. We should have just
made the announcement that they were sacked and then sent the
policemen to make sure they did not come in. What could they have
done then?

Interviewer: But surely . . .'
'I don't see anything that's wrong with that. Our judges are really
corrupt, you know, they would really deserve it![3]

Both in defence of Nkrumah and in other contexts, there has been a
questioning, at various levels of sophistication, of the relevance or at
least the weight, of some of the criteria of constitutional judgement:
where do they fit in assessing the performance of postcolonial governments whose object is a transformation of the internal and international structures that perpetuate the poverty and oppression of the
mass of the people.

My purpose here is not to make a critique of the constitutional
arguments invoked against Nkrumah, nor indeed to measure his or
any other governments by reference to any constitutional yardstick.
I have in an earlier paper[4] sought to criticize the limitations of "dominant" constitutional law discourse. Clearly many valuable ideals are
contained in the various doctrines of "the rule of law" and "human
rights" which constitute the substance of the standard constitutional lawyer's armory. But we need to note that these ideals express
elastic and somewhat contradictory ideas which require to be elaborated and qualified as regards each other to mould them into a relatively definite and coherent act of criteria. Thus, for instance,
chapter six of the 1979 Ghana Constitution, on Fundamental Human
Rights, begins in Article 19 as follows:

Every person in Ghana, whatever his place of origin, political opinions, colour, creed or sex, shall be entitled to the fundamental
rights and freedoms of the individual contained in this Article, but

subject to respect for the rights and freedoms of others and for the public interest.

The elaboration and qualification of these rights and freedoms in relation to each other has occurred not merely or even principally on the basis of the mental exertion of intellectuals but as part of the evolution through historical experience of definite societies.

There is too much that has been assumed in the invocation and application of constitutional criteria in our discussions. To clear some of the undergrowth that impedes the development of coherent, legitimate and viable constitutional criteria, it would be useful to construct an agenda of important issues which are assumed or are in controversy. This way it may be possible to have a meaningful debate, rather than a situation akin to that in the Biblical Babel, with many speaking in different tongues, none understanding the other. Towards that end, this paper seeks to identify important strands in relevant historical experience which bear upon both the assessment of constitutional practice, and the formulation of constitutional goals and institutions.

The investigation of history is important because, as it was put by Marx, one of the leading historians of the nineteenth century, "men make their own history but . . . not . . . as they please; they do not make it under circumstances chosen by themselves, but under circumstances directly encountered, given and transmitted from the past. The tradition of all the dead generations weighs like a nightmare on the brain of the living."[5]

The first strand of history that we examine relates to the colonial period. The work still needs to be done of elaborating from a critical distance and a many-sided and rounded perspective, the colonial constitutional order.

Suffice it here to remind ourselves of a number of elementary facts which relate to the constitutional heritage of colonial rule:

1. electoral representation in the legislative council, for a minority of unofficial members at that, was first introduced in the Gold Coast in 1923;

2. as late as 1946, the Gold Coast legislature was described by a not unsympathetic colonial observer as in "form . . . not parliamentary," and in "psychology . . . paternalistic and not democratic . . . The *ultima ratio* of the government in constitutional practice has hitherto been its official majority; its *ultima ratio* in controversy is an appeal for the recognition of its beneficent wisdom;"[6]

3. universal adult suffrage as a general basis for election to the legislature was not introduced till 1954, practically at the end of the decolonization period;

4. the first political party formed with the aim of forming a government, the United Gold Coast Convention, was only launched on 4th August, 1947;

5. the first party which expressed itself and operated as a modern mass-based party, the Convention People's Party, was not launched until 12th June, 1949;

6. the first Constitution under which a cabinet, selected from the majority party after elections, functioned was the 1954 constitution ;[7] and

7. the colonial judiciary, which began as a key weapon for the extension of colonial rule, remained for practically all its life an active part of the machinery of colonial government, and did not pretend to be a controlling arm against the administration — it enforced colonial legislation untrammeled by constitutional restraints save, rarely, determinations of the consistency of local legislation with Orders of the Crown in Council; its members were active in the formulation of colonial policy and legislation; they depended for career advancement on reports of the colonial bureaucracy; and many of their members as District, Provincial and Chief Commissioners performed at the same time judicial, executive and police roles.

We need to learn more about the institutions of force of the colonial state, and about the character of social and political relations, in the towns and villages, in workplaces, mines[8] and on the land, which were expressed in the form of the "law and order" which these institutions enforced.

On the state of the evidence it is hard to escape the conclusion that the ideas and institutions expressed in the independence constitutions required standing colonial constitutional history on its head. What these constitutions sought to do was to insert us into a different history — that of the development of bourgeois democracy in Western Europe.

In order to assess the viability of that project, we need to appreciate, not only the weight of the baggage of the colonial past; but also the historical processes by which bourgeois democracy arrived at its present. We do not, as of now, trouble to discuss the limits of the practice of bourgeois democracy. We content ourselves with the following observations:

1. Both universal adult suffrage as a basis of electoral representation and the mass based political party as the "hub of government"[9] are twentieth century phenomena in Western Europe;

2. the institutions of Western Government have had a history of
   continuity at a formal level for at least three centuries, but they
   have also changed significantly in substance over the period, in
   response to major social upheavals expressing definite and contending material interests; and

3. these institutions express, albeit in abstract ideological form, the
   balance attained between different social forces at definite
   moments in the history of their societies.

This last point needs to be elaborated. In the thoroughly respectable
work of Professor M. J. C. Vile's *Constitutionalism and the Separation
of Powers*,[10] we come upon the following startling passage.

> (I)t would be quite untrue to say that the (doctrine of separation of
> powers) does not have any class "bias." The theory of mixed gov-
> ernment (a preceeding and contending doctrine) had as its central
> theme a blending of monarchy, aristocracy and democracy. . .
> (Separation of Powers) assumes that the legislature will, or may, be
> taken over entirely by the democratic element, and that checks
> upon mob rule will therefore have to be applied by branches of the
> government largely or wholly outside the legislature. The battle for
> the control of the 'chief mark of sovereignty,' the legislative power,
> may be won by the proponents of popular rule, but there are meth-
> ods of ensuring that this power is subjected to limitations. . .

Louis Althusser expresses a similar idea in his own inimitable French
style in his observation that Montesquieu's doctrine separates and
balances off not only "pouvoirs" — functions, but also "puissances"
—social forces, "what is involved is above all a 'political' problem of
relations of forces, and not a 'juridical' problem concerning the definition of legality and its spheres."[11]

The implications of these comments is that issues about the
powers of and relations between the institutions of control and those
of "popular rule" are placed squarely into the arena of conflict
between contending social forces. The deadening weight of the past
and the formation of dominant constitutional discourse, on the other
hand, tend to convert these into a historical and abstract question.

Clearly, these are not matters to be settled by reference to authority. However, the purpose of these quotations is to challenge us to look at the evidence on which such observations as those of Vile and Althusser are based.

We now turn to the third strand of historical experience, that of indigenous society into which colonial rule intervened. We begin with an extract from Rattray, which is probably representative of prevalent ideology, even though written by a colonial anthropologist:

> To all outward appearances and to the superficial observer, the fiction indeed was often encouraged that (the chief) was a despot and an autocrat. In reality, every move, every command which appeared to emanate from his mouth had been discussed and agreed upon in private by every councillor who had a say in the affairs of state. These councillors, in turn, would also have taken care to sound their subjects right down to the Asafo. Nominally autocratic, the Akan constitution was in practice democratic to a degree, of which even now not many have any correct conception[12]

We have to remind ourselves that this purports to be an account of a constitutional system in which

    a. the highest and most powerful office was only open to a restricted segment of the society;

    b. that office gave the incumbent immense powers for creating and filling influential offices and allocating wealth and subjects to such office holders;[13]

    c. for a substantial portion of its history the resolution of issues of power at the highest levels involved violent struggle rather than consultation and an elaborate system which

    d. expressed the dominant ideas of a society in which the existence and consciousness of substantial differentiation was an important aspect of social and political life: slaves, commoners, wealthy nobles, chiefs, etc.

Rattray's idealist portrayal is reproduced in the modern "return to traditional institutions" ideology of right wing nationalism. In our submission any serious attention to the history of the various polities that make up modern Ghana, will show societies, which like others elsewhere,

    a. changed over time,

    b. contained different social groups with differential access to political power,

    c. in which force played a role in the motion of history.[14]

In relation to indigenous Asante constitutionalism an extract from the minutes of the Committee of Privileges of the Asante Confederacy Council muddies Rattray's simple picture. The Committee of Privileges investigated issues of the status of various Asante Chiefs after the restoration of the Confederacy in 1935. This extract is from the meeting of the committee held on 21st June, 1935, and concerned the elevation of the Asokorehene by the Asantehene. All the linguists and the chiefs who spoke agreed that:

(t)he Asantehene has the prerogative to elevate even a small boy to the highest position in the State.

(t)he Asantehene has the right to put even a senior chief under a junior chief, and he has also the right to elevate anyone to a senior position.[15]

The purpose of raising these historical questions is not to deny the possibility of moving forward: it is simply to enable experience, as opposed to building constitutional structures simply in one's head, based on one's wishes.

But it is not only the past which is a guide to the future, the present has its lessons. The past three and half years have seen some of the most intense political struggle that this country has had since the heydays of the anti-colonial struggle. New and unexpected units of political organizations have been introduced into our national life. In the activism, enthusiasm and initiatives which the people's defence committees exhibited certainly in the first year and a half of their existence, they exposed the vacuum in the representation of popular interests under the constitutional system of the Third Republic. Their practice suggests the relationship between popular political and constitutional institutions and the interests represented by those institutions.

If, as we have suggested, constitutions express albeit in abstract legal form, the resolutions related to "the clash of interests to be found in the real world,"[16] then in formulating criteria for assessing constitutional practice in our society, we must identify the important issues of social and political struggle, and integrate them into our criteria. Thus, for instance, in a country where about 70 percent of the population is in the countryside, issues of access to land and credit for agriculture are basic. Where do agricultural rent control and credit measures fit into the constitutional lawyer's assessment of governmental practice?

One of the principal limitations of much constitutional law work has been the failure to integrate material on social and political issues which are not explicitly about relations between the two internally undifferentiated categories of "government" and "citizen."

In the words of Kwame Nkrumah:

We must avoid the tendency to suppose that the form in which the law is administered is more important than the content of the law. Law is converted into a reactionary force once it is regarded as an abstract conception, which is in some mysterious way universally applicable without regard to the economic and social conditions of the country in which it is being applied. The reverse is true. The law should be the legal expression of the political, economic and social conditions of the people and of their aims for progress. It is the height of absurdity to attempt to assess the legal institutions of any country by adopting a formalistic yardstick which completely disregards the material content of the law . . . Unfortunately, such an approach too often marks the attitude of even the most eminent lawyers towards people with whose economic needs and social and political aims they do not see eye to eye.[18]

NOTES

1. Danquah, 1972.
2. Luckham, 1977 :190.
3. *Ibid.,*:222-223.
4. Tsikata, 1978 :17 .
5. Marx, 1979:103 .
6. Wight, 1947:82.
7. Amissah, 1981: ch.3 .
8. Crisp, 1984.
9. Barraclough, 1967.
10. Vile, 1967:33-34.
11. Althusser, 197 2: 90-91 .
12. Rattray, 1929: 406; and Busia, 1967: ch .2 .
13. McCaskie, 1980:189.
14. Kea, 1982; and Aidoo, 1977: 20.
15. Asante Confederacy Council: Proceedings of the Committee of Privileges, Kumasi, 18th June, 1935, to 3rd January, 1936.
16. Vile, *op. cit.*:l.
17. Tsikata, 1984.
18. Nkrumah, Speech at the formal opening of the Accra Conference on Legal Education and of the Ghana Law School, 4th January, 1962.

The Nkrumah Government and the Opposition on the Nation State: Unity vs. Fragmentation

Kwame A. Ninsin

Introduction

History seems to suggest that all ruling classes have fought for, and secured the establishment of a nation-state where none existed prior to their emergence.[1] The nation-state may therefore be described as the geo-political condition necessary for the political triumph of any class. It offers the territorial framework for the exercise of legitimate political power to control people and resources for the purpose of accumulation on a national scale.

In colonial Ghana the political geography of the nation-state had been decided, more or less, by imperial Britain. But the future ruling class lacked a virile economic base and its rate of accumulation was accordingly low. Control of the political institutions of the nation-state was therefore needed not only for accumulation but also for self-reproduction.

Where this future ruling class is divided, the internal structure of the state power is likely to become contentious. In Ghana the divisions within the nascent ruling class were determined by conflicting views about the extent to which state power could be utilized to promote social development; and they were fed on the concrete socio-economic and political conditions of the country. Among those conditions was the rather superficial sense of nationalism among the bulk of Ghanaians. This had been exacerbated by British colonial policy of unequal development and the generally conservative social policies which encouraged social backwardness, parochialism, mutual isolation of cultural collectivities, and in some cases cultural chauvinism .

And then also the concentration of cocoa wealth in a few of the regions reinforced the first and created a false sense of autonomy and sovereignty. This was strongest in the case of the Asante and Akirn Abuakwa. In the case of the Northern Territories it was rather the spectre of southern domination because of their relative natural backwardness than any sense of political autonomy, sovereignty or cultural chauvinism. The Trans-Volta Togoland on the other was encouraged by irredentist elements within and outside the region. In the struggle that ensued between the two leading class factions, the Opposition would actively exploit these two factors in the political environment to justify and strengthen its position.

This paper (i) examines some of the issues which were used to dramatize the controversy over the structure of state power; (ii) offers explanations for the development of that controversy; and (iii) assesses the results. The term "Opposition" is used to include all the political groupings, formal and informal, organized or unorganized, that stood against the CPP.

The Issues

From 1951 when the CPP formed the government of this country, the controversy about what form the structure of state power should take assumed growing importance. From that time the Opposition persistently accused the CPP of anti-democratic tendencies. To check this suspected tendency the Opposition made a number of stringent political demands. Those demands may be summarized as follows: (i) protection of chieftaincy as a viable indigenous institution for local government; (ii) diffusion of state power from the centre to regional political organs; and (iii) control over cocoa revenue. These demands were interrelated at the level of concrete political struggle and factional debate.

The agitation on the need to protect chieftaincy for example was originally legitimized and predicated on the need to evolve a democratic system of government rooted in the traditions of the people. The institution was in fact regarded as the basis for true self government. But it must be emphasized that as a political institution chieftaincy was bound up with the traditional political and economic order.[2] In this regard the aspect of the struggle that upheld this political institution was linked not only with property rights in land: It was also linked with that view of society in which chieftaincy embodied stability and individual liberties. And so the defence of chieftaincy became synonymous with the defence of liberty in the struggle against the hegemony of the CPP. As the anti-CPP struggle intensified the defence of civil liberties was carefully amplified and developed into the ideological basis of the struggle to secure the fragmentation of state structure as a means to contain what they dreaded: a dictatorial regime. A careful appraisal of the issues does, however, suggest that the struggle against the CPP can only be appreciated in relation to the Opposition's fear of imminent political demise which the formation of the CPP had come to represent. The creation of regional centres of political power in a federal constitutional framework as a bulwark for civil liberties was therefore regarded as the means to their redemption.

To render this demand legitimate and credible required that certain conditions be satisfied. Among these were such historical and cultural evidence of nationhood as common history, language and culture; and these could be sustained only around the existing traditional communities. Danquah, who was the leading mind within the ranks of the Opposition at the time did, for example, constantly return to the greatness, glory and power of the Akim Abuakwa state. In a letter to Seth Appiah of the Akim Abuakwa Youth Association (dated 4th February, 1952) he celebrated Akim Abuakwa as "the largest State in the Colony (and so) must also be the greatest in the Land." He added: "I am determined to have the Abuakwa name rehabilitated and to make Abuakwa lead the nation.'[3]

Since the traditional states were organized around chieftaincy, the Opposition's defence of these also meant defence of chieftaincy. This was categorically stated by Danquah when he proclaimed that any attack on chieftaincy was also an attack on the states.[4] Therefore the agitation for a federal system of government hinged as much on the survival of the traditional states as on chieftaincy. The two were inseparable. The interest of these powerful chiefs who were also against the CPP coincided with that of the political Opposition in this area.

But however linked the interests of the Opposition and chiefs was, the two were not congruent: they were just complementary. This was underscored in the persistent demand for a second legislative chamber which would be reserved mainly for chiefs. The principal justification for the federal system of government lay therefore in the aspiration of the non-chief elements of the Opposition for a territorial political framework within which they would exercise hegemony and be able to use regional state power for self-reproduction. In this regard the demand for a federal system of government was inseparable from the need to promote accumulation for private gain,[5] and that of controlling the economic potential of specific regions. This point was argued not without justification particularly in the case of Ashanti, Akim Abuakwa and, to some extent, of the Trans-Volta Togoland. These after all were the leading cocoa producing areas.

Democratization Vs. Chieftaincy

The first major confrontation between the CPP government and the Opposition occurred during the debate on the Local Government Ordinance of 1951. That moment exposed the contradiction between the government and the Opposition concerning the structure of the state power.

The government's position was determined by the need to democratize the machinery of government down to the grassroot. This, it was argued, had become necessary in view of the need for "a definite separation of the authorities responsible for ceremonial, ritual, constitutional and customary functions from those responsible for the administration of local government services." Local government institutions must therefore not only be modern: They must also be democratically constituted.[6] In order to ensure that the new popular local government organs possessed the necessary financial means they were also vested with power to manage stool lands as estate agents, and not as owners.[7]

It was evident that the bill was not intended to divest chiefs of their right as trustees of communal land. The Opposition nevertheless disputed the need to vest powers of control and management of stool lands in the proposed councils. They were concerned that it might jeopardize the allodial rights of chiefs — that "sacred right to enjoy one's own property,"[8] and eventually undermine chieftaincy itself. But their real concern was with the stability of chieftaincy. Reference to property rights was only for purposes of ideological legitimation and also because chieftaincy's survival hinged on the stability of existing land tenure. According to Magnus Sampson "stools and land are the essence of chieftaincy. Therefore if you take away the land you destroy the institution of chieftaincy."[9] In a letter to Sir Henry Coussey,[10] Danquah had also observed with dismay that ". . . one direct result of this Enactment (the Local Government Ordinance) will be to destroy Chieftaincy and tribal loyalties, and the State as such will cease to be."

Why chieftaincy? The Opposition's view transcended the mere sentimentalism often expressed by Danquah who defended it "because I love the institutions of this country . . . I feel strongly that . . . it is chieftaincy over which or around which our institutions are built"[11] Their position sprang from pure political considerations. In the view of Nana Ofori Atta, the chief's role is not just ceremonial: Chiefs "have been, are and will continue to be part and parcel of the Government of this country, and it is essential that they should have the opportunity to take active leadership in Government of the country."[12] Yet the Local Government Ordinance and subsequent ones such as the State Councils Ordinances of 1952 denied chiefs precisely the right to govern. They were left with only the power to deal with constitutional and civil matters related to customary law. It was because of this dramatic change in the powers of chiefs that the Opposition regarded those laws as effecting a de facto abolition of chieftaincy.

That controversy was significant for it exposed chieftaincy as the embodiment of a complex of rights which impinge intimately on the citizenship of the people of the country. Nene Azu Mate Kole summarized this significantly when he proclaimed in the debate on the Local Government Ordinance that the question of land is related to "the civil rights of our people. . ."[13] It would seem then that the CPP government was right in maintaining that the building of a modern nation-state required divesting chieftaincy of the right to represent and thereby usurp the rights of the people. This was indeed regarded as a necessary condition for restoring to the people their democratic rights. Besides, it was evident that in the past chiefs had used their judiciary claim to the rights of "their subjects" to play an influential role in colonial government and politics. The impulse towards democracy as the only credible basis of the modern nation-state therefore also required the dissolution of such an authoritarian structure.

But in that unfolding power struggle between the CPP and the Opposition, popular democracy was for the latter a perversion of civilized and orderly government; because members of the Opposition "had essentially the same attitude to the great masses of the African people that a liberal colonial official would have . . . And like the colonial officials, they sought the support of the Chiefs."[14] For them the masses were "only individuals" and their acclaimed role in modern politics was dismissed as mere emotion.[15] Chiefs on the other hand were hailed as the natural rulers, and constituted the only true source of legitimacy.[16] The Opposition therefore had good reason to resent what obviously were concealed attacks on chieftaincy.

Control Over Cocoa Wealth

In the course of the debate on the Local Government Ordinance the Opposition had not just deprecated but also repudiated the government's policy of controlling and managing stool lands through the new local government organs. In the words of a leading Opposition spokesman, that action amounted to "Confiscation of Property — Communism naked and unashamed."[17] In the end the government relented on the question of "control" but not on management. The same claim about land (i) as the property of individual communities as if such traditional policies still constituted equal and sovereign entities, distinct from the Ghanaian nation, and (ii) as the embodiment of the civil liberties of such collectivities had been raised earlier in the year.

The debate on the Gold Coast Cocoa Marketing Board (Amendment) Ordinance, 1951, provided the opportunity for the Opposition to advance such a position. On the one hand the government's conception of a unitary nation state directed by one strong central government affected its attitude toward cocoa revenue. For the CPP government, cocoa revenue was common national property. It therefore ought to be centrally controlled and utilized for common benefit. Accordingly it was important that the cocoa board was reorganized in order to ensure effective government control and direction of its policies through a responsible minister.

To that extent government did not consider the Ordinance an infringement on either individual or communal right to the free enjoyment of property. Mr. Ohene Djan, then ministerial secretary for Finance, summarized the government's view quite succinctly. According to him, the CPP government regarded the cocoa industry as the hub of the economy's health and the country's stability. The industry was for farmers as it was for the whole country. "Can we (therefore) separate the interest of the cocoa farmer from that of the rest of the country?" he asked. Talk about farmers' interest as if it were exclusive and regional was accordingly parochial and far too fantastic.[18]

But the Opposition disagreed. Danquah, for example, charged during the debate that the bill was in violation of the full enjoyment of private property. Its aim was to transform the Cocoa Marketing Board from a trustee to controller and manager of farmers' wealth so that government could use it for the development of the whole country. He declared: "The Board is not a Trustee for the Gold Coast people. It is a trustee for the cocoa producers." To reinforce this argument, he stressed further that the funds of the GCCMB were not "profits" accruing to government. They were farmers' earnings. Government could therefore control them only with the expressed consent of farmers.[19] Mr. Awuma (Rural Member for Akpini Asogli) affirmed this same view when he asserted that, "The Farmers of Togoland have always agitated first of all that their share of the accumulated profits of the fund should be calculated, declared and set aside for them. The second is that their cocoa should be sold under a separated account."[20]

The relationship between cocoa revenue and land is an intimate one. Both contain property rights.[21] Hence Danquah could lament that the Local Government Ordinance violated "that sacred right to enjoy one's own property" in the same way as the Gold Coast Cocoa Marketing Board (Amendment) Ordinance infringed the full enjoyment of private property.

This is the crux of the matter! If cocoa revenue and land could be legitimately considered as private property rights then whenever there was the slightest sign of violation of their private enjoyment the grounds for rebellion became incontrovertible. Then rebellion against constituted civil authority, that is, appealing to a higher justice, became justified. The agitation for a federal state system and bicameral legislature underscored this philosophical viewpoint. And so did the events which immediately preceded the formation of the National Liberation Movement (NLM), the highest organized expression of that agitation.

Federal Vs. Unitary State Power

By 1954 the agitation for a federal state system had erupted into a full-scale rebellion — almost a civil war. The dynamics of that rebellion and its philosophical underpinnings bore a strong semblance to the rebellion of the American colonies against imperial Britain. For example, Danquah had, on the question of independence for Ghana argued passionately for the colony to assert its "residual political sovereignty in the chiefs and people" to set up a constituent assembly. He had argued that this act of rebellion to "dissolve the

political bonds which have connected them with another" was justified whenever citizens are convinced that the end of government
has become destructive of their inalienable rights.[22] The declaration that gave birth to the NLM was nourished by this philosophical
claim. For the Opposition, it signalled the resumption of this residual political sovereignty which is presumably inalienable and
latent.[23]

In this regard, it is remarkable that after the Coussey Committee
Report the issue of federalism and a bicameral legislature should
resurface only during the debate on the government's July 1953
Motion for Constitutional Reform for the country. In fact the Coussey
Committee had dealt with the issue of regionalizing the political
administration of the country as well as a second legislative chamber. But both of them had been rejected under the 1951 Constitution.
This Constitution merely affirmed the conclusion of the Phillipson
Report.[24] Sir Phillipson (the sole Commissioner) had disagreed with
the Coussey Committee on the need to create such regional administrative regimes which would be vested with considerable autonomy and a wide range of powers. He was of the view that its adoption
would be an unnecessary impairment of the unitary character of the
Ghanaian state. He had therefore rejected any suggestion for a federal system and instead emphasized the need to strengthen the cen-
tripetal nature of the state. Contrary to the centrifugal implications
of the Coussey proposal, this Commissioner had recommended the
establishment of regional councils which would be "essential outly-
ing parts" of the central government.

Even so the Opposition had by 1953 come to the view that fragmentation of state power was a necessary weapon against the creeping dictatorship of the CPP. The debate on the Motion for
Constitutional Reform therefore provided the occasion for the
Opposition to revive the issue. During that debate the Government
clearly stated its unqualified commitment to upholding and defending the territorial integrity of the country. To this end, it was also
determined to find an amicable and democratic solution to the
Togoland question.[25] It had further assured all the traditional territorial entities of its respect for their respective integrity. But the
Opposition was not prepared to see the value and sincerity of the
government's declared position. They rather chose to commit their
energies to the defence and consolidation of traditional territorial
units as the basis of democratic representation of government.
Toward this goal they rejected electoral representation on the basis
of population and opted for representation on the basis of territor-

ial units—all equally. It meant that Ashanti, for example, would have the same number of representatives as Togoland or the Northern Territories.[26] All these claims were inconsistent with the government's view of the nation-state and of popular democracy. They were accordingly rejected just as other Commissions and Committees found it legitimate and necessary to do.

Directly related to regional representation was the demand for a separate legislative chamber for chiefs. In a statement issued on 28th March, 1953, the Asanteman Council argued that it was reversing its earlier position against the idea of a second legislative chamber in the light of "the present political situation." Earlier in the same month the Joint Provincial Council of (Chiefs) had issued a similar statement in which it called for a bicameral legislature "in the light of (recent) experience."[27] Obviously that "situation" or "experience" was the unbroken chain of interventions by the CPP government in the eminent domain of chiefs as well as its electoral successes over the Opposition at both national and local levels. It was these experiences, which according to Danquah, made the formation of the NLM inevitable as a means for demanding a federal form of government.[28] It would seem obvious then that even up to 1953 the demand for a federal system of government remained a latent part of the Opposition's demands. It was the frustration of persistent failure in realizing previous demands that compelled them to make a public declaration of it.

Two factors precipitated the federalist outburst. First; the failure of the Opposition in the 1954 general election, the first ever to be held on the basis of universal franchise. The Opposition had emerged from it as a weak, essentially tribal-regional group. Second; the Cocoa Duty and Development (Amendment) Ordinance, 1954. "The objects of the Ordinance were to provide for: (1) the establishment of three further development funds, (2) the allocation of amounts of money from general revenue, into which export duty on cocoa is paid to these new development funds, and (3) the alteration of the rate of export tax on cocoa."[29] But the Opposition misrepresented the Ordinance as fixing for cocoa farmers a maximum price of 72 shillings per 60 lbs of cocoa whereas, in fact, the government had rather assured cocoa farmers a minimum price of 72 shillings. In any case the Opposition effectively mobilized cocoa farmers, first in Ashanti and then in Akim Abuakwa, around what crystallized as a grievance—an unsatisfactory producer price, to promote their own political and economic aspirations. The result was the formation of the NLM in September 1954 to spearhead the federalist agitation. The NLM received the solid support of the Asanteman Council[30] and the Okyeman Council.[31] All the Opposition parties (viz. the NPP, GCP, MAP, TGP) also supported it but for different reasons. What united them was fear of the CPP.

The birth of the NLM fused the struggle for a federation and for a higher producer price for cocoa farmers. The two were labeled as a struggle for liberation from the misrule and dictatorship of the CPP; from a government that expropriated cocoa farmers, and that was above all corrupt. The House Select Committee on a Federal System of Government summarized the actual position of the Opposition in these succinct words:

> It was argued that in a federation each unit would be able to formu-
> late its own fiscal and economic policy. Ashanti, as a federal unit
> with its own government would be able, for example, to pay the
> farmer a much higher price for his cocoa. Prof. Busia put the farm-
> ers' case in these words: 'We have a central government which not
> only controls the price we get for our cocoa but also taxes the
> cocoa heavily and controls the spending of the money. We object to
> the present price, we object to the heavy taxes proposed and we
> are not satisfied with the way the money from cocoa taxes has been
> spent. We demand a greater say in the fixing of the price of cocoa,
> and in the use to which revenue from cocoa is put. We do not think
> the central government is serving our interests. We therefore
> demand a federal form of government in which we could curb the
> powers of the central government and have a greater say in the use
> to which our money, the revenue from cocoa, is put. In a federation,
> the component states or regions would have a larger measure of
> self-government; this would mean a larger control in managing our
> own affairs, and in the use of our resources; we would see more for
> our money.'[32]

It is therefore clear, as the Committee emphasized, that the demand for a federation was based on the economic advantage of Ashanti rather than on any practical and genuine considerations. For if Ashanti were at least endowed as the North, for example, that demand would not have been made. The same must be said for its advocates in Akim Abuakwa and to some extent the then TransVolta Togoland. That the federalist agitation was artificial was further underscored by its almost unanimous rejection by all the commit-tees and commissions appointed to investigate the whole or aspects of it.[33] Furthermore it contradicted the unitary character of the Ghanaian State and was therefore bound to collapse. But that the Opposition persisted in their demand for it even after they had been rejected at the 1956 general election underscores the motive behind the struggle against the CPP; namely their ambition to wrest power from the "Verandah Boys." Up to 1960 when the country became a republic, the Togoland Disturbances of March 1957, the anti-CPP campaign of the Ga Shifimo Kpee and the Awhiatey Amponsah-Apaloo conspiracy of 1958[34] represented instances of this anti-CPP struggle of which the goal of a federal system of government for the country constituted a mere starting point. And, in fact, judging from the historiography of the 1966 coup it may be argued that that coup was indeed the culmination of that long struggle against the CPP.[35] When we look back, on 19th April, 1956, the NLM had prophesied what was eventually fulfilled almost 10 years later. It had declared in a statement, warning the British government of dire consequences if the country attained independence under the CPP, that "as far as we can see (this would lead to a road that) makes for the country (one) of riot, rebellion, revolution; the road long ago taken by those unhappy countries where one can change only the Head of State or the people who govern by armed insurrection after underground conspiracy and sabotage."[36]

Explanation

Even though the House Select Committee rejected the overall claims of the Opposition, it was persuaded by the theory that the demand for federalism became necessary because of the Opposition's failure to secure the creation of a second chamber.[37] This is far from the truth. The demand for a second chamber was unrelated to cocoa revenue though it was related to chieftaincy. Rather the cause lay in the chain of defeats the Opposition had suffered at the polls since 1951, and also in their dissatisfaction with government policies relating to "land and capital."[38] These had increased the price of the direct exercise of power and the urgency to sweep the CPP from power to pave the way for them to implement their vision of a free and democratic society.

The position of Danquah on this subject is revealing. In a letter he wrote to the Secretary of the CPP on November 3, 1949,[39] he had rejected even the Coussey Constitutional Committee's mild recommendation for the setting up of regional administrative bodies which would be vested with considerable executive powers. He had argued that it would not be conducive to economy, smoothness and effectiveness in national political administration. And after the formation of the NLM, which he supported and defended, he still held passionately to the unity of the Ghanaian state.[40] Even so he was convinced that the rebellion was consistent with natural law.[41]

One must admit that Danquah, for example, had been a consistent advocate of the traditional institutions, ideas and practices of especially the Akim Abuakwa people. However, it must be emphasized that by the mid-1950's, this value of his had dovetailed into his personal political ambitions. This followed the growing realization on his part (and by the Opposition generally) that the CPP was destined to be the dominant political force and thereby render some of them politically ineffective. For example, in a circular to Akim Abuakwa chiefs in October 1950[42] he had merely regretted, without any signs of bitterness, the rejection of the Coussey Committee's proposal for representation in the Legislative Council on the basis of population, and for a bicameral legislature. He regarded it as a lost political advantage.

With the surge of the CPP to popularity and dominance, however, he began to talk about the need "to have the Abuakwa name rehabilitated and to make Abuakwa lead the nation," "feared and respected" and "loved by all."[43] On the eve of the 1954 general election, he wrote to Nana Kwabena Kena II exposing the essence of his "policy in so far as it affects Akim Abuakwa:"

> That policy is to defend the State and to foster and maintain its development, the progress of its people in all spheres of activity, the development of its lands and the security thereof, and, finally to see to it that Abuakwa Chiefs and people should have a full share in the new order of self-government which is rapidly coming to be ours in the Gold Coast, and in which I can truly claim to have played a part to make its coming a certainty.[44]

In the same spirit he had suggested to the House Select Committee on Federalism that among the issues to be resolved in an independent constitution were (i) "The place of the independent sovereign states and their State Councils in an independent Gold Coast" and (ii) "The place of the larger territorial units already recognized as administrative blocks with their own territorial capitals and territorial problems, institutions and economy."[45] The purpose of all this as stated by Busia was to secure control over their territorial resources.[46] This is why the birth of the NLM was regarded by the Opposition as the "hour of liberation." But the aim was not to liberate the country but themselves (the Opposition) as a group from imminent political extinction. Regionalization of state power was to be the basis of their liberation.

Conclusion —Triumph of Unity

The contradictory views of the CPP government and the Opposition on the role of the state in social development was the basis for the division within the ranks of the Ghanaian elite—a division that has dominated the political scene since 1951 . This divergence further determined their conflicting view on property, that is, whether one can maintain a rigid distinction between property which is social and that which is private. The conflict over policies on land and cocoa revenue originated from this. And so did it ultimately divide them on whether or not cocoa revenue could be used to attain the larger social goal of egalitarianism. The leading Opposition spokesman, Danquah, for example, believed that the privatization of such property was the condition for effecting "a revolution in the standards of living of the general mass of the people."[47]

The CPP government's view was the exact opposite. For them land and cocoa wealth are social property and should be utilized for the benefit of the whole. The measures which the government instituted to control land and cocoa revenue were aimed at ensuring the unencumbered realization of this goal. In this connection the massive investments in the development of social services like education, health, communication, and housing, which were made at the time, are lasting monuments to the foresight and courage of that regime and its leader, Kwame Nkrumah.

The vision of society held by the CPP government was one that would be united, free from tribalism and all feudal remnants, strong and prosperous. The latter was necessary for forging national unity and making the nation strong. These collective social purposes were a value far greater than individual or private advantage. The CPP government therefore committed its energies to their realization. Hence in a White Paper issued in 1959 the government registered its unqualified commitment to "the very existence of the state of Ghana by (not) allowing to go unchecked plots and conspiracies which might result in the destruction of the state itself."[48] Toward this goal the CPP regime was prepared to take special or emergency measures. Those measures were of two kinds: (i) the elimination of sectarian or sectional tendencies which militate against the unity and security of the Ghanaian state; and (ii) the elimination of the structural basis of the tendency toward national fragmentation. It was indeed for the same reason that the one-party system was instituted. As Kwame Nkrumah himself explained later, on 1st February, 1966, "A multi-party system introduced into Africa results in the perpetuation of feudalism, tribalism and regionalism, and in inordinate power struggle and rivalry."[49]

The implementation of those measures re-enforced earlier ones, and saved the new nation-state of Ghana from the danger of fragmentation and, possibly, collapse. Among them were "The Avoidance of Discrimination Act" of 1957 which prohibited racial, tribal, regional as well as religious and political organizations and propaganda. The government was thus, in one stroke, able to undercut the centrifugal tendencies which produced the NLM and the bloody strife of 1954–56. It, above all, produced the United Party and thereby laid the structural basis for the development of Opposition and other political parties which would become national in character, and whose activities would thenceforth reinforce the unity of the nation-state of Ghana. The consolidation process was advanced further by the enactment of the Nationality and Citizenship Act, 1957, (Act I) and the Preventive Detention Act, 1958, (Act 17) (PDA). The first clearly defined Ghanaian citizenship and thereby provided the legal framework that enabled the government to deport aliens who were engaged in activities inimical to the unity, security and stability of the Ghanaian state. The PDA, on the other hand, made it possible for the government to imprison, without trial, some Ghanaians whose activities were understood to threaten state security and stability. Though the PDA is still regarded with disdain, its value in safeguarding the interest of the state seems to have been appreciated and vindicated, as borne out by its repeated use under different titles, by successive governments after the fall of the CPP government on 24th February, 1966; and some of the regimes that have resorted to a revised version of the PDA have been the most devout and vehement critics of the CPP.

Finally, the government used its overwhelming support in the country to amend the 1957 Constitution in order to modify the powers vested in the Regional Assemblies.[50] The government did this because of its deepseated resentment against those extensive powers conferred on the Regional Assemblies under that Constitution. In its view it had decided to accept that Constitution as a compromise; it wanted to avert any further situation that might be used by the Opposition to delay the attainment of independence. The same consideration for a unitary state system prevailed here; because that amendment served to remove once and for all the regional base of the Opposition. By 1960 therefore the unitary character of the new nation-state had triumphed over the centrifugal demands of the Opposition. The new nation-state of Ghana had become entrenched; so that it has now become part of the consciousness of successive generations of Ghanaians. But ultimately, that victory created a unified territorial framework for the growth of a national economy and the rise into effective political and economic dominance of a ruling class which is truly national in outlook.

NOTES

1. Consider for example the unification movements in Italy, Germany, Greece, Poland and other parts of Europe.
2. For a discussion of this see Asante, 1975.
3. Danquah, Vol. III, pp. 29-31 and 63-64.
    (Compiled by Akyeampong, H. K.)
4 . Danquah, 1946-1951, Vol. II, pp. 140-141.
5. Danquah, Vol. III, *op. cit.* pp. 69-75.
6. *Gold Coast Legislative Assembly Debates,* 1951 Vols. 1-2, 52-53.
7. This was in conformity with the recommendations of the Coussey Constitutional Committee and the House Select Committees on Ashanti and the Colony. All three castigated traditional authorities for their mishandling of stool revenues.
8. Danquah, Vol. II, *op. cit.,* 141
9. *Gold Coast Legislative Assembly Debates, op. cit.,* 71
10. Danquah, Vol. II, *op. cit.,* 141
11. *Gold Coast Legislative Assembly Debates, op. cit.,* 106
12. *Ibid.*: 182
13. *Ibid.*: 115
14. See James in "Miller and Aya" (eds.), 1971:136 .
15. Declared Danquah in an Interview. See Wright, 1954: 220
16. *Gold Coast Legislative Assembly Debates,* 1953, Vol.2:342.
17. Danquah, Vol. II, *op. cit.,* 140.
18. *Gold Coast Legislative Assembly Debates,* 1951, *op. cit* ., pp. 474–475.
19. *Ibid.,* 468
20. *Ibid.,* 474
21. Danquah, Vol. III, *op. cit.,* 71, affirms this view
22. *Ibid.,* 96
23. For example, Danquah would say in apparent justification of that rebellion: the "Ashanti, for one, decided to join hands with the Gold Coast Colony upon certain understandings. If those understandings are abused or not respected by those in power today, it may be because they consider governing a people is cheap, especially with a people easily moved by the pangs of centuries of pain and suffering for something to liberate them." Danquah, Vol. III, 74.
24. Gold Coast Report, 1951.
25. See Government White Paper on the subject.
26. This was the position of the Asanteman Council as argued by their representative, Nana Boakye Dankwa, second Territorial Member for Ashanti in the Legislative Assembly. See *Gold Coast Legislative Assembly Debates,* 1953, 385-386.
27. See Memoranda submitted to government on the proposal for Constitutional reform in the country. In Gold Coast, 1953, Proposals, Appendix D.
28. Danquah, Vol. II, *op. cit.,* 99

29. Gold Coast, *Report*, 1955. para. 9.
30. See Ghana, *Report*, 1 958a.
31. See Ghana, *Report*, 1 958b.
32. *Report from House Select Committee on Federal System of Government.*
33. The Phillipson Committee; The House Select Committee on Federal System of Government; The All-Party Achimota Conference; The Regional Constitutional Commission; and the Constitutional Adviser (Sir Frederick Boume).
34. See Ghana, *Report*, 1959.
35. See, for example Afrifa, 1966. And political and economic policies of the NLC regime.
36. Quoted in Davidson, 1973:167.
37. *House Select Committee on Federal System of Government op. cit.*, para. 45.
38. Danquah, Vol. II, op. cit.: 71
39. *Ibid.*, 72-76.
40. See how he, for example, lamented the prospect that the formation of the NLM should negate all the efforts put into realizing the "miracle" of our Gold Coast unitary Government, Danquah, Vol. III, *op. cit.*: 74.
41. *Ibid.*
42. Danquah, Vol. II, *op. cit.*, 124-130.
43. Danquah, Vol. III, *op. cit.*, 29-3 t .
44. *Ibid.*, 64
45. *Ibid.*, 90
46. As quoted by *the House Select Committee on Federal System of Government, op. cit.*
47. Danquah, Vol. III, *op. cit.*, 73.
48. Ghana: *Report* 1959
49. Quoted in Davidson, *op. cit.*, 199
50. See the Regional Assembly Constitutional Amendment Act of 1958.

Nkrumah's Foreign Policy
1951–1966

Obed Asamoah

Mainsprings of Nkrumah's Foreign Policy

To understand and appreciate Ghana's Foreign Policy under
Nkrumah, it is necessary for background purposes, to look back to
the political cross currents in the Gold Coast and pre-independence
Africa, the situation of the black man in America at the time of
Nkrumah's stay there, the intellectual ferment among the blacks in
the diaspora which was manifesting itself in a Pan-Africanist movement in Britain and the Americas, the demonstrative impact of
Gandhi's life and thoughts and the Indian independence struggle,
and the new world situation created by the expansion of communist
influence and power after the Second World War and the Cold War
that developed as a consequence. These were all factors that shaped
Nkrumah's life and thoughts and affected the scope of his achievements. Of these, however, the single most important factor in the
development of his policies was the Pan-Africanist tradition.

At the time of Nkrumah's return to the Gold Coast, Ethiopia and
Liberia were politically independent and by that token free to manage their own affairs, but black Africa was, to all intents and purposes, considered the "dark continent" inhabited by people who,

according to some theories, were simply not considered capable of any cultural innovation much less of managing their own affairs. This view, as wilfully mistaken as it was unconscionable, taught that all works of excellence found on the continent were the creation of the white man and of his interaction with the blacks. Nor, was this an idle, academic exercise since in its varying interpretations and manifestations, the doctrine was used to justify the so-called civilizing mission of the white man in Africa and the continued subjugation and exploitation of the continent.[1]

Thus, even though the Gold Coast Soldier in the Royal West African Frontier Force could, as late as the Second World War, be sent into battle in defence of the so-called "free world" against the armies of the Axis Powers, he himself had no personal stake in or right to freedom, being nothing more than the white man's burden. Thus he returned home in the flush of victory only to be mowed down in a hail of bullets when he marched on the seat of the colonial administration at the Castle, Osu, to present his petition to the Colonial Governor in demand of his basic right to a decent life.

Similarly, in the Americas, even though our kinsmen had long been freed from slavery, the black man was still only nominally free with hardly any voice in the land of his enforced adoption or right to the wealth or opportunities his labors had helped to create in the New World. Voices of protest such as those represented at the series of Pan-African Congresses organized by scholars of African descent from 1900 onward, were beginning to heighten awareness of the plight of the black man throughout the world and it was only a matter of time that these should finally make common cause with the independence struggle in Africa.

In his autobiography, *Ghana*, Dr Nkrumah says he was influenced more by the the ideas of Marcus Garvey than by anything else in the Pan-Africanist movement, although he had read authors like Dr. duBois, Claud Mckay, Langston Hughes, David Diop and Dr. Edward Blyden, among others.[2] Garvey's "Philosophy and Opinions" and, in particular, his characterization of the African situation as being "not only peonage, and serfdom, but outright slavery, racial exploitation and alien political monopoly" exercised a profound effect on Nkrumah and reinforced his determination, as Garvey had urged, to bring "these crimes against our race" to an end.[3] In Garvey's view, "if Europe is for the white man, if Asia is for the brown and yellow man, then surely Africa is for the black man" and he advocated a return of all black men to Africa.[4] The cry "Africa for the Africans" in its varying echoes was to serve as a rallying theme in the independence struggle in Africa. Garvey's ultimate dream was of a free United States of Africa under one Government and as "a nation of our own, strong enough to lend protection to the members of the race scattered all over the world and to compel the respect of the nations and races of the earth."[5]

However, although it was Garvey's idea of a United Africa which in time became the cardinal theme of the Pan-Africanist Movement, it was not until the Sixth Congress held in Manchester in 1945 that the various concepts of the Movement were crystalized into a concrete programme of action. The historic Manchester Congress was attended by more than 200 delegates from all over the world and for the first time, the necessity for well-organized firmly-knit movements as a primary condition for the success of the national liberation struggle in Africa was stressed.[6] Significantly, Dr. Nkrumah was joint Secretary of the organizing Committee with George Padmore and it is a measure, not only of the growing affinity of interest in the two traditions of protest, but also, of the role Nkrumah was destined to play that from the Manchester Conference onward, the Pan-African Movement became transformed into an expression of African nationalism.

On account of its special relevance to the African liberation struggle and its ultimate impact on the foreign policy of Ghana under Nkrumah, the Pan Africanist programme may now be noted in summary form. Briefly, this called for:

i.   Africa for the Africans; complete independence of the whole of Africa. Total rejection of Colonialism in all its forms;

ii. United States of Africa: The ideal of a wholly unified continent through a series of inter-linking regional federations within which there would be a limitation on national sovereignty;

iii. Renaissance of African moral virtues and cultures: This was to take the form of a quest for the African personality, a determination to recast African society in its own traditional forms, drawing from its past that which is valuable and desirable and marrying it with modern ideas as may be deemed appropriate;

iv. African nationalism to replace the tribalism of the past: a concept of African loyalty wider than "the nation" and which would transcend tribal and territorial affiliations;

v.   The regeneration of African economic enterprise to replace colonial economic methods: a belief in a non-exploitative or communalistic type of socialism;

vi. Belief in democracy as the most desirable method of government based on the principle of "one man, one vote;"

vii. Rejection of violence as a method of struggle unless peaceful methods of struggle—Positive Action—are met with military repression;

   viii. Solidarity of black peoples everywhere and a fraternal alliance of coloured peoples based on a common history of struggle against white domination and colonialism;

   ix. Positive Neutrality (as it was then called) or non-involvement as partisans in super-power politics, but "neutral in nothing that affects African interests" or the peace of the world.

As can readily be discerned, it was these strands of Pan-Africanism which at Ghana's independence were woven into a pattern by Nkrumah and the Convention People's Party to form the main thrust of Ghana's foreign policy and which, with only slight modifications and shifts of emphasis here and there, have remained the basic tenets of Ghana's foreign policy ever since.

Summing up his impressions of Ghana's accession to independence on 6th March, 1957, a political commentator described the occasion as "the most important event in the history of modern Africa."[7] If that, perhaps, was a snap judgment at the time, events since then have more than justified this verdict and nowhere has this been more true than in the impact of Ghana's foreign policy on the rest of Africa and the world. What precisely then were the basic tenets of Ghana's foreign policy under Nkrumah?

Welcoming dignitaries to a state banquet on the occasion of Ghana's independence, Dr. Nkrumah remarked: "our country is no stranger to world affairs." More than anything else what Nkrumah sought to stress, was that the material basis for Ghana's independence existed. As he further explained: "we can stand on our own feet."[8] Indeed, from Nkrumah's point of view, the most significant consequence of independence was that Ghana could now have a foreign policy and this from the onset was defined as a dynamic process concerned with the broader ends of rebuilding Ghana both as a necessary objective in itself, and as proof of the black man's capability of managing his own affairs and also as a means towards the infinitely more challenging task of achieving economic emancipation, the independence and union of Africa, and rehabilitating the African personality within the comity of nations. He summed up the objectives of his policy to Parliament on the eve of Independence as "Dignity, Peace and Friendship."[9]

Following from this the main elements constituting Nkrumah's foreign policy were:

1. Economic Independence for Ghana
2. Elimination of Political Neo-colonialism
3. Total liberation of African from colonialism and racism

4. The attainment of African Political Unity and African Personality
5. Support for the United Nations
6. Non-alignment and positive neutrality
7. Support for the Commonwealth.

Economic Independence for Ghana

One of the primary pre-occupations of Dr. Nkrumah was the need to make political independence meaningful by achieving the economic emancipation of Ghana and of Africa. The aim was first of all to satisfy the expectations of the people of Ghana, second to modernize Ghana as a showpiece of African achievement and as a basis for his ambitious policy of African liberation. In this and in spite of whatever ideological inclinations he may have had and the subsequent adoption of socialism as state policy, Nkrumah remained essentially a pragmatist co-operating with the colonial administration before independence and working within the international economic structures of the day, accepting a role for private enterprise and actively wooing private investment, welcoming economic co-operation and support from the socialist countries, preaching maximum economic co-operation between African nations, welcoming the role of the UN and its specialized agencies in the development of Ghana, relying on Israeli technology and expertise and above all doing everything possible to ensure the coming into fruition of the Volta River dam. He told the National Assembly on 20th February, 1958, that: "It is my strong belief that the Volta River Project provides the quickest and most certain method of leading us towards economic independence."[10]

Nkrumah's commitment to the Volta River Project muted his criticisms of the West, explained his relations with Israel, slowed his approaches to the East and explained his commitment to United Nations operations in the Congo even after it was apparent that the UN was being used to further western interests and to frustrate his ally, Patrice Lumumba, and his objectives of African unity. Of course that is not the whole story. The Congo episode graphically illustrated the impotence of a small nation such as Ghana in the face of big power rivalry and big power interests.

Ultimately neither the Volta River Project nor the other impressive economic developments of the Nkrumah era could ensure Ghana's economic independence. The problem was much bigger than Ghana and Dr. Nkrumah's belated efforts to turn to the East yielded little results which were more than offset by the political complications that brought about, leading eventually to his downfall through western intrigue and subversion. Nkrumah's concern for the economic emancipation of Africa was the basis of his opposition to association of African nations with the EEC. In his speech on 7th April, 1960, to the Conference on Positive Action and Security in Africa, after castigating association with the EEC as "a striking instance of new imperialism" he called for the industrialization of Africa for her own sake and for the sake of a healthy economy as part of the process of ensuring African economic freedom. He continued thus:

> This can only happen if the artificial boundaries that divide her are broken down so as to provide for viable economic units, and ultimately a single African unit. This means an African common market, a common currency area and the development of communications of all kinds to allow the free flow of goods and services. International capital can be attracted to such viable economic areas, but it would not be attracted to a divided and balkanized Africa, with each small region engaged in senseless and suicidal economic competition with its neighbors.[11]

Nkrumah has been criticized for his decision to take Ghana out of such regional arrangements as the West Africa Airways Corporation, the West African Currency Board, the West African Cocoa Research Institute and the West African Court of Appeal which had been created during the British colonial administration to foster cooperation among the British dependencies in West Africa. According to his critics, this was a serious contradiction to his policy of maximum inter-African co-operation which only served to promote his personal political ambitions at home. However, if as Nkrumah argued at the time, these were colonial appendages which a sovereign, independent Ghana had to shed, there was no denying the fact that his policy blamed even some of his friends. This taken with missed opportunities such as the creation of a common currency zone with Guinea as advocated by Guinea and his opposition to East African regional co-operation reflected badly on the soundness of his tactics.

Elimination of Political Neo-Colonialism

The famous dictum of Dr. Kwame Nkrumah that Ghana's independence would be meaningless unless it was linked up with the total liberation of the continent may readily be seen as the most succinct summation and cornerstone of decolonization policy under Nkrumah.[12] On the occasion of Ghana's independence Dr. DuBois, then President of the Pan-African Congress wrote to Dr. Nkrumah saying: "I hereby put into your hands, Mr. Prime Minister, my empty but still significant title of President of the Pan-African Congress due. I trust, to meet you soon and for the first time on African soil at the call of the independent state of Ghana."[13] At the earliest opportunity in April, 1958, Dr. Nkrumah opened the First Conference of Independent African States in Accra to offer the Heads of State and Government assembled the opportunity to speak for themselves and to agree on a common programme for future action. As the first conference of its kind in Africa, this meeting not only served as an important landmark in evolutionary pan-Africanism, it also underscored Ghana's determination to be the torch bearer of the struggle for independence on the continent.

The All-African Peoples' Conference which followed in December 1958, therefore, came as the formal and concrete expression of Ghana's dedication to the freedom struggle in Africa and made it possible for representatives of freedom-fighters throughout the continent to assemble in a free, independent African state for the purpose of planning a co-ordinated assault on colonial and racist rule in Africa. The conference was particularly noteworthy for Nkrumah's appraisal of the tasks ahead. Addressing the meeting, Nkrumah called on the delegates to remember always that before the final objective of Pan-Africanism could be achieved, four stages had to occur. These were: the attainment of freedom and independence; the consolidating of that freedom and independence; the creation of unity and community among the African states, and finally, the economic and social reconstruction of Africa.

As the initial step, therefore, the over-riding imperative was to seek the "political kingdom" which would then serve as a basis for the attainment of the other objectives desired. In pursuit of this goal every conceivable assistance was made available to the liberation movements for the prosecution of the struggle against the colonial and racist regimes on the continent. Accordingly, a special fund was created for concerted financial assistance to the liberation movements; similarly the African Bureau was set up to offer direct financial, propaganda and military support to the struggle. Additionally refugees from South Africa, Namibia, Rhodesia and other colonial dependencies in Africa were granted placements, scholarships and other facilities in our educational institutions and even employment opportunities where necessary in order to help prepare them for the struggle ahead. Indeed, so dear was the liberation cause to the heart of Nkrumah that no less a body than the African Affairs Secretariat which, at the time, functioned as a separate and autonomous organ from the Ministry of External Affairs (as it was then called), was assigned responsibility under the direct supervision and control of Dr. Kwame Nkrumah himself for the formulation and direction of our African policy in this regard.

In the same manner, Ghana was instrumental at the United Nations and other international fora in spearheading the adoption of a number of measures against the colonial and racist presence in Africa; most notably, General Assembly Resolution 1514(XV) of 1960 on the granting of independence to colonial territories and Resolution 1716 at the 17th Session of the General Assembly in 1962 requesting Member States separately or collectively to apply diplomatic and economic sanctions including an arms embargo against South Africa as well as the establishment of the UN Special Committee on Apartheid which was assigned responsibility for reviewing UN policies on South Africa and assessing the extent of their effectiveness. Indeed, to an extent that none can gainsay and to which the unprecedented accession of 17 African countries to independence in 1960 alone bears ample testimony — it is largely to the credit of the liberation policy pursued by Ghana under Nkrumah that the acceleration of the process of decolonization in Southern and Eastern Africa owed it success.

In all this, it is significant to note that in the practice of Ghana's policy of decolonization, Nkrumah was as forth-right and uncompromising in his commitment to the basic objective of liberty for all, as he was principled in his pragmatism and preparedness to support a negotiated transfer of power to the black majority in the areas of colonial and racist domination such as the then Rhodesia. Some of you may even remember the little known fact of Dr. Nkrumah's invitation to South Africa to attend the First Conference of Independent African States in Accra in 1958 and his preparedness to establish diplomatic relations with that country. South Africa, as we know, frustrated both objectives.[14] Now, as the pressure mounts on the Pretoria regime in this last phase of the liberation struggle in Africa, I can only call on the racist regime even at this stage to acknowledge the urgent need in their own best interest to come down from their high horses to negotiate a meaningful transfer of power not only in Namibia but also to the black majority in South Africa itself. Nkrumah's struggle for the liberation of the African continent was a reflection of his aim of dignity for the blackman and of the oppressed generally. He was opposed to the war in Vietnam for that reason. As regards the impact of his struggle for the dignity of the black man the words of Mr. Ralph Bunche at the luncheon given in Nkrumah's honor at Harlem in 1958 by the Harlem Lawyers Association says it all

We salute you, Kwame Nkrumah, not only because you are Prime Minister of Ghana, although this is cause enough. We salute you because you are a true and living representation of our hopes and ideals, of the determination we have to be accepted fully as equal beings of the pride we have held and nurtured in our African origin, of the achievement of which we know we are capable of the freedom in which we believe, of the dignity imperative to our stature as men .[15]

It is significant that the rise of black power in the United States of America coincided with the liberation struggle in Africa.

The Attainment of African Political Unity and African Personality

A fundamental objective of Dr. Nkrumah to which the decolonization of Africa was a prelude was the political unity of Africa. The form this unity would take or the speed with which it should proceed did not have a consistent definition more particularly in relation to the degree of sovereignty to be surrendered by the component states. This is apparent from contrasting the Sanniquellie Declaration of the conference between Ghana, Guinea and Liberia in July 1959 with the results of the Conference of Independent African States in Accra in 1958, his address to the Conference on Positive Action and Security in Africa in 1960, and to the National Assembly on 3rd September, 1965, and in Dublin on 1~,th May, 1960. However, Nkrumah's commitment to African unity was an obsession. It was with this objective in view, among others, that he called the Conference of Independent African States and of All African Peoples and worked for the creation of the Ghana-Guinea Union as early as 1959. Envisaged as a nucleus of a Union of Independent African States the Ghana-Guinea Union was later joined by Mali. Other efforts towards African unity included the Sanniquellie conference, the wooing of Upper Volta (Burkina Faso), Togo and the Congo into political union and the formation of the Casablanca group. Nkrumah's desperation for union led him to woo support from political parties and to advocate the creation of an All African Trade Union Federation and the development of Pan African political consciousness through the setting up of the Ideological institute at Winneba.

However well intentioned Nkrumah was, his policy and tactics alarmed some people, aroused envy and provoked opposition from many African countries which led to charges of African imperialism, lack of realism and subversion of sister African states. With the prodding of imperialist forces the Monrovia group was formed as a bloc of so called moderate African states to champion devalued concepts of African unity and to undermine Nkrumah's influence. While the Brazzaville GIOUP at the Lagos and Monrovia Conferences were campaigning for an African organization based on a unity of aspirations and action, Ghana under Nkrumah continued to press for a more viable institution based on political interaction in which Africa would have a common foreign policy and a common economic and domestic policy buttressed by a High Command of the armed forces to defend the territorial integrity and sovereignty of our countries. It was a measure of Ghana's commitment to African unity that Nkrumah had enshrined in the 1960 Republican Constitution that Ghana was the nucleus of a union of the continent.[16] Eventually when the Organization of African Unity was set up in Ethiopia in 1963 it was based on the notion of functional or diplomatic unity rather than a fusion of sovereignty, but Nkrumah enthusiastically supported it. Half a loaf was better than none. That the rest of Africa did not seem to share Nkrumah's vision of a United States of Africa was only partially his fault. His opposition to Nyerere over the creation of an East African community and his dealings with political parties some of whom were in opposition to the Governments of other African states could not have been helpful in enhancing his prospects for a Union; and the opportunities missed in fostering unity with Togo particularly under Olympio did not do credit to his strategy. Whatever the tactical errors, Nkrumah's conviction was sincere and thanks largely to him, the concept of African unity gained currency and his dream lives on the reality that without it Africa is incapable of escaping from its position of economic servitude and political impotence.

If I appear to have dwelt at such length on Ghana's African Policy under Nkrumah, this is simply because of the central position Africa occupied in Nkrumah's foreign policy calculations, and that this was largely a contributory factor of his overthrow. Being the first sub-Saharan country to gain independence from colonial rule, Ghana under Nkrumah played a much larger role in African affairs than might otherwise have been expected of a country of its size. Of the many successor states in the post-colonial era in Africa none aroused so many hopes as Ghana and none came to independence with so extensive a commitment to the development of a forceful Pan-African policy.

Significantly, also, Pan-Africanism was brought to a state which at the time was well-endowed with natural and human wealth. Ghana supplied one-third of the world's cocoa as well as one-fifth of its gold. Our external reserves at independence were over half a billion dollars which was more than India, for instance, had at a comparative time in her history. This degree of wealth meant that the Nkrumah administration had no pressing need to seek massive aid anywhere.[17] It was against this background that Ghana under Nkrumah was transformed into the torch-bearer of African irredentism and unity, a matter of pride which we still cherish to this day. Nkrumah became a symbol of what Africa could be and of necessity a foe of imperialist designs on Africa. This, among other things, sealed his doom.

Let me now turn to the other elements of Ghana's foreign policy under Nkrumah which though, perhaps, not as central and all-pervading as our African concerns were, nonetheless, tenets of fundamental and compelling significance in their own right. I shall begin with Nkrumah's policy toward the United Nations.

Support for the United Nations

In a world of super-power rivalry and antagonisms, President Nkrumah saw the United Nations Organization as providing the most effective forum and machinery for small countries like Ghana to exert some measure of influence for peace and progress in the world. As Nkrumah saw it, in spite of the reach and range of modern communication, it was a matter beyond doubt that there would be neither a world moral opinion nor the means to express it if the United Nations did not exist. Therefore, given our stake in peace and the security we seek for our peoples, it was not only logical but also vital that Ghana should actively identify with the medium that the world body offered for us to make ourselves heard on issues that pre-occupied us. In an address to the US Senate on 24th July, 1958, he said: "On this great issue, therefore, of war and peace, the people and Government put their weight behind the peaceful settlement of disputes . . . We are willing to accept every provision of the United Nations Charter."[18]

Similarly, Nkrumah saw the world body as being not only an indispensable tool in the struggle against colonialism, neo-colonialism, racism and apartheid but also as a medium for social and economic development dedicated to raising the standard of living of all people and, in particular, the countries of the Third World. Thus, from the very moment of our admission into the world body, Ghana under Nkrumah sought to foster maximum co-operation with the

UN as well as its various agencies some of which, in time, came to establish their regional headquarters in Accra. One is also doubtless aware of Ghana's role in the peace-keeping operations of the United Nations beginning from the Congo crisis in 1960 and the honors won for the country by the brilliant performance of our men culminating in the appointment of a Ghanaian as Commander of the United Nations Force in the Middle East.

However, if Ghana was committed to the United Nations, Nkrumah was, nonetheless, only too well aware of how in the existing world situation, it was easy for a small country to be frustrated and its interests set at naught in the arena of international politics where the word of the big powers carried. Thus in the preface to his, *I Speak of Freedom*, he wrote:

It may be argued that the existence of the United Nations Organization offers a guarantee for the independence and territorial integrity of all states, whether big or small. In actual fact, however, the UN is just as reliable an instrument for world order and peace as the Great Powers are prepared to allow it to be.[19]

How then could a small country, like Ghana, maintain its independence in the midst of the prevailing super power rivalry and conflict? And how could Ghana co-operate with any of the Big Powers and at the same time manage to maintain her independence of initiative and action?

Non-alignment and Positive Neutrality

Ghana, to a considerable extent, was able to do so, that is, to maintain the right to act in the way she considered best by adopting a policy of Positive Neutrality and Non-Alignment. Nkrumah's role in the formation of the Non-Aligned Movement in 1961 has been well documented.[20] Simply put, this policy was dictated by the calculated refusal of the emerging countries of the Third World to enter into any military or political commitment with any of the great powers or for that matter, any alliance concluded in the context of Great Power politics. The positive objective of this refusal was to retain substantial freedom of policy and action in international affairs especially in relation to the policies and actions of the super powers. Specifically, this policy defined our policy towards NATO and the Warsaw Pact alike and also implied a doctrine of peaceful co-existence which in the precarious era of post-war confrontational nuclear politics had become a cardinal pre-condition for the peace and security of the world. If non-alignment meant that Ghana would not allow herself to become subservient to any power or in any way accept dictation from outside, Positive Neutrality, on the other hand, did not mean that being neutral, Ghana would then withdraw into her shell and not be concerned even by issues of burning urgency that affected her.

In addition to making us free and not being hamstrung in any way, this policy also required taking on the mantle of self-reliance even as we sought to diversify our sources of external aid and investment of the vital and self-sufficient type, which the country clearly needed in supplementation of our efforts at nation building.

Nkrumah summed up the policy of non-alignment and positive neutrality in his speech to the US Senate on 24th July, 1958, thus:

Non-alignment can only be understood in the context of the present atomic arms race and the atmosphere of the cold war. There is a wise African proverb: 'When the bull elephants fight, the grass is trampled down.' When we in Africa survey the industrial military power concentrated behind the two great powers in the cold war, we know that no military or strategic act of ours could make one jot of difference to this balance of power, while our involvement might draw us into areas of conflict which so far have not spread below the Sahara. Our attitude, I imagine, is very much that of America looking at the disputes of Europe in the 1 9th century. We do not wish to be involved . In addition, we know that we cannot affect the outcome. Above all, we believe the peace of the world in general is served, not harmed by keeping one great continent free from the strife and rivalry of military blocks and cold wars. But this attitude of non-alignment does not imply indifference to the great issues of our day. It does not imply isolationism. It is in no way anti-Western; nor is it anti-Eastern. The greatest issue of our day is surely to see that there is a tomorrow. For Africans especially there is a particular tragedy in the risk of thermo-nuclear destruction. Our continent has come but lately to the threshold of the modern world. The opportunities of health and education and a wider vision which other nations take for granted are barely within the reach of our people. And now they see the risk that all this richness of opportunity may be snatched away by destructive war. In any war, the strategic areas of the world would be destroyed or occupied by some great power. It is simply a question of who gets there first — the Suez Canal, Afghanistan and the Gulf of Aquaba are examples.[21]

In essence the policy was aimed at the avoidance of big power politics, keeping the cold war out of Africa, not taking sides in the ideological debate and creating conditions for peace and for the development of Africa; and it is predicated on the reality that Africa was impotent to affect the balance of power. This policy dictated Nkrumah's opposition to military pacts between independent African states and their former colonial master and also his call for an All African Trade Union Federation in order to avoid the practice whereby the Trade Union Organizations in Africa were affiliated either to the Western or Eastern controlled federation of Trade Unions. It was also the basis of his opposition to the supply of arms to India by Great Britain during the Sino-Indian war and the maintenance of an even-handed approach to East and West Germany and to North and South Korea. With regard to the Sino-Indian war, Nkrumah, however, went on to join the Afro-Asian group whose suggestion for ending the conflict, namely the Colombo proposals, were eventually accepted by the Indian Prime Minister and Parliament in July 1962 to bring an end to the conflict.

It was courageous to adopt non-alignment and positive neutrality in Nkrumah's day. This policy was described by Foster Dulles, the US Secretary of State, as immoral. This policy coupled with his strident anti-imperialism and openings to the East marked out Nkrumah as dangerous to Western interests and obviously contributed to his overthrow. Certainly the ideological rhetoric of the *Ghanaian Times* and the *Spark* and of many CPP functionaries of those days heightened western susceptibilities.

Ghana's Policy Towards the Commonwealth

On the attainment of independence, Ghana moved from colonial status to dominion status to become the first African member of the Commonwealth. The significance of the Commonwealth to Nkrumah is reflected in several of his speeches, most notably the ones to the National Assembly on his *Motion of Destiny* on 10th July, 1953, and on the eve of independence on 5th March, 1957, to the US Senate in 1958 and to the Commonwealth Prime Ministers' Conference in London on 9th July, 1965. In summary he saw in the Commonwealth:

1. An example of a free association of independent states and a demonstration of the sort of international relations Ghana wished to see.
2. An example of multiracialism.
3. An example of North-South co-operation through which he hoped, rather in vain, to sell his scheme of cocoa purchases by the older members in order to stabilize prices in recognition of Ghana's considerable contribution to the dollar earnings of the sterling area of the volume of 25 per cent in the 50s.

4. A vehicle for the transfer of technology and for economic and cultural co-operation.
5. "A pilot scheme," in his words to the National Assembly on the eve of independence, "for developing the most effective methods by which colonialism can be ended without revolutions or violence and under conditions in which the former colonial territory still retains a close and friendly association with the former imperial power."[22]
6. A platform for projecting African personality in world affairs.
7. A brotherhood of shared values and tradition.[23]

For Nkrumah, therefore, the Commonwealth represented the triumph of maturity over prejudice. It was also an association based not on any rigid rules or treaty but on tradition and consensus openly arrived at and on an equality of sovereignties whose collective wealth and diversity were matched only by the strength of its collective moral force. It is a reflection of his admiration for the Commonwealth that he made the singular contribution of suggesting the creation of the Commonwealth Secretariat.

Balancing Competing Interests — The dilemmas of Foreign Policy Formulation and Execution

If I have stated Nkrumah's foreign policy in terms of praise and admiration this is because by and large the policy was courageous and correct. However, we must recognize some weaknesses in the implementation or formulation of that policy that affected the success of the policy and the perceptions of others towards Ghana.

In his determination to achieve African unity in his lifetime he was impatient of others with dissimilar views and he assisted or dealt with opposition political groups in a number of states — Cote d'Ivoire (Ivory Coast), Togo, Nigeria, The Gambia, etc., as to arouse allegations of subversion and interference in their internal affairs. By the time of the military coup of 1966 Nkrumah's influence in Africa was waning precisely because of this and other reasons, and Ghana was suffering from some degree of isolation.

To what extent the assistance to opposition elements was conscious policy and to what extent it was forced upon him is difficult to say. The problem of political refugees continues to bedevil relations between African countries until today, long after Nkrumah's overthrow. Political refugees are often not invited into any country but they find their way there and international practice requires that they are given sanctuary. Once there they are a source of friction between the receiving state and the state of their nationality and where there are conflicts of interest they are useful tool for destabilization.

Another dilemma faced by Nkrumah was the problem of balancing his African policy with the need to maintain efficiency and stability at home. The policy of Africanization had therefore to be held in check with the result that the presence of British officers in the Ghana Army compounded his problems in the Congo. Moreover, as an officer of the British Army, General Alexander, who led the Ghana contingent had different perceptions of how to deal with the Lumumba Government than Nkrumah had. The role of the Ghanaian forces in the Congo could be defended in terms of their status as UN troops but this overlooks the fact that UN policy and Nkrumah's aims in participating in the UN operations were not always the same. Lumumba invited Ghanaian troops to the Congo to help maintain his regime and not to supervise the disintegration of his authority. In the end even though we went into the Congo as heroes we left with some disfavor and without having enhanced African Unity.

It is a marvel that Nkrumah achieved so much when he had so little to work with. The infant foreign service did not have the facilities or an adequate stock of skilled or committed men to sustain his pace. He therefore took direct charge by creating the African Affairs Secretariat under him. But this created problems as the Foreign Ministry and the Bureau of African Affairs were equally involved in policy formulation and execution.

A more devasting constraint on the success of Nkrumah's policies was the near impossibility then of exercising a truly independent judgment in the neo-colonialist situation into which many an African nation, including Ghana, was born on independence. Our economy was effectively linked with the west and was most vulnerable to pressures as a result of reliance on a single crop.

We have noted that on the eve of independence Nkrumah told Parliament that "Our foreign policy shall be based on three words: dignity, peace and friendship." These values were the basis of his policy, and they were noble. Dignity for the African and for the black man in general he achieved in large measure, peace eluded him as it has eluded mankind for centuries, friendship he achieved with many and not with some and these were powerful enough to destabilize his regime and to send him into exile. A dramatic end to a dramatic career.

Nkrumah certainly had his limitations and may have often misjudged the mood of his times, but he will go down in history as a pioneer without a peer.

NOTES

1. For a discussion of the more serious viewpoints on this subject, see, Luggard, 1965 . 617-618.
2. Nkrumah, 1957: 37
3. Jacques Garvey, 1969: 3 8
4. *Ibid.* 'S
5. *Ibid* . 3 9
6. Nkrumah, op. cit. 43
7. Zolberg, 1964: 219
8. Nkrumah, 1962c: 95
9. *Ibid.* 97
10. *Ibid.* 123
11. *Ibid.* 218
12. Midnight pronouncement of Independence, Accra 5-6th March, 1957.
13. du Bois Papers, Accra.
14. See Appendix 'A', *the papers relating to The First Conference of Independence African States,* Accra, 1958, Dei-Anang, 1 975.
15. Nkrumah, 1962c: 147
16. Article 2 of the Constitution of the (First) Republic of Ghana (1960).
17. Thompson, 1969: 17
18. Nkrumah, 1962c: 143
19. *Ibid.*
20. Mazrui, 1969: 164-175; also Legum, 1962: 112–17 and Nkrumah, 196b.
21. Nkrumah, 1962c: 143
22. *Ibid.* 101
23. For further reading on Nkrumah's views on the Commonwealth, See Mazrui, *ibid.,* chs. 4 and 9.

NKRUMAH

Part 3
ECONOMY

Nkrumah and State Enterprises

K. B. Asante

The Origins of Significant State Involvement in the Economy

Although the form and nature of state enterprises in Ghana were largely determined by Nkrumah's personality and political leanings, the establishment of public corporations in industry, trade and services was a historical necessity given the circumstances and what a shrewd observer has described as "the people's insistent demand for rapid development."[1]

The Influence of Guggisberg and Colonial Trends

State intervention in the economy of the Gold Coast in the twenties under the leadership of the colonial Governor, Sir Gordon Guggisberg, was so successful that the principle of Government responsibility for economic and social development has become deeply rooted in the Ghanaian mind. According to Omaboe, "if the tempo of development achieved in the country during 1920-27 had been maintained Ghana would now be enjoying a standard of living approaching that of some of the developed countries of the world."[2] But even before Guggisberg, the idea of tutelage, or engagement in social, political and economic upliftment, had been developing since the latter part of the

19th Century as the rationalization for colonial rule.

Concern for economic and social development heightened after the Second World War and measures such as the Colonial Development and Welfare Act were adopted to promote social and economic advances. But the tempo of development envisaged by these measures was far below the aspirations of the people of the Gold Coast. For example, in 1946 £3.5 million was allocated to the Gold Coast under the Colonial Development and Welfare Act to be expended during the next ten years. The Gold Coast Government planned to supplement it by approximately £4 million. The allocation may be viewed in the light of the estimated Revenue and Expenditure of the country for the 1946-47 fiscal year of £5.6 million and £6.1 million respectively. It may therefore be argued that the allocated amount was not paltry. It was, however, definitely not tuned to the needs of the times. But what was even more important was that no major structural change in the economy was contemplated. Education was properly given importance, but industry (and by industry I include the agricultural industry) received only peripheral treatment such as the planned promotion of industry through the furtherance of "local African manufacturing industries"[3] by the allocation of funds in the 1946-47 budget estimates for a "study of the role of gold in the art and culture of the Akan people."[4]

The Cocoa Marketing Board

A colonial initiative to promote social and economic welfare, which has had far-reaching influence on the policies of successive Ghana governments, including the evolution of state enterprises, was the establishment of the Cocoa Marketing Board in 1947 following the Cocoa White Papers of 1944 and 1946. By the Amending Ordinances of 1951 and 1952 under Nkrumah's pre-independence administration, the Board came under more effective and direct control of Government. The government and its successors were thus enabled to replace the difficult search for a sound financial policy by recourse to the resources of the Board.

Bauer[5] as early as 1954 warned about some of the possible adverse effects of the operations of the Board on the cocoa industry and on the economy. But here we are mainly concerned with the effects of the operations of the Board in drying up sources of savings for industrial and other enterprises. Savings for investment could most readily have come from the operators in the biggest industry in the country: cocoa farmers and the Ghanaian middlemen, most of whom performed economically useful functions. But efficient middlemen were replaced by organs of the Board; and the farmers were heavily taxed indirectly by low producer prices and the export tax on cocoa. Cocoa prices, fixed by the Board, on the prompting of Government, affected levels of income, the standard of living and the ability to save. Government was therefore constrained to assume the role of the entrepreneur. Rapid industrialization could in the circumstances only be most readily achieved through direct Government action in establishing state enterprises.

The Industrial Development Board/Corporation

In his address to the Legislative Council on March 12, 1946, Sir Allan Burns, the Governor, stated that "It is the Government's policy to develop local African manufacturing industries and the instrument which has been set up for the purpose is the Industrial Development Board."[6] The appendix to his address gave more details about the Board.

The Industrial Development Board was set up in October 1946 to initiate and build up commercially with a view to "handing over to local private enterprise," certain industrial projects such as the Togoland textiles scheme, high-class furniture and cabinet making, and leather-working and shoe-making. A Secretary and executive officer of the Board was appointed and an instructor in high-class cabinet work recruited from the United Kingdom.

The concept was too narrow for the mood of the times,but perhaps not for the capacity of the country as perceived by the colonial administration. For Nkrumah, who was soon to come on the scene, the colonial industrialization scheme lacked inspiration and depth. His vision was reflected in a speech on December 19, 1948:

> And across the parapet I see the mother of West African Unity and Independence, her body smeared with the blood of her sons and daughters in their struggle to set her free from the shackles of imperialism. And I hear and see springing up cities of Ghana becoming the metropolis of science, art, industry, philosophy and learning. And I hear mortals resound the echo and the rejoinder: 'seek ye first the political kingdom and all things will be added unto it.'[7]

For Nkrumah, therefore, the colonial industrial development plans might be accommodated and tried until independence after which the real strategy would be developed to build Ghana into a strong, prosperous industrial state.

The report of the activities of the Industrial Development

Corporation which succeeded the Industrial Development Board, dated 6th November, 1951, (the year Nkrumah took charge of Government Business but with expatriates effectively in control), stated that three subsidiary companies had been formed, each with an African Managing-Director. These were a laundry, saw-milling and hand-weaving companies. There were losses due to "delays in arrival and installation of machinery, lack of sales and initial problems of administration."[8] The problems of state enterprises therefore started before Nkrumah came on the scene and have been persistent since his departure. Solutions therefore lie not in polemics, but in objective analysis, a proper reading of history and the national character and appreciation of economic realities and managerial skills.

The Pre-independence Administration of Nkrumah 1951-57

As Leader of Government Business from 1951 to 1957, Nkrumah tried to implement the schemes and plans of the colonial administration. Generally, he accepted conventional wisdom. In spite of the rhetoric there were hardly any radical initiatives in the economic field. He gave popular interpretation to the development plans of the colonial administration and mobilized his large CPP followers to give enthusiastic support to the implementation of on-going projects and plans already prepared. The disappointing results strengthened Nkrumah's faith in greater direct state intervention in the economy.

The Lewis Report

In 1952, Nkrumah's energetic lieutenant, Gbedemah, then Minister of Commerce and Industry, invited the distinguished West Indian economist, Professor Arthur Lewis, to report on the "problems of industrialization and Economic Policy." Lewis advised that "a vigorous agricultural programme is needed, not because food is scarce but because this is the road to economic progress." He went on to state that "the secret of industrialization is rapidly progressing agricultural and more particularly food production." He carefully examined a number of possible industries and found that many of them would not be viable. He wrote:

> The list of "favourable" industries is very short because the Gold Coast does not have many industrial raw materials.

Yet on processing cocoa, Ghana's major commodity, he commented:

In so far as the whole bean is used in the consuming countries, the Gold Coast has little chance of entering successfully into processing. It lacks fuel and skill and is at a disadvantage climatically.[9]

The Professor, however, found favourable prospects for the production of beer which depended on imported inputs. In obvious reference to state enterprises, Professor Lewis advised that "The Gold Coast government is so short of money that it should be reluctant to take on ownership and operation of industrial undertakings except where this is inescapable." Such ventures would, however, be inescapable in the case of utilities and for the purposes of pioneering. Here, the professor gave support to the Industrial Development Corporation concept of government establishing industries and turning them over to private enterprise.

We have dwelt at length on the Lewis Report because it is believed by many that the economic situation of Ghana would have been better if Nkrumah had followed the advice contained m the report, that in particular he should have concentrated on agriculture and not wasted resources on state enterprises. This belief is not supported by the facts. Nkrumah did not neglect agriculture as we shall see later. He regarded agriculture and industry as complementary or mutually supportive. And, in any case, not all parts of the Lewis recommendations were out of tune with the tempo of the times and the aspirations of Nkrumah and most Ghanaians.

The CPP and Agriculture

Nkrumah inherited the Ten-Year Development Plan of the Colonial Administration. He adopted its main elements, which lay emphasis on infrastructure, education and agriculture, as the CPP Development Plan to be implemented in five years. The "Grow More Food" campaign was initiated in 1951; and the Minister of Agriculture and Natural Resources stated in Parliament that Government "was exploring all avenues to stimulate the growth of more food. Government will adopt any constructive ideas of Parliamentarians".[10]

On the question of improving the farming industry and possible shortage of foodstuffs, the Minister of Agriculture and Natural Resources, Mr. Casely Hayford, informed the Legislative Assembly – that the "aim of Government is to foster as many agricultural enterprises and industries as possible."[11] A chain of agricultural stations were to be set up for experimental purposes, with the aim, amongst others, of improving the old methods of shifting cultivation by trying to find better and improved methods of dealing with the land.

Cocoa was of special concern but crops such as coconut, citrus and oil palm were to receive great attention.

The strategy adopted produced results which were not satisfactory on the whole in that food and crop production was not increased sufficiently to support consumption, exports and industry.

The CPP and Management of Corporations

As Nkrumah himself put it, "when the CPP came to power in 1951 the pace of development was so slow and confused that we decided to speed it up by attempting to implement in five years the programme of reconstruction which was designed by the colonial administration to take place over a period of ten years. That programme was not a development plan. It was a collection of various individual petty projects that had to be built in preparation for future planning."[12]

The CPP government therefore viewed the industrialization proposals of the colonial administration as inadequate but necessary. The proposals and projects of the Industrial Development Corporation were carried out with vigour. Soon difficulties arose with regard to the very nature of the instruments of implementation. The solutions evolved at this early stage are of crucial importance. They continue to bedevil state enterprises today. Inefficiency and mismanagement in state corporations became so pronounced that a bill was introduced in Parliament to deal with the problem. The CPP reaction to the situation, although faulty, appears to be essentially a Ghanaian approach, because it had been followed by all subsequent governments. We therefore quote the Minister of Trade and Labor, Kojo Botsio, at length:

> Following enquiry into the Cocoa Purchasing Company, legislation relating to all statutory Boards and Corporations had been examined with a view to securing closer governmental control of these bodies and of their subsidiaries . . . Provision has accordingly been made in the Bill to permit the Minister responsible for Trade to give specific directions to the Industrial Development Corporation and to its subsidiaries.

The Bill provided for the "nomination of a General Manager by the Minister with the prior approval of the Cabinet..."

> Furthermore it is proposed that the Minister should in future control the appointment of employees of the Corporations and any of the companies in which it has controlling interest where the respec-

tive basic salaries are £1000 per annum and over. [14]

In the debate which followed, Braimah questioned whether giving power to the Minister would solve the problem and he cited the Jibowu Report[15] in support. Wireko blamed outside interference and nepotism. But most of the criticism was on the appointment of CPP supporters only, and on qualifications. Jatoe Kaleo set the tone by charging that "the government has an unenviable reputation of filling most of these Boards with ex-convicts, people who have been imprisoned for dishonesty and improper conduct in the discharge of their public duties. Another is to fill these Boards with its party members who have been defeated."[16]

Regional interests were stressed meaning that industries should be fairly distributed in and among the regions rather than sited on economic considerations. And Wiafe, a CPP member, complained that the "Head of the Corporation was a quartermaster in the army;" and concerning the establishment of a soap factory by UAC asked: "Are we going to allow foreigners to set up industries which we have facilities to establish ourselves?"[17]

This and other debates reflected the trend in the country which accepted Ministerial control, laid emphasis on "paper qualifications rather than on competence" and preferred "industries to be established by Ghanaians." It was also felt that "Ghanaians should head state enterprises," Nkrumah's government gave expression to these feelings and views before and after complete independence.

Strategy After Independence

As has already been stated, Nkrumah continued with the colonial plans and strategies after independence. The Industrial Development Corporation and the Agricultural Development Corporation were the main governmental instruments for promoting the agricultural and industrial policies of his government. But private enterprise was expected to play a very substantial role in economic development. Towards this end, tariffs and tax incentives for pioneer industries were designed to encourage private investment. This strategy changed markedly after Ghana became a Republic.

Private Enterprise

The five-year Development Plan launched by Nkrumah in March, 1959 was to provide the "solid Foundation to build the welfare state"[18] and by "encouraging investment" raise the standard of living of the people. Nkrumah had described himself as "a Marxist Socialist and a non-denominational Christian"[19] and some may perhaps consider this contradictory. The Marxist socialist character however did not manifest itself strongly until later. His aim in the early days was to establish a "welfare state" not a "socialist state" and although the state was to direct the economy and establish enterprises, private enterprise — local as well as external — was regarded as an important and necessary instrument in the building of the welfare state.

Under the Income Tax (Amendment) Bill and the Pioneer Industries and Companies Bill of 1959, privileges and reliefs as might be prescribed were accorded to undertakings declared pioneer industries or companies. As the Minister of Finance, Mr. K. A. Gbedemah, stated:

> The Government attaches great importance to the expansion of industrial activity in the country and the purpose of the Bill is to provide a machinery for the declaration of pioneer industries and for their general regulation. This Bill empowers the Governor-General in appropriate circumstances to declare an industry to be a pioneer industry and when so declared the industry shall be entitled to such privileges and reliefs as may be prescribed or allowed under any Act of Parliament.[20]

The Local Industries (Customs Relief) Bill also sought "to give further encouragement to the setting up of new industries in Ghana"[21] by partial or total remission of customs duties.

These measures did not step up industrialization to the satisfaction of the impatient Kwame Nkrumah. Unlike similar more successful measures today in countries such as Northern Ireland, there was no precision as to which industry would be declared pioneer. It was within the Minister's discretion and this created an element of uncertainty and the possibility of unhealthy lobbying and corruption.

The Statutory Corporations Act

Meanwhile public corporations were being established to promote economic and social progress. The volume of work they entailed in Parliament was so great that in November, 1959, it was decided to adopt a bill under which public corporations could be established without recourse, each time, to Parliamentary legislation. This Act was re-enacted with modifications in 1961 and 1964.[22] The Act provided for the establishment of bodies corporate by Executive Instrument and in many ways established the character of public corporations including State Enterprises.

Under the Act, corporations were "to observe general or specific directions given by a Minister" or the relevant authority. Provision was made for the appointment of members of the Board, exemption of the properties and activities of the corporation from tax, rate or duty, the transfer on "secondment of public officers" and the "remuneration allowances and pensions of officers" and "servants" of the corporation. The effect of the Statutory Corporations Act (cf. para. 2.3) was to centralize the control of the corporations and, in spite of contrary professed intentions, subject them to a regime similar to that of the Civil Service, and generally to give them a character different from that which obtained in commercial concerns.

And commercial viability was not of crucial importance to Parliament and perhaps the nation. The mode was to see Ghana as a nation with all the trappings of the modern state. Not surprisingly, therefore, even though Minister of Communications, Krobo Edusei, admitted that Ghana Airways Corporation was making deficits of about £G200,000 to £G300,000 yearly, Parliament on November 20, 1959, moved "That this House record its appreciation of the magnificent progress which has been made by the Ghana Airways Corporation during its short existence."[23]

Industrialization Policy

During the early years of full independence, the strategy of using largely indirect state intervention to achieve a measure of industrialization was employed but with state enterprises being accorded a greater role. As Minister Quaidoo said, the IDC was "one of the vital war horses at the head of our plans to make Ghana an industrial nation."[24] The IDC was still (i) "to pioneer in fields of industrialization where private enterprise does not enter," and (ii) "to apply new techniques to existing industries."[25] It was to achieve these two objectives "by carrying out research, establishing itself and also by assisting private industrialists with loan finance."

It would be observed that these aims and objectives made it difficult to assess the achievement of the corporation objectively in financial terms. Be that as it may, by the middle or 1959, subsidiary companies of the IDC had been established and the Corporation was engaged in laundries, manufacture of tobacco, matches, soap, furniture, saw-milling and the running of cinemas.[26] A brick and tile factory which had foundered was being resuscitated and the Corporation had investments in the remolding of tires, airborne surveys, refining of oil, manufacture of biscuits and building materials and the management of cold stores. The corporation had also given financial assistance to companies engaged in cereal processing, baking, engineering and electrical works, pottery, printing, tailoring, dressmaking, shoe-making and leather works.

Prevalent Development Strategies

Although Nkrumah was initially prepared to adopt any viable strategy and instruments which would help build Ghana into a modern state, his socialist beliefs increasingly came to the fore. He came more and more to believe that action must be guided by a philosophy; but he was no slave to ideology. He was a man of ideas. He had the talent for grasping new ideas and the weakness of giving them form and calling them his own. He was conversant with the mainstream of the development theories and models in vogue and found natural sympathy with the prevalent highly interventionist school. As Tony Killick put it, this school:

> established powerful theoretical and practical arguments against reliance upon the market mechanism and advocated a strategy of development which placed the state in the centre of the stage. A central planning agency was to provide inducements or commands superior to the price signals of the market. There was much less agreement on whether the instrumentalities of the state should be largely indirect i.e. modifying but working through the market mechanism by such means as tariff policy and the provision of tax incentives for investment, or direct, i.e. replacing the market by administrative controls and the establishment of state-owned industries. It is not possible, in my view, to identify a consensus on this issue. But there was virtual unanimity on the large role of the state—a unanimity which extended to Ghana.

Nkrumah opted for a predominant role by the state after his visit to the Soviet Union and the Socialist countries of Eastern Europe.

Socialist Transformation of the Economy

In his address to the National Assembly on March 4, 1959, Nkrumah linked control of the modern state with control of the means of production and called on those responsible for "running our affairs" to "acquire a socialist perspective and a socialist drive." But it was some two years later after his Eastern European tour that he went all out for a "socialist transformation" of the economy and attempted to accord a dominant role to state enterprises.

The Dominance of Ideology

The visit to the Soviet Union, China and the socialist countries of Eastern Europe in 1961 had a profound effect on Nkrumah. The story is told of Nkrumah requesting the Soviet authorities to arrange a private visit to Lenin's tomb after he and his entourage had paid the usual official visit. Nkrumah went alone to the mausoleum and meditated for about half-an-hour.[29] He became deeply disappointed with the pace of development in Ghana, especially when compared with the transformation of the Soviet Union from a "backward" state into a modern state through "socialist planning" in a little over a generation. He pondered over the methods used by Lenin and Stalin and came to the conclusion that the tradition, culture and the circumstances of Ghana precluded treading a similar path.[30] He however became convinced that the socialist transformation of the economy through the rapid development of the state and cooperative sectors was paramount and that the "colonial structures" of the economy should be eliminated.

In retrospect Nkrumah lamented the past as shown above. As he himself stated,[31] at the conclusion of the Five-Year Reconstruction Programme, his government paused for two years because it became quite clear that the solution to the reconstruction of Ghana lay, in the long run, in the adoption of a socialist and cooperative programme for industry and the mechanization and diversification of agriculture.

Nkrumah often tried to show that he was always consistent and had a grand plan and design which he followed faithfully but whose implementation had to take account of circumstances and realities. "One step backward, two steps forward," he used to say. Nkrumah was, however, a realist and as he said when presenting the 7-Year Development Plan, Ghana would operate a mixed economy for sometime during which vigorous public and cooperative sectors would operate alongside the private sector. His ideology was tempered with pragmatism. It was a means to an end, and what he wanted above all also was to turn Ghana in a "relatively short period" into a "modern industrial nation providing opportunities for all and a standard of living comparable to any in the world."[32]

Ideology in Context

Nkrumah was aware that planning and state enterprises were not exclusive preserves of socialism. He was an avid reader and enjoyed the company of intellectuals and men of ideas, especially those whose views were similar to his own. Nkrumah was therefore aware of the trends of development economics, and as Killick put it, during this period, "Mainstream development economics was at many points highly congenial to Marxists. This is of considerable importance when we turn to examine economic policies in Ghana during the Nkrumah period, for Nkrumah called himself a Marxist and was clearly influenced by Marxian ideas. . . Perhaps the congruence of mainstream development economics and Marxian views was not surprising, for inequality has long been one of the principal concerns of Marxian thought, and the hidden value premise of development economics is an egalitarian one . . . Whatever the reason, it is probably true to say that contemporary Marxian thought was in general agreement with the main tenets of mainstream development economics."[33]

Nkrumah and his lieutenants, however, gave the impression that state enterprises were a consequence of their socialist leanings and not dictated mainly by Ghana's circumstances, experience and aspirations. This was unfortunate. The linkage of socialism with state enterprises remains strong in many Ghanaian minds and debates about the failures or achievements of state enterprises often degenerate into arguments about the relative merits of socialism and free enterprise. Knowledge of state enterprises in countries which follow the free enterprise system is often restricted to superficial acquaintance with the nationalized industries in Britain. The extent of state intervention in the economy in most countries, and more particularly the existence of reasonably successful state enterprises in such countries as France and Canada, is often not fully appreciated.

Nkrumah made state enterprises a part of his ideology. But state enterprises had already been found in Ghana's circumstances to be an indispensable tool in the industrialization of the country, and successive governments have not found it possible to disengage from industrial, commercial and agricultural enterprises. Indeed,the number of state-owned enterprises has increased since Nkrumah's departure. It is therefore necessary to attempt an appraisal of efforts to deal with the ills which plague state enterprises today—ills which were apparent long ago in the days of the Industrial Development Corporation. Putting the state enterprises debate in an ideological context is unhelpful.

The Objectives

From the early sixties onwards Nkrumah got annoyed with anyone who referred to Ghana as an agricultural country.[34] This was a reaction to paternalistic and unconvincing "expert" advice. But

Nkrumah was not against agricultural development His establishment of State Farms testifies to this. Nkrumah saw rapid industrialization as the path to modernity and state enterprises were the instruments for achieving this transformation and assisting in the national control of the economy.

For Nkrumah industrialization was a means to an end. As he said during the Sessional Address on 25th September, 1963, the aim of his government was "as far as possible" to establish industries in the rural areas "to stimulate economic activity in these areas." The objective was to carry work to the people and thereby "arrest the steady drift of the population into the cities and big towns from the countryside." And in pursuit of this a number of small-scale industries such as the bamboo factory had started or were nearing completion, he stated.

Another objective in establishing state enterprises was to provide "concrete employment opportunities" and to "enhance foreign exchange earnings." The time of pious hope that someone else would provide the jobs for the growing number of unemployed and partially employed was over. But it was not the aim of Nkrumah to squeeze out private enterprise. He did appreciate the enormity of the task and the necessity of tapping all available resources. As he stated "private investors continue to play active role in industrial development" and he explained how the Capital Investment Act consolidated all the measures taken to stimulate economic activity. In his view investors "continue to flock in" but in retrospect we can say that this was an optimistic assessment and that not all the investors who flocked in promoted desirable economic activity.

The Problems

As we have already seen, the perennial problems of inefficiency and losses in state corporations surfaced in the colonial days. When these problems became acute and compounded, Nkrumah sought to deal with them by exhortation, through ideological orientation and by strengthening Ministerial and Presidential control.

Failings Identified

The failure of state enterprises was a major blow to Nkrumah's grand design for the economy. One can do no better than allow Kwame Nkrumah himself to speak on the subject:[35]

> We have already established many industrial projects and enterprises, as a means of securing our economic independence and

assisting in the national control of the economy. I must make it clear that *these state enterprises were not set up to lose money at the expense of the tax payers.*[36] Like all business undertakings they are expected to maintain themselves efficiently, and "to show profits." Such profits should be sufficient to build up capital for further investment as well as to finance a large proportion of the public services which it is the responsibility of the state to provide.

In every socialist country, state enterprises provide the bulk of state revenues and we intend to follow the same pattern here. Our state enterprises will set up yearly financial and production targets so that they may work towards definite objectives and goals and thereby given every stimulus to operate efficiently and profitably. Here the managers of our state enterprises and those in charge of our state organizations and apparatus should be men trained in management; honest and dedicated men; men with integrity; men who are incorruptible.

When we have succeeded in establishing these principles, Government will then be in a position to lower taxes progressively, to lessen steadily the burden of taxation on the people and eventually to abolish many of them, if not all of them.

Good management, probity and integrity were correctly identified as prerequisites for the successful running of state enterprises which should generate sufficient resources or profits for further investment and help finance services without increasing the tax burden on citizens. Nkrumah found that these prerequisites were lacking and what was worse, the state enterprises were being subsidized instead of making money. Having identified the problems Nkrumah sought solutions which were not successful but which are of great relevance today because the fundamental structures he established have not been changed much.

Central Control

In spite of the shortcomings of state enterprises, Nkrumah pressed on with the extension of state ownership. As he asserted at the opening of the National Assembly on 12th January, 1965:

State enterprises are the main economic pillars on which we expect to build our socialist state. We will continue to expand the public sector of the economy by establishing more state-owned enterprises both in industry and agriculture. We have at present 35 state enterprises in operation and additional new ones are being established right now which will bring the total to 60. Also we have shareholding in nine joint enterprises . . . and discussions are going on to add three more.

Having decided to expand state enterprises, Nkrumah proceeded to put things right by greater political control. And yet many of the ills which afflicted and continue to afflict state enterprises can be traced to inept political or ministerial control. But Nkrumah believed that those imbued with socialism were incorruptible and would always seek the public interest. Even if they took 10 per cent it would be for the party's coffers and would therefore be in the national interest since a strong party was indispensable to the attainment of his socialist goals and the prosperity of the masses.

The Legal Instruments

As his lieutenants failed or disappointed him and as problems mounted, Nkrumah intervened more and more directly in the running of state enterprises. Authority was sought in various legal instruments promulgated in accordance with the Statutory Corporations Act. The general pattern of control was to invest the Minister responsible for the corporation or enterprise with powers to give directions and to appoint the Board and chief personnel with the approval of or in consultation with the State Enterprises Secretariat and the Cabinet. This in effect meant that Nkrumah himself assumed greater control since at that time no Minister would take a substantial decision without consulting him. Moreover, Nkrumah's powers were explicitly stated by provisions which allowed the President to exercise reserve powers at any time.

Political Control

As an illustration of the political control authorized by legal instruments, we may take the Ghana National Construction Corporation Instrument, 1965. Under Part VII(2), "All appointments to any post in the Corporation of General Manager or Manager or to any other post of a similar category in the Corporation shall be made by the Minister with the approval of the Cabinet." Under Part IV, Article 3, "The Minister shall appoint to be Chairman of the Board, such member of the Board as the Cabinet may approve and may with the approval of the Cabinet revoke any such appointment." Under Article 4, "The members of the Board, other than the Managing Director, . . . may with the approval of the Cabinet, be removed from office at any time by a direction in writing given by the Minister." The Managing Director himself is appointed "with the approval of the Cabinet by the Minister and upon the recommendation of the State Enterprises Secretariat."

And the members of the Board are appointed "by the Minister with the approval of the Cabinet."

Moreover, under Parts Xl and XI11(2)

> The Minister may, subject to the provisions of this Instrument, give directions of a general character to the Corporation as to the general policy of the Corporation and the Corporation shall be bound to comply with such direction.

And the Minister had to consult the ultimate authority for,

> No direction, instruction, requisition, approval, authorisation or other things shall be given or made by any member empowered to do so under this instrument,
> a. To the Corporation or any employee thereof
> b. To be Board or any member thereof;
> c. To the Auditor-General or any auditor appointed by him under Part X of this Instrument except after consultation with, and through the medium of the State Enterprises Secretariat.

Nkrumah in Effective Control

It should be noted that the State Enterprises Secretariat was under the direct control of President Nkrumah and was located in his office at Flagstaff House, which was known in those days as "the Power House." Therefore the President had effective control of state enterprises. To underline the powers of Osagyefo, the instrument made it quite clear that the President was indeed the ultimate authority. Part XIV stated:

> Notwithstanding anything to the contrary in this Instrument, the President may at ally time it he is satisfied that it is in the national interest so to do. take over the control and management of the affairs or any part of the affairs of the Corporation and may, for that purpose;
> a. Reconstitute the Board
> b. Appoint, transfer, suspend or dismiss any of the employees of the Corporation, and
> c. Do, in furtherance of the interests ol the Corporation, any other act which is authorised or required to be done by any person under this Instrument.

Objectives of Control

As we have found, Nkrumah was unhappy about the short-comings of state enterprises and kept repeating what he wanted these enterprises to achieve. He deprecated the shortcomings of state enterprises which he insisted should make profits for further capital investment and repeated that unprofitable state enterprises would be closed down.[37] He sought more direct control of state-owned enterprises to inject more purposefulness and efficiency into them but unfortunately, in the process, established an apparatus which strengthened outside control instead of giving each enterprise sufficient autonomy to run on "sound commercial lines."

We quote Nkrumah himself to show that he inspired the legal instruments which established political control over state enterprises and that his measures were in practice at variance with his objectives:

> In view of the special requirement for the staffing and organisation of state enterprises, a special procedure will be established for the recruitment, training and discipline of staff of all state enterprises. The employees of these state enterprises will be removed from the control of the Civil Service Commission and the Civil Service Regulations and Procedures.

> In accordance with the Instrument of Corporation under which the state corporations are being set up, appointments to the corporations will be made by the Boards of these corporations. The State Enterprises Secretariat will, however, ensure that these appointments are proper and that the salary scales fixed for them fit into the general pattern of salaries and working conditions which is being worked out for state enterprises. Appointments to positions of Manager and comparable posts will be made by the Minister with the approval of the Cabinet and upon the recommendations of the State Enterprises Secretariat.[38]

He added that the aim was "to make our state enterprises efficient and profitable state organizations and to run them on sound commercial lines."

The intentions were unexceptionable. But experience has shown that the action was a typically Ghanaian way of dealing with problems. And Nkrumah was the archetypal Ghanaian. Not surprisingly many of his acts, establishments and procedures which many Ghanaians deprecate have continued nineteen years after his departure from the scene. Indeed we continue to repeat them.

The typical Ghanaian way of dealing with inefficiency, abuse of authority or discretion, and even corruption, is not to improve or design better systems while vigorous action is taken in accordance with the existing rules, but to concentrate authority in one person. Thus we find Managing Directors and the like signing chits to authorize sales of scarce commodities and a routine process in organizations halted because the chief is absent. It is also taken for granted that authority should be concentrated in the hands of the Minister or the President; and arbitrary action by authority is generally accepted. It is to Nkrumah's credit that he endeavored to act within the law. What is of interest and contemporary relevance is that the laws and structures he established to govern state enterprises have not been questioned by successive governments. Ministers, Commissioners and Secretaries still like to be in a position to dismiss heads of state enterprises for any reason whatsoever and they also like to give directives to these organizations. The pettiness, arbitrariness, lack of discipline and disregard for procedures and the national interest of the political heads of Ministries are largely responsible for the failure of most of our state-owned enterprises.

Concluding Observations

State enterprises were the only available instruments for the rapid transformation of the economy of Ghana which Kwame Nkrumah sought. Later, Nkrumah saw in the socialist transformation of the economy and state institutions the quickest path for the modern Ghana of his dreams. He believed that "socialism is the only pattern that can within the shortest possible time bring the good life to the people."[39] He saw socialism as the cure for corruption and lack of motivation and purpose. Therefore he sought to appoint to key positions in state institutions including state enterprises, persons who were "dedicated socialists." Nkrumah however believed in efficiency and capability and the first two persons he appointed to lead the State Enterprises Secretariat were experienced, capable and mature public officers — Mr. J. V. L. Phillips and Mr. H. P. Nelson. In general, however, Ghanaians are not noted for their willingness to suffer for principle. Many became ardent socialists overnight to secure top appointments. Needless to state that it was the not-so-good who paraded their socialism. And these often made a mess of things when they obtained key posts in state enterprises, while they could hardly be touched because of their socialist credentials and party activism.

Now Nkrumah was a political animal and understood the need of political support. And despite his popularity with grassroot CPP supporters, Nkrumah appreciated the importance of key elements in the party such as Ministers and party activists in key posts. He would scold and threaten a Minister or a key functionary only to send aides and able and trusted Civil Servants like T. K. Impraim to find out how the victim took the incident and whether it had affected his loyalty to the President. Indeed Nkrumah was afraid of some Ministers and key functionaries.[40] He was also not an ungrateful person. He was conscious of help given or work done in the past and was most reluctant to take action against friends who had done so much for him and the party in the past. These qualities became weaknesses when applied to state enterprises which had become inefficient through bad management and corruption.

Nkrumah did consider foreign management in some state organizations but was not in favor of this because he believed that Ghanaians should have the opportunity to learn. He believed the problems prevailing to be teething troubles and, above all, he had faith in the abiding cure of socialism which he promoted with more vigour. Naturally, he never at this stage thought of selling off state enterprises which were doing badly even he threatened to close them down. He was aware of the mood of Ghanaians which was manifested later when attempts were made to sell state enterprises after he was overthrown. The Acheampong Government re-iterated the prevailing mood when it stated "we shall detest the concentration of shares in the hands of a few Ghanaian businessmen."[41]

No successful solution to the present crisis in the management and viability of many state enterprises can be found in simplistic prescriptions such as straightforward privatization which do not take account of the prevailing political and social trends and the history of the evolution of state enterprises. But lasting solutions are possible provided we search without prejudice and with open minds. We have for too long blamed Nkrumah for bequeathing us problems. He might have done better than build a corned beef factory near Bolgatanga where there were no sizeable herds of cattle, we complain. But we forget that we clamored and still clamor for fair distribution of enterprises in and among the various regions and even today we decry the exodus to the big cities and towns. Nkrumah did try to do something about these problems. But as in medicine, many drugs have side-effects. So we have to deal with the residual problems created by state enterprises. These enterprises are national assets and we must at least make most of them work. Our inability to profit from the state enterprises bequeathed to us by Nkrumah's efforts, and added on since his departure, is a serious indictment on our generation. We are like children who moan about the size and maintenance problems of houses bequeathed to us by a generous and hardworking father, instead of making these houses earn money for us. The state enterprises are a challenge to us. We cannot fail our children. With realism and hard-work, we are capable of making the assets bequeathed to us work for us.

NOTES

1. Harvey, 1960: 12.
2. In Birmingham, Omaboe and Neushadt, Vol. 1, 1966: 441.
3. Lewis, Report, 1953.
4. *Ibid.*
5. Bauer, 1954.
6. Legislative Council Debates: 1946.
7. Blueprint of our Goal, Launching of the Seven-Year Development Plan, 10th March, 1964.
8. Parliamentary Debates, 21st January, 1957.
9. Lewis, *Report,* 1953: pp. 3, 71.
10. Legislative Assembly Debates, November 22, 1951.
11. *Ibid.*
12. Address to the National Assembly, March 4, 1959.
13. Legislative Assembly Debates, 21st January, 1957.
14. *Ibid.*
15. Mr. Justice Jibowu of Nigeria investigated the activities of the Cocoa Purchasing Company and issued a very critical Report Exposing a number of malpractices. See *Report of the Commission of Inquiry into the Affairs of the Cocoa Purchasing Company Ltd.*, Government Printer, 195 0, part II of Gold Coast: Commission of Inquiry into the Affairs of the CPC.
16. Parliamentary Debates, 21st January, 1957.
17. *Ibid.*
18. In the National Assembly, March 4, 1959.
19. Statement to a Press Conference (February 13,1950) quoted by Bankole Timothy in his "Kwame Nkrumah and his Rise to Power". 195 5: 3 2.
20. *Parliamentary Debates,* First Series Vol. 17, 1957.
21. *Ibid.*
22. Statutory Corporations Act 1959 (No. 53) and the Acts of 1961 (Act 41) and 1964 (Act 232).
23. *Parliamentary Debates* 20th November, 1959.
24. *Parliamentary Debates,* 30th July, 1959: Statement by P. K. K. Quaidoo, Minister of Commerce and Industry.
25. *Parliamentary Debates,* First Series, Vol. 15.
26. Personal observation.
27. Killick, 1978: 24.
28. *Ibid.:* 24.
29. Confirmed by T. K. Impraim, a member of the touring team and one of the team of able and trusted civil servants Nkrumah assembled at Flagstaff House, Nkrumah's offices.
30. Personal observation.
31. *Blue-print of our Goal-Launching of the Seven-Year Development Plan,* 10th

March, 1964.
32. Sessional Address: First Parliament of the Republic, 1st July, 1960.
33. Killick, *op. cit.:* 25 .
34. Building a Socialist State—Address to the CPP Study Group, April 22, 1965 .
35. Address on 11th February, 1961, at the opening of Nzima Oil Mills.
36. Author's italics.
37. See Note 35.
38. *Ibid.*
39. Building a Socialist State, address to the CPP Study Group, April 22, 1961.
40. Personal Knowledge
41. Statement on the Investment Policy Decree 1975 (NRCD 325) and the Ghanian Enterprises Decree (NRCD 30).

Public Sector Manpower Development During the Nkrumah Period 1951-1966[1]

Joseph R. A. Ayee

Introduction

One of the major administrative problems which faced the Nkrumah government during the country's advance to self-government and subsequent independence was the Africanization of the Public Service. By all accounts, the colonial bureaucracy in Ghana compared favorably with similar public services elsewhere in Africa. The senior service of the bureaucracy was mainly staffed by expatriates, while the junior service was filled by local personnel. Since there was a dearth of skilled African manpower in the higher branches of the public service, the need for recruitment and training of African public servants to take over from the departing expatriates assumed a critical dimension. This need was further accentuated by the expansion of the bureaucracy between 1954–1957, which was required to implement the series of development plans launched by the Nkrumah government.

The burden of this paper is to examine Nkrumah's public sector manpower development programme during the period 1951–1966, since the question of administrative manpower development was one of the crucial problems which confronted the Convention People's Party (CPP) government.

The Colonial Government's Policy Towards Africanization

As stated, the colonial bureaucracy was divided into two classes; namely, the senior and junior services. The former was recruited mainly from British personnel who formulated and decided on policy, and managed and controlled the bureaucracy, while the latter service was recruited locally and performed the more routine tasks.[2] In this way, Africans were excluded from responsible senior positions in the government. This exclusion naturally led to a feeling of inferiority and frustration among Africans.

The colonial government did not make any conscious and concerted effort to Africanize the public service. Earlier attempts by Governors Guggisberg and Alan Burns to increase the number of Africans holding "European Appointments" did not yield substantial results.[3]

In 1941, the Lynch Commission was set up to carry out a survey of departments and to make recommendations on the number of senior appointments, specifying the grades in each department that should be filled by Africans in the following fifteen to twenty years. It was also to make recommendations on qualifications needed by African candidates for the grades which would be opened to them. Although unable to complete its work, the Commission made two important recommendations. These were the launching of a scholarship programme, and the policy of Africanization by giving preference to Africans for appointments over expatriates.[4] In 1945, a Scholarship Selection Board was set up to replace a number of other Boards for different scholarships and to centralize the government's scholarships training programme.[5]

To make it possible for Ghanaians to study abroad, a scholarship scheme was introduced. This was, at first, restricted to a few candidates. From the mid 1940s, however, the number of scholarship awards rapidly increased in order to build up an efficient number of African officers who would be able to take over the functions of British expatriate officers.[6] Scholarships were awarded to persons who were given places at educational institutions abroad to pursue a wide variety of courses. After the successful completion of their studies, these people (as well as private students) were absorbed into the bureaucracy. Scholarships were also awarded to those who gained admission to the then University College of the Gold Coast.[7]

As a result of the scholarship scheme, the earlier wide gap between supply and demand for qualified local officers, excluding many specialized fields, was narrowed somewhat.

At the end of the Second World War, the colonial administration assumed new responsibilities such as finding jobs for the large number of African soldiers returning home. The inability of the colonial government to secure jobs for the soldiers, the non-fulfillment of promises made to them while they were in service, insufficient pension rates and the "snail's pace" of the Africanization of the Gold Coast Regiment contributed to the 1948 riots.[8] After the disturbances, the Watson Commission was set up to inquire into the causes of the riots. It attributed the disturbances to the socio-economic and political conditions in the country. The Watson Commission recommended Africanization of the public service and more opportunities for African participation in government.[9] The Commission noted that out of 1,400 Senior positions in the civil service, only 98 were held by Africans.[10]

In April 1949, a Select Committee of the Legislature on Africanization of the Public Service was set up under the Chairmanship of Mr Saloway, the Colonial Secretary. The Committee's terms of reference were:

> to draw up a comprehensive scheme for the progressive Africanization of each department of the public service during the next ten years and for the education and training necessary to provide suitably qualified African officers in adequate numbers to take up senior appointments in the public service and further to make recommendations for its implementation.[11]

The Saloway Report was published in 1950. It recommended the setting up of a statutory Public Service Commission (PSC) to advise the Governor on all matters relating to the public service. The functions and role of the Commission should be such that it could not be interfered with by party politics. The Committee also endorsed the policy of the interim Public Service Commission for the recruitment of Africans to senior posts in preference to expatriates.[12]

The Saloway Committee also made a number of recommendations covering the development of secondary, technical and higher education, and the provision of scholarships in order to ensure, as quickly as possible, the supply of suitable Africans. As regards the award of scholarships, the Committee recommended that the Public Service Commission take it over from the existing Scholarship Selection Board.[13] This was to ensure fair and co-ordinated awards.

A further recommendation was the establishment of a Commission to review the structure of the public service so as to abolish the distinction between the junior and senior services and to give more responsibilities to a greater number of local officers. One other major recommendation of the Committee was the appointment of a full-time Commissioner of Africanization to act as an executive officer of the PSC with responsibility for ensuring that a maximum number of suitable and qualified African candidates became available for appointment to the higher grades of the public service.[14]

These recommendations were put into effect and by Article 67 (I) of 1950 Orders-In-Council, the PSC was given a legal status. A two-member Commission was also appointed in September 1950, under the Chairmanship of Sir David Lidbury, to review the structure of the Public Service.

The Lidbury Commission recommended three things. The first was that the public service should not be subjected to undue political interference in its internal management. This recommendation was necessitated by the fact that under the new Constitution of 1951, ministers were going to be responsible for departments. There was, therefore, considerable fear among public servants that their conditions of service would be decided on political grounds.[15] Secondly, the Commission saw the need for a balance between the powers of the PSC and the Chief Establishment Officer.[16] To avoid overlapping, the Commission decided that the PSC ought not to encroach on the day-to-day administration of the Chief Establishment Officer. The PSC was to act as a consultant to whom important issues would be referred for advice.[17] Thirdly, the Lidbury Report also stressed the need for the PSC to remain absolutely impartial and advocated severe penalties for attempts to influence the Commission outside the prescribed channels.[18] A further recommendation was that the functions of the Commissioner for Africanization be absorbed into those of the new post of Director of Recruitment and Training in the office of the Establishment Secretary.[19]

It is important to note that the various commissions and committees established were the result of intense political pressure on the colonial government. Strong pressure arose from well organized nationalist movements which challenged the colonial government's lackadaisical policy of absorbing, from time to time, a number of Africans into the senior service.[20]

Nkrumah's Manpower Development Policy

When the Convention People's Party (CPP) under Dr. Kwame Nkrumah assumed power in 1951, it was committed to socio-economic development objectives as well as to the policy of Africanization of the public service. However, it became apparent that these were conflicting objectives; the government could not give priority to development and rapid Africanization at the same time. Another aspect of this dilemma was that the advance towards independence was outstripping the Africanization of the administrative process. This situation led to criticisms in the National Assembly about the government's Africanization policy.[21]

The government was thus faced with very strong political and social pressures to Africanize quickly, while at the same time, it needed to retain a number of expatriates to cope with the development programme and also to provide for such a smooth administrative handing over that expatriates would leave only when Ghanaians had been fully trained to assume their responsibilities. To do this successfully, the government had to satisfy both groups in the public service—Africans and expatriates—by ensuring that their legitimate job interests and aspirations would be fairly met. The pressures meant that from time to time the government had to justify and defend its Africanization programme. Significantly, the government's objective was to achieve swift Africanization while at the same time preventing an exodus of expatriates and thereby a disruption of the administrative service.

In 1951, a Commissioner for Africanization was appointed by the Nkrumah government in keeping with the recommendations of the Saloway Committee. He was given executive authority to introduce training schemes for Africans. He also had a say in expatriate recruitment so that the maximum number of suitable and qualified African candidates would be available for appointment.[22] The Commissioner also acted as the chief executive officer of the PSC in that he was called upon by the PSC to report on the progress made in carrying out decisions arrived at by the Governor on the advice of the Commission and to ensure that they were pursued to conclusion. The Commission deemed it necessary to continue with the appointment of overseas officers especially in the fields of medicine, agriculture and engineering.[23]

With the implementation of the Lidbury Report, the functions of the Commissioner for Africanization were absorbed into the new post of Director of Recruitment and Training. But the existing structural relationship of the Commissioner for Africanization with the

PSC was not altered in any significant way with the change of title to Director of Recruitment and Training. The Director still worked in close co-operation with the PSC. However, his functions were enlarged. He was the responsible executive officer within the government for ensuring that the Africanization programme was accelerated with the object of building up a local public service staffed by local personnel capable of maintaining appropriate standards and a high level of efficiency. Under the Director of Recruitment and Training, a Working Party was set up to review the Africanization programme, to examine the staffing position in each department, and to advise on training and introduction of training grades and the award of scholarships. This was an important step, for it was essential to the service both to recruit Africans in preference to expatriates and to offer training within the service in order to promote Ghanaians to positions hitherto held by expatriates.[24]

The Nkrumah government also adopted a special recruitment policy which laid it down that when a vacancy occurred for any post, other than a post normally filled by promotion of a serving officer, no consideration should be given to the recruitment of an expatriate unless a suitable indigene could not be found.[25] It should, however, be emphasized that in spite of the urgency of Africanization, "the government in no way encouraged any lowering of standards— in fact the policy was to maintain and enhance standards."[26]

A Standing Committee on Africanization of the Legislative Assembly was appointed to undertake an adequate study of the Working Party's reports. In July 1953, Dr. Nkrumah made an important statement in the Assembly. He said:

> The Africanization of the public service has made great strides in recent times and the Government is doing everything possible compatible with efficiency to accelerate the pace of Africanization. We have more than laid the foundations of the African Civil Service of the future.[27]

The following table indicates the progress of Africanization of the public service. It relates to senior posts, i.e. posts carrying salaries of £680 per annum and over.[28]

Year	1952	1953	1954	1955	1956	1957	1958	1959	1960
Africans	620	898	1043	1277	1553	1941	2984	2320	2766
Expatriates	1332	1350	1350	1241	1123	984	880	859	749

Note: These figures include both pensionable and contract posts, but exclude development and non-permanent posts.

Pensionable and non-pensionable posts in December 1958 were as follows:

Nationality	Pensionable Staff	%	Non-Pensionable	%
Africans	1852	86.5	132	18
Expatriates	289	13.5	591	82
Total	2141	100	723	100

It can be seen from the tables that between 1952 and 1958, the total number of senior officers increased by nearly 1,000, but the proportion of expatriates dropped from approximately two-thirds to one-third.[29] Again, out of the 880 overseas officers serving on 31st December, 1958, only 289 were pensionable, about 100 of them being young officers who had not served long enough to retire with compensation.[30]

The reduction of pensionable expatriates also proceeded steadily from about 1952 onwards. This is shown by the following figures for some intermediate dates:[31]

July 1955	March 1957	Feb. 1958
800	519	400

Throughout the whole period, therefore, there were between 500–700 expatriates serving on contracts and on project work.[32]

The period also witnessed considerable concessions given to expatriate public servants by the 1954 Constitution. For instance, a retiring overseas officer was entitled to, apart from earned pension or gratuity, "either (a) a compensatory pension or (b) a lump sum compensation for loss of career calculated either at the operative date of his retirement or whichever shall be more advantageous to him."[33] Sub-section (12) of Section 58 of the same Constitution gave an additional concession to expatriate officers:

An overseas officer shall, if he can show to the satisfaction of a Secretary of State that he has reasonable grounds for anxiety regarding the future of his career in the public service, be eligible to retire and receive compensatory pension or compensation for loss of career.[34]

These concessions were aimed at protecting the interests of expatriate public servants and no doubt contributed to accelerating the rate of expatriate voluntary retirements.[35]

In 1955, a "freezing" provision was announced by the Nkrumah government allowing an expatriate officer to retain until July 1959 the right to retain lump sum compensation at the highest figure to which he would become entitled at any point during the four-year period. This provision slowed down the rate of retirements, but it threatened to cause a sudden large scale exodus when the period ran out.[36] Sensing the danger, the Nkrumah government in March 1958 published a new statement of policy, the Overseas Entitled Officers (W.P. No. 2/58).[37] In this paper, it was stated that about 370 entitled overseas officers remained in the Ghana Public Service, 85 as administrative officers and 285 in technical and professional grades. It was anticipated that owing to the operation of the compensation scheme, half of these would give notice within the next 16 months.[38] Despite rapid progress in Africanization, such a rate of departure would make it necessary for the government to recruit a substantial number of replacements from abroad in view of the requirements of the Second Development Plan. The Nkrumah government accordingly decided to make proposals which would induce more of the existing overseas staff to remain, provided that the government could choose the officers whom it wished to retain, and that the arrangement did not cost more than recruiting new staff from overseas.[39]

The new scheme was applicable to all overseas entitled officers in the public service on 1st April, 1958, and they had three months to apply for selection under the new terms. Each application was examined, in order to see whether a suitable Ghanaian was not available for the post. When selected, the officer converted from permanent to temporary terms of service for a contract period not exceeding five years, the post, salary and period all being specified in the contract. Under this scheme, 170 officers applied for contracts and about 120 were accepted.[40]

No vacant post in the public service was filled by recruitment from overseas unless the PSC was satisfied that no suitable Ghanaian was available. Moreover, the duration of any contract offered to an overseas applicant was related to the estimated length of time required to train a Ghanaian for the post. There was little overseas recruitment of purely administrative staff. However, overseas recruitment of professional and technical officers continued for a considerable length of time. For instance, overseas recruitment was in progress on 31st December, 1958, for 239 vacancies[41] and the most numerous categories were:

Public Works Department	41
Health	39
Education	25
Agriculture	14
Railways	14

It needs to be pointed out that Ghana went through a period during which a large number of overseas officials either resigned or retired. The country suffered from this by way of a drop in efficiency, but not the breakdown of any services. Difficulties arose mainly from the rapid increase in governmental activity and from the growing demands of the development plans. The agreement whereby in May 1958 most officials converted from pensionable to contract terms seemed somewhat expensive in the short-run, but it produced the result required and probably represented the most satisfactory arrangement at the time.

Higher Education and Training

Africanization was made more difficult because the educational system was not sufficiently developed in the inter-war period to meet the demands that were to be made upon it after 1945. The Nkrumah government, on assumption of office, recognized the crucial role of higher education in meeting the manpower requirements and in the general development of the country. Considerable changes, therefore, took place in the realm of higher education during the Nkrumah period. This was the result, to some extent, of the Commission on University Education created in 1960 and the appointment of the National Council for Higher Education. It was during the Nkrumah regime that the University College of the Gold Coast, now the University of Ghana, was granted full University status as the University of Ghana. Again, under his regime, the Universities of Science and Technology (UST) and Cape Coast (UCC) and the Ghana Institute of Management and Public Administration (GIMPA) were established. While the University of Science and Technology was set up to produce scientific and technological personnel which are of utmost importance for industrialization, the University of Cape Coast, on the other hand, was to meet the man-

University of Cape Coast, on the other hand, was to meet the manpower requirements of second cycle institutions in the country.

During the late 1950s, the Ghanaian bureaucracy was faced not merely with the maintenance of existing services but the complexities of social and economic development. Most of those who were recruited did not have adequate knowledge of the developments in the "science of management."[42] Training of senior personnel in administration in the public service was neglected. Subsequently, the Nkrumah government decided to establish a College of Administration (now School of Administration, Legon), the aim of which was to provide further studies, training and research in business subjects and public administration. Later, another institute, the Institute of Public Administration (now Ghana Institute of Management and Public Administration, GIMPA) was set up to replace the then Administrative Academy. The establishment of GIMPA was seen as the

> Consummation of the Nkrumah government's belief that the success of its plans for social and economic development depended on a good, efficient, strong and honest administrative system and that such a system could best be developed through giving young graduates newly recruited to the higher echelon of the civil service a thorough grounding in the principles and techniques of administrative planning and management before they take on their duties.[43]

The following table (page 283) indicates the number of graduates and diplomats produced by the Universities of Ghana, Legon, Science and Technology, Cape Coast and GIMPA.

Judging from the number of graduates produced by the various institutions, it ought to be seen that the Nkrumah government took keen interest in higher education as a means of meeting the manpower requirements of the country.

State Enterprises

Increasing participation of the State in the economy by the establishment of more state enterprises after independence was regarded by Nkrumah as necessary for the creation of a socialist society and was, therefore, central to his economic strategy. By the end of 1965, there were some 198 Central Government units — presidential secretariats, departments, divisions, etc.— of which 60 were of the public corporation type.[44] This proliferation of governmental structures was the result of the ambitious plans for a statist regime to mobilize the country's material and human resources with maximum speed.

Year	U of G Degree	U of G Diploma/Cert	UST Degree	UST Diploma/Cert	UCC Degree	UCC Diploma/Cert	GIMPA Diploma	GIMPA Cert
1951/52	25	26						
1952/53	52	32						
1953/54	54	34						
1954/55	54	36						
1955/56	73	38						
1956/57	39	38						
1957/58	59	33	-	7				
1958/59	77	35	2	7				
1959/60	138	37	11	7				
1960/61	148	41	15	18				
1961/62	151	35	26	47			22	
1962/63	201	48	21	87			10	10
1963/64	194	69	34	131		30	24	44
1964/65	363	84	107	58	40	49	16	36
1965/66	395	106	102	62	51	84	33	43
Total	**2,023**	**692**	**318**	**424**	**91**	**163**	**105**	**133**

Source: University of Ghana Registry, University of Cape Coast Statistics 1962/63–1974–75; GIMPA Registry. The Diploma course is for graduates entering the Administrative class and the Foreign Service and it lasts for 9 months. The Certificate course is for professionals, e.g. Agricultural Officers and lasts for 3 months.

In 1964, the State Enterprises Secretariat was established as a presidential agency charged with the responsibility for exercising general supervision over various public corporations, in order to ensure their efficient operation, and looking after government's interests in the state — private joint enterprises. In 1966, there were 20 state enterprises and 10 state/joint private enterprises under this secretariat.[45] Persons engaged in state manufacturing enterprises comprised a small proportion of the employees of the public services though during the period from independence to the 1966 coup, there was a marked increase. In 1956, there were 9,827 public corporation employees and by February 1966, when Nkrumah's government was toppled, the number had risen to 131,180.[46] From 1951 to 1961, the proportion of government employees to the total number of wage earners in the country rose from 43 per cent to 61 per cent. By 1961, some 189,990 persons were employed in the public sector, 19,494 more than in 1959 and nearly two and a half times the 1950 figure which stood at 77,375.[47]

Conclusion

Initially, the purposes and procedures of Nkrumah's manpower development policy or programme were relatively straightforward. The policy was designed to phase out British colonial service officials wherever they could be replaced by qualified Ghanaians, and to increase the percentage of Ghanaians in the top positions of the public service. In both respects, the programme appeared to be a marked success. For example, between 1949 and 1954, the percentage of Ghanaians holding senior officer grades in the public service rose from 13.8 per cent to 38.2 per cent and by 1965, Ghanaians comprised nearly 87 per cent of the senior ranks.[48]

It must be noted, however, that there was a rise in the absolute number of expatriates in Ghana's senior public service between 1949 and 1965: 1,068 in 1949, 1,490 in 1954 and not less than 1,900 by 1,965.[49]

At the time of independence, the number of British Civil Servants in Ghana had actually declined somewhat from preceding years. The rising expatriate figures since then could be attributed chiefly to the subsequent arrival of large numbers of Russians, Poles Chechs, Yugoslavs, Italians and United Nations personnel.[50] Also military personnel from the Soviet Union and China were brought in to help train "African Liberation fighters" at several secret camps around the country and although they were not included in official figures, their numbers were felt. Hence by the 1960s, it appeared to many Ghanaian public servants that the net effect of Ghanaianization had been to cede the "managerial and technical heights" of the economy and the administration to foreigners. Certainly, the presence of hundreds of expatriates "who often spoke different languages," could only undermine the Ghanaians' sense of efficacy and increase their sense of job insecurity.[51] It is on record that in 1959, Dr. Nkrumah partially purged the senior public service by dismissing several key persons, including Dr. Robert Gardiner, the British-trained Ghanaian, who headed the Establishment Secretariat.

The proliferation of agencies during the period was accompanied by a shortage of trained personnel to fill the newly created positions, and administrative "shortcutting" contributed greatly to a decline in co-ordination and communication within the public sector resulting in an erratic and disorderly decision making process. In the words of Elliot Berg:

> There were thirty-one ministries, and Statutory Corporations were scattered all over the place. It is not certain that at any one time, anybody knew just how many there were. Key operating ministries were cut up periodically, their functions divided, then shuttled back and forth. Agriculture was the best example: between the old ministry the State Farms Corporation, the United Ghana Farmers Council and the Agricultural Wing of the Workers Brigade and twenty-five other agencies, lines of authority hopelessly tangled, co-ordination inexistent and personal access to political figures more important in decisions than technical or economic issues.[52]

By 1965, therefore, one is tempted to say that Ghana had become almost a "classic example of an administrative system on the verge of collapse." The large number of graduates produced by institutions of higher learning was not enough to meet the manpower requirements of the many public agencies created during the Nkrumah period.

FOOTNOTES

1. Not read at the symposium.
2. Adu, 1965:21.
3. Greenstreet, 1963:24.
4. A Statement on the Programme of the Africanization of the Public Service, 1954.
5. Greenstreet, *op. cit.:* 25
6. *Ibid.:* 25.
7. *Op. cit.*:30.
8. Watson Commission Report: 120–123.

9. *Ibid.:* 30.
10. *Ibid.:* 30.
11. The Gold Coast Legislative Council Debates Session Issue No. 1, 1949:222.
12. Saloway Commission Report: 16.
13. *Ibid.:* 19.
14. *Ibid.:* 21.
15. Lidbury Commission Report: 47.
16. *Ibid.* : 47 para. 176.
17. *Ibid.:* 48 para. 178.
18. *Ibid.* : 48 para. 180.
19. *Ibid.:* 49 para. 182.
20. Greenstreet, op. cit.: 26.
21. *Ibid.:* 26.
22. *Ibid.:* 26.
23. File No. R.168 Vol. 1,: P.67 (Establishment Secretariat). See also File No. PSC 28:42.
24. Greenstreet, *op. cit.:* 27.
25. *Ibid.:* 27.
26. *Ibid.:* 27.
27. The Gold Coast Legislative Council Debates, Issue No. 2, 1953: 145.
28. Younger, 1960:52.
29. *Ibid.:* 53.
30. *Ibid.:* 54.
31. *Ibid.:* 54.
32. *Ibid.:* 55.
33. Gyandoh, Jnr. and Griffiths, 1972:118. Also see The Gold Coast (Constitution) Order in Council, 1954: Section 58 subsection 2(b).
34. This concession was not included in the 1957 Constitution. However, the other benefits in the 1954 Constitution were retained.
35. The figure on compensation or benefits paid to retiring expatriates are not available.
36 . Younger, *op. cit.:* 56.
37. *Ibid.:* 56.
38. *Ibid.:* 57.
39. *Ibid.:* 58.
40. *Ibid.:* 58.
41. *Ibid.:* 55.
42. Greenstreet, 1978:5.
43 . *Ibid.:* 6.
44. Greenstreet, 1973(a):21.
45 . Greenstreet, 1973(b):12.
46 . Birmingham, Neustadt and Omaboe, (ed), 1966 :124–125 .
47. Le Vine, 1975: 198.
48. *Ibid.:* 198.
49. *Ibid.:* 198.
5 0. *Ibid.:* 199.
51. Berg, 1971:209.
52. *Ibid.:* 211.

THE DEVELOPMENT AND PATTERNS OF MANUFACTURING INDUSTRIES IN GHANA 1951-1965

S. Asamoah Darko

Introduction

The period 1951—1965 constitutes a significant landmark in the socio-economic history of Ghana. It was during that time that Ghana underwent crucial social and economic transformations. Many of these changes found expression in the cultural landscape in the form of the physical expansion of towns and cities, improvement in road and marine transport facilities, the emergence of modern factories, housing estates, resettlement schemes, etc. They also affected the expansion and distribution of such socio-economic amenities as employment, water supply, electricity, health facilities, and education. The man at the centre of those changes was Kwame Nkrumah who, within the period, successively held office as Leader of Government Business, Prime Minister, and President. Nkrumah was also a significant figure because his political thinking was at variance with that of many eminent Ghanaians who, before him and during his time, concerned themselves with political matters, including opposition to colonialism. He described himself as a socialist. While some people agreed with him on his socialist stance, others were of the view that he was essentially an anti-colonial nationalist and that his claim to socialist ideology was only a rhetoric.[1]

Nkrumah was ousted from power in 1966, and died in exile in 1972. Criticisms of his administration immediately after his overthrow were profuse and loud. He was blamed for almost everything that went wrong. Comments about his handling of economic issues were particularly devastating. We can take advantage of this occasion, which is in commemoration of the 75th year of his birth, to reflect on an aspect of his economic performance, namely, industrialization in Ghana during his tenure. It is also almost twenty years since his overthrow. We are, therefore, some distance away from the time he performed and, with our knowledge and experience of what has taken place since 1966, can now assess him more objectively. We propose to throw some light on his industrialization policy and practice against the back-ground of his political views and the conditions which unfolded themselves in the manufacturing field as the years rolled by. The thesis of this paper is that Nkrumah demonstrate much pragmatism in his handling of issues relating to industrialization in Ghana during his tenure, and that many of the decisions he took were dictated by the prevailing conditions, the situation in which he found himself, and his political convictions.

Attitude of Metropolitan Powers to Manufacturing Industries in the Colonies

Nkrumah's assessment of the attitudes of metropolitan or colonial powers to manufacturing industries in their colonies can be found in his writings. In this connection, his book entitled *Towards Colonial Freedom* written during 1942–1945 and published in 1962 is particularly significant.[2] Nkrumah thought, first, that the main objective for securing colonies was economic and emphasized in particular, the procurement of raw materials from, and the sale of manufactured goods to, the colonies. To ensure continuity in the supply of raw materials, the colonial authorities pursued the following policies;

i.   Preventing the colonies from engaging in manufacturing;
i.   Preventing colonial subjects from acquiring knowledge of modern techniques for developing their own industries
iii. making the colonial subjects simple producers of raw materials; and
iv. prohibiting the colonies from trading with other nations.[3]

Secondly, he identified three stages in the development of colonial economies, namely, the mercantile stage, the free-trade stage and economic imperialism. The operation of wages in the last period was such that the capitalist producer in seeking high profits limited his wage bill so that domestic market for the products became restricted. As a way out, the capitalist producer found ways and means of making the colonies viable markets. To achieve this objective, the producer, among other things, killed the indigenous art and craft industries and emphasized the need and importance of specialization in primary production in which the colonies had comparative advantage.

Thirdly, the capitalist investor derived some of his easiest profits not from establishing industries in the colonies, which might compete with the home industries and necessitate a drastic rise in wages and in the cost of living. Instead, the metropolitan governments and private financiers might push loans on the colonies for the construction of railway, harbor, roads, etc. so long as these constructions assured them of their profits and safeguarded their capital. It is important to note that these infrastructures were usually provided in localities where they could effectively help to assemble raw materials for shipment to the metropolitan countries and to distribute manufactured goods to consumers.

In the specific case of the British colonies in general and Ghana in particular, Nkrumah remarked that the marketing of produce and manufactured goods was done by European merchants through a "pool" system. As a result of the operation of this kind of monopolistic combine and other agencies, for example the mining companies, gold and money were regularly taken out. Consequently, opportunity for capital formation was crippled. Industrial and commercial aspirations and growth in the colonies were thus thwarted and crushed.

Manufacturing Industries before 1951

Whether one agrees with Nkrumah or not, the fact remains that until 1951, manufacturing was essentially of the craft type. Attempts made by the early missionaries at technical and craft training was not given any serious encouragement by the colonial government. Also, the Art and Craft Department of Achimota College were not meant to produce potential industrialists, because the efforts of interested trainees to go commercial were nipped in the bud by cheap imported manufactured products. The result was that the products turned out of the craft workshops were for use only in the homes of peasants and other ordinary folk. They were replaced with imported substitutes as one advanced on the social and economic ladder.

In the 3rd edition of his book, *An Elementary Geography of the Gold Coast,* published in 1940, D. T. Adams had hardly anything to say about modern manufacturing industries in Ghana.[4] His chapter on secondary industries dealt almost exclusively with home industries which were of the craft type. This situation, characterized by the preponderance of craft industries which were inefficiently run, is distressing because Szereszewski notes that evidence of modern manufacturing activity existed in Ghana before 1904, following the establishment of a saw mill in the Sekondi District, a mineral water plant in Cape Coast and a workshop for the repair and conversion of launches at Ada.[5] What this means is that modern industrial development was for a long time not a matter of any serious concern to the colonial government.

The situation had only slightly changed by 1950 when, in terms of organization, three types of industries had emerged, namely domestic handicraft and workshop industries, in which the owner might be the only worker, and the factory industries, which the latter employed several workers in each plant, and used power driven machinery. Also they needed much capital, and the level of managerial and production efficiency must be quite high.

Industries organized on factory basis at the time were very few and included cocoa and salt processing, saw milling, brewing, the making of bricks, roofing tiles and coolers, and the manufacture of shirts. In addition, there was the processing of minerals, e.g. gold, diamonds, manganese and bauxite.

Table 1

Manufacturing Establishments, Persons Engaged and Capital Formation

Period	No. of Establishments	Persons Engaged	Capital Formation. $'000
Before 1900	1	1,237	17
1900-1909	10		
1910-1919	3	515	22
1920-1929	19	983	47
1930-1939	18	898	46
1940-1949	53	1,953	767
1950-1959	130	8,232	1,466

All these activities were performed by about 53 establishments (Table I) scattered in the southern half of the country with the greatest concentrations in Accra, Kumasi and Sekondi-Takoradi.

Nkrumah's reasons for the extreme paucity of modern manufacturing industries in Ghana during the colonial period have been discussed. Other reasons which may be considered more acceptable to economists, etc. may be mentioned. It was felt that Ghana had several handicaps which made large-scale modern manufacturing activities uneconomical.[6] These included lack of fuel and skilled labor, and the type of climate. The last problem, which is Ghana's climatic disadvantage, may be illustrated. Although Ghana was producing large quantities of cocoa, only a small fraction of the total output was being processed in the early 1950s into cocoa butter and cocoa cake which could be used in the manufacture of theobromine. According to Prof. Lewis, existing process of manufacturing theobromine was uneconomical in Ghana, since it required large quantities of water at a temperature of 14°C (57°F) which could not be cheaply obtained in the country.[7] Another reason, which seemed equally plausible, was given by Harrison Church to explain the lack of manufacturing efforts in the colonies. In his view, in agricultural societies as found in almost all colonies, industrialization might seriously impair food production and cause bad husbandry by the withdrawal of an undue proportion of able-bodied males from the land.[8]

It is important to note that it was in normal times that vested interests in metropolitan countries emphasized the handicaps and disadvantages of the dependencies for manufacturing industries. In times of crisis, environmental and other problems had been played down and some manufacturing industries set up. As Harrison Church observed, the difficulty in war time of importing manufactured products was an incentive to simple industrialization in Zimbabwe where a cotton mill was set up in the Second World War to produce, inter alia, sanitary towels and singlets.[9] In Ghana, the difficulty of importing roofing materials in the war necessitated the setting up of a factory to produce roofing tiles and water coolers.[10]

A significant lesson which the colonial government of Ghana learned during the Second World War was that some serious attention should be paid to local industries. This need arose from the difficulty in getting imported commodities from overseas. Accordingly, an Industrial Development Board was set up in 1945 to help in the establishment of local industries.[11] This was an aspect of a larger modernisation plan. Other features of the package were the provision of better marketing facilities for agricultural products, the setting up of the Cocoa Research Institute and the initiation of research into the methods of fighting cocoa diseases.[12]

The Industrial Development Board achieved very little. Its place was, therefore, taken by the Industrial Development Corporation in 1947, when the discontent which resulted in the disturbances of early 1948 was building up. The inauguration of the corporation marked the first conscious effort on the part of the colonial government to play some part in the process of industrialization which seemed to be in serious disarray. The institution was charged with the responsibility of conducting investigation, formulating policies and carrying out projects for developing industries in Ghana.[13]

Preparing for a Plunge

Following the 1948 disturbances in Ghana, a Commission of Enquiry was set up under the Chairmanship of Mr. Aiken Watson. The Commission provided an opportunity for the discussion of complaints on diverse issues, including industrialization. In their report, the Commission ruled out heavy industry, saying:

> ... the establishment of heavy industry on the Gold Coast capable of finding an export market must remain a dream. [14]

In assigning reasons for this dis-recommendation, they stressed:

> With an enervating climate in the torrid zone, lacking coal and other basic minerals the prospect is so barren that not even the greatest enthusiast could suggest to us a method of accomplishment.[15]

In the view of the Commission, there was room for many other secondary industries. They recommended that in these areas, there was considerable scope for bold planning on imaginative lines. They also, by implication, suggested some state participation when they remarked that in a country which was rapidly passing to a money economy, the fact ought to be faced that the intense individuality of the Africans notwithstanding, unbridled private enterprise would at best lay the foundation of future social strife.[16] It is significant to observe that in a White Paper on the Report, His Majesty's Government of the United Kingdom, the metropolitan power, endorsed the recommendations on industrialization and directed that they should be passed on to the newly created Industrial Development Corporation for study.[17]

It was partly on the basis of these recommendations and comments that the colonial government of the Gold Coast initiated a 10-year Development Plan in early 1951, which would, among other things, help to provide the necessary infrastructure for a plunge into full productive activity including industrialization in the immediate future. On coming into power in the same year, Nkrumah who became Leader of Government Business, and his colleagues quickly made some modifications in the Plan, which received the approval of the Government. For example, the total estimated expenditure of £75 million under the original Plan was altered to £108 million with more emphasis placed on the improvement and expansion of basic services. The execution of the revised Plan went so well that in 1952 it was decided to complete it in five years instead of ten.[18] The first 10-Year Development Plan was accordingly ended on 30th June, 1957. This was, however, followed by a period of consolidation during which some improperly finished projects were completed at an additional cost of £10 million.

Certain steps were taken during the period of implementation of the First Development Plan to further aid industrialization immediately or in the foreseeable future. In the first place, Nkrumah felt the need for expert direction on the issue of industrialization, so that no sooner had he assumed duty as Leader of Government Business than he caused to be invited Prof. A. W. Lewis of Manchester University, to advise the Government on industrialization and economic policy. His report on "Industrialization and the Gold Coast" which was published in 1953 and given very wide publicity, gave some guidance. In it, he laid stress on the processing of primary products. It was, therefore, not surprising that the processing of local timber into sawn timber, veneer, furniture etc. took place and expanded considerably in southern Ghana. In addition, there were palm oil extraction, the manufacture of lime juice and the refining of vegetable oil.

Secondly, in order to familiarize industrialists and investors in the Americas with investment opportunities in Ghana, a team of New York Consultants was invited into the country.[19] Members of the team were to carry out an investment survey with a view to determining the possibilities of attracting private foreign capital to supplement local effort. It was unfortunate that the response given to the team's report in the New World was not very encouraging.

Thirdly, with a view to stimulating the development of new industries in the country, relief was given to "pioneer" companies (companies which started new industries).[20] The relief took the form of exemption from taxation on profits for five years in the first instance. If a loss was incurred over the tax holiday period, it might be carried forward and set against subsequent profits. Some industries certified as "Pioneer" ones, including the manufacture of cigarettes, wire, nails, bricks and tiles, and the refining of vegetable oils were set up.

Fourthly, the functions of the Industrial Development Corporation became more clearly defined. It was, among other things, charged with the following responsibilities:

i. promoting subsidiary companies in which the IDC would be the principal share-holder;
ii. associating with other companies in which the IDC would be a minority holder;
iii. encouraging small businesses by way of loans; and
iv. exploring the possibility of establishing industrial estates.[21]

These were almost in accord with the recommendations of Professor Arthur Lewis.

Finally, realizing the vital role foreign investment might play in his industrialization effort, Nkrumah took steps to make his policy on expatriate capital known to interested and potential investors. He declared early in the plan period that it would be many years before the Gold Coast would find from its own resources people who combined capital with experience for industrial management. His government would, therefore, wish to give every encouragement to foreign investors. Much as he was interested in foreign investment, he made it crystal clear, however, that it would not be accepted on any terms. "It should be understood," he stressed, "that the degree of worth with which any enterprise is welcome will be conditioned by arrangements proposed for the employment, training, and promotion of Africans, for it is my government's policy to ensure a future steady increase in the number of qualified Africans in senior technical, professional and managerial posts."[22] On nationalization, he assuaged the fears of prospective investors with the following words: "The government has no plans on nationalization, but if a future government should consider nationalization of a particular industry essential, steps will be taken to ensure adequate compensation."[23]

Post Independence Trend: I

Nkrumah's acceptance of the 10-Year Development Plan to work with, on coming to office in 1951, has been interpreted as a weakness. Some observers consider the acceptance as indicative of his having nothing to offer by way of economic development proposals.[24] Nothing can be farther from the truth. Nkrumah knew what he was about, and sought advice where he felt one was needed. In 1959, the

Second Development Plan, prepared at his instance, was launched. Significant highlights of the new plan were several. In the first place, it was felt that sufficient infrastructure and public services had been developed to enable profitable manufacturing industries to be started. To this end, the plan stated, inter alia, that high priority would be given to the promotion of the establishment of not less than 600 factories of varying sizes producing a range of over 100 different products.[25] Indeed, there was to be a doubling of productive capacity from 10 per cent under the first Development Plan to 20 per cent under the second. Since there were about 500 concerns employing less than 5 persons each, it was decided that some of the manufacturing business being contemplated should operate on large scale. Secondly, although the private sector was still to be encouraged, it was felt that the state, through the IDC, should begin to play a more positive role in the manufacturing effort.

The result of the effort of the IDC was, however, not very reassuring. Studies made in 1961 into about 8 IDC industries showed the following results: 4 made losses up to 1960–61, 3 went into liquidation, and one was put on care and maintenance basis.

We may now consider the reasons assigned to the poor performance of the state industries. There was inadequate demand for some of the products of the state enterprises at the prices they were being offered. The poor quality of the products made their prices very uncompetitive. The unexpectedly low demand caused some of the factories to operate well below capacity. A few examples may be given. The quality of the products of the Brick and Tile Factory was low because the clay deposits being used were unsuitable, lacking sufficient homogeneity for the types of products planned. The problem was traced to inadequate feasibility studies, including faulty analysis of data. Another concern plagued with enigma was the Soap Factory. Demand for its products was low because the local palm kernel oil used as raw material was poor in quality, seasonal in availability and uncertain in quantity. The principal lesson learned from these experiences was that when projects were being planned, the supply of raw materials should be treated as part of the projects themselves. To treat the two as semi-independent was to invite trouble.

Associated with the poor performance of the state industrial concerns were also capital, technical and managerial problems. Inadequate liquid capital and the frequent break-down of machinery greatly impeded the flow of production. The rampant break-down of machinery and equipment was partly the result of the type of machinery and equipment purchased and partly the outcome of poorly trained technical personnel. To rectify the situation, the IDC undertook some training of its technical personnel, but this was often haphazardly organized. Besides, there were several irregularities, including pilfering,which management was unable to control effectively. Ineffective management was partly due to the high turnover of managers and the use of part-time managers in a number of cases.

Part of the problem which plagued the country stemmed from improper financial control. At the start of the implementation of the plan, an amount of £100 million was made available from the country's reserves. The expenditure of the amount was not properly programmed; the link between need and availability in any one year disappeared and the annual estimates no longer provided any guide or automatic check. The technocrats who were expected to provide good guidance did very poor work, in that many of the projects planned were grossly underestimated. The result was that much more money than was anticipated had to be released during the process of implementation. Also some of the proposals were very vague, a factor which allowed much latitude for extending the scope of some projects. The factors enumerated offered opportunity for corruption and led to much over-expenditure and the dissipation of scarce resources.

Two other factors which led to even greater over-expenditure may be mentioned. The first, over which neither the technocrats nor the politicians had any firm control, was a quick rise in the prices of imports in 1960–61. This put many estimates into disarray. Much more money had to be released if several planned projects were to be implemented or completed. The second was the introduction of the minimum wage legislation, which added between 5 and 10 per cent to the cost of the plan.[26] It was difficult for a government which claimed to seek the welfare of workers and was aware of what was being paid to them to resist a request to grant a minimum wage, which could ensure some decent living.

The provision of more infrastructure and a greater participation in production meant that the government must maintain a high level of public investment. The government also had to spend a lot of money on the maintenance and use of completed projects. Unfortunately, from the start of the plan period, the country began experiencing deteriorating foreign exchange conditions. While the import bill rose from £95 million in 1958 to £165 million in 1961, earnings from export experienced only a slight change from £110 million in 1958 to £122 million in 1961. The budget deficit increased from £8 million in 1959 to £29 million in 1961.[27] What was worse, the inflow of capital after independence reduced to a tickle. Indeed, there was a net out-flow of £2 million in 1960. In the main, inflow of capital reduced to the barest minimum. Two reasons could be assigned to explain that state of affairs. In the first place, many investors were doubtful of the good intentions of the government so far as its nationalization policy was concerned. Secondly, the ease with which consumer goods could be imported into the country alarmed potential investors about the market for their products.

Post Independence Trend: Increased State Participation

By the early 1960s, Nkrumah had become convinced that state participation had to be stepped up significantly. In the first place, all attempts to assist Ghanaian businessmen to overcome their problems did not yield much dividend. Serious entrepreneurial spirit was still lacking, as most African businessmen continued to operate on a small scale. Indeed, he found that there was very little prospect of fostering the growth of an indigenous entrepreneural class capable of industrializing the country.[28] Secondly, foreign private capitalists did not seem to him to be a reliable alternative. They were hesitant in entering fields with limited opportunity for profits. Besides, they were more interested in repatriating profits than in ploughing them back into the expansion of their business. Thirdly, it had become clear to him that socialism was the form of government which would help to transform the country. With socialism, the state's role in all spheres of economic activity would be increased. Finally, he saw increasing state participation as a means of modernizing the economy and decreasing the country's economic dependence.

Although earnings from exports were almost static, Nkrumah remained hopeful that the trend might change for the better. He was also confident that external assistance might be obtained to finance manufacturing. Furthermore, he was convinced that capital could be generated through the creation of surpluses in annual government budgets. He expected that 44 per cent of the planned investment would be contributed by the government.

Nkrumah was aware that active involvement of the government in economic activities was an interference. He, however, did not consider the action unusual and quoted Myrdal to support his view that interference of the type he was contemplating was necessary in all developing countries.[29]

Nkrumah sought to put into effect his socialist ideas through the Seven-Year Plan which was launched in 1964. Industrialization retained prominence in the plan, which, inter alia, postulated an increase of 83 per cent in the output of industry and construction by 1970. Almost all the five main objectives of the plan highlighted the dominant role industrialization was to play in the economic modernization of Ghana. In the first place, as much as possible, domestic substitutes were to be produced for those manufactured staples of consumer demand for whose supply Ghana was almost entirely dependent on foreign sources and expended large sums in foreign exchange each year. Secondly, the building materials industry should be expanded and modernized to enable it to support the inevitably increased activity in construction. A start should also be made on the development of other basic industries in the field of metals and chemicals. Thirdly, contemporary industrialisation should prepare the ground for further industrialization under subsequent plans. To this end he emphasized that a beginning should be made in the field of machine making, the manufacture of electrical equipment and electronics. Fourthly, industrialization in Ghana should not be carried out in isolation. It must be organized in such a way that it might fit with development in other parts of Africa. Finally, agricultural and mining commodities which were being exported mostly as unprocessed primary products should be progressively processed before export.

In the Seven-Year Development Plan, Nkrumah realized the importance of agriculture and sought to shift to it some government investment away from social overheads. He did not deny the desirability of agricultural development, but he was vehemently against the view that industrialization should wait for agricultural development to take off first. Among other things, he considered industrialization as one of the surest ways of reducing unemployment. The relative importance of types of ownership as shown in the percentage of gross output in 1962 and 1966 is worth studying (Tables 2 and 3). In the same way, it is crucial to draw attention to changes in the sectoral distribution of public investment under ten-year, five-year and seven-year plans (Table 4).

The role of private Ghanaian entrepreneurship decreased from 13.0 per cent in 1962 to 10.0 per cent in 1966, while that of the state increased from 12.0 per cent to 20 per cent in the same period. Industrial entrepreneurs have been characterized by various partnerships. The output of concerns jointly owned by private Ghanaian and foreign entrepreneurs increased from 5.0 per cent to 9.0 per cent while that of concerns jointly run by the state and foreign cap-

italists rose from 7.0 per cent to 13.0 per cent. What is most significant was the improvement in total Ghanaian contribution which rose
from 25.0 per cent to 30.0 per cent and a relative fall of purely foreign contribution from 63 per cent in 1962 to 48.0 per cent in 1966.

The Sectoral distribution of Public Investment from 1951 to
1965 shows some change in emphasis. In the first place, the relatively
dominant role of social services in the 1951–1958 plan had reduced
in the Seven-Year Development Plan. Secondly, the attention given
to infrastructure was fairly constant throughout the period. Finally,
the productive sectors of manufacturing and mining, and agriculture received more attention in the Seven-Year Development Plan
than in any of the previous plans.

Other Features of the Seven-Year Development Plan

The salient objectives of the Seven-Year Development Plan and
the dominant role the state was expected to play has been discussed. Other features which need mention are the plan's priorities,
and problems of implementation. The plan had four stated priorities,
namely:

1. attainment of maximum utilization of existing plant capacity;
2. expansion whenever possible of the productive capacity of existing (state) enterprises in preference to the setting up of entirely
   new factories;
3. completion of projects in the process of construction; and
4. the erection of new buildings and installation of new machinery
   to commence entirely new industries.

In the implementation of the plan, however, first priority was
given to the construction of new projects. In the allocation of foreign
exchange, the construction of new projects was given precedence
over the supply of industrial raw materials and spare parts to operational concerns to raise their utilization levels.

Socialism was not to be achieved by killing the private sector,
but by maximizing the growth of the public sector; nor was it to be
fulfilled by nationalizing private concerns. Socialism through industrialization was to be achieved by the state creating new enterprises.
Several problems arose from this policy. The building of new factories which the non-nationalization of private concerns encouraged
caused new projects to appear, which had never been envisaged in
the plan. Several contractors emerged who were prepared to pay
heavy commissions to persons who accepted their projects. The

contractors were attracted by the generally ambitious nature of the plan and the country's enormous potential in mineral and agriculture resources. Projects were started without adequate feasibility studies and without competitive tendering. Failure to carry out adequate feasibility studies meant a repetition of some of the problems which characterized the implementation of earlier plans. In that state of confusion, new industries were distributed among party functionaries as "grants" which might enable them to give patronage to their relatives, friends and supporters.

Table 2

Type of Ownership	Percentage of Gross Output	
	1962	1966
Ghanaian		
Private	13 .0	9 .7
State	11 .8	20.5
Total Ghanaian	24.8	30.2
Mixed		
Private-foreign	4.9	8.7
State-foreign	7.1	12.7
	12.0	21.4
Foreign	63.2	48.3

Table 3

MANUFACTURING INDUSTRY—VALUE OF GROSS
OUTPUT IN CURRENT PRICES ¢ '000 (AND PERCENTAGES)

	1962	1963	1964	1965	1966
State owned	8,444(11.8)	13,266(14.3)	14,916(13.9)	20,687(17.2)	27,665(19.5)
Joint State/Private	5,080(7.0)	6,844(7.4)	7,784(7.3)	12,029(10.0)	14,996(10.5)
Co-operative	80(0.2)	261(0.2)	610(0.6)	282(.3)	386(.3)
Private	57,765(81.0)	72,668(78.1)	83,702(78.2)	87,118(72.5)	98,963(69.7)
TOTAL	71,369(100.0)	93,039(100.0)	107,012(100.0)	120,116(100.0)	142,010(100.0)

(Figures are from large establishments with 30 or more persons engaged)

Table 4

DISTRIBUTION OF PUBLIC INVESTMENTS

	10-Yr Plan (1951-58)	5-Yr Plan (1959-63)	7-Yr Plan (1964–65)
1. Agriculture	6	7	10
2. Manufacturing and Mining	4	21	26
3. Infrastructure and Public Service	45	32	41
4. Education	13	9	5
5. Health, Social	13	13	7
6. General Government	19	18	11
	100	100	100

There was not much co-ordination in the implementation, and the planners were unable to influence the balance of payment policy. Although they had advised that the country's reserve should not be reduced below 1963 level, its international liquidity dropped from £211 million in 1963 to £170 million in 1964 and £59 million in 1965.[30] This situation was partly the result of the unpredictable variability of world cocoa prices. Cocoa prices fell during the period of implementation of the plan, a situation which greatly destabilized the country's capacity.

Although Nkrumah made it clear that much of the investment in manufacturing industries was to be generated locally through budget surpluses, taxation, etc., a factor which gave him encouragement was the willingness of European companies and governments to supply on credit the factories, equipment, and sometimes technical and managerial expertise which was beyond Ghana's capacity to organize and finance. By this arrangement, the Ghana Government was able to raise on hard terms the external resources which it could not raise through long-term aid. It is sad to observe that in some cases, the factories and equipment supplied were old, reconditioned, out of production or the wrong type.[31] It was this willingness to supply and install on credit factories, equipment, etc. which plunged the country into its huge debts.

Conclusion

That Nkrumah played a leading and important role in reshaping the economy of Ghana from 1951 to 1966 cannot be gainsaid. He provided a reasonably adequate and appropriate social and economic infrastructure for the economic transformation of the young, developing country. Many foreign economists have derided the efforts of newly independent countries to diversify their economies by increasing the level of industrialization as prestigious and ambitious. It is significant to note that where these efforts have not been made, the countries concerned have oftentimes suffered for being essentially primary producers. Although Nkrumah, from his writings, seemed to have socialist tendencies, he did not emphasize socialism as a strategy of economic development until he had convinced himself that the *laissez-faire* and purely market-oriented policy would delay development. He brushed aside African private entrepreneurship and emphasized state participation when the former failed to take advantage of the assistance of the Industrial Development Corporation, and of the Industrial Promotion Unit, set up in 1957, with the aim of interesting investors in the development of manufacturing and processing in Ghana. In spite of the facilities offered by these and similar institutions, most Ghanaian businessmen operated on small-scale basis. Even when Nkrumah became convinced of the suitability of socialism as a vehicle of change, he was cautious in enforcing it so that the existing structure might not be unduly destabilized. For example, he encouraged state participation in industrialization not through nationalization and confiscation but through the state moving into areas it considered neglected or not adequately provided for.[32]

Nkrumah relied on his technical experts, sought advice and sometimes subjected his decisions to scholarly debate before implementing them. His Seven-Year Plan was directed by both internal and external experts. Although his external experts came mainly from the East, an opportunity was given in an International Conference on the Plan for men like Albert Hirschman, K. N. Raj, H. C. Bos and Joszef Bognar to express their views.[33] Many of his earlier decisions had been influenced by such men as W. A. Lewis, Dudley Seers and Nicholas Kaldor.[34]

His import-substitution policy was, in a measure, self-reliance which is now a household word in most developing countries. One of his problems was that he lived well ahead of his time so that some of the measures he suggested and introduced, but which were condemned. are now being encouraged. In this connection, one is bound to refer to his direction that Ghana's plans for industrialization should fit into that of Africa. In effect, Nkrumah was all the time thinking about south-south dialogue, which is now being encouraged and pursued.

After 1962, Nkrumah was said to have run the economic engine at a very high speed, resulting in serious overheating of the engine. This statement refers to the heavy investments made into both manufacturing industry and agriculture, which were in accord with the current view that a high level of investment was a crucial component of a big push needed to break the vicious circle of poverty in most third world countries. The problem lay in the dishonesty of most foreign and local contractors and their agents who took advantage of Nkrumah's genuine concern about the poverty of the people of his country to enrich themselves.

The outcome of Nkrumah's industrialization policy and the heavy losses incurred by many of the state enterprises have served as a lesson. To abate industrial losses, the PNDC government encourages the appointment of competent staff, including managers, and the enforcement of discipline at all levels of production. Also, such techniques as worker participation in decision making are strongly advised as a means of increasing the productivity of labor. Furthermore, wherever possible, management of state industrial concerns is encouraged to develop and rely on local raw materials in order to reduce overdependence on external sources, the limited supply of which results in many factories operating below capacity.

NOTES

1.   Killick, 1978:39.
2.   Nkrumah, 1962(d).
3.   *Ibid.:* 10.
4.   Adams, 1940.
5.   Szereszewski, 1965.
6.   Lewis, 1953:3.
7.   *Ibid.*
8.   Church, 1963:77.
9.   *Ibid.:* 77.
10. *Ibid.* :77.
11. British Government (HMSO), 1957 :19.
12. *Ibid.:* 19.
13. Birmingham et al (eds.), 1966 .
14. Watson, 1948.
15. *Ibid.*
16. *Ibid.*
17. British Government (HMSO), 1948.
18. Ghana Government, Ten Great Years, 1951—60.
19. British Government, 1957:32.
20. *Ibid .:* 3 .
21. Gold Coast Government, 1954.

22. British Government (HMSO), 1957 :32.
23. British Government (HMSO), 1957:32.
24. Krassowski, 1978:18.
25. *Ibid.:* 18.
26. *Ibid.* : 39.
27. *Ibid.* : 43.
28. Nkrumah, 1965a: 111.
29. *Ibid.* : 167.
30. Killick, 1978:48.
31. Nkrumah, 1963a: 27.
32. Killick, op. cit. :48.
33. *Ibid.:* 52.
34. *Ibid* .: 52.

Agricultural Development Strategy under Nkrumah

J. A. Dadson

1. Overview/Abstract

This paper evaluates Ghana's experience with socialized agriculture, the model which Nkrumah adopted as a modernizing device. The factual analysis is conducted in terms of the following: the economic environment which stimulated it; initial preparation and acquisition of resources; production and distribution of commodities; the transfer of technology; working arrangements governing labor and farm management; and organization, administration and control of the socialized sector.

The account shows that the programme of technical modernization and socialist/structural transformation was frustrated by inconsistent objectives, inappropriate methods, inadequate management capacity, and dysfunctional political interference. It also suggests that the model itself was inappropriate for Ghana and points to the need to re-examine alternative approaches.

2. Introduction: The Problem, And The Model

In their search for practical ways of mobilizing resources for the rapid development of their predominantly agrarian economies, emerging countries such as Ghana have had to face an issue of strategic importance — that of finding the institutional mode of resource organization for rapid and continuing growth under conditions of dynamic efficiency and equity. The options are wide: from the existing traditional smallholder farming to large-scale controlled production. In the early 1960s, Ghana attempted to develop its agriculture on the socialist model, having chosen socialism as its goal.

Prior to the choice of socialized agriculture in 1961, two different approaches to farm modernization had been tried. Under the first, the aim was to support and improve the existing traditional system with a range of services, research and development of improved techniques, and extension. Under the second, it was to experiment with government plantations as primary producers and as models of modernization. For the latter approach, an Agricultural Development Corporation (ADC) was set up, whose functions were: to demonstrate the use and possibilities of modern technology to surrounding traditional farmers; and to assist, with initial technical and supervisory services, those farmers who might wish to establish their own modern farms.

Over the period, agriculture failed to grow as expected, and a widening gap between domestic output and demand emerged: local foodstuffs prices rose rapidly, while food imports, which reflected a change in the structure of food demand towards high-protein foods (e.g. meat, dairy products, fish) more than doubled.

In contrast to the stagnation in agriculture, population was growing at over 3 per cent per annum. More seriously, there was a strong drift of the potentially more productive rural educated youth to the urban areas in search of non-agricultural employment, opportunities for which were, however, limited. Socialized agriculture, operating under centralized planning and direction, appealed to the Party as a more efficient means of mobilizing the rural economy— that is, of realizing agricultural productivity and output, and solving the problems of rural exodus and unemployment.

Traditional Agriculture

Traditional agriculture was, as it still is, characterized by small-scale production by farm families, which comprised some 60 per cent of the working population. Production, characterized by mixed cropping and incidental livestock holdings, was "basically" subsistence oriented, the only and major cash crop being cocoa. It was based on an ample supply of land and on labor technology—farm implements being quite rudimentary—and on land rotation (or "shifting cultivation") which was consistent with the favorite man/land ratio existing and also with the communal tenure system, but could hardly generate capital for growth and development.

The only important attempts at introducing new technology into non-cocoa agriculture prior to 1961 were, (a) a bullock-plough scheme designed to encourage mixed farming in the northern savanna, and (b) a scheme of subsidized mechanized service for all farmers. The former was initiated in 1938, and, by 1961, had reached only 4,000 farmers. The latter was begun in 1953. The highest acreage ploughed was 4,000 in 1961.

Thus, traditional agriculture was in 1961 still characterized by rudimentary methods and low productivity. It could not meet the increasing demand for food, rising standards in nutrition, or the requirements of an expanding economy. It could also not retain its own rural educated manpower. Yet its mobilization appeared difficult because of the number of independent farmers involved, their spatial spread, and their level of literacy.

Socialized agriculture, on the other hand, appeared to offer the advantages of economies of scale, of centralized management and decision-making, and of co-ordination and control. Consequently, it was expected to be a more efficient means of transferring technology and meeting national requirements. Above all, socialized agriculture was an ideological choice, in response to past colonial development and the quest for a new social and economic order.

The model of socialized agriculture, as historically derived from socialist development experiment, may be sketched in terms of its preconditions, the institutions characteristic of it, and the strategy of development in it (Karcz; Wilber). The preconditions include severance of bonds with colonial and foreign capitalists, and a social revolution in favor of workers and peasants (small-holders). The old political and economic institutions and mechanisms are destroyed, and new socialist forms substituted, namely: collectivized units in place of landed estates and peasant or smallholder proprietorship; comprehensive central planning; centralized distribution of inputs; and a system of administrative controls, incentives and pressures on enterprises partially supplanting the market mechanism to ensure compliance with the plan. The strategy of development encompasses high rates of capital formation; priority of industrialization; bias in favor of modern capital-intensive technology combined with labour-intensive techniques in selected operations; target setting and extraction, and others.

The role of the socialized sector as described in the Seven-Year Development Plan was (1) to raise agricultural output and efficiency by introducing technology into agriculture, and by expanding the area under cultivation; (2) to alter the structure of commodity production in favor of industrial and export crops, and livestock; (3) to supply the urban populations with low-cost foodstuffs; (4) to attract the rural educated youth into agriculture, and thus to reduce unemployment and improve the quality of human resources in agriculture.

The sector comprised four agencies—the State Farms Corporation (SFC), the Workers Brigade (WB), the United Ghana Farmers Council (UGFC), and the Young Farmers League (YFL). All these bodies, except the SFC, had been established already for various non-agricultural functions—the Brigade as a para-military training organization for the unemployed, the UGFC as a farmers' political organ and a cocoa buyer, and the League as a farm training organization for the educated youth. All were integral parts of the ruling Party, and continued to perform various other political and non-economic functions. The SFC and WB operated state or parastatal farms, the UGFC co-operative farms, and the League youth collective camp farms.

3. Socialization Process and Experience

To get its programme under way, the Government dissolved three important Divisions of the Ministry of Agriculture which traditionally served the existing agriculture, namely, Extension, Economics, and Cocoa, in order to transfer the Divisions' resources, including skilled manpower, to the new sector. A greater portion of the agricultural development resources was also concentrated on the new sector.

Apart from this step, socialization which preceded the Seven-Year Development Plan by two years, was launched without any preparation whatsoever. Predictably, it ran into immediate implementation difficulties, and preceded without co-ordination. The main problems of the first year of socialization were the following: (a) an extreme shortage of skilled manpower in charge of management and technical operations due to the speed of socialization and the refusal of the agencies' directors — because of a distrust of civil servants — to place the transferred personnel in responsible positions where they could be effective; (b) inadequate supplies of plantings, spares, etc.; (c) poor marketing organizations; (d) for the SFC and WB, the difficulty of acquiring contiguous unallocated land and their refusal to follow established procedures to acquire land; and (e) the harmful role of politics in recruitment procedures, which resulted in the hiring of excess labor and untrained tractor operators and managers.

Though initial progress was hampered by these factors and was poor, a large number of farms were established. The SFC, having acquired 42 developed projects (9,000 acres) from the former ADC, the Ministry of Agriculture, and private foreign estates, had grown to 112 by the end of 1964; the Brigade had 43 farms, the UGFC had 992 societies operating 1,732 farms, and the League 39 camps.

By the end of 1964, nearly one million acres had been acquired for socialized agriculture. Of this, only 20 per cent was cleared, half of which was cultivated. The SFC led with 47 per cent of the cultivated acreage, followed by the League and UGFC co-operatives with 25 per cent each and the Brigade with 3 per cent.

In 1965, the total area cultivated by the sector rose by 16 per cent. The increase was recorded by the public sub-sector, particularly the SFC, which rose by 28 per cent. The UGFC co-operatives declined by 23 per cent. They also fell in aggregate membership by 41 per cent, and in number per society by 33 per cent, in contrast to substantial gains recorded in the public sub-sector. The League declined less, but was still insignificant. In sum, the sector was able to account for only about 1 per cent of the national total cultivated area by the end of 1965: it had expected to cultivate at least 10 per cent by then.

In regional terms, the greatest progress was made in the Western Region, where rubber was expanding fairly rapidly before socialization. The northern savanna, with greater stretches of undeveloped land, was almost entirely ignored. In other words, socialized agriculture failed to develop new land, that is, to expand the total cultivated area significantly or to attract farmers.

It failed also to alter the structure of production as anticipated. Firstly, annual and food crops dominated, although the public sub-sector showed expansion in rubber, oil palm and coconut in 1965. Industrial crops, on the whole, were still insignificant. Secondly, livestock production, except poultry by the SFC, was almost totally insignificant. Poor seed and stock supply were partly responsible for these problems. But lack of preparation, planning and organization are also important explanatory factors. Indications are that yields of crops per acre were generally below levels in the traditional peasant sector. The new sector was in fact a deficit and inefficient producer. But it tried to fulfill its objective of supplying low-cost foodstuffs to urban consumers by arbitrarily charging artificially low retail prices for its produce.

The attempts to introduce new technology also ran into difficulties. The most important new method promoted was mechanization. The introduction of mechanization was unsuccessful for several reasons, of which the following were important: (1) imports of machinery (tractors, etc.), which began in large numbers only in 1961–62, were haphazard, so that machinery and parts arrived at different times, causing much idleness and under-utilization of machines; (2) a multiplicity of models and makes were imported, making adequate servicing difficult; (3) servicing was poor because of restricted importation of parts; (4) most imported machinery were unsuited to tropical conditions; (5) the distribution of machinery was poor; and (6) there was a shortage of adequately trained operators. Idleness and breakdown of machines were high. The level of under-utilization was about 80 per cent; in 1966, it was assessed that about 60 per cent of the machinery were beyond repair.

The other input of significance which the sector tried to introduce was fertilizer. This also failed partly because of poor distribution, but more importantly because knowledge regarding suitability and application was poor. Irrigation was also being studied, and was insignificant as an input, as also were genetic inputs.

In sum, knowledge regarding the use of new inputs was inadequate while it was being transferred; and the transfer effort failed as much because of this as of defective organization.

Working arrangements on the farms inhibited productive effort. On SFC farms, the manager was severely constrained by several internal and external committees and officers to whose authority he was subjected: (a) on the farms by two committees—one technical, the other political—whose decisions regarding farm operations were binding; (b) outside the farm by different managers-at-large, based in Accra, who were responsible for decisions regarding the growing of specified crops, and by district and regional committees as well as directly by headquarters in Accra. Basically, the same arrangements obtained on Brigade farms. On co-operative farms, the UGFC officials who supplied managerial advice to co-operative producers were themselves untrained and inexperienced, and lacked interest in the co-operative enterprise because of the greater importance to them of their family farms. Indeed, more time was spent by farmers on the latter than on the co-operative enterprise. League farms were managed by regional organizers who were in managerial charge of all the farm camps in the region. Supervision was therefore weak. Lastly, management on all farms was hampered by the absence of statistical or other technical information.

Labor productivity was also low because of defective working arrangements which impaired effort. SFC, WB and YFL farmers worked by civil service scheduled hours. Co-operative members worked only 2 days in the week for short hours (about 2 hours) on each occasion, and worked little. The SFC tried to solve the problem of low effort by its workers by resorting to "contract" work. But implementation and supervision were so poor that the system failed. On all farms, party political meetings and affairs took precedence over farming and interfered with it.

In sum, both management and labor were unproductive on socialized farms. And given the high level of labor employed at institutionally determined wages, the labor cost was extremely high.

Finally, the administration, organization and control of the sector were grossly inefficient. Each agency had a number of divisions or departments at its headquarters, all in Accra. These divisions exercised functions over different aspects of the agricultural operations of the agency as a whole. Each division had its own sub-divisions or counterparts in the regions (8), districts (40) and on the farms, which were run by several committees on which Party representatives served. However, within the agencies, co-ordination of divisions was weak, and technical information and feedback hardly flowed down or up. And between the agencies, there was no co-ordinating link whatever, save that all the agencies were part of the ruling party.

Further, they had no links with any government or planning body, with the exception of the Brigade, which was under the dual control of the Ministry of Defence and the Office of the President who exercised direct control over it, often interrupting its farm operations for political activities. The Ministry of Agriculture was particularly weakened through re-structuring. It was dismembered into 5 separate Ministries, none of which had links with the sector. Civil Servants were isolated from the sector because their loyalty to the Party's ideology and programme was suspect. On their part, the civil servants and other professionals were skeptical of socialized agriculture. The result was that technical expertise was denied the sector, and the sector operated without adequate reference to any plan.

Lastly, undesirable political influences and pressures had adverse effects on the sector's farm operations. They led to irrational recruitment procedures, wrong siting, land seizure, and generally dysfunctional activities. Much of the poor progress of socialized agriculture must be explained by this factor.

Pressures for reform of the system mounted as sector performance and overall agriculture declined. In response, the Government particularly restored the technical leadership of the Ministry of Agriculture and proposed other measures of reform and adjustment. This, however, did not signify retreat. Rather, as it quickly became clear, it was heralding an even bolder scheme of collectivization involving whole villages and larger production units announced in 1965. But that was not to be: early 1966, the Government was overthrown and the socialist development programme terminated. The Nkrumah chapter was closed.

4. Evaluation and Conclusion

There are two schools of thought on the value and effectiveness of the experience analyzed above. One school holds the view that the socialist experiment, while not successful, was certainly not a failure either, and that the rejection of socialized agriculture was premature and ill-advised. They argue that the experiment had not had time to settle, and that the experience was too brief to permit conclusive appraisal. Major social programmes such as this, the argument continues, have long gestation periods and can only proceed by trial and error.

There is a point there. Revolutions and transformations cannot be accomplished overnight. But it is worthy of note that, except for the period 1966 to 1972 (of the NLC and Busia era), when Nkrumah's socialist and state interventionist policies were rejected, post Nkrumah Ghana has been under leaders who, without exception, have claimed and proclaimed their commitment to Nkrumah's ideology and policies. Yet, the system has not been restored.

True, some attempts have been made to re-introduce "command farming" in some form or other, notably under certain phases of Acheampong's agricultural programme code-named "Operation Feed Yourself" (OFY), and more recently in the early period of the PNDC. Recall, for example, the following: the attempted entry of the military into commercial agriculture in the 1970s; the creation of the Ghana National Reconstruction Corps (which absorbed the Young Farmers League) for youth agricultural and industrial production; the formalized *nnoboa* and crop association schemes of OFY; and the community, institutional and people's farms of 1982/83. One is talking of abortive programmes; all failed. One hardly needs reminding that the state farms and Brigade (now Food Production Corporation) farms are still in operation; and that for all the policies of restructuring and rationalization, they are inefficient, deficit, unsuccessful producers. The record clearly does not support the viability of "command farming" in Ghana. And that is the view of the other school of thought.

In the opinion of this writer, socialized agriculture as a model, adopted as it was without study and without adaptation to suit local conditions and capabilities, was and is inappropriate and unsuited to Ghana. This view is based not simply on the fact that the system failed to achieve factor productivities above existing levels or to contribute to capital formation, among other factors; it is based on reasons that are fundamental and also derive from the experiences of other African and underdeveloped countries which have also tried it. For one thing, it involves replacing the existing land tenure system, which provides fairly equitable if imperfect access to farm land for all farm families, with a system which in equity terms is inferior. (Note that seizure of land was the method of acquisition used; and predictably it alienated the rural people. See *Report* on the Brigade). For another, Ghana lacks the capabilities of planning and management as well as the discipline demanded for implementing the system, at least at this stage of our development. Also, the system does not provide adequate incentives to stimulate its operators to sustained productive effort, in contrast with family farming conditions. And it is notoriously slow in transmitting correct signals to producers on the one hand, while, on the other, it seems to tolerate tardy, distorted interpretation of signals, and inappropriate policies and responses.

All this is not to question Nkrumah's intentions regarding his commitment to development, or his stature and achievement; only that this strategy lacked sufficient study and appropriate policies. There is little question that socialized agriculture did at least partially solve certain of his objectives, like youth unemployment. But these were short-term gains. In the long-term, the effectiveness and viability of the path was doubtful.

Given the high capital intensity and disappointing productivity trends associated with it, it would seem appropriate to consider and explore alternative systems of agricultural resource organization. In this regard, the existing traditional system is the one that was too hastily set aside. Numerous studies indicate its potential and viability as a base for development. The increasing recognition of this fact in Ghana, though belated, is welcome.

NKRUMAH

NKRUMAH AND THE DECOLONIZATION OF GHANA'S EXTERNAL TRADE RELATIONS 1956-1965

Kwesi Jonah

Introduction

About two decades after the overthrow of the Nkrumah regime, the essence of the social, economic and political experiment it was trying to carry out in Ghana remains a controversial issue. One study divides the Nkrumah phase in Ghana's politics into two. There is an earlier non-marxist phase during which official association with marxist socialism was carefully avoided, even though Nkrumah himself was evidently under some marxist influences.[1] In the second phase, caution was officially abandoned and marxism fully embraced.[2] However, in most of the studies, substantial doubts have been cast on Nkrumah's socialism. Some interpretations reduce it to a petty bourgeois mystification[3] while others claim that it was nothing more than an anti-colonial economic and political strategy, the application of which was conditioned by the availability of favorable circumstances.[4] A later re-appraisal threw it even farther into the shade.[5] Certainly, a more scientific and overall assessment of this very important and formative period in Ghana's post-colonial history cannot be confidently tackled without detailed studies of all aspects of Nkrumah's strategy of development. Even after this, it can be expected that a really impartial judgement will still be hard to make. Nevertheless, the task of providing adequate and informed basis for an evaluation of the period must continue. This brief work is intended to contribute a widow's mite towards this end.

Objective

This is a study of efforts made by the Nkrumah Government to alter the external trade pattern it inherited from colonial rule in Ghana. It is essentially a study of the changes in the structure of external trade relations as it had evolved at the time Ghana became a sovereign state. It does not aim at studying the distribution of internal trade among multinational trading firms, Levantine and other foreign traders on the one hand and indigenous Ghanaian traders on the other—a task which Garlick[6] has performed complementing thereby Bauer's monumental work covering the greater part of colonial rule in British West Africa.[7] Neither is it a study of indigenous Ghanaian markets, their historical evolution and significance, to which much time and attention has already been given by our historians and anthropologists.[8] This study belongs to the general area of studies in economic decolonization. Within this general area of study, so much attention has been focussed on the set of policies aimed at reducing foreign domination of the Ghanaian economy.[9] It cannot be claimed that emphasis within this general area has been unduly concentrated. Nevertheless, the extension of attention to other aspects of the problem should be beneficial to all engaged in the search for a greater understanding of the Ghanaian political, social and economic reality. This essay should be seen primarily as geared towards broadening our understanding of the full dimensions of anti-imperialism of a nationalist leader whose actual impact on Ghana and Africa has as yet not been fully assessed.

Argument

The substance of this essay is that trade relations established during the period of the Nkrumah regime reflected a clear and consistent anti-imperialist strategy of development. Trade policy and practice of the Nkrumah Government was anti-neocolonialist, anti-racist and pan-Africanist. It is already known that between 1957 and 1960, Nkrumah's economic policy was characterized by an unquestioned adherence to Arthur Lewis'[10] proposals of continuing dependence on imperialism. From 1960 onwards, very rapid changes began to occur. The thrust of these changes was to reduce dependence on imperialism, strengthen the country's independence and freedom of choice, as well as make available from a wider area of the international system more resources for national development. It is necessary to provide a back-drop to these changes by going further back in time, to Ghana's pre-colonial and colonial trade relations. As it will be seen, Ghana's thriving trade ties with her close neighbors were increasingly cut off, first, by mercantile traders from Europe, further by free trade imperialism and later, to a much greater extent, by the colonialization of the country in the period of monopoly capital.

Pre-Colonial Trade

Ghana has a long history of trade with the outside world. Some attempts have even been made to establish the existence of commercial contacts with the ancients (Phoenicians and Carthaginians).[11] Nothing seems to have come of such efforts. Naturally, Ghana's strongest trade links were with her immediate neighbors. Ghana maintained extensive trade links with her immediate neighbors with which the bulk of her exchanges took place. Through the ancient kingdoms of the Western Sudan, Ghana also maintained commercial contacts with Europe. Dike has observed that "The history of modem West Africa is the history of five centuries of trade with Europe."[12] While this observation is substantially correct, it also overlooks, in a sense, the importance of trade among West Africans themselves. Ghana's pre-colonial trade was carried on with her neighbors to the north, west and the east. The northern trade consisted not only of Ghana's participation in the trans-saharan trade in which gold from the country's forest belt was a crucial commodity.[13] This trade was certainly beneficial to the western Sudanese commercial entrepots and some Ghanaian commodities. Equally important was the trade between the Gonja of Northern Ghana and the people of Northern Nigeria. This trade made available to the northem Nigerian markets fresh kola nuts from Ghana's forest belt.[14]

With the appearance of European mercantile traders on the coast of Ghana, the trade in gold was diverted southward to the sea. Similarly, under colonialism, in later years, Ghana's kola nuts continued to reach Nigeria not by Gonja caravans and traders plying overland routes in the north but by European boats. Ghana's trade with Benin in the past largely involved the matrilineal Akan peoples exchanging handicrafts for female slaves, with the Portuguese playing temporarily, the role of intermediaries. The Ghana-Benin commercial chain was soon to be broken and subordinated to European interests. Horizontal trade links between two African neighbors were replaced by vertical trade links between individual African communities and Europe.[15]

The same is true of the trade links between Ghana and her western neighbor, Cote d'Ivoire (Ivory Coast). This trade was broken by the Portuguese who set up a commercial port at Axim and so prevented the two neighboring peoples from trading with each other. It is a great credit to the perseverance of these African neighboring communities that as late as 1637 when the Dutch captured Axim, the trade was still going on.[16] Like the Portuguese, they immediately took measures to subordinate it to their own interests. Even in this early phase of commercial contact with Europe, mercantile interests of that continent had already begun to cut off horizontal trade links existing between Ghana and her neighbors and to reorient them vertically to serve European needs. This phase of the subordination of Ghana's trade with her neighbors was closed with the introduction of the infamous traffic in human beings—the European slave trade. The abundant supplies of gold and silver discovered in the Americas could only be exploited when a hard working people accustomed to settled work could be found nearby. Africa, the nearest continent, whose people were already engaged in settled agriculture and used to disciplined labor, was to serve as the source of slave labor. To recount Ghana's role in this trade will be wasteful repetition as original accounts have already been given by our historians.[17]

The birth of industrial capitalism in Europe was to transform European needs in Africa from slave labor to industrial raw materials. With the advent of industrial capitalism, a new stage in the subordination of Ghana's external trade to European needs was reached. Palm oil and other raw materials needed in Europe could be produced only when labor was put to agricultural use rather than exported. Daaku and Reynolds have produced a detailed account of Ghana's role in this new phase of trade with Europe.[18] For our purposes, it is important to note that Ghana further became deeply integrated into European trade conducted along the West African coast by small competitive firms. An even greater proportion of Ghana's trade was captured by European companies. An important consequence of this trade was the emergence of a class of African traders who derived their fortunes from serving as middlemen between the Europeans on the Coast and the rest of the peoples in the interior.[19] Today, it can only be speculated that these "merchant princes" could have developed into the forebears of a full-blown indigenous bourgeoisie if monopoly capital had not displaced them under colonialism. This speculation is, of course, founded in the belief that competitive capitalism was less ruinous to African development in general than its monopoly successor.

Colonial Trade

The story of the colonialization of Ghana is the story of the total take-over of the economy by European monopoly companies and the development of the economy as a raw material production appendage of the British economy. Outside of agriculture, every single sector of the economy—mining, commerce, banking and insurance, shipping and industry etc.—was in the hands of European monopolies.[20] Trade, retail, wholesale and import-export, were even more monopolistic. Bauer and Howard both described the economy as "oligopolistic," controlled as it was by about a dozen trading companies under the leadership of the UAC, Unilever's subsidy. Colonization of Ghana by Britain also meant that all trade was as far as possible to be redirected to Britain. In conditions of imperialist economic domination, international trade is largely trade between different units of monopoly companies. Trade between Ghana and her West African neighbors which in the past constituted almost the whole of her international trade now came to represent a drop in Ghana's ocean of external commercial transactions. On the contrary, Ghana's trade was now carried on with Britain. Only a small proportion of trade was carried on with other foreign countries, even less with Ghana's neighbors. Analysis of Ghana's colonial trade will be done within the framework of a two-phase division, i.e. the pre-World War II period and the post-World War II period.

Ghana's pre-World War II external trade pattern was characterized by a high proportion of trade with the colonial mother country — Britain — with Germany, the USA, Holland and France accounting for small proportions. This was true of both import and export trade, and remained largely the case till the outbreak of World War I when this situation was modified slightly. The proportion of Ghana's imports originating from Britain after World War I remained high but exports to Britain were drastically reduced. This trend is very clearly demonstrated by the trade figures before and after World War I.

Table I

PRINCIPAL FOREIGN COUNTRIES' SHARE IN GHANA'S
IMPORT TRADE BEFORE WORLD WAR I IN PERCENTAGES

		1910	1911	1912	1913
1.	United Kingdom	75.00	72.00	70.00	69.99
2.	Germany	12 .00	10.00	11.00	NA
3.	USA	1.00	6.00	7 .00	5.09
4.	Holland	9.00	6.00	6.00	NA
5.	France	1.00	1.00	1.00	0.94

Source: Report on the Trade of the Colony for the year 1912 and 1913.

Table II

PRINCIPAL FOREIGN COUNTRIES' SHARE IN GHANA'S
EXPORT TRADE BEFORE WORLD WAR I IN PERCENTAGES

		1910	1911	1912	1913
1.	United Kingdom	70.00	69.60	67.70	64.77
2.	Germany	18.00	16.00	18.00	NA
3.	USA	1.00	1.00	2.00	3.40
4.	Holland				
5.	France	8.00	11.00	1.00	8.39

Source: Report on the Trade of the Colony for the years 1912 and 1913.

These figures bear eloquent testimony to Britain's undisputed leadership in Ghana's foreign trade in the pre-World War I period. The colonial mother country accounted for between 64 per cent and 75 per cent of both import and export trade. In spite of this obvious dominance, the colonial state was increasingly worried over what it considered as stiff competition by other European countries. Therefore, in August 1912, the acting Comptroller of Customs, Mr. Mitchell, submitted a memorandum on "foreign competition with British goods in the market of the colony." The memorandum largely laid the blame for this "foreign competition" on the expensive trade practices of British Companies in Ghana and their unwillingness to accept and act on advice from their agents in the Colony. But clearly, the memorandum indicated the desire of British Colonialism to appropriate an even larger proportion of Ghana's external trade.[21]

After World War I, Britain lost a considerable proportion of her import trade with Ghana. Unlike in the period before the War, Britain could no longer absorb her accustomed proportion of Ghana's exports though she maintained somehow her position as the Colony's leading source of imports. The following figures of the Post-World War I trade of Ghana speak for themselves.

Table III

SHARE OF GHANA'S PRINCIPAL TRADE PARTNERS IN HER EXPORT TRADE IN PERCENTAGES

		1920	1922	1923	1925	1926
1.	UK	47.48	42.26	34.53	31.33	29.84
2.	USA	20.68	25.61	2 6.02	22.01	24.72
3.	Germany		12.68	7.13	16.95	18.34
4.	France	12.67	6.68	7.99	8.12	5.46
5.	Holland	NA	NA	17.58	13.10	13.21

Source: Report on the Trade of the Colony for the years 1920-1926.

It is obvious from these figures that after World War I, Britain's ability to take the greater part of Ghana's export trade was reduced. Correspondingly, the USA and other European powers increased their share in Ghana's export trade. On the other hand, Britain's share in Ghana's import trade remained at about the same level as before the war — 78.05 per cent in 1920, 75.76 per cent in 1922, 69.08 per cent in 1923. It seems that the impact of World War I as far as Ghana's trade was concerned was to reduce the capacity of the British economy to absorb Ghanaian imports while Britain's exports to Ghana remained at pre-War levels. World War II had a much more damaging impact on Britain's monopoly of Ghana's external trade.

Slight but significant changes in the structure of Ghana's external trade occurred after World War II. The substance of these changes was that Britain's share increasingly fell while other European countries and the USA picked up what Britain had lost.[22] For example, in import trade, Britain gradually yielded ground to other European countries, a development entirely due to World War II. World War I had affected only Britain's import of Ghanaian goods. In 1950, about 56.4 per cent of Ghana's total imports were of British origin. It was 53 .5 per cent in 1951, 5 6.3 per cent in 1952 and 54.9 per cent in 1953 but only 48.3 per cent in 1954. In 1957, the year of Ghana's independence, Britain was only able to absorb 40.7 per cent of Ghana's imports. Over the period, other European countries increased their share in Ghana's imports from 22.6 per cent in 1950 to 25.6 per cent in 1957. Their dependencies and the USA also improved their position in Ghana's import trade.

Similar adjustments occurred in the structure of Ghana's export trade. About 40 per cent of Ghana's exports went to Britain in 1950 but in 1957, this was down to 37.3 per cent. Other European countries increased their share in Ghana's exports from 19.3 per cent in 1950 to 27 per cent in 1957. The USA showed a decline. From the end of World War II to the time of independence, the main change in Ghana's external trade was that Britain lost part of her share to the USA and other European countries. On the whole, western Europe maintained her dominant position in Ghana's trade. This period then seems to have been marked by an uncritical adherence to the doctrine of *laissez faire et laissez passer* free production and free distribution. This doctrine reigned supreme in Ghana until 1960 when conscious efforts were made to alter the situation. Nkrumah could no longer put up with a situation in which he had occasion to pass critical comments: "Our trade . . . is not between ourselves. It is turned towards Europe and embraces us as providers of low-priced primary materials in exchange for the more expensive finished goods we import."[23]

Neo-Colonial Trade Dependence

The situation graphically portrayed here is one of neo-colonial trade dependence, i.e. the dependence after political independence of an underdeveloped country's trade on a few advanced capitalist countries with which the bulk of its external trade transactions take place. Neo-colonial trade dependence originates from colonial trade dependence. But unlike trade dependence under colonialism, the position of the capitalist countries other than the ex-colonial mother country is considerably enhanced. As a general rule, trade dependence is characterized by increasing balance of payments difficulties for the underdeveloped countries whose trade terms are susceptible to notorious fluctuations and often very unfavorable largely because they export mainly primary produce and import mainly manufactures. The price of raw materials exported by the underdeveloped countries is most unstable. On the other hand, the manufactures imported by them show constantly rising prices. A wide array of mechanisms are available to the advanced capitalist countries for maintaining trade dependence. Among them are the system of preferences, financing policy and monetary relations. Above all, the underdeveloped country is discouraged from diversifying its trade relations.[24]

Nkrumah on Neo-Colonialism in Trade

The concept of neo-colonialism cannot be discussed without reference to Nkrumah, who perhaps more than anyone else, contributed to its birth and development. In the second year of Ghana's independence, precisely in April 1958, Nkrumah, in his welcome address to representatives at the Conference of Independent African States held in Accra, warned that Africa had to contend with not only "old forms of colonialism" but also the "new forms of colonialism."[25] There is a high probability that the Resolutions on Neo-colonialism adopted by the All African Peoples Conference (held in Tunis, January 1960), had considerable Ghanaian input which could be attributed to Nkrumah. Even before his famous *Neo-Colonialism, the Last Stage of Imperialism* came out in 1965, he had devoted a full chapter in *Africa Must Unite* (1963) to the concept. In both *Neocolonialism, the Last Stage of Imperialism* and *Handbook of Revolutionary Warfare,* neo-colonialism was conceived as a condition of economic dependence and exploitation in the period of political independence. As it related to trade, he explained that the international trading system operated to the disadvantage of the underdeveloped countries because of monopoly capital's control of the world market as well as of the prices of commodities bought and sold there. Therefore, for a leader like him whose "fundamental guide is the need for economic independence,"[26] strong and persistent efforts to break out of this system was a vital need.

Perhaps, it is necessary to highlight the dangers of trade dependence. Trade dependence can be turned into a dangerous political weapon against an underdeveloped country. After the recent experience of Nicaragua, this point should not be hammered too hard. It is important to point out that in cold war conditions, international trade can no longer be naively regarded as a simple act of economic exchange. One dangerous development in modern times is what the former West German Chancellor Helmut Schmidt has described as "the turning of trade . . . into a political instrument or some valve that could be opened or closed, depending upon the political situation."[27] The persistent refusal to apply trade sanctions against apartheid South Africa and the ease with which trade embargo has been slammed on Nicaragua and other revolutionary countries are cases in point.

What makes trade dependence particularly dangerous is the

tendency to resort to protectionism in the advanced countries. If trade can be used as a political weapon against revolutionary countries, it is at least clearly evident by now that third world countries that are not in any way revolutionary, and in some cases are anti-revolutionary, have suffered as much, if not more, from protectionist policies of advanced industrial countries. Protectionism in the industrialized countries of the north has increasingly resulted in the reduction of third world countries' manufactured exports to the markets of the north. The few third world manufacturers that have entered the markets of the north have done so against very high import duty. Protectionism is hardly motivated by political reasons. On the contrary, it is an attempt to protect inefficient industries in the north even if this means heavy governmental subsidies or higher consumer prices. In the words of Castro, "the invisible hand of market forces which is the heart and soul of the capitalist economic system is conveniently forgotten."[28] Mr Malcolm Baldridge, the US Secretary of Commerce, has pointed out that "more than 100 pieces of protectionist legislation —all opposed by the Reagan administration—were pending before the US Congress when it adjourned in October 1984."[29] As Mr. Baldridge frankly admits,

> Protectionism won't make the problems of adjusting to fundamental shifts in an economy any easier. It won't make non-competitive industries competitive. It won't bring down costs. It won't increase employment. It will raise costs, lose jobs and allow uncompetitive industrial sectors to continue to stagnate. It will divert resources from efficient industries to inefficient ones.[30]

Another cost of trade dependence is unequal exchange—the tendency for more and more third world produce to exchange for the same quantity of manufactured goods from the north. The Ghanaian Head of State, Flt. Lt. Rawlings, captured the essence of this phenomenon when he explained: "over the years, the prices we pay for things have gone up higher than the prices we receive for our agricultural products. That is to say, if in 1960 we needed one ton of cocoa to exchange for one tractor, today we need ten tons of cocoa to exchange for the same tractor."[31] What does unequal exchange really imply? It means, according to Castro, that an under-developed third world country "has transferred merchandise, economic values without receiving anything at all in exchange."[32]

Third World's External Trade

Recent research has invalidated certain major assumptions about the external trade of third world countries. For example, Jalee had established in the past that not only was the third world's share in the export trade of the world small but that this share was dropping with passage of time.[33] Tochir has observed an increase in south-south trade as a whole relative to south-north trade. More propitiously, the expansion in south-south trade is greater in manufactured than in other goods. What is more, this trade has increased at a much faster rate (16 per cent) than that between south and north (13 per cent).[34] This means the share of the north in third world trade especially in manufactured goods is shrinking. At the same time, the share of the south in industrial exports bound for southern countries is increasing.[35] In both directions, important changes have taken place in the third world in recent times. At the same time, the fact should not be overlooked that a small number of third world countries account for this increase in third world industrial exports to other third world countries. Moreover, some of these third world countries serve only as relay stations for western multinational productions.[36]

However, in the 1960s with which this paper is largely concerned, most of Jalee's observations were valid. Third world countries played only a marginal role in international trade, traded less among themselves than with the advanced capitalist countries and exported largely raw or semi-raw materials.[37] These features made external trade much more important, in fact crucial, to the economic growth of countries like Ghana than it was for advanced industrialized countries.

Specific Features

In his analysis of the restrictive foreign trade regime in Ghana, Leith paid little attention to the specific features of Ghana's external trade.[38] Killick, however, points out the excessive dependence of the Ghanaian economy on foreign trade, the predominance of manufactures in her imports and raw materials in her exports, the dependence of her export earnings on one produce characterized by notorious price fluctuations and the direction of trade towards European and American markets.[39] Killick's point that the direction of Ghana's trade is a function of the composition of her production is at best controversial. The composition and direction of trade were largely politically determined. The political courage of Nkrumah in attempting to change the structure of internal production and redirect external trade in itself is a clear indicator that Killick's position cannot be accepted without qualifications.

For our purposes, certain specific features of Ghana's external trade deserve emphasis.

At the global level and within the African context, Ghana's neocolonial trade dependence had certain characteristic features. First, about 80 per cent of her external trade was carried on with a few West European countries and the USA. Second, trade with the socialist countries was virtually non-existent. Third, at the level of the African continent, Ghana's trade with her immediate neighbors was very limited; and, fourth, Ghana's African trade was dominated by one country, apartheid South Africa. These features point to certain obvious policy implications for any government desirous of building a more independent national economy capable of utilizing resources from all corners of the world for national development, and to strengthen her political independence. From 1960 onwards, Nkrumah's Government began to take bold steps to reduce dependence on the west and increase trade with the socialist countries (centrally planned economies). In African trade, Ghana's doors were closed to South Africa and trade links with other African countries strengthened or established. Ghana's external trade was deflected away from imperialism to benefit socialism and from apartheid to benefit other countries. To show how this was done, we shall examine first, the expansion of trade links with the socialist bloc.

Eastward Expansion

Trade between Ghana and the socialist countries was negligible before Ghana's attainment of political independence. This, however, is not to say that Ghana did not have any historical trade links with the whole or part of the countries that later became socialist. For example, in 1923, Ghana under British colonial rule imported from Siberia about £305 of goods falling in the categories of food, drinks and tobacco and in 1925, about £44 of raw goods were imported from Russia.[40] Though the documents are not very clear on this matter, this is obviously a carry-over of trade with pre-revolutionary Russia. In the same year, 1925, goods of varying values were imported from some of the countries which later turned socialist. That year, imports from Poland were worth £3,634, from Czechoslovakia £1,923 and from Cuba £1,164. Imports of smaller value came from China (£79) and Yugoslavia (£19).[41] It seems that this trend continued for some time, and ceased when these countries turned socialist. If that indeed was the case, then it would seem to suggest that at some point in Ghana's history as a Colony of imperial Britain, there must have been some degree of de-easternization of her external trade relations.

Whatever might have been the case, in 1956 Ghana exported £1.05 million of goods to the Soviet Union. This was equivalent to 2.4 per cent of Ghana's total exports. In 1957, this went up to £6.25 million or about 6.8 per cent of total exports. Import from the USSR was nil. On the other hand, Czechoslovakia which did not make any purchases from Ghana sold about £1.13 million and £1.41 million worth of goods to Ghana in 1950 and 1957 respectively, representing 1.3 per cent and 1.5 per cent respectively of Ghana's total imports. This good start in Ghana's trade with socialist countries did not see consistent development, for, in 1958, Ghana's exports to the USSR measured only up to 0.4 per cent of her total exports. By 1965, trade with the socialist countries which in 1956 was negligible had risen to 26.3 per cent of Ghana's total exports and 24.2 per cent of her imports in 1964. Before the 1960s, Ghana had no policy on trade with the socialist countries; now one was about to emerge.

Phenomenal Expansion

Ghana's trade with the socialist bloc of countries expanded phenomenally; from a total of £3.18 million in 1956, it shot up to £7.74 million in 1957. However, the really phenomenal growth was yet to take place. From 1959 onwards, trade with the socialist countries entered a period of steady growth; in 1959, only 3.3 per cent of Ghana's imports came from the socialist countries. This climbed first to 4.3 per cent in 1960 and then to 5.7 per cent in 1961. The year 1961 marked a watershed in Ghana's trade with the socialist bloc. That year, Ghana Trade Missions toured and signed bilateral trade agreements with the socialist countries, namely Albania, Bulgaria, China, Czechoslovakia, Hungary, Poland, GDR, Romania, USSR and Yugoslavia. A new era in Ghana's external relations had begun.

These bilateral agreements gave a new vigour to Ghana-socialist bloc trade. Hence, in 1962, Ghana's imports from socialist sources went up to 7.15 per cent of her total and in 1963 to 11 per cent. The next year, 1964, the figure was 15.8 per cent. The really big leap occurred in 1965 (the last full year of the Nkrumah regime), when a good 26.3 per cent of Ghana's imports came from these countries. As with imports, so with exports. Ghana's exports to the socialist countries were 1.9 per cent of total export value in 1959 and 7.2 per cent in 1960. There was a sharp decline in 1961 to 1.5 per cent, but by the end of that year, bilateral trade agreements between Ghana and individual countries of the socialist bloc had been concluded. From that time onwards, trade with the socialist countries began to leap forward, reaching 8.1 per cent of total value in 1962 and 13.7 per cent in 1963. In 1964, it almost doubled to 24.2 per cent. Such was the nature of the exponential expansion that occurred in Ghana's trade with the socialist community.

Trade, even increasing trade with the socialist countries, is not necessarily evidence of a country's socialist orientation. However, a redirection of trade away from the leading capitalist countries towards socialism is positively anti-imperialist. This was the essence of Ghana's changing trade relations under Nkrumah. In 1950, the UK accounted for 56.4 per cent of Ghana's imports and in 1952, 57.6 per cent. By 1965, only 25.8 per cent of Ghana's imports came from the UK. In 1952, a good 40.1 per cent of Ghana's exports went to Britain but by 1965, this had been whittled down to 20.8 per cent. Ghana's other West European trade partners also lost their positions. Whereas in 1961 they appropriated 31.9 per cent of Ghana's exports, in 1965 they were down to 27.5 per cent. This was also the case with the Dollar Area with which Ghana's trade declined uninterruptedly. The chief beneficiaries of this reduction in trade with the West were the socialist bloc countries with which Ghana had signed bilateral agreements.

Features

The characteristic feature of Ghana's trade with the socialist bloc of countries was that, in accordance with the bilateral agreements, each of the countries agreed to supply at Ghana's request, certain types of goods to be paid for over a number of years through the supply of Ghana's products, mainly raw materials. Ghana, therefore, did not need to find scarce hard currency before it could import needed goods. At a time when Ghana was compelled to buy increasingly expensive manufactures from the west with diminishing cocoa revenues due to falling prices, Ghana's eastern trade enabled her to import the industrial goods badly needed to carry out the Seven-Year Development Plan. By 1965, imports from socialist countries consisted of mainly industrial equipment. It seems that trade with the socialist countries introduced qualitative changes in Ghana's imports. The proportion of consumer goods in total imports dropped from 50 per cent in 1961 to 40 per cent in 1963, while that of industrial goods and equipment shot up from 50.6 per cent of total imports in 1961 to 60.6 per cent in 1963. For purposes of overcoming Ghana's under-development, the qualitative change in the content of imports was rather rational. The exchange of goods in each case was balanced. At the beginning of the year, quantities and values of goods to be exchanged were agreed upon. Therefore, Ghana knew in advance how much it would derive from this trade and how much it would buy from each bilateral trade partner.[42] This trade was mutually advantageous, for no longer did the socialist countries have to buy Ghana cocoa from the capitalist market. They could now buy directly from Accra. To realize fully the benefits of trade with the socialist bloc, certain institutional changes in the Ghanaian economy were considered very necessary. In 1961, the Government set up a state-owned monopoly trading company, the Ghana National Trading Corporation (GNTC), to exercise monopoly control over Ghana's trade with the socialist bloc as well as over the internal distribution of goods coming from this and other sources.

Barter trade or counter-trade of the type Ghana carried on with the socialist countries has been attacked on many grounds. The chief case against counter-trade is that it does not lead to any increase in resources. It is only a straightforward exchange of goods. However, in a situation where free trade leads to the loss of resources by poor third world countries, counter-trade becomes the only indispensable means for achieving national developmental objectives. If free trade served the national interest of third world countries, there would be no need to engage in counter-trade. Developing countries have turned to counter-trade only after free trade has become a hinderance to the attainment of national developmental objectives.

Push Factors

The major factor in the shift towards stronger trade links with the socialist community was the deteriorating balance of payments position and the acute shortage of convertible currency which became a feature of Ghana's post-colonial economy. After the attainment of political independence, Ghana plunged headlong into a deep balance of payments crisis from which it never recovered until the end of the Nkrumah regime in 1966. With the single exception of 1958 when Ghana recorded a surplus of £10,787,000 in her current account, every year after independence showed a deficit. The biggest deficit was registered in 1965, the last full year of the Nkrumah Government. The deficit of £81.5 million in 1965 was an all-time high. Until then, it had been thought that the 1961 deficit of £52.7 million and the 1964 one amounting to £32.6 million were quite alarming. Presented below is Ghana's current account position for 1956–1965.

GHANA'S BALANCE OF PAYMENTS POSITION 1956–1965
(in thousands)

1.	1956	£13,342	6.	1961	£52,700
2.	1957	£14,431	7.	1962	£28,300
3.	1958	£10,787	8.	1963	£45,800
4.	1959	£8,258	9.	1964	£32,600
5.	1960	£20,558	10.	1965	£81,500

Source: Ghana Economic Survey, Ministry of Finance and Central Bureau of Statistics, Accra.

It is clear from this table that unfavorable balance of payments was one economic circumstance in which Ghana s political independence was inaugurated. It ought to be pointed out that this was not a post-colonial development. Even under Colonial rule, the disease was there. From 1952, every year showed a reduced surplus in the balance of payments until 1956 when a dwindling surplus gave way to deficits. By 1960, the point had been reached where Ghana's capacity for the importation of both producer and consumer goods had been stretched to the limit. Perhaps matters would have been different if Ghana had resorted early to selective borrowing from abroad. Until 1960, Ghana's trade and development were financed entirely from her own resources. It was only in 1959 that the first negotiations for loans to finance the Volta River Project and other important projects began. Depletion of reserves was the consequence of increasingly unfavorable balance of payments. The terms of trade were extremely bad for Ghana. In 1961, import duties were raised and import restrictions introduced. To ensure sustained development in these difficult times, the importation of essential consumer goods and vitally needed producer goods had to be continued. Bilateral trade agreements helped sustain essential imports without the use of scarce convertible currency.

Political considerations in the decision to expand trade with the socialist bloc cannot be ruled out. First, many countries in the third world have gone through similar economic problems without "playing the eastern card." Second, given the strong anti-imperialist character of Nkrumah's politics, as evidenced by both his early writings on the colonial question and later work on neo-colonialism, strengthening trade and other economic relations with the leading anti-imperialist countries was all too logical. Finally, in domestic politics, Nkrumah had pledged to build socialism in Ghana.

Problems and Pressures

Trade with the socialist bloc was a new development in Ghana's external economic relations and, as such, it presented its own problems some of which were soon to be overcome. Initially, some of the products from the socialist countries were not familiar to the Ghanaian consumers and so did not move fast enough. Added to this was the problem of delivery dates which suppliers did not keep, apparently due to the long distances involved. These two problems combined to exert a negative effect on demand. Therefore, while Ghana supplied her bilateral trade partners with the value of products agreed upon, she could not utilize her earnings with them. The result was that at the end of 1962, Ghana had a credit balance of £1.7 million with her bilateral trade partners. This presented a ridiculous situation in which a poor underdeveloped country beset with intractable problems of balance of payments with the west was giving an interest-free loan to industrialized socialist countries. But it was hoped that it would not be long before this problem was eliminated. However, at the end of 1963, Ghana's surplus credit had not disappeared but increased to £1.8 million. Partly because of this situation and also because of Ghana's clear-cut leanings towards bilateralism in trade relations as opposed to the multi-lateralism favored by the leading capitalist countries, Ghana came under pressure from the international financial agencies of which she was a part.

Soon after gaining her political independence, Ghana joined the Bretton Woods system—the IMF and the World Bank—all of which stood for multilateral trade and system of payments. Particularly, it was to avoid the bilateralism of the 1930s that the IMF was set up in the difficult conditions of the post-World War II era. More importantly, Ghana became a contracting party to the General Agreements on Tariffs and Trade (GATT) which prohibit bilateral trade and discriminatory trade practices and uphold multilateralism. By implication, Ghana was to give all countries equal access to her trade without discrimination. It was evidently clear that persistent balance of payments crisis had brought Ghana's ability to stick to GATT provisions under severe strains. The bilateral trade agreements with socialist countries and imposition of import restrictions on the goods from the west were all clear indications that Ghana's adherence to trade liberalism and multilateralism could no longer be taken for granted by the international financial and trade organizations of which she was a member. At the same time, Ghana's worsening financial difficulties forced her to seek assistance from these institutions. These institutions would assess Ghana's title to their assistance partly by the extent to which it pursued multilateralism, free trade and liberalization. By 1963, Ghana frankly admitted that she had not been able to stick scrupulously to these principles.

> As a member of GATT, Ghana's foreign trade policy is based generally on the concept of free trade and multilateral co-operation as well as the liberalization of trade and payments. In principle, however, the trade policy of Ghana has been characterized by measures aimed at achieving an expansion in domestic production and promoting internal development at a fast rate. It has not therefore been possible to pursue her obligations in GATT to the full.[43]

In 1962, Ghana took her first IMF loan of $14.25 million to keep her out of the woods. By 1965, her balance of payments problems had assumed crisis dimensions. Ghana applied to the Fund and the World Bank for assistance. A Fund team arrived in Ghana to examine the economy and make recommendations prior to making available the Fund's financial resources for adjusting the Ghanaian economy. One of the recommendations of the Fund team was that trade with the socialist countries should be reconsidered. The Fund team recommended inter alia that: "The present bilateral and barter arrangements should be reconsidered with a view to reducing their harmful impact on Ghana's economy." [44]

The World Bank team made similar recommendations which the Government of Ghana could not accept. Shorn of its diplomatic language, the Fund's recommendation was a clear warning to scale down drastically or halt altogether trade with the socialist bloc. This was only one side of the coin.

Powerful external opposition to Ghana's trade with the socialist block was reinforced by an equally fierce internal opposition from established business interests in the Ghana National Chamber of Commerce. The Ghana National Chamber of Commerce was opposed to the idea of giving monopoly over imports from the socialist bloc to a state-owned monopoly trading company (GNTC). Moreover, private business interests argued that highly competitive prices could be quoted by companies with trade links outside the socialist block. These then were the main sources of opposition to trade with the socialist bloc of countries. In reality, the two streams of opposition were one. The Ghana National Chamber of

Commerce was dominated by the large European trading firms some of which had over a quarter century of trading experience on the west coast of Africa. Prior to independence, there were two separate chambers, one for indigenous Ghanaian traders, the other for the large international trading companies with operations throughout West Africa (some in East Africa). This opposition to trade with socialist countries is actually the opposition of these large European firms which controlled Ghana's internal trade, i.e. retail, wholesale, and import-export. This was clearly evident from their memorandum on Ghana's trade with the socialist countries. It stated inter alia:

> Some of the importers are trading . . . organizations with many
> years of West African experience and world-wide connections. They
> buy not only from Ghana but for the whole of West Africa and by
> the volume of their imports can quote extremely competitive
> prices.[45]

A clear case for the big firms. The small scale sole Ghanaian proprietors who were members of the chamber obviously did not have world-wide trade connections. Neither did they buy for the whole of West Africa nor have many years of West African experience. Only the huge European trading companies—UAC, SCOA, CFAO, UTC etc. would meet such a description. Opposition to Ghana's trade links with the socialist community then was essentially opposition by imperialism. We may now turn our attention to Ghana-South Africa trade.

The South African Connection

After the victory of the National Party in the 1948 South African election, racial discrimination in that country developed rapidly into the apartheid system—a complete system of racial discrimination with the requisite substructural and superstructural elements. Incidentally, it was after this time that South Africa increasingly became integrated as a powerful link in Ghana's colonial and neo-colonial trade dependence on world capitalism. It has been already pointed out that compared with Ghana's trade with the advanced capitalist countries, trade relations with African countries before independence in 1957 were negligible. The only notable exception was trade with apartheid South Africa. Though certainly not as important as trade with Western Europe and the USA, trade with South Africa ranked in importance as trade with the Nordic countries, particularly Sweden and Norway and was comparable with

Ghana's trade with other Commonwealth countries, especially Australia. Ghana's trade with South Africa got off with a flying start after South Africa's trade Commissioner had paid a brief visit to Ghana in 1956.[46] By the end of 1956, about £1.21 million of South African goods were imported to Ghana and in 1957, the figure shot up slightly to £1.58 million. Apartheid South Africa had already become an important trade partner of Ghana, and was accounting for a fairly good proportion of Ghana's import trade— 1.4 per cent in 1956, 1.5 per cent in 1957 and 1.8 per cent in 1958.

Export trade with the apartheid republic showed a similar rate of increase. South Africa picked from Ghana £1.34 million of goods in 1956 and £1.31 million in 1957, equivalent to 1.5 per cent and 1.2 per cent respectively of Ghana's total export trade. In 1959, there was a drop to 1 per cent of Ghana's total export value. Viewed within the context of Ghana's total trade, this still represents a very low level of trade.

South Africa's position in Ghana's external trade is better appreciated only when set within the context of Ghana's total African trade. Though Ghana's total African trade was on the whole very small, South Africa, at the distant southern end of the continent, appropriated a disproportionately large share. In 1959, Ghana's total imports from African countries was £13,955,000. South Africa alone appropriated £5,871,000 or 42 per cent of it. In 1960, South Africa's share went up to 46 per cent; South Africa's share in Ghana's import trade was not only higher than any other African country's but it increased at a much faster rate. Within one year, 1959–1960, Ghana's import trade with South Africa shot up to 30 per cent. In 1959 Ghana's total exports to all African countries were a meagre £3,352,000 of which South Africa alone accounted for 36.8 per cent. Between 1959 and 1960, Ghana's trade with South Africa went up from £1,300,000, a whopping 113 per cent increase. By contrast, Ghana's export to all African countries increased by 75 per cent, i.e. from £2,232,000 to £4,072,000. Altogether, by 1960, South Africa accounted for about 40 per cent of Ghana's total exports to all African countries. Growing trade co-operation with South Africa was reflected in political attitudes toward the apartheid republic. South Africa was invited to the First All-African Peoples Conference held in Accra in 1958. She refused to attend only because her condition that "other responsible powers" on the African continent, i.e. the colonial powers, should also be invited, was not met.[47]

The image of black Africa's first independent country doing brisk business with South Africa where discrimination against black people is official policy defended by law must have been very embarrassing to the Nkrumah Government. After the Conference of Independent African States in April 1958, Ghana had already taken the path of radical Pan-African politics. This was rapidly followed with other Pan-African Conferences. First, the All-African Peoples Conference in Accra in December 1958, then the Second All-African Peoples Conference in Tunis in January 1960; another Conference of Independent African States in Addis Ababa in June 1960 and the famous Casablanca Conference of January 1961. Nkrumah's Government was the foremost critic of Colonialism and racism on the continent; strengthening apartheid through trade would seem to suggest that the Government did not mean what it said. Early in 1960, the Government imposed a ban on trade with South Africa, trade which gathered momentum during the dyarchy and increased from year to year thereafter. This trade, however, could not die suddenly in spite of the embargo. In 1961, Ghana still exported about £229,000 worth of goods to South Africa, a sharp decline indeed. Imports had been whittled down to almost nothing (i.e. about £10,000). The Nkrumah Government thus brought its African trade policy in line with its militant Pan-African, anti-racist, anti-colonial politics. The South African trade connection was thrown overboard. However, cutting trade links with apartheid South Africa would not be sufficiently Pan-Africanist if the chief beneficiaries were to be countries outside Africa.

Nkrumah's Government made extra hard efforts to increase trade with African countries after severing trade relations with South Africa. We shall, therefore, examine Ghana's trade relations with Africa as they were developed during the Nkrumah regime.

Ghana's African Trade

It ought to be recounted that Ghana's integration into the world capitalist system entailed both the subordination of her production and the re-orientation of her exchange relations to the needs of this system. Trade relations forged over long periods with Ghana's African neighbors, namely, the medieval kingdoms of the Western Sudan, the people of Northern Nigeria, Benin, Cote d'Ivoire and Burkina Faso etc. were relegated to insignificant positions. In their place, trade links with advanced capitalist countries were forged. This was also the pattern with which Ghana negotiated the transition from colony to neo-colony.

Soon after political independence, the Nkrumah Government embarked on determined efforts to change this situation and improve trade relations with African countries, particularly Ghana's immediate neighbors. Nkrumah's policy in this regard was not a reactionary one of restoring medieval trade routes, caravans and socio-economic groups. It was a progressive effort aimed at restoring imperialist destroyed trade links and establishing new ones in the modern conditions of a politically free Africa. It was a policy to build Ghana's economic independence and strengthen her political freedom. Burkina Faso (Upper Volta) was the first neighbor with which strong trade relations were developed after independence. In 1957, Burkina Faso was the source of 2.3 per cent of Ghana's total imports. The next year, this had dropped to 1.9 per cent, a level which was maintained throughout 1959. Ghana's exports to this northern neighbor, however, were not substantial—0.1 per cent of total in 1957; 0.3 per cent in 1958 and down to 0.2 per cent in 1959. Some trade links were also developed with Cote d'Ivoire (Ivory Coast) and Nigeria. Cattle, sheep, goats and fish were imported by Ghana which in turn exported kola nuts, timber and re-exported imported textiles and other manufactured goods. Trade with Ghana's neighbors was gratifying to the Nkrumah Government. But compared with the level of trade with South Africa, Ghana's trade with her neighbors was still very small.

However, in 1961, a year after Ghana had placed an embargo on trade with the apartheid republic, Ghana's trade with her immediate neighbors increased dramatically. Ghana's imports from Burkina Faso went up by 34 per cent and export by 107 per cent. To encourage increased trade with Ghana's northern neighbor, the Government of Ghana abolished duties on re-exports from Ghana and ordered a refund of duties collected in 1962. Much of the trade with her immediate neighbors consisted of re-exportation and semi-barter exchanges carried on by itinerant traders. Goods exchanged were kola, timber and manufactured re-exports from Ghana. Cattle, sheep and goats came from Ghana's neighbors. Further afield within the continent, Nkrumah's Government pursued a vigorous (not to say aggressive) policy of expanding trade with as many African countries as possible. Ghana established trade relations with more African countries and Ghana's African trade increasingly claimed a higher proportion of her total trade until 1965 when Ghana's exports dropped sharply.

The expansion of Ghana's trade links with African countries followed a very interesting pattern. Geographically, the directions of expansion was northward; Egypt, Morocco and Libya became Ghana's trade partners. The other trade partners were all within the

West African sub-region — Burkina Faso, Nigeria, Mali, Niger and Togo. The choice of trade partners was also politically interesting. Egypt, Libya and Morocco attended the 1958 Conference of Independent African States held in Accra and are among the oldest independent states in Africa. They met again at the Casablanca Conference in January 1961. At the same time, strong commercial ties with these Arab countries in Africa underscored the fact that Nkrumah's Pan-Africanist angle of vision was not limited to sub-saharan Africa. Notably absent in Ghana's trade relations at that time were Southern and Eastern African countries. Apart from the presence of white minority regimes in these two regions, political independence arrived there late.

On the whole, Nkrumah's trade policy reflected an anti-neo-colonist, anti-racist and Pan-Africanist orientation. This is not surprising. These, after all, are some of the main themes in Nkrumah's political writings — *Africa Must Unite* and *Neo-Colonialism: the Last Stage of Imperialism* — both before and after his overthrow. His struggle against neo-colonialism, his quest for African unity — both of them had the primary purpose of building an economically prosperous and politically strong Africa. And yet, in spite of all efforts by Ghana to develop extensive trade relations with African countries, Africa's share in Ghana's external trade remained small. Primarily, this is due to the fact that all African countries are underdeveloped neo-colonial dependencies without a developed industrial sector. They specialize in primary production for the world capitalist market and within the framework of the imperialist-imposed International Division of Labor. The main outlets for the mineral and agricultural raw materials turned out by African economies are the advanced capitalist countries. African countries do not have developed industries to absorb each other's raw materials or supply each other's requirements of manufactured goods. Neither have they developed specialized industries complementary to rather than competitive with those of sister African countries. African countries have all launched into MNC-directed import substituting industrialization behind high tariff walls, the same range of light consumer goods for domestic elite consumption.

By 1965, persistent balance of payments problems had weakened Ghana's capacity for increased trade with sister African countries. Matters became worse when Ghana's relations with the IMF strained in 1965. An application for a stand-by credit was rejected and in the face of acute balance of payments difficulties, Ghana's ability to pay for her imports was in serious doubt. Ghana's African trade seems to have been impeded by political factors as well, particularly, President Nkrumah's Pan-African politics. The same driving force behind the expansion of Ghana's trade turned into an obstacle. Wide-spread suspicion, no doubt fuelled by imperialist and neo-colonialist propaganda, gained ground among Ghana's neighbors that there was nothing Nkrumah would not do to achieve a political union of Africa under his leadership,and subversion was believed to be his main weapon. Trade and other links with Ghana were cut down. Earlier positive measures came to nought; for example, the removal of trade barriers between Ghana and Burkina Faso and the refund by Ghana of all customs duties collected on re-exports bound for that country. Trade with neighboring Togo fell into similar political difficulties and the border was closed.

Largely because of these political obstacles, trade between Ghana and other African countries fell to a very low level in 1965, the year the OAU Summit Conference was to be held in Ghana's capital city. The decline in trade followed a definite political pattern. In absolute terms, there was an overall decline in Ghana's African trade partners mainly her immediate neighbors. Ghana's immediate neighbors which were naturally her leading trade partners abandoned their leading positions in Ghana's trade to more distant neighbors. Certainly immediate neighbors had more reason to fear real or imagined subversion coming from next-door. It also reflected a common decision of the Afro-Malagasy Common Organization (OCAM) and other French-speaking States. In 1965, they decided to boycott the OAU Summit in Accra because of the "unfriendly policy" of the Ghana Government towards them.[48] In 1962, Burkina Faso and Togo were the first and second major sources of Ghana's African imports. About 38.2 per cent of it came from Burkina Faso and 22.4 per cent from Togo. Spanish controlled Canary Islands came third with 11.8 per cent and the Kingdom of Morocco fourth with 9.8 per cent; Nigeria accounted for only 5.3 per cent and Egypt 3.6 per cent. At the bottom were Mali and Niger appropriating 1.9 per cent and 0.9 per cent respectively.

In 1965, politically induced changes had occurred in the position of Ghana's leading trade partners. Nigeria moved up from close to bottom position in 1962 to be the leading trade partner in 1965—a leap from 5.3 per cent of Ghana's imports of African origin to 30.1 per cent. In a similar fashion, Mali made a long leap from 1.9 per cent supplier of Ghana's African imports to the second position accounting for some 19.7 per cent. Burkina Faso's share in Ghana's African imports dropped by more than half, i.e. from 38.2 per cent in 1962 to 19.0 per cent in 1965 — decline from first to third position. Libya which had no strong trade links with Ghana in 1962 became Ghana's largest supplier in 1965, accounting for some 9.6 per cent of Ghana's total imports of African origin. Egypt made a little upward move from 3.6 per cent in 1962 to 5.2 per cent in 1965. Niger which supplied less than 1.0 per cent in 1962 turned into a 4 .4 per cent supplier in 1965. On the other hand, Togo by 1962, the second major source of Ghana's imports, was by 1965 supplying only 0.8 per cent of Ghana's African imports.. These dramatic political changes in Ghana's trade relations were most unfortunate and regrettable.

A dynamic Pan-Africanist, anti-neocolonial African trade policy would require an increase in both absolute and relative terms of all African countries' share in Ghana's overall external trade. An unplanned and even chaotic shift in trade partners, one African country picking all or part of what another African country had lost is more divisionist than unifying and undermines rather than pro- motes African trade as a whole. But then, such were the contradic- tions of Ghana's African trade policy under Nkrumah's rule—the means employed or believed to be employed obtained the very opposite of the intended goals. Larger questions obviously beyond the very limited scope of this paper come to mind. Would there have been a more successful African trade policy if economic co-opera- tion rather than political union had been the goal of Nkrumah's Pan- Africanism? Would a successful economic co-operation have laid the foundation for a political or organic union of African States? The accumulated experience of the whole world in matters of this nature, i.e. the East African Community, ECOWAS, EEC, CMEA etc. should provide social scientists the basic elements for a comprehensive answer. Needless to repeat, these issues, however interesting, lie outside the scope of this present work.

In Lieu of Conclusion

The story of Ghana's external trade relations is the story of five centuries of integration into the world capitalist system from its early mercantilist phase to its present multilateral stage. Integration into this system has entailed for Ghana increasing de-Africanization of her external trade relations once almost completely African. De- Africanization of Ghana's external trade links reached its peak in the heydays of colonial rule in Ghana. The Nkrumah Government's bold attempts to restructure Ghana's dependent external trade pattern were both inspired and constrained by political and economic factors. At the global level, these attempts consisted of redirection of Ghana's trade away from the advanced capitalist countries towards the socialist community of states and African trade from apartheid South Africa towards other African countries. This diversification nf trade partners was not only compatible with non-alignment but also true national independence. Besides, racial discrimination and apartheid are universally abhorred. The isolation of racism is a vital political demand of the entire Peace loving mankind. Therefore, Nkrumah's trade policy was consistent with the policies of national independence, peace and racial equality.

And yet, these anti-imperialist and anti-racist tendencies in trade could not be allowed to continue indefinitely. In February 1966, the regime was violently overthrown through a coup d'etat. Powerful economic interests would not permit the dismantling of a trading system constructed by them and for them. In particular, imperialism was strongly opposed to any transformation of Ghana's "traditional" external relations including trade relations. Nkrumah's struggle against Ghana's neo-colonial trade patterns was an anti-imperialist struggle. Anti-imperialism in trade would succeed only if it is correctly linked with a neo-colony's anti-imperialist struggle in general. While this is not the main subject of this paper, it may be stated in passing that a neo-colony's anti-imperialist struggle entails unifying all forces with scores to settle with imperialism and welding them into a single potent anti-imperialist force. The isolation of imperialism from the popular forces whose unity and strength must be consciously built is the key to success in this enterprise. No doubt Nkrumah knew the anti-imperialist character of his trade policy and also understood its connection with Ghana's anti-imperialist struggles in general. But did he know and understand the full implications of this connection?

NOTES

1. Folson, 1977a.
2. Folson, 1977b:3
3. Fitch and Openheimer, 1966.
4. Genoud, 1969.
5. Ninsin, 1977. See also *Ufahamu,* Vol. ix(i) 1979.
6. Garlick, 1972.
7. Bauer, 1963.
8. Arhin, in Meillassoux (ed.), 1971:379.
9. Esseks, 1967, also by same author, 1971, Jonah, 1980.
10. Lewis, 1953.
11. Claridge, 1964; pp. 19—29 .
12. Dike, 1956:9.

13. Wilks, 1962 .
14. Hodgkin, 1960:89.
15. Rodney, 1972:580.
16. *Ibid.*
17. Boahen, 1970, also Priestly, 1969 and Daaku, 1970.
18. Reynolds, 1974.
19. Detailed accounts of the activities of "Merchant Princes" have been provided in Daaku, *op. cit.* and Reynolds, *op. cit.*
20. Esseks, op. cit.:581: Howard, 1978 and Kimble, 1963, all provide accounts of this development.
21. Government of the Gold Coast, 1963.
22. *Ghana Economic Survey* (Central Bureau of Statistics), 1954, 1955, 1966.
23. Nkrumah, 1963 a: 160.
24. Discussion on this section draws on Szentes' (1970) treatment of the concept.
25. Nkrumah, 1958.
26. *Ibid.*
27. Quoted in Stepanov, 1981:43 .
28. Castro, 1985:2.
29. Baldridge, 1985:21.
30. *Ibid.*
31. Rawlings, 1984: 2.
32. Castro, op. cit.: 2.
33. Jalee, 1969:62.
34. Tochir, 1983: 24.
35. *Ibid.*
36. *Ibid.*
37. Jalee, op. cit.; pp.62—70.
38. Leith, 1974.
39. Killick, in Birmingham, et al (ed.), 1966:33 and also Asante, 1985 :40.
40. Government of the Gold Coast; 1925 :26.
4 1. *Ibid.*
42. *Ghana Economic Survey,* 1968 :38.
43. *Ghana Economic Survey,* 1963 :39.
44. *Ghana Economic Survey,* 1965 .
45. *Ghana National Chamber of Commerce Second Annual Report, 1963—1964:8 and Ghana Economic Survey,* 1965:38.
46. Wallerstein, 1967:27.
47. *Ibid.* :10 1.
48. *Ibid*

GENERAL BIBLIOGRAPHY

Books and Pamphlets

Adamafio, T., *By Nkrumah's Side: The Labour and The Tears*. ACCM: Waterville, 1982.

Adams, D. T., *A Geography of the Gold Coast*. London: 1940.

Adu, A. L., *The Civil Service in New African States*. London: Allen and Unwin, 1965 .

Afrifa, A. A., *The Ghana Coup*. London: Frank Cass, 1966.

Agyeman, D K, "Africanization and the Frontiers of Africanization Through Education" in *African Studies Journal*, Cape Coast: UCC, 1975.

Aidoo, A. A., "Order and Conflict in Asante Empire" *African Studies Review* I, April. Los Angeles: African Studies Association, 1977.

— "Women in the History and Culture of Ghana". *Research Review* Vol. I, No. 1, Legon: Institute of African Studies, 1985.

Althusser, L., *Politics and History*. London: New Left Books, 1972.

Amin, S. and Cohen, R., *Classes and Class Struggle in Africa*. Nigeria: Afrografika Publishers, 1977.

Amissah, A. M. E., *The Contribution of the Courts to Government*. London: OUP, 1981.

Anquandah, J., *Together We Stand and Reap Accra:* Asempa Publishers, 1979.

Apter, D., *Ghana in Transition*. New York, Altheneun, 1963.

Arhin, K., "Atebubu Markets, 1884—1930" in Meillasoux (ed.): *The Development of Indigenous Trade and Markets in West Africa*. London: OUP, 1971.

— "Transit Market in Asante Hinterland in the late 19th Century". *Odu New Series*, No. 9, 1974.

— "The Pressure of Cash and its Political Consequences in Asante in the Colonial Period", UCLA. *Journal of African Studies,* Vol. 3, No. 4, 1976/66.

— "The Political and Military Roles of Akan Women" in C Oppong (ed.), *Female and Male in West Africa*, London: Georye Allen and Unwin, 1983.

— *Traditional Rule in Ghana: Past and Present.* Accra: Sedco, 1985.

Arthur, J., *One Africa,* Leipzig, GDR, n.d.

Asante, S. K. B., P*roperty Law and Social Goals in Ghana, 1844— 1966.* Accra: Ghana Universities Press, 1975.

— *The Political Economy of Regional Integration in Africa*. New York: Praeger, 1985 .

Austin, D., *Politics in Ghana, 1946—1960*. London, 1964.

Baldridge, M., "A Case for Free Trade," *Amanee*. Accra: US Information Services, 1985 ..

Balme, D. M., *The University of the Gold Coast 1948—1951*. London: Thomas Nelson and Sons Ltd., n.d.

Barraclough, G., *An Introduction to Contemporary Politics.* London: Penguin, 1967.

Bauer, P. T., *West African Trade: A Study of Competition, Oligopoly in a Changing Economy*. Cambridge, 1954.

Beckmann, B., *Organizing the Farmers.* Uppsala: Scandinavia Inst. of African Studies, 1976.

Bening, R. B., "The Development of Education in Northern Ghana, 1908— 1957". *Ghana Social Science Journal* Vol. 1, No. 2, 1972.

Berg, E. J., "Structural Transformation Versus Gradualism: Recent Development in Ghana and the Ivory Coast" in Philip Foster and Aristode Zolberg (eds.), *Ghana and the Ivory Coast: Perspective on Modernization* Chicago: University of Chicago Press, 1971.

Birmingham, W., Neustadt, I. and Omaboe, E. N. (eds.) *A Study of Contemporary Ghana: The Economy of Ghana* Vol. 1, London: Allen Unwin, 1966.

Boahen, A. A., *Topics in West African History*. London: Longman, 1970.

Boserup, E., *Women 's Role in Economic Development*. London: George Allen and Unwin, 1970.

Bretton, H. L., *The Rise and Fall of Kwame Nkrumah—A Study of Personal Rule in Africa*. London: Pall Mall Press, 1967.

Buhl, W., Evolution *Und Revolution—Kritik der Symmetrischen Soziologie*. Muchen: Goldman, Verlag, 1970.

Busia, K. A., *The Position of the Chief in the Modern Political System of Ashanti*. London: OUP, 1951.

— *Africa in Search of Democracy*. London: Routledge and Kegan Paul, 1967.

Castro, F., *There is no other choice: The Cancellation of Debt or the Death of Democratic Processes in Latin America*. Havana: Editora Politica, 1985.

Claridge, W., *A History of the Gold Coast and Ashanti*. London: Frank Cass, 1964.

Crisp, J., *The Story of an African Working Class*. London: Zed Press, 1984.

Cutrufelli, M. R., *Women of Africa: Roots of Oppression*, London: Zed Press, 1983.

Daaku, K. Y., *Trade and Politics on the Gold Coast 1608—1720, A Study of the African Reaction to European Trade*. Clarendon: OUP, 1970.

Dadson, J. A., *Soclalized Agriculture, The Ghanaian Experience* (Forthcoming). Based on unpublished dissertation, Harvard University, 1970.

"Farm Size a.nd Modernization of Agriculture in Ghana," in I. M. Ofori (ed.). *Factors of Agricultural Growth*. Legon: University of Ghana. ISSER, 1973.

Danquah, J. B., *Journey to Independence and After: Letters* Vol. 1, and 2. Compiled by H. K. Akyeampong. Accra: Waterville Publishing House, 1972.

Davidson, B., *Black Star—a View of the Life and Times of Nkrumah*. London: Allen Cane, 1973.

de Wilde, J. C., *Experience with Agricultural Development in Tropical Africa* Baltimore: Johns Hopkins Press, 1967.

Debrunner, H. W., *A History of Christianity in Ghana.* Accra: Waterville Publishing House, 1967.

Dei-Anang, M., *Ghana Resurgent.* Accra: Waterville Publishing House, 1 964.

— *The Administration of Ghana's Foreign Relations, 1957—1965, A Personal Memoir.* London: Athlone Press, 1969.

Dickson, K. A., *Theology in Africa.* London: Darton, Longman and Todd/New York: Orbis Books, 1984.

Dike, D. O., *Trade and Politics in the Niger Delta, 1830—1875.* London: OUP, 1956.

Drah, F. K., "The Brong Political Movement" in Kwame Arhin (ed.,) *Brong-Akyempim: Essays on the Society, History and Politics of the Brong People.* Accra: Institute of African Studies and African Publications, 1979.

Dumor, E. "Women in Rural Development in Ghana" *Rural Africans,* No. 17, 1983.

Engels, F., Socialism *Utopian and Scientific-Marx-Engels-Selected Works.* Moscow: Progress Publishers, 1975.

Esseks, J. D., *Economic Independence in a New African State: Ghana 1956—1965* Ph.D. Thesis (unpublished), Harvard University, 1967.

Fanon, F., *The Wretched of the Earth.* London: Penguin Books Ltd., i970.

Fitch, R. and Oppenheimer, M., Ghana: *End of An Illusion.* New York: Monthly Review, 1966.

Folson, B. D. G., "The Developm.ent of Socialist Ideology in Ghana, 1949—1958" *Ghana Journal of Social Science.* Vol. 5, No. 5, 1977.

— "The Marxist Period in the Development of Socialist Ideology in Ghana, 1962—1966". *Universitas* Vol. 6, No. 1, 1977.

Fortes, M, "The Political System of the Tallensi of the Northern Territories of the Gold Coast" in Fortes and E. E. Evans-Pritchard (eds.), *African Political Systems.* London: OUP, 1940.

Foster, P. and Steiner, H., *The Structure of Algerian Socialized Agriculture.* University of Maryland: Miscellaneous Publications, No. 527, 1964.

Garlick, P., *African Traders and Economic Development in Ghana.* Clarendon: OUP, 1972.

Garvey, A. J., *Philosophy and Opinions of Marcus Garvey*. London: Frank Cass, 1969 .

Genoud, R., *Nationalism and Economic Development in Ghana*. New York: Frederick A Praeger, 1969.

George, B. S., *Education in Ghana*. Washington: US Department of Health, Education and Welfare, 1976.

Graham, C. K., *The History of Education in Ghana*. London: Frank Cass, 1971.

Greenstreet, D. K., "The History of the Ghana Civil Service," *Journal of Management Studies*. Vol. 20, No. 2, September, 1963.

— "Public Corporations in Ghana in the Nkrumah Period". *The African Review* Vol. 3, No. I, I 973 a.

— "The Government and the Manufacturing Sector in Ghana, 1957—1966," *Nigerian Journal of Social and Economic Studies* Vol. 15, No. 3, November 1973b.

— "African Experiment, Public Administration and Higher Education in Ghana, 1960/70," *School of Administration Working Paper Series*. No. 13, Reprinted from the *International Review of Administrative Science*. Vol. 38, No. 1, 1972, 1978.

Greenstreet, M., "Employment of Women in Ghana." Geneva: *International Labour Review,* Vol. 103, 2, 1971.

Gyandoh Jnr. S. O. and Griffiths, J., *Source Book of the Constitutional Law of Ghana 1925 to present*. Vol. 1. Accra: Catholic Press, 1972.

Hachten, W. A., *Muffled Drums*. Ames: Iowa State University Press, 1971.

— *World News Prison*. Ames: Iowa State University Press, 1981.

Hagan, K. O., *Mass Education and Community Development in Ghana: A Study in Retrospect 1943–1968.* Legon: Institute of Adult Education, 1975.

Harper, R. D., "The Revolutionary Process—A Frame of Reference for the Study of Revolutionary Movements" in R. H. Turner and L. M. Killian (eds.) *Collective Behaviour*. New Hampshire: Prentice Hall, 1957.

Harrison-Church, R. J., *West Africa: A Study of the Environment and Man's Use of it*. London: Longmans, 1963.

Harvey W. B., *Law and Social Change in Ghana*. Princeton: Princeton University Press, 1960 .

Hayes, C., *Nationalism: A Religion.* New York: Macmillan, 1960.

— *Essays on Nationalism.* New York: Russell and Russell, 1966.

Hodgkin, T., *Nigerian Perspectives.* London: OUP, 1961.

— *African Political Parties.* London: Penguin African Series/OUP, 196 1.

Howard, R., *Colonialism and Underdevelopment in Ghana.* London: Croom Helm, 1978.

Hyden, G., *Beyond Ujamaa in Tanzania.* London: Heinemann, 1980.

Irizarry, R. L., "Overpopulation and Unemployment in the Third World: The Paradoxes." *Comparative Education Review* Vol. 24, No. 3, October 1980.

Jalee, P., *The Third World in World Economy.* New York: Monthly Review, 1969.

James, C. L. R., "Colonialism and National Liberation in Africa: The Gold Coast Revolution" in Miller, N. and Aya, R. (eds.). *National Liberation.* New York: Free Press, 1971.

— *Nkrumah and the Ghana Revolution.* London: Allison and Busty, 1977.

Jonah, K., *The Politics of Economic Decolonization: The Case of Ghana's Indigenization Policy.* MA Thesis (unpublished). Legon: Department of Political Science, University of Ghana, 1980.

Jones-Quartey, P, "The Effects of the Maintenance of Children Act on Akan and Ewe Notions of Paternal Responsibility." *Legon Family Research Papers* Vol. 1. Legon: Institute of African Studies, 1974.

Karcz, J F, "Organizational Model of Command Farming," in E. Bornstein (ed.). *Comparative Economic Systems: Models and Cases.* Homewood, Ill: Irwin, 1974.

Kea, R. A., *Settlements, Trade and Politics in Seventeenth Century Gold Coast.* Baltimore and London: Johns Hopkins University Press, 1982.

Killick, T, "External Trade" in Birmingham, Walter *et al* (eds.). *A Study of Contemporary Ghana.* London: Allen and Unwin, 1966.

— *Development Economics in Action: A Study of Economic Policies in Ghana.* London: Heinemann, 1978.

Kimble, D., *A Political History of Ghana: The Rise of Gold Coast Nationalism* 1850—1928. Clarendon: OUP, 1963.

Kohn, H, "A New Look at Nationalism." *Virginia Quarterly Review* 32. Summer, 1956.

Konings, P., *Peasantry and State in Ghana: The Example of the Vea Irrigation Project*. Leiden: African Studies Centre, 1981.

Krassowski, A., *Development and the Debt Trap*. London: Croom Helm in association with the Overseas Development Institute, 1974.

Le Vine, V., *Political Corruption: The Ghana Case*. Stanford: Hoover Institution Press/Stanford University Press, 1975.

Legum, C., *Pan-Africanism: A Short Political Guide*. New York: Praeger, 1962.

Leith, J. C., *Foreign Trade Regimes and Economic Development* Vol. 2. New York: National Bureau of Economic Research.

Lenin, V. I., *What Must Be Done*. Peking: People's Publishing House, Beijing 1965.

Lent, J. A., "A Third World New Deal Part One: Guiding Light." *Index on Censorship*. Vol. 6, No. 5, September—October 1977.

Lewis, L. J., *Educational Policy and Practice in Tropical Areas*. London: Thomas Nelson and Sons Ltd., 1954.

Little, K., *Urbanisation as a Social Process*. London and Boston: Routledge and Kegan Paul, 1974.

Lowe, J. (ed.), *Adult Education and Nation Building*. Edinburgh: Edinburgh University Press, 1970.

Luckham, R., "The Administration of Justice." *Review of Ghana Law* 9, 1977.

Luggard, F. P., *The Dual Mandate in Tropical Africa*. London: Frank Cass edition, 1965.

Marais, G., *Kwame Nkrumah as I Knew Him*. Great Britain: JANAY, 1972.

Marx, K., "The Eighteenth Brummaire of Louis Bonaparte" in *Marx and Engels, Collected Works*. Moscow: Progress Publishers, 1979.

Mazrui, A. A., *Towards a Pax Africana: A Study of Ideology and Ambition*. London: Weidenfeld and Nicolson, 1969.

McCaskie, T. C., "Office, Land and Subjects in the History of the Manwere Fekuo of Kumasi." *Journal of African History* 21, 1980.

McManners, J., *Church and State in France 1870–1914*. New York: Harper and Row, 1973.

McQuail, D., *Mass Communication Theory*. London: Sage Publications, 1983.

Merrill, J. C. and Lowenstein, R., *Media, Messages and Men*. New York and London: Longman, 1979.

Metcalfe, G. E., *Great Britain and Ghana: Documents in Ghana History 1807–1957*. London: Thomas Nelson and Sons, 1964.

Mikell, G., "West African Women and Men — Roles and Interaction". *Ghana Studies Bulletin*, No. 3, Birmingham, 1985 .

Ninsin, K. A., "Nkrumah's Socialism: A Re-appraisal." *Seminar Papers*. Department of Political Science, University of Ghana, 1977.

Nkrumah, K., *Ghana: The Autobiography of Kwame Nkrumah*. London: T H Nelson, 1957.

— *Speech at the Opening of the Hall of Trade Unions*. Accra: Government Printer, 1960.

— *Address by Dr Nkrumah during the Opening Ceremony of the Nzima Oil Mills* (IDC). Accra: Ministry of Information, 1961a.

— *I Speak of Freedom*. London: Heinemann, 1961b.

— *The Noble Task of Teaching Accra:* Government Printer, 1961c.

—*Voice of Africa*. Accra: Ministry of Information and Government Printer, 1961d.

—*Building a Socialist State*. Accra: Ministry of Information, 1962a.

—"Dr. Nkrumah States the Neutralist Case." *Africa Report* Vol. 7, No. 5, 1 962b.

— *I Speak of Freedom*. London: Mercury Book, 1962c.

— *Towards Colonial Freedom*. London: Panaf Books, 1962d.

— *Africa Must Unite*. London: Heinemann, 1963a.

— *Our Civic Duty*. Accra: Government Printer, 1963b.

— *Revive Our Virtues*. Accra: Government Printer, 1963c.

— *Strength and Power*. Accra: Government Printer, 1963d.

— *The African Genius*. Accra: Government Printer, 1963

— *Torch Bearers*. Accra: Government Printer, 1963g.

— *Consciencism*. London: Heinemann, 1964a.

—*Laying the Foundation Stone of Ghana's Atomic Reactor*. Accra: Government Printer. 1964b.

— *Sessional Address to Parliament*. Accra: Government Printer, 1964c.

—*Why the Spark?* Accra: The Spark Publications, 1964d.

—*Bright Future For All*. Accra: Government Printer, 1965a.

— *Neo-Colonialism*. New York: International Publishers, 1965b.

— *Sessional Address to Parliament*. Accra: Government Printer, 1965c.

— *Speech on Inauguration of GBC-TV*. Accra-Tema: State Publishing Corporation, 1965d.

— *Dark Days in Ghana*. London: Panaf, 1968a.

— *Handbook of Revolutionary Warfare*. London: Panaf, 1968b.

— *Dark Days in Ghana*. New York: International Publishers, 1969.

— *Class Struggle in Africa*. New York: International Publishers, 1970a.

— *Consciencism*. New York: Monthly Review Press, 1970b.

— *Ghana: The Autobiography of Kwame Nkrumah*. New York: International Publishers, 1971.

—*Africa Must Unite*. New York: International Publishers, 1972.

— *Ghana: The Autobiography of Kwame Nkrumah*. London: Panaf, 1973.

—*Revolutionary Path*. London: Panaf Books Ltd./New York: International Publishers, 1973.

Obeng, S. (Compiler), *Selected Speeches of Kwame Nkrumah*. Accra: Ministry of Information, 1961.

Oduyoye, A., "Socialisation through Proverbs." *African Notes* Vol. I, Ibadan, 1981.

Ollenu, N. A., "Chieftaincy Under the Law" in W. C. Ekow-Daniels and G. R. Woodman (eds.) *Essays in Ghana Law 1876–1976*. Accra: Ghana Publishing Corporation for the Faculty of Law, University of Ghana, Legon, n.d.

— *The Law of Testate and Intestate Succession in Ghana*. London: Sweet and Maxwell, 1966.

Padmore, G., *Pan-Africanism or Communism?* Garden City, NY: Doubleday, 1957.

Pettazzoni, R., *Essays on the History of Religions*. Leiden: E. J. Brill, 1954.

Pobee, J. S. (ed.) "Church and State in Ghana." *Religion in a Pluralistic Society*. Leiden: E J Brill, 1976.

— "Bible and Human Transformation." *Mission Studies*. Vol. I—2.

Powell, E., *Private Secretary (Female) Gold Coast*. London: C Hurst and Co., 1984.

Priestly, M., *West African Trade and Coast Society: A Family Study*. London: Oxford University Press, 1969.

Rattray, R. S., *Ashanti Law and Constitution*. London: Oxford University Press, 1929.

— *Tribes of the Ashanti Hinterland*. 2 Vols. London: OUP, 1952.

Rawlings, J. J., "Boosting the Morale of Farmers" in *Forging Ahead* Vol. 2, Accra: Information Services Department, 1984.

Reynolds, E., *Trade and Economic Change in the Gold Coast*. Harlow: Longmans, 1974.

Rivers, W. C., *The Adversaries: Politics and the Press*. Boston: Beacon Press, 1970.

Rodney, W., *How Europe Underdeveloped Africa*. Dar es Salaam: Tanzania Publishing House, 1972.

Rossler, R., "Kirche und Revolution in Russland: Patriach Tichos und der Sovietstaar," *Beitrage Zur Geschichle Osteuropas* Vol. 7, Koln, Wien: Bohlau Verlag. 1897 .

Sarbah, J. M., *Farlti Customary Law*. London: Frank Cass,1968, 1897.

Schumacher, E. F., *Small is Beautiful: Economics as if People Mattered*. New York: Harper and Row, 1973.

Seidman, A., *Ghana 's Development Experience*. Nairobi: East African Publishing House, 1978.

Senghor, L. S., *"Les Foundements de l'Africanist ou Negritude et Arabites."* *Presence Africaine,* Paris, 1967 .

Siebert, F. S., Peterson, T. and Sohramm, W., *Four Theories of the Press*. Urbana: Universities of Illinois Press, 1974.

Songsore, J., "Structural crisis, dependent capitalist development and regional inequality in Ghana." *ISS Occasional Papers*. The Hague: Institute of Social Studies, 1979.

Stepanov, G., "East-West Business Ties: A Sphere of Co-operation Not An Instrument of Blackmail." *International Affairs* (Moscow) No. 12, 1981.

Szentes, T., *The Political Economy of Underdevelopment*. Budapest: Academiao Kiado, n.d.

Szereszewski, R., *Structured Changes in the Economy of Ghana 1891—1911*. London: Weidenfeld and Nicolson, 1965.

Thomas, R. G., "Forced Labour in British West Africa: The Case of the Northern Territories of the Gold Coast." *Journal of African History*, X;IV, 1973.

Thompson, W. S., *Ghana's Foreign Policy 1957–1966: Diplomacy, Ideology and the New State*. Princeton: Princeton University Press, 1969.

Tillich, P., *Theology of Culture*. New York: Oxford University Press. 1959/Galaxy Books, 1964.

Timothy, B., *Kwame Nkrumah and His Rise to Power*. London: Allen and Unwin, 1955.

Tsikata, E., *Agricultural Rent Control in Ghana*. Long Essay, Faculty of Law, University of Ghana, Legon, 1984.

Tsikata, F., "Limits of Constitutional Law" in *Ghana University Law Journal*, No. 15, 1978.

Vellenga, D. D., "Attempts to Change the Marriage Laws in Ghana and Ivory Coast" in Foster and Zolberg (eds.), *Ghana and Ivory Coast: Perspectives on Modernisation*. Chicago: University of Chicago Press, 1971.

Vile, M. J. C., *Constitutionalism and the Separation of Powers*. London: OUP, 1967.

Wallerstein, E., *Africa: The Politics of Unity*. New York: Random House, 1967.

Watson, A., *Report of the Commission of Enquiry into the Distribution in the Gold Coast*. London: HMSO, 1948.

Wight, M., *The Gold Coast Legislative Council*. London: Faber and Faber, 1947.

Wilber, C. K., *The Soviet Model and Underdevelopment*. Chapel Hill: University of California Press, n.d.

Wilcox, D. L., *Mass Media in Black Africa: Philosophy and Control*. New York: Praeger Publishers, 1975.

Williams, R., *Communications*. London: Penguin Books, 1962.

Wilks, I., *The Northern Factor in Ashanti History*. Legon: Institute of African Studies, University of Ghana, Legon.

Wontumi, I., "Women in the Civil Service in Ghana." NCWD *Background Papers for Seminar on Ghana Women in Development*. Accra: NCWD, 1978.

Wright, R., *Black Power*. New York: Harper and Brother, 1954.

Yachir, F., "South-South Co-operation: An Alternative?" *Third World Forum Bulletin*. No. 2, October, 1983.

Younger, K., *Public Service in New States: A Study in Some Trained Manpower problem*. London: OUP, 1960.

Zolberg, A. R., *One Party Government in Ivory Coast*. Princeton: Princeton University Press, 1964.

Reports

Coussey Committee, *Report on Constitutional Reforms*. Accra: Government Printer, 1949.

Ghana, *Report of the Commission Appointed to Enquire into the Affairs of the Kumasi State Council and the Asanteman Council*. (By Justice Sarkodee-Addo). Accra: Government Printer, 1958a.

Ghana, *Report of the Commission of Enquiry into the Akim Abuakwa State Affairs* (By Mr. Justice J. Jackson). Accra: Government Printer, 1958b.

Ghana, *Report of the Commission Appointed to Enquire into the Matters Disclosed at the Trial of Benjamin Awhaitey before a Court-Martial and the Surrounding Circumstances*. Accra: Government Printer, 1959.

Ghana, *Ghana National Chamber of Commerce. Second Annual* Report. 1965.

Ghana, *Report of the Commission of Enquiry into the Workers Brigade*. Accra: Government Printer, 1969.

Gold Coast, *Government of Gold Coast Departmental Report* 12. Accra: Government Printer, 1913.

Gold Coast, "Summary Statement of the Value of Import into the Colony of the Gold Coast." *Government of the Gold Coast, Department Report.* Accra: Government Printer.

Gold Coast, *Regional Administration* (Report by the Sole Commissioner, Sir Sydney Phillipson), 1951.

Jibowu Commission, *Gold Coast Commission of Enquiry into the Affairs of the Cocoa Purchasing Company.* Accra: State Publishing Corporation, 1956.

Lewis, W A, *Report on Industrialisation in the Gold Coast.* Accra: Government Printer, 1953.

Ollenu Commission, *Summary of the Report of the Commission of Enquiry into alleged Malpractices in the issue of Import Licences.* Accra: Ministry of Information, 1967.

Watson Commission Report, *Commission of Enquiry into Disturbances in the Gold Coast.* Accra: Government Printer, 1948.

Other Sources

Acts of the First Republic.

Annual Volumes of Laws of Ghana.

Bills of the First Republic of Ghana.

"Cultural Policy in Ghana," Unesco, 1975.

"Daily Graphic" various issues.

"Evening News" various issues.

Ghana Economic Surveys (1954, 1963, 1965 issues). Published by the Central Bureau of Statistics.

Ghana Parliamentary Debates, various issues.

Ghana's Seven-Year Development Plan 1963/64l—1969/1970.

"The Ghanaian Woman," a Journal of the National Council on Women.

The Gold Coast Legislative Council Debates, various issues.

The Government Proposals for Constitutional Reforms, 1953.

"The Party", a Journal published by the CPP's Bureau of Information and Publicity.

INDEX